The Governance of Privacy

The Governance of Privacy
Policy Instruments in Global Perspective

Colin J. Bennett and Charles D. Raab

The MIT Press
Cambridge, Massachusetts
London, England

MIT Press books may be purchased at special quantity discounts for business or sales promotional use. For information, please email special_sales@mitpress. mit.edu or write to Special Sales Department, The MIT Press, 55 Hayward Street, Cambridge, MA 02142.

This book was set in Sabon by SNP Best-set Typesetter Ltd., Hong Kong and was printed and bound in the United States of America.

Library of Congress Cataloging-in-Publication Data

Bennett, Colin J. (Colin John), 1955–.
  The governance of privacy : policy instruments in global perspective / Colin J. Bennett and Charles D. Raab.—[2nd and updated ed.]
    p. cm.
  Includes bibliographical references and index.
  ISBN 0-262-52453-8 (pbk.)
  1. Data protection—Government policy—OECD countries. 2. Privacy, Right of—OECD countries. I. Raab, Charles D. II. Title.
JC596.2.O43B45 2006
323.44'8309177—dc22
                                                                    2005058021

10 9 8 7 6 5 4 3 2 1

Contents

Preface

This book is the culmination of more than a decade of collaboration on research on privacy protection policy. At the end of the 1980s, our mutual interests and prior work led us to think about writing a lengthy analysis of data protection based upon the experiences of the United Kingdom (UK), whose Data Protection Act had been legislated in 1984 and was still in the relatively early days of implementation. As political scientists, we thought we could build upon the work of lawyers, computer scientists, social theorists and philosophers, but take it in a different direction, one that was more in line with the preoccupations and analytical outlooks of empirical social science and policy studies. We thought it would be a fresh approach to consider the various roles of the UK's Data Protection Registrar as the regulatory instrument responsible for overseeing the Act, and to consider different facets of the privacy protection afforded to a "data subject" caught up in various domains of data processing. We interviewed officers of leading UK data-using organizations in a variety of industries, as well as regulatory officials and consumers' spokespersons, and collected a vast quantity of written documents. We also attended practitioners' conferences and other gatherings where we were able to observe the discourse and debates of the various policy protagonists as well as make contacts with many who could help us as informants and interviewees. These activities gave us a great deal of material to analyze over the first few years of research.

As the 1990s evolved, however, the landscape of data protection changed dramatically, and so did our conception of the book. For one thing, the policy agenda of data protection was deeply affected by the emergence in draft form of the European Union Data Protection Directive early on in our work, by the political debates it engendered, and by its subsequent revisions. Secondly, the development of the Internet, and especially the World Wide Web, had a transformative effect on the subject under study. Once again, it moved the center of gravity farther away from the experiences of one country and broadened the array of issues and analytical perspectives. But it also posed sharper questions about the relationship between technological change, globalization, and privacy protection. This gave an object lesson of the predicament of trying to research policies and developments in a field where the pace of change—technological, legal, political, economic, and others—is extremely rapid. While continuing our research, we revised our framework of issues several times, each outline losing its luster with the further development of both our thinking and the world of privacy protection. Some anchors in a shifting sea were provided by the continued prominence on the scene of many of the same groups and policy actors, although new organizations at various levels continued to enter the policy arena.

Meanwhile our involvement in other research and practical endeavors within and outside of the scope of the subject helped us to deepen and broaden our ideas and knowledge. Colin Bennett's intensive policy-related work on the Canadian privacy standard and on a possible equivalent at the international level drew his attention to the analysis of more innovative policy instruments for the "governance of privacy." Some of Charles Raab's energies were absorbed in investigating and advising on the privacy implications of government's use of information and communication technologies, in studying the emergence of the concepts of risk, trust, and equity in policy discourse on information policy, and in collaborative study of European police cooperation. A further project was our involvement with two other colleagues in a European Commission study of the "adequacy" of data protection in third countries. These "distractions" paid rich dividends in terms of new understandings and insights as well as fresh interview and documentary material. At the turn of the millennium, we settled on one plan and began, finally, to re-assess draft chapters as well as to revisit some of the ideas that we meanwhile had released into the public domain. Addi-

tional joint research—again with colleagues—on geographical information systems, funded by the National Science Foundation (US), has more
recently added a further set of issues for consideration in terms of the
possibilities of privacy regulation, although that work is not directly
reflected in this book.[1]

We have incurred a large number of debts in the preparation of this
book. Not the least are the funding bodies whose indispensable and
generous assistance has underwritten our efforts to amass and to analyze
a very large amount of data within several projects that have contributed, directly or indirectly, to the production of this book. First, we
acknowledge with gratitude the early assistance of the Nuffield Foundation (UK) and the Moray Fund of the University of Edinburgh, which
sustained our ability to carry out a large, initial wave of interviews and
document collection. Subsequent funding from the Social Science and
Humanities Research Council of Canada[2] and from the UK's Economic
and Social Research Council (ESRC)[3] provided major funding for projects of direct relevance to the subject of this book,[4] as well as temporary
release from teaching and administrative duties. Colin Bennett was
fortunate to spend a sabbatical year at the Harvard Information Infrastructure Project at the Kennedy School of Government, and was therefore able to draft some of the chapters within one of the richest and
exciting intellectual environments in the world for the analysis of the
social impacts of information technologies. For a short time, Charles
Raab was Visiting Professor at Tilburg University in the Netherlands,
where the Centre for Law, Informatization, and Public Administration
provided a supportive and congenial environment for similar writing,
and for discussing the book's topics with scholars who are at the forefront of multidisciplinary research on issues related to our concerns.

We cannot name here the hundreds of persons who have assisted us
in one way or another over many years. A large number were the subject
of formal interviews that have informed the background of our analysis,
while others gave us the benefit of their knowledge, views, and further
contacts, in less formal discussions and conversations. Our endeavors
were encouraged and supported by a wide variety of fellow academics
as well as practitioners. Many of them shared their knowledge of
specialized topics in the broad field of information policy and politics,

and commented usefully and critically on our ideas. None is, of course, responsible for any errors or for our interpretations.

At the risk of invidious mention of just a few members of this vast network, we should particularly like to thank (in alphabetical order) Francis Aldhouse, Diana Alonso Blas, Jonathan Bamford, Bojana Bellamy, Christine Bellamy, Peter Blume, Monica den Boer, John Borking, Danièle Bourcier, Vivian Bowern, Ulf Brühann, Giovanni Buttarelli, Herbert Burkert, Lee Bygrave, Ann Cavoukian, Ulrich Dammann, Alexander Dix, Wim van de Donk, Bärbel Dorbeck-Jung, Stewart Dresner, Jos Dumortier, Dag Elgesem, David Flaherty, Elizabeth France, Robert Gellman, Marie Georges, Gordon Graham, Jan Holvast, Melanie Howard, Eric Howe, Peter Hustinx, Rosemary Jay, Stephen Lau, Klaus Lenk, Laura Linkomies, David Lyon, Gustav Mahler, László Majtényi, Viktor Mayer-Schönberger, Dame Sheila McKechnie, Michael Moran, Jim Norton, Margriet Overkleeft-Verburg, Pablo Palazzi, Stephanie Perrin, Nick Platten, Yves Poullet, Chris Pounder, Corien Prins, Priscilla Regan, Joel Reidenberg, Simon Rogerson, Paul Schwartz, Spiros Simitis, David Smith, Ignace Snellen, Michael Spencer, Blair Stewart, Graham Sutton, Ivan Székely, Alastair Tempest, Stefan Walz, Nigel Waters, John Woulds, and Perri 6. We have also been very fortunate to have had the research assistance of Gary Williams at the University of Edinburgh, and of Peter Walker, Martin French, Sanda Farcas, and Ben Gonzales at the University of Victoria.

The first (hardcover) edition of this book was published by Ashgate Publishing Limited in 2003. This second and updated edition for The MIT Press has been necessitated by evolving events in the world of privacy protection, in part precipitated by the terrorist attacks of 11 September 2001. We are very grateful to Valerie Geary of The MIT Press for helping us to bring this new edition to publication.

As with the first edition, we dedicate the book to our wives, Robin Bayley and Gillian Raab, to whom we owe a large debt of gratitude for their forbearance and support during the preparation of this book and during the years of research that preceded it.

List of Abbreviations

ACM	Association for Computing Machinery (US)
AHAG	Ad Hoc Advisory Group of the International Standardization Organization
AICPA	American Institute of Certified Public Accountants
ALA	American Library Association
APEC	Asia-Pacific Economic Cooperation
APPCC	Asia-Pacific Privacy Charter Council
BBB	Better Business Bureau
CA	Certification Authority
CBA	Canadian Bankers Association
CBBB	Council of Better Business Bureaus
CCTV	Closed Circuit Television
CDT	Center for Democracy and Technology (US)
CEN/ISSS	Comité Européen de Normalisation/Information Society Standardization System
CENELEC	Comité Européen de Normalisation Electrotechnique
CICA	Canadian Institute of Chartered Accountants
CITU	Central Inspection Technology Unit (UK)
CLHIA	Canadian Life and Health Insurance Association
CMA	Canadian Marketing Association
CNIL	Commission Nationale de l'Informatique et des Libertés
CMC	Computer-Mediated Communication
CoE	Council of Europe
COPOLCO	Consumer Associations' Committee of the International Standardization Organization

CPO	Chief Privacy Officer
CSA	Canadian Standards Association
CTSC	Cable Television Standards Council (Canada)
EC	European Commission
ECOM	Electronic Commerce Promotion Council of Japan
EFT	Electronic Funds Transfer
ENC	Electronic Network Consortium (Japan)
EPIC	Electronic Privacy Information Center (US)
ESRC	Economic and Social Research Council (UK)
ETSI	European Telecommunications Standards Institute
EU	European Union
FEDMA	Federation of European Direct Marketing Associations
FIPs	Fair Information Principles
FIPR	Foundation for Information Policy Research (UK)
FTC	Federal Trade Commission (US)
GATS	General Agreement on Trade in Services
GILC	Global Internet Liberty Campaign
HTML	Hypertext Mark-Up Language
IATA	International Air Transport Association
IBM	International Business Machines
ICTs	Information and Communications Technologies
ICX	International Commerce Exchange
IETF	Internet Engineering Task Force
IFIP	International Federation for Information Processing
ILO	International Labour Organization
INRA	International Research Associates
IP	Internet Protocol
IPC	Information and Privacy Commissioner (Ontario)
IPSE	Initiative on Privacy Standardization in Europe
ISATs	Intelligent Software Agent Technologies
ISO	International Organization for Standardization
ISTPA	International Security Trust and Privacy Alliance
JIPDEC	Japanese Information Processing Development Center
JISA	Japan Information Technology Industry Services Association

MITI	Ministry of International Trade and Industry (Japan)
NADPO	National Association of Data Protection Officers (UK)
NIM	National Information Market
NTIA	National Telecommunications and Information Administration (US)
OECD	Organisation for Economic Co-operation and Development
OPA	Online Privacy Alliance
OPC	Office of the Privacy Commissioner (Canada)
OPS	Open Profiling Standard
PETs	Privacy-Enhancing Technologies
PGP	Pretty Good Privacy
PIA	Privacy Impact Assessment
PIAC	Public Interest Advocacy Centre (Canada)
PICS	Platform for Internet Content Selection
PIPEDA	Personal Information Protection and Electronic Documents Act (Canada)
PISA	Privacy Incorporated Software Agent
PKI	Public Key Infrastructure
PLB	Privacy Laws & Business (UK)
PPM	Privacy Protection Mark (Japan)
PPSC	Privacy Protection Study Commission (US)
P3P	Platform for Privacy Preferences
QMI	Quality Management Institute (Canada)
RFID	Radio Frequency Identification Devices
S/MIME	Secure Multipurpose Internet Mail Extension
TACD	Transatlantic Consumer Dialogue
TMB	Technical Management Board of the International Organization for Standardization
TTP	Trusted Third Party
XML	Extensible Mark-Up Language
WTO	World Trade Organization
W3C	World Wide Web Consortium

Introduction

This book addresses the politics of privacy protection with regard to personal information. It is motivated by the argument that privacy-related problems are as much political and public policy issues as they are legal and technological ones. It is also based on the observation that the ability of any one jurisdiction to protect the privacy of its citizens through public policy is inescapably linked with the actions of public and private organizations that operate outside its borders. The development of the range of different processes that are embraced by the concept of *globalization* gives the protection of personal information a character that is far wider than can be contained within the borders of single states. In a "borderless world" public policies to protect personal privacy are inextricably interdependent.

This regulatory interdependence could hypothetically produce two possible broad dynamics. On the one hand, countries would progressively fashion their privacy protection policies according to the highest possible standard, a "trading up" or a "race to the top." Conversely, countries might consider that a less-regulated climate would attract global businesses that would want to circumvent the higher standards at work elsewhere. This competitive deregulation would lead to a race to the bottom, as countries progressively weaken their standards to attract global investment in the information technology and services industries. The main research question that directs the analysis within this book—and which we address explicitly in the final chapter—is whether, in the field of personal privacy protection, there has been a "race to the top," a "race to the bottom," or something less unidirectional and more complex.

To answer this question we offer a broad interrogation of the politics of personal privacy protection in contemporary advanced industrial states. We begin by analyzing the goals of privacy protection policy, and the changing discourse surrounding the issue. The body of the text is devoted to an analysis of the contemporary policy instruments that together comprise the inventory of possible solutions to this complex problem. In our conclusion we ask the "so what?" question. Does all of this policy activity at international, national, and corporate levels mean higher "levels" of privacy protection? How do we then conceptualize and measure "levels" of privacy protection? How do we judge whether there is a "trading up" or the opposite?

The Global Information Revolution

One popular cliché, often repeated in unreflective usage, is that we live in an "information society."[1] This concept has a variety of mythic and ideological representations. In its popular manifestation, the concept is simply used as a shorthand to describe some of the fundamental effects of new information and communications technologies (Negroponte 1995, Toffler 1981). Whether indeed the information society represents a structural transformation in late capitalism is also the subject of a more profound debate in the scholarly literature (for example, Beniger 1986). The contemporary academic debate has been heavily influenced by Castells's theory of the "network society." A new information technology paradigm with information as its raw material, based on a pervasive, convergent, and flexible networking logic, has reconfigured our conceptions of space. Society is now constructed around the "space of flows": "flows of capital, flows of information, flows of technology, flows of organizational interaction, flows of images, sounds, and symbols. Flows are not just one element of the social organization: they are the expression of processes *dominating* our economic, political and symbolic life" (Castells 1996, p. 412, emphasis in original).

We do not need to explore the wider implications of Castells's theory to emphasize the simple point that information now flows more freely, knows fewer national attachments, and indeed represents one of the significant forces behind the processes of globalization. Of course, *glo-*

balization, perhaps like *privacy*, is an ill-defined and controversial word and is currently the source of a range of controversies with respect to its conceptualization, causal dynamics, socioeconomic consequences and implications for state autonomy (Held et al. 1999, p. 3). These larger disputes led Held and his colleagues to search for greater analytical precision in order to gain a better purchase on the nature of the global changes in question. We return to these issues later, but briefly, these authors contend that globalization implies, first, "a *stretching* of social, political and economic activities across frontiers such that events, decisions and activities in one region of the world can come to have significance for individuals and communities in distant regions of the globe" (Held et al. 1999, pp. 15–16; emphasis in original). Second, globalization implies that these connections are not random or intermittent, but are regularized such that there is a "detectable *intensification*." Third, globalization implies a *speeding up* of global interactions as new communications processes increase the "velocity of the global diffusion of ideas, goods, information, capital and people" (Held et al. 1999, pp. 15–16). Fourth, each of these processes contributes to the deepening enmeshment of local, national, and regional institutions, such that local events can come to have global *impacts*. Conceptualized in this manner, globalization can be distinguished from other forms of transnational interactions. These concepts provide a more precise description of the trends that underlie the policy problems addressed in this book.

Hypotheses about globalization, however, tend to be based, not on research into the control over *information*, but on studies of the flow of *money*—foreign direct investment, capital mobility, trade balances, and so on. They also deal with other forces of production, such as skilled labor, managerial talent, and scientific knowledge. This is unsurprising since, in political science at least, the thesis has primarily been debated among students of comparative and international political economy, and is centered squarely within wider disputes between neoliberal and structural Marxist accounts of international capitalism. Of course, the power of information and communications technology is universally recognized as a crucial force behind the liberalization of financial markets, with concomitant implications for national regulatory and economic power. But how does the globalization hypothesis fare when the resource being studied and regulated is not money, but *information*, a commodity that is even more fluid and perhaps difficult for the state to control?

One of our aims is to submit the basic globalization thesis to examination with reference to a class of policies and practices that concern the flow of information—not information as "ideas" or "knowledge," but information as a commodity or resource for which the search for appropriate levels and instruments of control constitutes the core of a global policy process. Much of that process consists of attempts to forge regimes to govern flows of information of a nonpersonal kind, including works of literature, entertainment products, software, and other commodities constituting intellectual property. But an important part of the flow is that of *personal* information, and it is this that forms the subject of this book. Particularly in the emergent era of electronic commerce, privacy protection policies are central to debates over the structure of the international political economy.

For the last thirty years, states have been attempting to regulate the collection, use, storage, and dissemination of individually identifiable personal data. In recognition of the power of new information and communication technologies in the hands of large public and private agencies, governments began to pass information privacy, or data protection, statutes. These were designed to give individuals greater control over the information collected about them, and to stem the erosion of personal privacy. Most advanced industrial states have now passed such statutes, embodying a basic set of information privacy principles applied to every organization that processes personal data, regardless of the technologies involved. Most laws also establish privacy or data protection agencies with a variety of advisory, regulatory, educational, and complaints-resolution responsibilities (Flaherty 1989, Bennett 1992, Raab 1996).

With the rise of the transnational corporation employing private and public international networks, as well as the advent of distributed computing and data processing severely challenging traditional assumptions about legal liability, the privacy problem has recently assumed a far more complicated and global profile. Thus, the enforceability of information privacy laws is obviously undermined if organizations can escape strict regulatory responsibilities by instantaneously transmitting those data to other jurisdictions for processing.

These general considerations led to some of the central research questions of this book. How have the debates over privacy protection changed as a result of the stretching, intensification, and speeding up of flows of personal information? What is the range of policy instruments (transnational, regulatory, self-regulatory, and technological) for the protection of personal information within the contemporary "toolkit"? How can we compare these instruments and understand their relationship to the international policy community that now makes and implements privacy protection policy? Has there been a "trading-up" of standards, a search for the bare minimum, or something else? In any case, can objective judgments about "levels" of privacy protection be made?

A Public Policy Focus

The book is also informed by the perception that the collection of laws, codes, guidelines, conventions, and practices that together regulate the processing of personal information now constitutes a distinct *policy sector*.[2] Our analysis stems from a conviction that political scientists need to pay closer attention to the regulation of personal information as a major "currency" of both the contemporary capitalist organization and of the modern state. We contend that the nature and resolution of this complex policy problem can be effectively illuminated with the aid of theories and concepts drawn from the political science and public policy literatures. We believe that the understanding of the privacy issue has only been marginally influenced by the questions that most political scientists would find interesting, and by the approaches that are typically used for the analysis of other pressing policy problems.[3]

By the same token, there is no tradition of studying information privacy within the academic discipline of political science, and thus no identifiable tradition or cumulative literature upon which to draw. Indeed, most of the relevant questions about privacy have been posed by scholars affiliated with other academic specialties, such as sociology, law, and computer science, as well as by nonacademics, including journalists and civil-liberties advocates. Moreover, as we have argued elsewhere (van de Donk, Bennett, and Raab 1996), privacy tends to span the traditional subfields within the discipline. It is an issue of political theory, of public policy–making, of political behavior, of public administration, of comparative politics, and of international relations. Our experience is that studying the politics of privacy requires some familiarity, albeit superficial, with conversations at these "separate tables" (Almond 1988). In this book, therefore, we hope to convince the privacy community of academics and practitioners of the value of political science approaches, and political scientists of the importance of privacy protection as a subject of analysis. We also hope to provide insights for regulators and other participants in the social, political, technological, and other constructs that shape privacy as an issue in the contemporary world.

Implicit in our efforts is a concern with the way privacy protection has been studied in the past. It has become trite to observe that information and communication technologies are being innovated and applied with astonishing speed and creativity. The task of the privacy policy community has always been to comprehend these emerging technologies, to study their impact on privacy, and to formulate appropriate responses. These activities have understandably been focused on the pressing practicalities of the moment, and have tended to react to events and developments rather than to anticipate them.

This phenomenon is probably more true in the new millennium than it was in the 1960s, when the protection of personal information first appeared on modern policy agendas as a result of the growing importance of the computer. The centralized mainframes of that period were discrete and uncomplicated compared with the bewildering variety and decentralized application of new technologies that contemporary privacy analysts have to contend with: smart cards, call-management features in telecommunications, genetic testing, video surveillance, data mining, vehicle tracking, mobile telephony, encryption, the Internet and its "cookies," Radio Frequency Identification Devices (RFIDs), and so on. Personal information has rapidly taken on a new importance as an exploitable resource for states and businesses, and has given rise to a host of new practices fueling the contemporary information economies.

The world's privacy commissioners, as regulatory authorities, discuss and attempt to deal with a vast range of technologies and processes, most of which were never anticipated by the data protection laws that have to be implemented nor even contemplated as being their responsibility. With some exceptions, neither they nor the small (but growing) international group of privacy advocates are sufficiently resourced to anticipate technological changes and to study their likely effects upon privacy.

In addition, the analysis of privacy and public policy has tended to be ahistorical. To be sure, some historians have shed light on the social conditions of our ancestors and demonstrated that privacy is a deep-seated and intrinsically human concern (for example, Flaherty 1972, Sennett 1977, Seipp 1978, Ariès 1985). However, in focusing on the latest technology, law, or international agreement, the historical perspective on today's and tomorrow's policy issues risks being lost. Reflecting on these historical developments leads to the conclusion that, even though enormous weaknesses remain in some laws and other policy instruments, the issue has made rapid strides in terms of public policy over a relatively short period. Yet an understanding of contemporary threats to privacy, stemming from the growth of "surveillance society" and from new preoccupations with personal, national, and global security, is enriched by historical analysis.

Another characteristic of the privacy literature is that it is often noncomparative. This can be seen in two different senses. On the one hand, there has been very little systematic comparison of the response of different states with different cultures and institutions to the same technological challenges. Yet privacy protection is an excellent issue for comparative studies of how the same problems are resolved in different countries, and what this says about their institutional and cultural capacities to shape technological change.

The discourse is noncomparative in a second sense, in that privacy protection tends to be discussed, and indeed dealt with on a practical level, as a discrete issue without resemblance to or resonance with other policy fields. It has become a distinct policy sector characterized by a separate set of statutory instruments, regulatory bodies, a network of legal experts, a hardy band of journalists and activists ready to expose information abuses, a growing academic community with expertise in data protection and privacy, and a range of international arenas in which the policy community exchanges ideas and collaborates. The result of this "ghettoization" of the policy is that few comparisons are made with related fields, and sight is often lost of the lessons that can be learnt from them. There are some very interesting cross-sectoral parallels, as well as contrasts, to be drawn with policies of environmental and consumer protection, for example, in terms of the nature of risk assessment, technological change, policy instruments, and the role of the media and public opinion. Comparative analyses that brought the question of privacy protection in from the cold would do a service to the broad field of policy studies.

Finally, the discourse about the politics of privacy is heavily descriptive. The predominance of legal scholarship and comparative legal analysis have reached the point where descriptions abound concerning the scope and coverage of laws, their treatment of difficult definitions, the powers of enforcement authorities, the rights of citizens or consumers, and the like. We do not deny the value of these analyses, but we believe that their preponderance carries some dangers. In particular, this discourse may overlook the fact that the specifications of law are only one factor influencing the behavior of those who process personal data in public and private organizations. The more elusive, but sometimes more important, cultural and institutional factors that exert profound influences on the development and implementation of privacy protection tend to be forgotten in debates over the most appropriate legal and regulatory responses to new technological invasions of privacy. Empirical research into information practices is underdeveloped, and the contributions of organizational sociology and public administration to the analysis of these phenomena have yet to be fully realized.

One further aspect of the privacy literature requires a brief comment here. It is an almost ritual feature of any analysis of privacy—in which we ourselves have participated—to begin with a warning about the inherent difficulty, perhaps impossibility, of defining exactly what *privacy* is, and of disaggregating its various dimensions. For some, this is a show-stopper: if it cannot be defined, how can it be studied? Yet it would be misleading and confining even to try to provide a general definition of *privacy* to focus our analysis. All definitions of privacy, to some extent, are based on questionable assumptions about individualism, and about the distinction between the realms of civil society and the state. Many gloss over essential cultural, class-related, or gender differences among those whose privacy is invaded or protected. It is those very assumptions that require careful interrogation if the "politics" of privacy are to be unearthed.

Valuable attempts have been made to specify the various roles that privacy may perform within modern political systems.[4] Privacy is also said to embrace a number of dimensions: privacy of the person, privacy of personal behavior, privacy of personal communications, and privacy of personal data (Clarke 1998). A useful distinction can also be made between, on the one hand, privacy as an intrinsic or aesthetic value, or the "restriction of personal information as an end in itself" (Rule et al. 1980, p. 22) and, on the other, privacy as an instrumental or "strategic" value where the aim is perhaps to ensure that "the right people use the right data for the right purposes" (Sieghart 1976, p. 76). There is also a distinction between the claim to privacy and a "right of privacy" (McCloskey 1980). Nearly forty years of semantic and philosophical analysis, however, convey the clear message that privacy is a deeply and essentially contested concept, whose parameters are inevitably shaped by the differing contexts within which personal information is processed (Nissenbaum 2004).

Outline of the Book

This book represents the culmination of our individual and collective reflections on the politics of personal privacy protection over the last fifteen years. Our empirical examples are drawn from a number of advanced industrialized states over different historical periods in which different generations of information and communications technologies are apparent. The sweep must be broad if we are thoroughly to explore and interrogate the political theory and practice of privacy protection on a global dimension.

Part I discusses the goals of privacy protection. The first chapter elaborates and critiques the prevailing paradigm for understanding, promoting, and protecting the privacy of personal information. We contend that this paradigm is based on essentially liberal and individualist assumptions, and can be critiqued from a number of perspectives. Our analysis indicates that the privacy paradigm tends to be state-centric. Privacy, as traditionally defined, is a right or interest that citizens possess by virtue of their citizenship within liberal democratic states. Traditionally, the threats to privacy have stemmed from within the boundaries of the single state and from its use of personal data in public administration and law enforcement. Regarding the private sector's processing of personal information, the paradigm conceives of citizens in their role as individual consumers, perhaps armed with rights, but also as persons whose privacy is deemed a preference to be exercised without regard to any wider social consequences. As a policy problem, personal privacy protection has been treated as a value that states, primarily, have the obligation to protect.

Chapter 2 considers the much-neglected relationship between privacy and social equity; the individualist assumptions behind the privacy paradigm have tended to overshadow the question of the distribution of privacy protection (and conversely of surveillance) in modern societies. We therefore broach the question whether privacy protection can be construed as social policy, creating tensions with the legal, economic, and philosophical frameworks that are applied to it. Chapter 3 argues that there has been something of a paradigm shift with a renewed emphasis on promoting trust and confidence in new technologies, and particularly in the Internet. The way in which the risks of privacy invasion are conceptualized and accommodated in business and government practice, and are reflected in privacy-protection systems, is an important part of this emphasis.

How has the privacy-protection problem been reformulated under conditions of globalization, where personal information flows instantaneously across the boundaries of states for processing in multiple and remote locations? In Part II, we describe and evaluate the policy instruments that have attempted to grapple with the global privacy-protection problem. A range of different guidelines, codes, and agreements has been struck over the past thirty years with profound consequences for the shaping of information privacy laws in economically advanced countries and, more recently, in other states as well. Chapter 4 considers the transnational instruments that have originated from a number of prominent international organizations. By far the most important has been the 1995 Directive on Data Protection from the European Union (EU). Central to the rationale of this Directive is the belief that personal data should not be transmitted outside of the EU unless the receiving jurisdiction can guarantee an "adequate" level of protection. The implications of this provision for the international political economy are potentially very considerable, and the policy instruments we analyze in the subsequent chapters have been strongly influenced by the Directive's provisions.

Chapter 5 describes and compares the development of legal instruments that have treated privacy protection in terms of a top-down, command-and-sanction approach. We demonstrate how laws have increasingly converged around a common set of substantive and procedural principles, so that they represent variations on a theme. Nevertheless, the way they have been implemented in practice, through specific machinery and in different territorial contexts, has given rise to global divergences, as well as to doubts about the efficacy of statutory approaches in coping with the challenges of rapid technological and other developments that have significant consequences for privacy. Chapter 6 therefore analyzes the phenomenon of self-regulation, which continues to play an important role within this policy sector, and is regarded by many as the way forward for privacy protection in the global "information age." Codes of practice, standards, and privacy protection seals on Internet websites are the central, self-regulatory components of the "privacy toolbox."

In chapter 7, we show that technologies themselves can operate as policy instruments. The explosion in electronic transactions has produced a number of privacy-enhancing technologies that may have important domestic and international implications. They may supplement regulatory and self-regulatory instruments; they may also be used to avoid or pre-empt regulation; and—in the hands of individuals—they may enhance the ability of citizens to protect their own privacy.

Following these descriptions of the range of policy instruments in the international "toolbox," Part III focuses on several issues concerned with policy impact. Chapter 8 tries to evaluate the policy instruments and their interrelationships as mutually supportive or conflicting components in privacy-protection systems. It brings these together in terms of a more comprehensive understanding of the governance of privacy, involving action and interaction at many levels and through an orchestration of the instruments. An integral vehicle of governance is the international privacy protection regime, the policy community of public and private actors that now make policy on this subject in the international arena. Those actors may be state officials with explicit authority to make and implement public policy on this subject. But they may also be nonstate actors, including media and privacy advocacy groups. Global corporations also make privacy protection policy. The policies and activities of an IBM or a Microsoft may have far greater potential than the actions of nation states, both to endanger privacy and possibly to protect it in the context of their commercial dealings.

Chapter 9 addresses the issue of how we might evaluate whether privacy protection policy is having its desired effect. In practice as well as in academic analysis, public policy and what has been called the "new public management" (Hood 1991) are increasingly focused upon policy outputs and outcomes, rather than on the inputs. Public accountability, and indeed reward, for the results of official actions—in terms of achieving objectives and affecting society—have become increasingly important. This poses a dilemma for an objective that is so ephemeral as protecting privacy, specially where privacy is seen as a human right, as it has come to be in the eyes of policy and legal discourse. Nevertheless, we believe that the search for procedures for making such judgments is a necessary practical effort that academic study can assist.

In chapter 10 we move from the present to the future. Bennett and Grant (1999, pp. 265–266) argue that there are four possible visions of privacy protection for the future. The first, consistent with the "race to the bottom" thesis, is that of the *surveillance society*, in which the individual would have little or no control over the collection and circulation of his or her personal information. The second possibility is one of an *incoherent and fragmented patchwork* of privacy protection, where the pressures towards surveillance would continue, but would be punctuated by periodic and unpredictable victories for the privacy value. A third vision sees a world of *privacy haves and have-nots*, in which some countries trade up to higher standards of protection while others become data havens for those organizations that wish to process personal data free from data protection restrictions. The fourth, consistent with the "trading-up" thesis, would envisage a world of *global privacy standards*. In conclusion, therefore, we interrogate the global dynamics that might push privacy protection in those different directions. Central to our effort is an attempt to understand the complicated relationship between policy goals, policy instruments, and policy impacts, and how each is defined and redefined by the large, pluralistic, and transnational policy community engaged in the governance of privacy.

I
Policy Goals

1
The Privacy Paradigm

Introduction

There is plenty of anthropological and sociological evidence that human beings have always needed a degree of privacy. That need is manifested to different degrees and in different ways from culture to culture (Moore 1984, Bok 1982). These questions continue to interest social scientists, for the quest for privacy can tell us a great deal about social relations and structures, now and in the past. However, this book does not address these questions. Instead, we are interested in the processes by which privacy has become a *political* value and a public policy goal, and in what it means to protect privacy when information can flow freely across organizational and jurisdictional borders.

It is first necessary to establish the theoretical tradition from which the contemporary justification for information privacy was derived, and to present the various critiques of this position. Whatever the psychological or sociological evidence for the importance of privacy, the contemporary political justifications overwhelmingly rest on general assumptions about the continued viability of a *liberal* political philosophy and epistemology. We first discuss how those assumptions have been reflected in the privacy literature in different countries. These assumptions entail a number of policy implications. We then review some of the major critiques of the *privacy paradigm* and conclude by suggesting that some of the principal assumptions behind the privacy paradigm require reformulation as a result of some key shifts in the nature and scope of the privacy issue under conditions of globalization.

Privacy and Liberalism

We use the word *paradigm* to denote a set of assumptions about a phenomenon or area of study that generally go unquestioned. These assumptions collectively set the agenda for research and for policy prescription.
The paradigm produces an agreed understanding about the nature and
scope of a particular problem. Paradigms are rarely explicitly interrogated, unless discoveries in knowledge and science force a community
of scholars to confront their long-held and preconceived assumptions
(Kuhn 1970). Sometimes that interrogation can occur through the
conduct of scientific inquiry; sometimes it can occur because of revolutionary changes in technology. The point is that paradigms are rarely
questioned, because for the most part there is no necessity. We would
argue that there is a set of unquestioned assumptions that surrounds
the modern analysis of privacy protection in Western societies. We also
hope to show that these assumptions are in need of careful scrutiny and
revision in the light of recent technological developments in the use of
personal data in the state and the economy.

The privacy paradigm rests on a conception of society as comprising
relatively autonomous *individuals*. It rests on an atomistic conception of
society; the community is no more than the sum total of the individuals
that make it up. Further, it rests on notions of differences between the
privacy claims and interests of different individuals. Individuals, with
their liberty, autonomy, rationality, and privacy, are assumed to know
their interests, and should be allowed a private sphere untouched by
others. In John Stuart Mill's terms, there should be certain "self-
regarding" activities of private concern, contrasted with "other-
regarding" activities susceptible to community interest and regulation
(Mill 1859).

The modern claim to privacy, then, is based on a notion of a boundary between the individual and other individuals, and between the
individual and the state. It rests on notions of a distinction between the
public and the private. It rests on the pervasive assumption of a civil
society comprised of relatively autonomous individuals who need a
modicum of privacy in order to be able to fulfill the various roles of the
citizen in a liberal democratic state. Thus, as Warren and Brandeis

comment in their seminal article on the right to privacy: "Still, the protection of society must come mainly through a recognition of the rights of the individual. Each man is responsible for his own acts and omissions only" (Warren and Brandeis 1890, pp. 219–220).

Shils is a twentieth-century proponent of this view that privacy reinforces the barriers between the individual and the state and within the contours of civil society (Shils 1956, pp. 154–160). Privacy, for Shils, is essential for the strength of American pluralistic democracy because it bolsters the boundaries between competing and countervailing centers of power. Westin (1967) has provided perhaps the most eloquent statement of the importance of privacy for liberal democratic societies. In contrast to totalitarian regimes,

[A] balance that ensures strong citadels of individual and group privacy and limits both disclosure and surveillance is a prerequisite for liberal democratic societies. The democratic society relies on publicity as a control over government, and on privacy as a shield for group and individual life. . . . Liberal democratic theory assumes that a good life for the individual must have substantial areas of interest apart from political participation. (Westin 1967, p. 24)

Westin goes on to address the specific functions that privacy plays. It promotes freedom of association. It shields scholarship and science from unnecessary interference by government. It permits the use of a secret ballot and protects the voting process by forbidding government surveillance of a citizen's past voting record. It restrains improper police conduct such as "physical brutality, compulsory self-incrimination, and unreasonable searches and seizures" (Westin 1967, p. 25). It serves also to shield those institutions, such as the press, that operate to keep government accountable.

Westin also argues that different historical and political traditions among Western nations were likely to create different results in the overall balance between privacy and government. In his view, England exhibits a "deferential democratic balance," a combination in which there is "greater personal reserve between Englishmen, high personal privacy in home and private associations, and a faith in government that bestows major areas of privacy for government operations." West Germany exhibits an "authoritarian democratic balance" in which "respect for the privacy of person, home, office and press still gives way to the claims of official surveillance and disclosure." The United States exhibits an "egalitarian democratic balance, in which the privacy-supporting values of individualism, associational life, and civil liberty are under constant pressure from privacy-denying tendencies toward social egalitarianism, personal activism, and political fundamentalism" (Westin 1967, pp. 26–27).

Whether or not these generalizations from the 1960s were, or still are, valid, it is no doubt interesting to hypothesize that the way the balance between privacy and community obligations and duties is struck within different democratic societies will vary according to different cultural traditions. The belief in privacy is arguably related to wider attitudes about participation in public affairs and about trust in the authority of governmental agencies. These questions have attracted considerable attention from students of comparative politics (for example, Almond and Verba 1965, 1980), as well as from more anthropological perspectives on social and cultural history (Moore 1984). Unfortunately, we have little systematic cross-national survey evidence about attitudes to privacy with which to investigate the nature and influence of wider cultural attributes. Much of this argumentation tends, therefore, to invoke anecdotes or cultural stereotypes: "the Englishman's home is his castle," and so on. As we will see in chapter 3, sample surveys on privacy in many countries suggest superficially that populations everywhere have high, and increasing, levels of concern about privacy. These seem mainly to be driven by fears of new technology, and by people's distrust of public and private institutions to use that technology with sufficient respect for the civil liberties of the individual. That distrust may be rooted in different historical experiences, but it appears to be pervasive and strong (Bennett 1992, pp. 37–43).

We would therefore observe that privacy protection is normally justified in individualistic terms in the academic literature and in the popular mind. We each have a right or claim to be able to control information that relates to ourselves. Privacy has an aesthetic and humanistic affinity with individual autonomy and dignity. It can be justified in political terms in that it promotes the institutions of liberal democracy, and it has a number of utilitarian values by way of fostering the principle that "only the right people use the right data for the right purposes" (Sieghart

1976). Whether justified in philosophical, political, or utilitarian terms, privacy is almost always seen as a claim or right of individuals that is threatened by a set of social and technological forces. Privacy is something that "we" once had; now it is something that public and private organizations employing the latest information and communications technologies are denying us.

This paradigmatic theme is represented in a large corpus of polemical literature, written mainly by journalists, activists, and academics. Orwellian metaphors and imagery are naturally prolific, even though 1984 came and went without any palpable change in the attention paid to privacy questions. Among the early examples of the popular American literature are Packard's *The Naked Society* (1964) and Brenton's *The Privacy Invaders* (1964). Continually over the past thirty years or more, publishers in North America,[1] Britain,[2] and elsewhere have been attracted by this more polemical genre. The literature also encompasses a shifting anxiety over emerging technologies. This ranges from apprehension over the "snooping devices" of the 1960s, to worries about the sophisticated trade in personal information revealed in Rothfeder's *Privacy for Sale* (1992), to the more contemporary concerns about the Internet discussed by Diffie and Landau (1998) and by Garfinkel (2000), or about the excessive responses to 9/11 (Rosen 2004).

The importance of this literature arguably lies in its cumulative impact and message. A steady flow of horror stories about the intrusive nature of modern technology, about the abuse and misuse of personal data, and about the size and interconnectedness of contemporary information systems has probably had a steady impact on public and political consciousness (Smith 1993). Moreover, many of these stories have then been picked up by the print and visual media, especially television. Big Brother imagery, together with accounts of how the powerless can be denied rights and services through the wrongful collection, use, and disclosure of personal data certainly make good copy; they also make good films.[3]

The contexts may change, the technologies may evolve, but the message of this genre is essentially the same: privacy is eroding, dying, vanishing, receding, and so on. Despite privacy laws, conventions, codes, oversight agencies, and international agreements, privacy (as typically defined) is something of the past, to the extent that a prestigious magazine can proclaim in an editorial (The *Economist* 1999, p. 16): "Privacy is doomed . . . get used to it."[4]

Policy Implications of the Privacy Paradigm

The pervasiveness of liberal assumptions within the literature has had a number of political and policy implications. Assuming that we each have privacy rights and interests, how can one frame a public policy to protect those rights? Philosophers, academic lawyers and other scholars have debated the meaning of *privacy* from a variety of standpoints (for example, Young 1978, Schoeman 1984). As a policy problem, however, the discourse settled around *information privacy*, a concept that arose in the 1960s and 1970s at about the same time that *data protection*, derived from the German *Datenschutz*, entered the vocabulary.

Concerns obviously differed among a number of advanced industrial states. However, a closely knit group of experts in different countries coalesced, shared ideas, and generated a general consensus about the best way to solve the problem of protecting the privacy of personal information (Bennett 1992, pp. 127–129). The overall policy goal in every country was to give individuals greater control of the information that is collected, stored, processed, and disseminated about them by public and, in some cases, private organizations. Essentially, the common view was that this goal necessitates a distinction between the *subject* of the information and the *controller* of that information. This distinction is one of role rather than of person: although we are all "data subjects," many of us are also "data controllers" or "data users." By the 1980s, therefore, it is possible to discern the set of key assumptions upon which information privacy policy development rested.

The first assumption was that privacy is a highly subjective value. Concerns about the protection of personal information vary over time, across jurisdictions, by different ethnic subgroups, by gender, and so on. Consequently, public policy cannot second-guess the kinds of personal information about which a given population or group will be concerned at a given time. Public policy and law can only establish the rules, principles, and procedures by which any individually identifiable personal information should be treated, and by which the worst effects of new technologies can be countered. Information privacy policy is based inevitably, therefore, on *procedural*, rather than *substantive*, tenets. It can put in place the mechanisms by which individuals can assert their own privacy interests and claims, *if they so wish*, and it can impose obligations on those who use personal data. But for the most part, the content of privacy rights and interests have to be defined by individuals themselves according to context.

It is generally difficult to define a priori those data that are inherently worthy of greater protection ("sensitive data"). It is often the shift of context—detaching personal data, through processing, from the circumstances of their original collection—rather than the properties of the data that lead to privacy risks when false conclusions are drawn about persons (Simitis 1987, p. 718). In addition, the same information can take on very different sensitivity levels in different contexts. Our names in the telephone directory may be insensitive; our names on a list of bad credit risks or of sex offenders may be very sensitive. A name and address in a telephone directory may be insensitive for most people, but may be very sensitive for vulnerable persons who do not want to be monitored and tracked down. Whereas the name "P. J. O'Reilly" is not particularly conspicuous in the telephone directory of an Irish town, it stands out in the telephone directory of a Chinese town. Little wonder that many people prefer to have unlisted telephone numbers. Examples of such people would be battered wives, doctors who perform abortions, celebrities, child protection staff, police officers, and so on.

For the most part, therefore, public policy cannot draw a definite line between those types of information that should remain private, and those that may be in the public domain. Law cannot easily delineate between those types of data that are particularly worthy of protection and those that are not. Some data protection laws have indeed distinguished between what are generally agreed to be sensitive data—religious beliefs, political opinions, sexual preferences, health, and the like—and the rest. But this distinction, and the inventory of data deemed sensitive, has remained controversial.

A second conclusion stemmed from the observation that personal information cannot easily be regarded as a property right. Classic economic theorizing would contend that an imperfect marketplace can be rectified in one of two ways. First, one can give a value to personal information so that the costs and benefits of transactions are allocated more appropriately. But it is very difficult to establish personal information as property in law, and then to define rights of action over its illegitimate processing. Consumers may have some bargaining power with a direct marketing firm that wants to trade lists of named individuals; citizens, however, have no bargaining power when faced with a warrant or any other potentially privacy-invasive technique backed by the sanctions of the state. Let us recall that, at the outset of the privacy debate, it was the power of government agencies that were considered to pose the most significant challenges. It was therefore hard to resist the conclusion that the imbalance could only be set right by regulatory intervention. Consequently, information privacy was generally defined as a problem for public policy, rather than as an issue for private choice.

More recently, as critiques of the dominant approach have surfaced, the personal data processing practices of the private sector have arisen as equally significant concerns. Moreover, as Internet communications and e-commerce have risen to prominence, so a variety of market-based solutions have been proposed, all of which have been based on the premise that personal information can be given a property value, to be traded and exchanged within the personal information market (Laudon 1996, Rule and Hunter 1999, Lessig 1999). Such arguments had, however, very little influence on the experts and legislators that grappled with the information privacy problem in the 1970s.

A third assumption concerned the relationship between information privacy and information security. These and related concepts (data protection, data security, confidentiality, etc.) have caused considerable confusion. Clarke notes:

The term "privacy" is used by some people, particularly security specialists and computer scientists, and especially in the United States, to refer to the security of data against various risks, such as the risks of data being accessed or modified by unauthorised persons. In some cases, it is used even more restrictively, to refer only to the security of data during transmission. These aspects are only a small fraction of the considerations within the field of "information privacy." More appropriate terms to use for those concepts are "data security" and "data transmission security." (Clarke 1999, p. 3)

In other words, data security is a necessary but not a sufficient condition for information privacy. An organization might keep the personal information it collects highly secure, but if it should not be collecting that information in the first place, the individual's information privacy rights are clearly violated. Over time, it became clear that the European concept of *data protection* was being used in much the same way as the term *information privacy*. Some, however, see this term as overly technical and concentrating on the *data* rather than the *person* as the object of protection.

Finally, there has been a consensus that the focus of protection should be the individual, or the "natural person" rather than some other entity. Therefore, organizations and corporations cannot have privacy rights. Some societies—in Scandinavia, for example—have attempted to embrace the rights of natural and legal persons in their data protection legislation, and Westin himself was certainly open to the possibility that groups and organizations could have privacy "claims" (Westin 1967, p. 7). Nevertheless, information privacy policy did develop, domestically and internationally, on the assumption that the interests of groups, corporations, and other organizations and the information about them can and should be dealt with through other legal instruments.

These assumptions might not be accepted by every scholar and commentator. They were and are deeply contested. The basic point at this juncture in the analysis is that privacy protection policy was set on a particular trajectory as a result of some common assumptions about the nature of the information privacy problem. It is particularly noteworthy that the privacy paradigm is not only shared by intellectuals and popular commentators, but also by those who make and implement privacy protection policy in advanced industrial states. The policy responses that developed—data protection or information privacy statutes—were driven for the most part by a shared understanding among policy elites about the nature of the problem they were facing. Those shared assumptions, based on fundamental liberal principles, have had profound and widespread policy implications in every advanced industrial state.

The "Fair Information Principles" Doctrine

From these realizations flows the doctrine of "fair information principles" (FIPs), enjoining upon data controllers norms for the collection, retention, use, and disclosure of personal information. The codification of these principles has varied over time and space. They appear either explicitly or implicitly within all national data protection laws, including those that, in the United States, Australia, New Zealand, and Canada, are called Privacy Acts. They appear in more voluntary codes and standards (for example, CSA 1996). They also form the basis of international agreements, which will be discussed in chapter 4. These include the 1981 *Guidelines* of the Organization for Economic Cooperation and Development (OECD 1981), the 1981 *Convention* of the Council of Europe (CoE 1981), and the *Directive on Data Protection* of the European Union (EU 1995). Over time, there has emerged a strong consensus on what it means for the responsible organization to pursue fair information practices responsibly.

While the codification of the principles may vary, they essentially boil down to the following tenets (Bennett and Grant 1999, p. 6). An organization (public or private)

• must be *accountable* for all the personal information in its possession;
• should *identify the purposes* for which the information is processed at or before the time of collection;
• should only collect personal information with the *knowledge and consent* of the individual (except under specified circumstances);
• should *limit the collection* of personal information to that which is necessary for pursuing the identified purposes;
• should not use or disclose personal information for purposes other than those identified, except with the consent of the individual (the *finality* principle);
• should *retain* information only as long as necessary;
• should ensure that personal information is kept *accurate, complete, and up-to-date*;
• should protect personal information with appropriate *security safeguards*;

• should be *open* about its policies and practices and maintain no secret information system;

• should allow data subjects *access* to their personal information, with an ability to amend it if it is inaccurate, incomplete, or obsolete.

These principles are, of course, relative. However conceptualized, privacy is not an absolute right; it must be balanced against correlative rights and obligations to the community, and can be overridden by other important values and rights. Hixson (1987) conceptualizes *balance* as the "continuing struggle over the meaning of private and public, the jurisprudential debate over individual autonomy and collective welfare, between the person and the state, the individual and the community" (Hixson 1987, pp. xv–xvi). An assumption of balance underlies many of the official investigations into privacy policy. The US Privacy Protection Study Commission, for instance, began its analysis by declaring that "the Commission has constantly sought to examine the balance between the legitimate, sometimes competing, interests of the individual, the record-keeping organization, and society in general" (PPSC 1977, p. xv).

However, this concept is problematic both as a verb and a noun (Raab 1999a). It does not discriminate between divergent conceptions of what it means, in practice, *to balance*; nor does it provide criteria for judging when a balance has been achieved. It is therefore not very informative to hear that "a balance must be struck between privacy and the public interest," or that "we have found the right balance" between the one and the other. Different people may go about finding a balance in different ways, and arrive at different substantive points of reconciliation between competing values, as we shall see shortly. Although the concept is related to the terminology of judicial decision, the achievement of a balance may ultimately be a matter of political negotiation, perhaps arriving at a consensus; or, alternatively, of authoritative assertion.

There are, however, many cross-national divergences in the content of privacy protection policy. Privacy regimes, discussed in chapter 8, involve a number of different participants who may play subtly different roles depending on the jurisdiction within which they exist and the political factors that have shaped these regimes. Moreover, not all advanced industrial states have accepted the logic behind privacy protection policy for every kind of personal data controller; the private sector is still largely unregulated in the United States, for example.

Critiques of the Privacy Paradigm

Not all commentators have accepted the logic outlined above. From the outset of the modern debate, there has been a lively but often marginalized critique of liberal political theory as a basis for privacy. This critique has come from at least four overlapping theoretical positions. First, some skeptics have noted that there is a definite negative dimension to the notion of privacy as the "right to be left alone." On the one hand, it draws attention to why one might want to be left alone, and invites the criticism that privacy rights are predominantly asserted by those who have the most to hide. Here is a quote from an early article by Arndt (1949): "The cult of privacy seems specifically designed as a defence mechanism for the protection of anti-social behaviour." He equates privacy with the almost pathological obsession with possessive individualism: "The cult of privacy rests on an individualist conception of society, not merely in the innocent and beneficial sense of a society in which the welfare of individuals is conceived as the end of all social organisation, but in the more specific sense of 'each for himself and the devil take the hindmost'" (Arndt 1949, p. 70).

A similar critique of the theory of information privacy was presented in a famous article by Posner (1978). Posner's central point is that the application of the principle of information privacy has an unfortunate corollary, namely that it allows people to conceal personal information in order to mislead and misrepresent their character. Others, including government institutions, "have a legitimate interest in unmasking the misrepresentation." "It is no answer," he continues, "that, in Brandeis's phrase, people have 'the right to be let alone'. Few people want to be let alone. They want to manipulate the world around them by selective disclosure of facts about themselves. Why should others be asked to take their self-serving claims at face value and prevented from obtaining the information necessary to verify or disprove these claims?" (Posner 1978, p. 20).

A second line of attack has come from those who find the distinction between public and private problematic. They cannot be treated as separate entities but are complex concepts that operate on different dimensions according to whether one is analyzing access to information, the capacities in which agents enjoy that access, or in whose interest the access is sought.

By extension, feminists have criticized privacy for reifying a distinction between a private, domestic (female) world, and a public sphere that is chiefly the preserve of men (Pateman 1983, Allen 1985, Boling 1996). Allen and Mack (1990) criticize Warren and Brandeis on these grounds: they "were not critical of the ways in which home-life, assertions of masculine personality, and norms of female modesty contributed to women's lacking autonomous decision-making and meaningful forms of individual privacy." They advocated "too much of the wrong kinds of privacy—too much modesty, seclusion, reserve and compelled intimacy—and too little individual modes of personal privacy and autonomous private choice" (Allen and Mack 1990, p. 477).

Thirdly, and from the perspective of democratic theory, some would also contend that the liberalism of Locke and Mill, upon which the theory of information privacy rests, represents just one version of democratic theory. Pateman (1970), for example, has contended that there are two general traditions of democratic theory. One is a liberal tradition rooted in eighteenth century natural rights theory; the other is derived from the view that the test of a democracy is not the protection of individual or minority rights, nor the degree of competition between centers of power. Rather, the test is the degree of participation, cooperation, community consciousness, and so on—values that are not necessarily promoted by asserting the "right to be let alone."

This argument finds current reflection in the renewed interest in the communitarian theorizing of Etzioni (1999), which has resonated with contemporary political elites of the left and the right in both Europe and America. Etzioni explicitly attempts to point to a new "communitarian concept of privacy"—"one that systematically provides for a balance between rights and the common good" (Etzioni 1999, p. 15). His analysis of privacy builds on "the sociological observation that although ideologies can be structured around a single organizing principle—like liberty, or a particular social virtue—societies must balance values that are not fully compatible" (Etzioni 1999, p. 200). He contends that, insofar as the public sector is concerned, the balance is too often struck in favor of privacy, while private sector abuses often go unchallenged.

A communitarian position might even argue that some of the most creative civilizations in history—such as ancient Greece and Rome, and Renaissance Italy—flourished despite, or maybe because of, the lack of individual privacy. Public philosophies, including communitarianism, do not spring from an emphasis on the "right to be let alone." If information privacy, as it is conventionally construed, is a precondition of democracy, it is not of democracy per se but of a particular form—liberal democracy, the theoretical justifications for which were provided by Locke, Madison, and Mill, rather than by Jean-Jacques Rousseau. However, there are alternative ways of looking at privacy, and these can serve other notions of democracy. We touch upon this again in the conclusion to this chapter, and develop it at greater length in chapter 2.

A final, and more recent, critique emerges from those who argue from poststructuralist assumptions that the essential ontological premise about the central autonomy of the subject is misguided. In explicating Foucault's (1979) notion of the "panopticon," as a new form of everyday surveillance and social control, Poster explains the postmodern and poststructuralist argument as follows:

Foucault taught us to read a new form of power by deciphering discourse/practice formations instead of intentions of a subject or instrumental actions. Such a discourse analysis when applied to the mode of information yields the uncomfortable discovery that the population participates in its own self-constitution as subjects of the normalizing gaze of the Superpanopticon. We see databases not as an invasion of privacy, as a threat to a centered individual, but as the multiplication of the individual, the constitution of an additional self, one that may be acted upon to the detriment of the "real" self without that "real" self ever being aware of what is happening. (Poster 1990, pp. 97–98)

Poster's (1990) analysis places the *mode of information* and especially the surveillance capacity of modern information technology at the heart of contemporary social transformations. For him, the theory and language of information privacy is irrelevant. As Lyon puts it, the more profound question for the postmodern era is nothing less than "where the human self is located if fragments of personal data constantly circulate within computer systems, beyond any agent's personal control" (Lyon 1994, p. 18). We take up this thread in the next section.

Thus the privacy debate has sometimes raised some insightful and controversial theorization about the concepts *public* and *private* and has echoed some of the claims and counterclaims within political theory generally. For the most part, however, political theorization about privacy has operated within the basic liberal paradigm. The privacy literature has assumed a distinction between the realms of the public business of the state, and the private spheres of individual life. It has also remained relatively unaffected by deeper questions about cultural relativity, or bias according to class, gender, race, or other social categories.

To some extent, this is explained by the fact that much of the more philosophical debate about privacy has originated in or has been directed toward the political and legal arena. It has been said—normally by those trained in European schools—that most American political theory is but a footnote to the Constitution. In the privacy area, there is some truth in this. The bulk of the more abstract and conceptual literature was prompted by the need to understand the emerging "right to privacy" that the US Supreme Court was in the process of developing and applying to private decisions about intimate family concerns such as contraception and abortion. In the tradition of Warren and Brandeis (1890), much of the philosophy of privacy is, therefore, understandably directed towards emerging legal doctrine (for example, Prosser 1960, Fried 1968, Parker 1974, Gavison 1980, Parent 1983). It has remained relatively untroubled by deeper questions about the nature of the *self* in modern or postmodern conditions. The political theory of privacy, in both the United States and Europe, has largely operated within a liberal paradigm and has not yet confronted more profound ontological, epistemological, and sociological issues. The links between the vast tradition of political theory, including its rich and multifaceted critique of the many varieties of liberalism, and the theoretical and practical literature on privacy are, therefore, tenuous.

Surveillance and the Collective Threat to Individual Privacy

As we have just mentioned, some scholars have argued that the contemporary problem confronting advanced industrial states can only be imperfectly addressed and resolved if it is defined in terms of *privacy*. Rather, they claim, the problem is *surveillance*, or excessive and illegitimate surveillance. Thus a sociological tradition has attempted to equate the loss of privacy with some deeper forces associated with modern or postmodern life. Underlying much of the sociological literature is the Foucauldian concept of "panopticism" as a phenomenon that operates as a process of disciplinary classification and control (see Gandy 1993, pp. 3–13).

"Rather late in the day," Lyon argues (1994, p. 219), "sociology started to recognise surveillance as a central dimension of modernity, an institution in its own right, not reducible to capitalism, the nation-state or even bureaucracy." The argument that the institutions of surveillance constitute a theme within modernity, separate from industrialism, capitalism, and the control of the means of violence, is principally associated with the writings of Giddens (1991), who says that each of these forces can be "distinguished analytically from the institutions of surveillance, the basis of the massive increase in organisational power associated with the emergence of modern social life" (Giddens 1991, p. 15). But, for Giddens, surveillance always operates in conjunction with what he terms "institutional reflexivity," the continual need to monitor what is going on, which becomes a constitutive element in an institution's identity and self-reference. Thus, "[s]urveillance plus reflexivity means a 'smoothing of the rough edges' such that behavior which is not integrated into a system . . . becomes alien and discrete" (Giddens 1991, p. 150).[5]

Within political science, the analysis of surveillance has surfaced in relation to the description and critique of authoritarian or totalitarian regimes. This critique spans the centuries, from the use of spies within Imperial Rome, to the systematic monitoring of individual behavior within Stalinist and Fascist systems (Westin 1967). To a certain degree, and perhaps particularly in Europe, the interest in privacy among scholars was motivated by a desire to build institutional and cultural barriers against the comprehensive monitoring of private life that appeared—before the Second World War and during the Cold War years—as a necessary condition for the functioning of totalitarian or authoritarian regimes. Only in post–Cold War times has the pervasiveness of secret-police surveillance in Eastern and Central Europe come into clearer focus through the dismantling of state-security institutions in several countries, and through the accounts of writers like Ash (1997).

In liberal democratic states, however, rather different questions have been raised about the insidious growth of sometimes more subtle forms of surveillance. What is the nature of contemporary surveillance using new information technologies, and to what extent is it different from the practices of the past? What explains the rise of "surveillance societies"? Is it due to an inexorable extension of Weberian bureaucratic rationality? Does it flow from the deterministic logic of technological application? Or is it more rooted in the demands of the capitalist mode of production, and in the responses of even liberal states to threats to national security? Maybe all of these. Perhaps Foucault's point, reflected in Lyon (2001), about the ubiquitous and "everyday" nature of power relations in which individuals unwittingly subscribe to their own surveillance within the "panopticon," provides the central, all-encompassing insight, albeit perhaps too sweeping as an explanation.

From the perspective of those social scientists interested in understanding and curtailing social control, the formulation of the privacy problem in terms of striking the right balance between privacy and organizational "demands" for personal information hardly addresses these wider questions. The liberal political theory that underpins the "fair information practices" places an excessive faith in procedural and individual remedies for excessive intrusions. Thus privacy and data protection laws can only have a marginal impact on the development of surveillance societies; some even would contend that they serve to legitimize new personal information systems and thus extend social control.

A formidable critique of the liberal theory of information privacy is given by Rule and his colleagues (1980). They claim that privacy and data protection laws are all well and good, but that they frame the problem in too narrow a fashion. The argument is that public policies that seek to balance privacy rights with organizational demands for information may produce a fairer and more efficient use and management of personal data, but they cannot control the voracious and inherent appetite of all bureaucratic institutions for more and more information on individuals. They cannot halt surveillance, in other words. On the contrary, there are persuasive cases of the enactment of data protection law being used to legitimate the introduction of new surveillance systems. The essential problem for Rule, then, is the inherent tendency of bureaucratic organizations to want to collect and store more and more increasingly detailed personal information. This dynamic of complex organizations has its roots in the eighteenth century, and in the move towards rationalization and control of resources that accompanied industrialization (Beniger 1986). Thus the "solution" to increasing surveillance can only come from the cultivation of a looser, less discriminating and less efficient relationship between organizations and their clientele.

The idea that advanced industrial societies are creeping inexorably toward an unacceptable level of surveillance has influenced writers from a number of disciplinary and national backgrounds. Flaherty, a Canadian scholar of legal history and subsequently Information and Privacy Commissioner of British Columbia, gave the title of *Protecting Privacy in Surveillance Societies* to his comparative analysis of the operation of data protection laws (Flaherty 1989). He begins: "The central theme of this volume is that individuals in the Western world are increasingly subject to surveillance through the use of data bases in the public and private sectors, and that these developments have negative implications for the quality of life in our societies and for the protection of human rights" (Flaherty 1989, p. 1). Flaherty demonstrates how countries that have established data protection agencies, including Germany and Sweden, have a better chance of stemming the tide than do countries like the United States, whose privacy protection regimes rely solely on the individual assertion of privacy rights through the courts, and on weak oversight mechanisms. But his overall conclusion is skeptical. Echoing Rule's analysis, he suggests that "[a]t present, data protection agencies are in many ways functioning as legitimators of new technology. For the most part, their licensing and advisory functions have not prevented the introduction of threatening new technologies, such as machine-readable identity cards or innumerable forms of enhanced data banks; they act rather as shapers of marginal changes in the operating rules for such instruments of public surveillance" (Flaherty 1989, p. 384).

As technological tools became smaller, less expensive, and more decentralized during the 1980s, other analysts have stressed rather different aspects of the problem. Marx's (1988) study of undercover police surveillance is a case in point. He demonstrates how incremental changes in technology, social values, and the law encouraged covert and deceptive police techniques with a variety of intended and unintended consequences. He shows how all covert surveillance has the tendency to blur the distinction between law enforcement and the lawless activities it is supposed to curtail. The range of new surveillance practices that Marx discusses allows him to suggest some more general characteristics of these new forms of social control.[6] "The awesome power of the new surveillance," Marx summarizes, "lies partly in the paradoxical, never-before-possible combination of decentralized and centralized forms" (1988, pp. 217–219). This analysis led him, in more recent writing, to propose a completely revised "ethics for the new surveillance" to replace what he regards as the outmoded and limiting "fair information principles" doctrine (Marx 1999).

Two other writers who have directed their attention as much to private as to public sector practices see other trends at work. Gandy (1993) draws upon a diversity of traditions to try to understand the implications for social control of new and sophisticated practices for the collection, classification, and manipulation of personal information in both sectors. He points out that a number of social theorists (Karl Marx, Ellul, Giddens, Weber, Foucault) contribute to an understanding of the system of disciplinary surveillance that continually seeks to identify, classify, and evaluate individuals according to ever more refined and discriminating forms of personal data: "[t]he panoptic sort is a difference machine that sorts individuals into categories and classes on the basis of routine measurements. It is a discriminatory technique that allocates options and opportunities on the basis of those measures and the administrative models that they inform" (Gandy 1993, p. 15). Gandy's analysis leads him to the conclusion that real consumer choice can only be implemented through "opt-in" (positive consent) rather than "opt-out" (negative consent) provisions.

Lyon (1994) employs more visual imagery to address similar questions about surveillance. Drawing inspiration from much the same literature as does Gandy, he too contends that surveillance cannot be reduced to one social or political process. But whereas Gandy relies on contemporary empirical analysis of the surveillance practices of modern corporate and bureaucratic organizations, Lyon adopts a more historical approach. He links surveillance to theories of modernity, and speculates on the possibilities and implications of a more communitarian postmodern condition as a way to avoid the dystopic visions of both Orwell and Foucault. In this light, surveillance may have positive, as well as negative, ramifications (Lyon 2001, pp. 53, 136–137).

The arguments of those who stress information privacy, and those who stress surveillance, have often been posited as diametrically opposed political stances. However, the distinction should not be exaggerated. The difference stems more from the starting-point: whether it is from the erosion of privacy and how the institutions of a liberal society might cope with the most dangerous and intrusive threats from new technologies, or whether it is from an interest in the changing impact and nature of social control and disciplinary practice. The processing of personal data by private and public institutions is, from this latter perspective, a way to shed light upon broader social and technological trends.

The privacy and surveillance literatures can often be regarded as two sides of the same coin. With few exceptions, most of the literature we have reviewed would share the following four assumptions:

• that privacy is an individual right;
• that privacy is something that we once had and is now eroding;
• that the source of the privacy problem is structural—the set of impersonal and remote forces that together contribute to the declining ability of individual agents to control the circulation of information that relates to them; and
• that the organizations that are responsible for privacy invasion can be observed, resisted, and regulated because they are subject to a set of obligations that stem from principles as embodied in the laws of discrete and bounded liberal democratic states.

In the conclusion to this chapter, we raise questions about each of these assumptions.

Conclusion: Privacy and the Liberal Democratic State

The privacy paradigm, based on a conceptualization of distinct private and public realms, almost inevitably leads the debate to a discussion of how privacy conflicts with social or community values; this debate is prompted, for example, by the first assumption that we have identified. It often leads to the view that privacy and social values such as sociability, internal security, social welfare, or government efficiency are necessarily antithetical. The problem here is not only the deeply contested and ambiguous quality of these concepts, but also that the promotion of privacy can itself be socially important.

Regan (1995) has gone far to develop the theory of privacy as a value for entities beyond the person. She writes:

> Most privacy scholars emphasize that the individual is better off if privacy exists; I argue that society is better off as well when privacy exists. I maintain that privacy serves not just individual interests but also common, public, and collective purposes. If privacy became less important to one individual in one particular context, or even to several individuals in several contexts, it would still be important as a value because it serves other crucial functions beyond those that it performs for a particular individual. Even if the individual interests in privacy became less compelling, social interests in privacy might remain. (Regan 1995, p. 221)

Regan makes the important point that "[p]rivacy is becoming less an attribute of individuals and records and more an attribute of social relationships and information systems or communication systems" (Regan 1995, p. 230). In this sense, it can be argued that excessive surveillance is bad not only for individuals, but also for society. Take a contemporary example: video-surveillance cameras (CCTV) in public places can be justified as a necessary remedy to deter and detect crime. On an individual level, they can be criticized as being overly intrusive, and may lead to mistaken identification with adverse consequences. On a societal level, we might properly question whether, as a society, we wish to go about our daily affairs with cameras recording our every movement, and enabling the compilation of comprehensive records of what we do, with whom, when, and where.

Moreover, such surveillance may have a chilling effect on associational activity, to the detriment of society. This argument is made in a similar critique by Schwartz (1999), who elaborates a theory of "constitutive privacy" to replace "the traditional liberal understanding of information privacy, which views privacy as a right to control the use of one's personal data" (Schwartz 1999, p. 1613). In analyzing a variety of recent practices on the Internet, Schwartz is persuaded that the silent collection of personal information in cyberspace "has a negative impact on individual self-determination; it makes it difficult to engage in the necessary thinking out loud and deliberation with others upon which choice-making depends" (Schwartz 1999, p. 1701). As we saw, Westin's (1967) account of privacy also highlights certain political values, including freedom of association and the secret ballot. Among his "four states of privacy" (Westin 1967, pp. 31–32), intimacy and anonymity imply the ability of individuals to engage others, rather than signifying their withdrawal from society. These two "states" therefore sustain participation in collective political life, including such modes of activity as associating politically with others or voting without the fear of surveillance.

As seen in analyses such as these, this relationship between privacy and political participation opens an avenue, even within the conventional paradigm, for considering privacy as a value for society beyond the single individual or beyond a simple aggregate of individuals. In a related fashion, we argue that excessive surveillance can lead to the erosion of trust, that it can exacerbate risk, and that it can lead to social inequities. Each of these values (equity, trust, and risk) can be promoted when privacy protection is viewed as social policy. In chapter 2 we elaborate Regan's (1995) argument and investigate how privacy protection policies can promote equity; we consider the reduction of risk and the promotion of trust in chapter 3.

The second of the four assumptions is that our privacy is eroding, vanishing, diminishing, and so on. We question such fatalism from a number of perspectives. We simply do not know whether we would have enjoyed higher "levels" of privacy in the past. How does one calibrate a "level" of privacy? Who are "we"? These measurements are surely highly subjective and dependent on a range of diverse contextual circumstances, as we will touch on in chapter 9. The mediaeval village and nineteenth-century industrial town were not particularly privacy-friendly places. The argument about the erosion of privacy depends on the starting-point. Typically, the fatalistic contention means that organizations simply know more about our lives than they did in the past. If one were to reckon the sum total of information that external structures "know" about us, that aggregation would be far greater than it would be for our predecessors who lived and worked in feudal and industrial societies. We therefore have less control over the amount and quality of the information that relates to us. Stated in this fashion, the problem becomes less one of stemming the collection of information, and more one of ensuring its appropriate use and disclosure. To the extent that this is so, the problem is inherently about social relations and their management.

Thirdly, therefore, the privacy value relates to more than the loss of human agency in the face of impersonal structural forces, whether bureaucracy, capitalism, or technology. We would insist that the privacy problem has its roots in human agency as well as in structural conditions: "[p]rivacy problems arise when technologies work perfectly and when they fail. They arise when administrative, political, and economic elites have worthy motives, and when they do not. They arise through both human fallibility and infallibility" (Bennett and Grant 1999, p. 4).

The scope of the privacy issue can be heuristically demonstrated through a four-cell matrix as depicted in figure 1.1. One axis displays

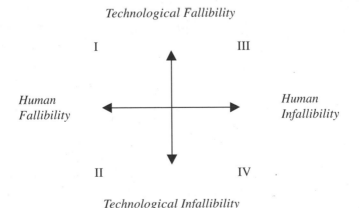

Figure 1.1.
A matrix of privacy problem sources

a difference in the fallibility of human agents; the other shows a difference in the fallibility of structures, which might be technological or organizational. Our point is that "privacy problems" can occur within each cell of the framework. Because each axis is a continuum, positions may be found in any part of each cell. We think, however, that in practice most positions will be found nearer the crossing than the extreme corners in each cell: few human agents, and few technical systems, are either perfect or imperfect.

Most privacy-related problems tend to be seen where human fallibility combines with technological fallibility (I): excessive collection of personal data, inaccuracies, inappropriate disclosures, and so on. To reverse Sieghart's (1976) formula, problems arise when the "wrong data are used by the wrong people for the wrong purposes." The long-held concern about a "Chernobyl" for privacy is also premised on an assumption of human and technological fallibility. But where technologies and humans combine perfectly to pursue organizational goals (IV), there is not necessarily a concomitant lowering of the risk to privacy. Indeed, the fear of the "surveillance society" in which our personal data can be matched, profiled, mined, warehoused, and manipulated for a range of social and economic ends is premised exactly on the fear that human agents and new technologies will combine *as intended* to reach new levels of intrusiveness, and from which there is no escape. Examples of this are the often surreptitious extraction and processing of personal data on Internet websites, and the sharing of personal data by government agencies to provide a range of services to the citizen. Of course, the "infallibility" of these systems may only be an aspiration that is never fully achieved in practice.

On occasion, the quality of human performance can be very high, but the technologies may fail (III); for instance, databases may be obsolete or highly inaccurate, or data-processing capacity may be deficient, or computer systems may be vulnerable to a variety of malicious attacks. On the other hand, technologies may perform as intended, while human agents err (II): they may draw the wrong inferences or conclusions from outputs of data produced by the system, whether because of inadequate training, the biases inherent in the pursuit of certain organizational goals, the pressures of reward systems in the organization, or some other reason related to the workings of human agency.

This simple framework, which could obviously be made more complex, is offered to counter the position that privacy-related risks stem from only one source. Their complexity may have increased as a result of the use of high technology in complex organizations. But they may just as easily relate to human fallibility—a perennial condition that can cause paper medical records to appear on rubbish tips, or damaging faults to appear in the most sophisticated computer program. Thus, the picture of an embattled individual trying to stem the tide of surveillance flowing from a range of impersonal and invulnerable structural forces makes good rhetoric for the privacy cause, but it distorts reality and oversimplifies social and political analysis.

Finally, and relating to the fourth underlying assumption about the role of the state, we wish to investigate the implications for privacy analysis and policy prescription when personal information knows neither organizational nor national attachments. The privacy paradigm, like liberalism, tends to be state-centric. We mean this in two different senses. First, the right to privacy is generally regarded as a benefit of state citizenship. These rights are conferred on us by virtue of our identities as Americans, Britons, Canadians, Germans, or whoever. The privacy and data protection laws that provide us with certain guarantees about our personal information reflect some essential principles of liberal democracy that are either enshrined in constitutions (such as the US Fourth Amendment) or are deeply embedded in the cultural and historical experiences of different societies.

Second, there is still an assumption that the primary threat to these rights emanates from within the state in which one is living, stemming from practices occurring within the boundaries of discrete states, whether in public agencies or in the private sector. This view was prevalent twenty years ago, when many of the European data protection laws were being promulgated, but contemporary discourse and policy prescriptions are still generally dictated by a paradigm that suggests that our personal information still tends to be held within organizations that are easily identifiable, stable, and that reside and operate within the boundaries of modern territorial states. However, many scholars, inspired by various themes prevalent in the literature on postmodernity, have questioned the empirical and theoretical reliance on the state for policy prescriptions in a range of policy sectors—the environment, consumer protection, taxation, and so on. We raise similar questions with respect to privacy protection. Information and communication technologies, systems, and practices involving personal data have changed dramatically over the past twenty years or so. When the problem is increasingly unbounded by state borders, how has this problem been redefined? What are the new policy instruments that have arisen? And what are the prospects for promoting this essential value within a globalized economy?

2
Privacy Protection as Social Policy

Introduction

In chapter 1 we signaled our argument that excessive surveillance can lead to social inequities. This statement has meaning only to the extent that comparisons can be made among individuals in terms of their relative enjoyment of privacy as a value. Looking at privacy in this way does not deny its abstract quality as a right, or even as a preference. However, it allows us to consider privacy issues beyond the conventional paradigm. That paradigm comprehends the individual's privacy and its protection almost completely in terms of individual rights or choices, as if protecting the exercise of one's right to, or choice of, a "level" of privacy could be the only objective of public policy. Yet, even to the extent that privacy *is* a value for individuals to enjoy, it would still be relevant to ascertain who enjoys what privacy, and why. This is because the extent to which individual values are, or can be, satisfied is influenced by social, economic, and political factors beyond individuals themselves, which can be shaped by evidence-based public policy. These factors have distributive consequences for individuals, and thus for society as a whole.

The knowledge basis for informing privacy policy is underdeveloped, and seems to be further advanced for information policy more generally. In academic circles, the economic and social implications of the "information revolution" are being analyzed and projected in considerable detail (Castells 1996, Dutton 1996, 1999, Shapiro 1999, Lessig 1999). Although a long-neglected issue, this analysis now includes investigation of the question of unequal access to the benefits of the "information revolution" and the skewed distribution of its disadvantages, both at the global level—across societies—and among groups of the included and excluded within single societies. As Loader (1998, p. 3) remarks, "[t]alk amongst the technologically elite of advanced capitalist societies of joining the Information Superhighway is a discourse which has little meaning in many regions of the globe where even intermediate telecommunications are underdeveloped." Writing in 1996 of the diffusion of the Internet and of computer-mediated communication (CMC), Castells (1996, p. 359) expected that CMC "will remain the domain of an educated segment of the population of the most advanced countries, numbered in tens of millions but still counting as an elite on a global scale."

Not only is there a "digital divide" on a world scale, but there are deep social inequalities in access to information technologies and resources within the United States (US, NTIA, 2000), the UK (Aurigi and Graham 1998, pp. 61–63), Canada (Ekos Research Associates 2001) and most other advanced industrial societies. Statistics are constantly being revised,[1] but the basic "digital divide" generalization remains sound, although there are alternative hypotheses that access to new information and communication technologies within advanced countries will spread in a more egalitarian fashion that empowers the disadvantaged (see Castells 1996, p. 360). An additional issue concerns the effect of the broadband Internet on the distribution of access and the ability of all to engage in political and other communication online. The Center for Democracy and Technology's (2000) report on this explains the technical reasons why the broadband Internet creates a "significant risk" that "the major means of broadband distribution will be the proprietary domains of large companies or wealthy speakers." The technologies "could ultimately destroy the rough equality among speakers worldwide so vital to the Internet's promotion and facilitation of democracy" (Center for Democracy and Technology 2000, p. 31; see also Morris and Berman 2000). This effect of the move from narrowband to broadband Internet would be felt not only between countries, but within countries as well.

Rather than acquiescing in these maldistributions as the inevitable consequence of the onward march of technology or capitalism, commentators and policy-makers are considering ways of redressing certain of these imbalances—for instance, providing public computing and Internet-accessing facilities to those who can least afford to buy them. Whether these remedial measures can help to erode social inequalities remains a matter for skepticism and debate. However, there is at least greater familiarity with the issues and problems so that new technological, commercial, and governmental developments can be assessed in the light of a broader range of criteria that include the distribution of social, economic, and political outcomes. Although privacy protection is not an issue born of the current "information age," who gets what privacy—and the "privacy divide," if it exists—can be construed as a matter for public policy. In this chapter, we contend that, by failing to consider the social distribution of privacy, the conceptual apparatus used in conventional discourse and regulatory practice has produced a gap in both the understanding of privacy protection and in the ability of public policy to be applied effectively.

The Privacy Paradigm and the "Data Subject"

The case of privacy's distribution is less clear than the broader assessment of who benefits or loses from the "information revolution." We can certainly comprehend the effects on privacy that innovations will have—for instance, mobile telephony, data matching, genetic screening, video surveillance, or the use of smart cards. People will be tracked more comprehensively, more of their personal details will be fed into labyrinthine channels of which they know little and control perhaps even less, and important decisions will be made without their knowledge or consent: so goes the broad-brush scenario found in countless critical books, articles, and media presentations. But the conventional paradigm that we explored in chapter 1 makes it all but impossible to get inside the question of what categories of people risk what privacy invasion and receive what privacy protection. That is because the paradigm conceives of people as undifferentiated "data subjects" or "citizens." Regulatory policy therefore has no place for systematically comprehending variations in their privacy-related experiences, much less for tailoring privacy protection to the needs of these different population segments. As we have argued elsewhere (Raab and Bennett 1998), to do this we need to reconstruct the abstract "data subject" into someone more three-dimensional.

This task is difficult on the basis of what is known at present. For instance, what privacy protection is enjoyed by a married, middle-aged ethnic-minority male working in a managerial post in a small town, and accustomed to buying many goods and services over the Internet? Is it equal to, or different from, that of everyone else in the same society? Are his movements less likely to be monitored in public places by legally unregulated surveillance cameras than those of, say, his teenage, football-fan son? Or more likely than those of a member of the ethnic majority? These persons, and an infinite variety of others, are all equally "data subjects" whose privacy is, in principle, safeguarded by the same laws and, to the extent that they all come within the scope of certain sectors and their information systems, by the other privacy-protecting instruments that are in use there. Yet, whether through compulsion, choice, or simply the differentiated circumstances of life, these different persons and categories differ in terms of the extent and frequency of their exposure to information-processing systems. Therefore, variations in the quality of privacy they experience are likely to occur. It seems reasonable to suppose that, as with other social values, some inequality in the distribution of privacy does exist. Whether this inequality is so serious or so structural as to warrant remedy beyond individual redress are political questions.

There is anecdotal "evidence" about media or other invasions of the privacy of, for instance, royalty, politicians, celebrities, and contest-winners, and sometimes of benefit claimants, gay persons, or other vulnerable groups who may be the targets of surveillance by public authorities. Sometimes, even the routine workings of technologies in interaction with certain categories of persons may expose them to greater privacy risks, albeit unintended and undesired by operators of these technologies and systems. Yet systematic, comparative knowledge is scarce concerning the interaction of information and communications technologies with society in ways that produce group or individual disparities in the privacy of various sections of the population. It is not certain whether these variations are systematic for various categories of people, such that it would be possible to talk of patterns of cumulative disadvantage or privilege, or indeed, therefore, of "privacy classes." Alternatively, it is impossible to calculate whether the privacy of any real individual or group is very well protected with regard to, for example, their banking details, moderately well protected in the health service, but poorly protected online, giving them a hypothetical privacy "score." Nor is it known how or why any such patterns or scores change over time.

Existing survey findings can perhaps be interpreted as showing that data protection is spread unevenly across society, and that the level of risk of privacy invasion varies across social categories. Surveys are not only able to map privacy at levels more finely grained than that of the "citizen" or "data subject," but can also venture to explain privacy experiences in ways that might lead to improvements in privacy practice and policy. However, the surveys that have been conducted have only marginally been designed to address questions of the distribution of privacy, as against the distribution of perceptions and attitudes towards privacy, new technologies, and so on. Therefore, there is generally insufficient, and insufficiently specific, evidence to underpin particular strategies of policy or practice that might be related to a conception of privacy and data protection, or the operations and effects of regulatory bodies, in terms of equality. This means that, at the present time, policies addressing inequities in the enjoyment of privacy protection would lack a secure basis of evidence. They would be ineffective without an accompanying move towards specifying the criteria by which improvements could be tracked, and also without a strategy indicating how, and with what instruments, they could be implemented. References to research findings about inequities are helpful, although it is difficult to disentangle these from the questions of public trust and variations in perceptions of, and exposure to, risk, which is addressed in chapter 3. We therefore reserve a discussion of survey evidence for that chapter.

Why do we need to know more about data subjects? One reason is that such knowledge could inform ways of leveling the playing field between data controllers and data subjects. It is obvious that privacy regulators are better organized to comprehend the activities of those who use personal data—data controllers—in the great variety of "sectors" in which they operate than they are to understand the circumstances of the people—data subjects—whose data are collected, processed, and transmitted. Privacy regulators have more highly developed "detectors" (Hood 1983) for learning about the practices of credit-reference agencies, banks, social-services agencies, electronic-commerce companies, universities, the police, and many other sectors. The work "desks" of regulatory bodies may even be constructed, and work undertaken, in terms of overseeing the activities of particular industries or sectors. The second reason is that, in political terms, the functional sectors of data controllers are in many cases better organized to articulate their interests and to engage in dialogue and negotiation with policy-makers and regulators over issues of compliance and control. Many of them—for example, the credit-reference and direct-marketing industries—are represented by clearer and louder political voices than are most data subjects, who are typically less able to bring a sharply focused or nuanced point of view to the political process through which policies are made and implemented. In short, in terms of the way they are comprehended and dealt with in policy and regulatory circles, data controllers tend to be better "known" than are data subjects. The latter are far more shadowy and one-dimensional: the abstract "citizens" or "customers" of the worlds they inhabit. Yet, as we shall see, many data controllers themselves rely on the construction of refined and differentiated categories of members of the public in order to market or control them.

This discrepant situation has consequences for practical knowledge and action in the policy systems for information privacy. Not all data controllers are equally or highly visible or influential, but they are arguably more able to mobilize themselves politically than is the public at large, as is always evident when national laws and international agreements are being negotiated. In contrast, citizens and consumers—data subjects—are less organized and less sophisticated as political actors. This is so despite the important and often successful efforts of privacy pressure groups that speak loudly and clearly on behalf of data subjects. It remains the case that data subjects are normally underpowered in the political arena, and that they are perhaps particularly disadvantaged in transnational decision arenas.

Currently, there is little distinction, conceptually or institutionally, between the individual data subject and all data subjects. On those occasions in the implementation of policy when distinctions *are* drawn among data subjects, it is mainly with reference to the attributed roles they play in those functional sectors by which the data controllers are identified. They are then seen as credit-seekers, depositors, welfare recipients, online consumers, students, suspects, and the like. But these are ascribed and derivative identities: they are not ones that indicate any available knowledge about their outlooks, interests, and sociodemographic characteristics. In addition, they are not necessarily ones that they might themselves adopt or around which they might organize. Thus the institutionalization of ways of classifying the world of the data controllers shapes the way data subjects are viewed. Classification schemes are potent (Bowker and Star 1999): among other effects, they may construct certain opportunities for comprehension and action, and inhibit others that may be based on different ways of categorizing the world. They lay down the tramlines for the way organizations understand things, and for the way in which people understand themselves and their relations with institutions.

We do not argue that the conventional categories of data subjects, and of data controllers, are absurd, but they do need to be seen in interaction with other ways of looking at society if the distributive questions are to be asked and answered. After some thirty years, data protection regimes and their instruments have too heavily institutionalized these categorical and sectoral ways of thinking and acting for this framework to be disregarded. It may, after all, be an effective and efficient way of relating protection to certain kinds of need. Data controllers, regulatory officials, and data subjects themselves can readily recognize these identities and can guide their conduct in terms of them; action and mutual expectations are conveniently shaped and simplified in these grooves. On the other hand, they may be insufficient to address wider issues of privacy protection in which these conceptions of data subjects in their sectoral variety mask, or ignore, other characteristics of populations. These would include gender, ethnicity, social class, age, income, or other typical socioeconomic and demographic categories. On the other hand, although some headway is being made through survey research, as we show in chapter 3, too little is known as yet about data subjects in *these* terms for it to be argued with confidence that there are invisible privacy-protection needs that go unaddressed, or undiscovered interests that go unrepresented, within regulatory regimes.

The absence of such a data-protection perspective on the data subject is ironic, when one considers that industries engaged in marketing to consumers are becoming ever-more sophisticated in their knowledge of the population, and are able to target them with considerable precision concerning their personal preferences, habits, and characteristics that are related to sociological and related typologies (Gandy 1993). Affinity marketing techniques are able to compile increasingly fine-grained and differentiated pictures of target populations, based on actual purchasing behavior. This technology results in the availability of some extensive and highly specific knowledge about customers. Abacus, for example, a major consumer database provider, analyzes some 3.5 billion catalog transactions from 90 million US households to determine precisely how many transactions are made by households in each of seven age groups, and how much on average is spent per transaction by each group. Abacus monitors changes over time in these behavior patterns, including shifts from catalog to online transactions, and the effect of the 11 September 2001 terrorist attack on these commercial activities, including geographical effects. The president of Abacus exhorts potential users of their databases that "[t]he more you know about your customers, the better equipped you'll be to develop short- and long-term marketing strategies, improve your profitability and increase your market share."[2]

The detailed categorization and profiling of consumers' habits and preferences by firms such as this abound in the burgeoning industry of marketing. We know of no equivalent impetus on the part of regulatory agencies to know systematically more about those whose privacy they are protecting. Privacy-protection organizations do not base their work on such refined intelligence about data subjects. They tend to have insufficient resources to mount research inquiries that would gather such information, and the external supply of such research, in any case, is very meager. Moreover, the legislative framework within which they work does not encourage regulators to expand their remit in this direction, nor is there typically any public policy pressure from the political system to make such a move. It is therefore difficult for regulators to target their assistance and advice to specific nonsectoral categories or groups of data subjects. Cognitive limitations join with other political, financial, and administrative restraints to keep regulatory practices focused upon broad, often low-level, objectives in privacy protection. These aims and achievements are not to be disparaged; however, their adequacy can be questioned. To improve upon this, knowledge about the different sorts of persons within the sectorally defined identities—or even independent of these—would need to enter the conceptions and practices of privacy-protection regimes. It would enable novel questions to be asked with a view to acting on their answers with alterations of policy and implementation.

The Distribution of Privacy and the Policy Agenda

What difference would it make to consider how privacy invasions and protections are distributed among types of data subjects within society, or indeed across societies? On the global level, we might envisage the world's population in the future divided, however crudely, into a world of privacy *haves* and *have-nots*. Such a division is already with us, construed in terms of countries that have legal instruments in place to protect privacy and personal data, and those that do not. The former would apply instruments of privacy protection, often comprehensively and vigorously. In terms of the 1995 EU Data Protection Directive, they would offer their citizens an "adequate level of privacy." In other countries, however, privacy protection policies and measures would be applied in a reactive manner, only as the issue became politicized. Pockets of these would act as "data havens," permitting organizations to process personal data without regard to data protection standards (Bennett and Grant 1999, p. 266). On the other hand, we might also imagine a future in which the distribution of privacy protection does not map onto distinctions between the geographic areas we call nation states. We could also conceive of a world in which privacy is unequally distributed *within* societies, such that, in whichever jurisdiction one lives, one may enjoy the fruits of a more private, less monitored, life if one is relatively more affluent, a member of the dominant ethnic group, male, well educated, and so on. We cannot say that that world is already with us; the picture is undoubtedly far more complex and paradoxical.

A better understanding of these distributions can underpin questions about whether inequalities can be justified and whether they can be altered by public policy and its implementation by public agencies, and at what jurisdictional level. Privacy protection can thus become part of *social* policy, at least within specific jurisdictions and perhaps more widely. In this idiom, privacy protection can be debated—as with the case of welfare, education, or health—in terms of alternatives such as public or private provision, costs and benefits, responsibilities and entitlements, and the best way to "deliver" privacy. Awareness of the importance of distributive questions would also underpin attempts to evaluate the impact of specific policy instruments or combinations of instruments, and of privacy-invasive technologies, upon different sections of society, and not just leave us with our current understanding of policy impacts in aggregate terms for a population as a whole. For instance, for *whose* privacy do privacy-enhancing technologies (PETs) make a real difference? What kind of person is best able to understand data-protection law and to take advantage of its opportunities for complaint and redress? Are they the same categories as those who understand "cookies"[3] and how to switch off these covert data-collection devices in order to minimize surveillance on the Internet?

In the early years of public policy analysis, Lowi (1964) made an important, and much-cited, distinction between distributive, redistributive and regulatory policy. The analytical assumption behind these categories was that different types of policy might be associated with different political and administrative processes or "arenas of power." We draw on this conceptualization in our subsequent discussion of regulatory approaches. Privacy protection is traditionally regarded as a regulatory policy (Bennett 1999). But how is it perceived if the purpose is to be redefined to include redistributive effects? Implementing the recognition that who wins and loses from privacy protection is a central issue would alter the policy playing field, the actors who may be mobilized, and hence the "politics" of privacy.

However, we are not aware that privacy-as-social-policy has yet seriously entered the conceptual and practical thinking of the privacy policy community, whether in official policy circles, among privacy advocates, or within academia. To be sure, there are examples where privacy regulators and pressure groups have attempted to comprehend differences among data subjects, to tailor or target their advice and help, or to mobilize subpopulations in campaigns over privacy issues. Thus, surveys in Australia have shown the privacy concerns of the aboriginal population and the problems that disabled persons have had over access to their medical records (Australia, Office of the Federal Privacy Commissioner 1995, p. 9). The Office of the British Columbia Information and Privacy Commissioner has translated its guidance materials into both Mandarin Chinese and Punjabi.[4] In addition, some civil liberties advocates explicitly see their role in terms of "helping the little guy," such as the welfare recipient whose privacy is threatened by government data-matching to reduce fraud (Westwood 1999). However, the "little guy" is still too easily seen as an abstract "everyman" and not as a type that comes in a variety of shapes and sizes—and genders, and whose privacy problems are specific to the ways in which these categories are comprehended within the government, the society, and the economy.

A quite obvious complexity is that any profile of privacy *haves* and privacy *have-nots* is not certain to coincide with conventional pictures of socioeconomic inequality. It would be tempting, but misleading, to offer a hypothesis that those groups in society who have been economically and politically marginalized in the past (the "little guys") are more likely to be the subjects of higher levels of surveillance. Undoubtedly this is true with regard to many forms of governmental data collection and processing. Research on closed-circuit television surveillance, for example, has exposed the not surprising finding that those individuals deemed worthy of monitoring are predominantly young males of "subcultural" backgrounds (Norris and Armstrong 1999). Similarly, government data-matching and profiling practices tend to impact those who are more dependent on government welfare programs. But then consider surveillance on the Internet, discussed in chapter 7: the surreptitious extraction and profiling of consumer data through the logging of cookies files and other spyware is directed principally to those presumed to have the most money to spend. Other marketing practices obviously have similar targets. We can obviously debate which form of data surveillance is of more abstract harm to the individual, but the point remains that the "privacy divide" does not map neatly onto the "digital divide." It is precisely that privileged minority who possess the luxury of broadband access who have most to fear from the varied and innovative forms of personal-data extraction on the Internet (Bennett 2001).

Misapprehension of this owes much to the fact that it is all the easier to avoid distributional questions altogether if one's conception of privacy is based on the individualist precepts concerning the right to privacy that we explained in chapter 1, as if the exercise of one person's privacy rights had no consequences for another person's exercise of theirs. These questions are far less easy to avoid if it can be argued that privacy has a *social* value in addition to its value to the individual. In chapter 1, we pointed to the importance of Regan's (1995) powerful argument about privacy's social value in the context of a critique of the conventional paradigm. We return to it at greater length here in view of its centrality to the present discussion. It will also be germane to the evaluation of the range of privacy instruments that we undertake in Part II.

Regan's (1995, p. 233) observation is particularly apt: "[i]f one individual or a group of individuals waives privacy rights, the level of privacy for all individuals decreases because the value of privacy decreases." She argues that "privacy's importance does not stop with the individual, . . . a recognition of the social importance of privacy will clear a path for more serious policy discourse about privacy and for the formulation of more effective public policy to protect privacy" (Regan 1995, p. 220). She supports this argument by treating privacy as having common, public, and collective value. All individuals have a common interest in privacy, reflected in shared meanings and perceptions of when it is under threat—even though they may differ over what its substance is or where they would draw its boundary. Whereas this value of privacy is still within the individual realm, the public value of privacy has to do with its instrumental worth in underpinning democratic institutions and practices. The case for this is made in terms of the importance of privacy for safeguarding participation in the affairs of the democratic polity.

The literature Regan cites (1995, pp. 225–227) concerns freedom of association and speech as well as limiting government's arbitrary power. But it also emphasizes the importance of privacy in preventing the fragmentation of the public realm by allowing individuals to operate within it on the basis of their commonality rather than their differences. Related arguments concerning privacy, democracy, and public values are also made elsewhere by several writers (for example, Raab 1997b, Bennett 1992, pp. 29–33). Regan (2002) deepens the discussion with reference to cyberspace as a "commons," while Schoeman (1992) sees privacy as indispensable for "social freedom" through its functioning within and among a variety of associations in a pluralist society.

We would hold that these two attributes of the social importance of privacy are, however, threatened to the extent that some categories of persons experience less privacy than others. For instance, the political, public realm is harmed if restraint on arbitrary power can only be exercised by certain, perhaps privacy-privileged, persons or categories. It is also harmed if the ability to form associations is possible only for them by virtue of their greater enjoyment of privacy through, say, the workings of patterns of social discrimination. Commonality is also incomplete to the extent that such patterns exclude certain groups from sharing in common perceptions and interests concerning privacy.

For the argument of this chapter, however, it is the *collective*, indivisible value of privacy that is particularly important, and which is perhaps especially vulnerable to attack by inequities. As a collective value, privacy cannot easily be provided to one person without its being enjoyed by others. Rather like street lighting, to provide for one is to provide for all. Regan (1995, p. 230) also observes that "some minimum level of privacy may be indivisible" because of the way information and communication systems are designed. Although many technologies and information systems exacerbate social differences, Regan (1995, p. 237) shows how the creation of "privacy haves" and "privacy have-nots" can be inhibited. This social division is likely to happen unless privacy's collective value is explicitly recognized in organizational practice and built into the construction of information and communications technologies and systems. However, this value could be subverted if some people were better able than others to buy protective information technologies for their own use, in keeping with the individualist paradigm. This would be the information society's equivalent of "gated communities."

The outcome of the "contest" between the individual and the social value of privacy is therefore far from decided. The social value is under-powered and survives precariously unless it can be specifically rein-forced by a change in the privacy culture, for it is powerfully challenged by the legacy of the conventional paradigm and by forces that tend to the protection of privacy seen as an individual value, if a value at all. Such a change would acknowledge this social value and act upon it through policy-related measures and/or technological design aimed at raising the minimum level of privacy and preventing its decollectivization.

Despite the inherently collective-value nature of some information systems, the opportunities for social division show signs of winning out as we move further into the era of electronic commerce and the growing acceptability, in business and policy circles, of market solutions and their accompanying ideologies and technologies of individual choice and tailor-made preferences. These offer individuals the real possibility of uncoupling "their" privacy from that of everyone else's, although, as Regan (1995) points out, there are strong constraints on realizing this in practice; moreover, it may be chimerical if the negation of privacy as a social value negates individual privacy as well. Be that as it may, even if market solutions, which involve individuals choosing their own privacy "level," were predicated on the assumption of a well-informed consum-erate, it is likely that such knowledge and awareness would be unevenly distributed unless supported by effective and deliberately egalitarian policies of "consumer" or citizen education.

For the sake of argument, suppose one were to envisage a "mixed economy of protection" in which those who can afford to do so, or who wield sufficient market power, negotiate the protection of their own privacy, while the rest are protected by the state or by data controllers' self-regulatory processes, which may arguably be of lesser quality. The merits and demerits of such a policy approach cannot be evaluated within the prevailing paradigm, because the question of inequities, their justification, and their remedy rarely, if ever, arises. Is an uneven distribution of privacy protection acceptable on social and political grounds? There are few arenas in which such an issue can be addressed. To paraphrase Schattschneider (1960, p. 71), some privacy issues and approaches may be "organized into" the regulatory policy-making process while others are "organized out"—a "mobilization of bias" that might leave certain needs for privacy protection unrecognized and unmet.

The privacy issues typically addressed by laws and the activities of regulatory bodies are those that correspond to the major functional and organizational divisions of society and the economy, or to particular technologies like telecommunications. The effects of the conventional conceptual paradigm, together with the relatively low salience of privacy issues in politics, the limited resources of regulatory agencies to point out and tackle neglected problems, and the power of major institutions result in many issues and approaches slipping through the net. This may be an instance of what Bachrach and Baratz (1962) regard as the second face of power, in which there are potential issues on which decisions are prevented. Or perhaps, beyond this, it is an instance of what Lukes (1974, pp. 21–22) shows to be the third dimension of power, in which "the bias of the system is not sustained simply by a series of individually chosen acts [as in Bachrach and Baratz's view], but also ... by the socially structured and culturally patterned behaviour of groups, and practices of institutions, which may indeed be manifested by individuals' inaction." An important difficulty here, of course, is establishing a convincing case that it is in disadvantaged people's "real interest" to put privacy inequities on the agenda for political solutions and thus to raise latent conflict to the status of an issue. But if privacy is a human right, the case may be strong, and the actions of privacy advocates in placing privacy on the agenda are not misplaced or presumptuous.

The salient point, however, is that the implementation of these remedial perceptions and reinforcements is not inevitable. There is little in the way the policy instruments and the theoretical paradigm of privacy are currently constructed that would encourage the adoption of new solutions, based on different values, unless they were deliberately brought to attention as possibilities for public policy; in other words, unless mere "situations" of inequity became "problems" and were then shaped into issues for action. As we have seen, privacy advocates have done just this for privacy as such—calling attention to the privacy abusiveness of "normal" business or state practices. However, they have done so largely within the prevailing framework of individualist conceptions of privacy in which the distributional issue of haves and have-nots has largely been left out of account, or has been only crudely articulated.

Therefore, a second conclusion is that the more that technological and information systems do come to embody the inequity-inhibiting properties that Regan (1995) has outlined, the more that this allows not just a view of privacy as a *collective* value but also as an *egalitarian* one. It strengthens the argument that privacy should be seen as a value whose unequal distribution is a societal problem. If it is a problem, it is one for which it would be appropriate to explore a range of remedial or preventive policy options as well as to debate the question of where responsibility should lie for doing something about it. Moreover, the rationale for this framework of conception and action would be reinforced by the comprehension of privacy as a right requiring equal protection and equal provision. To date, none of these departures have been undertaken within the communities involved in the policy process.

In complementary ways, these arguments suggest that privacy must be understood in terms of purposes that transcend that of individual benefit, without however denying the importance of the latter or sacrificing it to some supposed social good that must take precedence. Individual privacy is only truly achievable in a society in which privacy is considered socially valuable and which reflects that esteem in its collective decision-making—in other words, in its political and governmental activity. The question here is how societal arrangements can be devised that promote privacy in this sense. Morally, this means that citizens should so recognize the importance of privacy to other citizens, and to society as a whole, that they would support the protection of their privacy even if they do not value it for themselves, and—more controversially—even if particular instances of its enjoyment by others interfered with the full satisfaction of their own interests. This, of course, is not to foreclose a debate between conceptions of "equality of opportunity" and "equality of result," as in other realms of social policy. It may be sufficient—and perhaps the only possible avenue—to work toward ensuring the former conception, especially if the latter cannot be so easily measured. Equality of opportunity is more likely to be approached where underpowered individuals are not left to their own devices to protect their information; among other reasons, such self-protection is not widely available in an online, networked world. This is why the provision of privacy instruments beyond those wielded by individuals is important in the light of questions concerning equity, and why an examination of how they work, which we address in Part II, is relevant to normative considerations about privacy.

Conclusion: Equity—The Consequences for Policy and Practice

Beyond designing privacy into technologies and information systems lies shaping the discourse and designing the instruments of privacy protection in accordance with revised conceptions of privacy as a value. Away from the field of privacy protection, in the wider world of public-sector accountability, it is encouraging that there is some acknowledgment of the importance of employing a broader range of evaluative criteria than the usual ones of efficiency, effectiveness, and economy. The latter constitute a familiar discourse in the world of administration and accountability, and may be essential criteria for judging the success of policies and organizational behavior in many fields, including that of privacy. But the further development of evaluative theory and practice in public sector management also aims to incorporate a concern to even out the distribution of services, and for quality as well (Pollitt 1988).

We reserve for chapter 9 our main discussion of the evaluation of the quality of privacy protection. Although the theoretical and practical basis for this evaluation remains to be developed, it is unlikely that a single summary indicator would give a full picture, especially if the improvement of regulation were one of the aims of evaluation. As far as the equitable distribution of privacy is concerned, the use of relatively crude performance measures, even if they are broken down into different sectors of data usage such as credit-referencing, direct marketing, or health services, may reflect only what hard-pressed regulatory bodies can do with limited evaluation resources, few guidelines as to what parliaments or the public may deem important, and no mandate to develop wider-ranging, three-dimensional accounts of their performance. If it is therefore very difficult to know how far privacy is actually better protected as a result of laws, court cases, codes of practice, technological safeguards, or other devices, it is harder still to say with any reliability *whose* privacy is better protected and whose is not. Yet, because equity as a criterion has an established place in general political discourse, it points up the political choices that inhere in the provision of public services, including privacy protection.

Those choices cannot be ignored, since privacy itself is a political value in the sense that it corresponds to a view of the proper relationship among persons and between persons and society. Now, it is nothing new for public policy about privacy to raise political questions. It does this when the allocation of resources to regulatory tasks is at issue. But are such resources allocated according to explicit choices as to whose privacy to protect? Is everyone's privacy of equal worth to protect, or should some receive greater protection than others? Should the categories used in such allocative decisions reflect the variety of functional systems of information-collection, processing and use, or, instead, the variety of social categories within populations? Even among these systems, should more energy be spent regulating the data processing of direct marketers or public housing agencies, than of employers or Internet service providers? Or should greater attention be paid to protecting types of data that are deemed more sensitive, without regard to whether the way such data types are aligned with categories of persons protected would thereby result in a widening or a narrowing of the gap in the distribution of protection? The EU Data Protection Directive (1995), upon which all new European data protection law is based, certainly signals in this direction. Article 8 stipulates that "Member States shall prohibit the processing of personal data revealing racial or ethnic origin, political opinions, religious or philosophical beliefs, trade-union membership, and the processing of data concerning health or sex life." The exceptions to this prohibition are drawn more narrowly than with respect to non-sensitive forms of data.

Whether data protection "works" may depend on how questions like these are answered within regulatory regimes, in which policy and implementation choices could be made in the light of better knowledge about who is affected by which data practices, given the likelihood that privacy invasions are socially structured or patterned and are not randomly or evenly distributed. Take, for instance, the availability of channels of complaint against the misuse of personal information. Systems of data protection may provide such avenues of redress, but a knowledge of one's rights and of the opportunities for exercising them, plus the ability to take advantage of them, might be prerequisite to using them. This may depend upon possession of the social or cultural capital to do so—qualities that are very unevenly spread across society. Yet the arcana of data protection are difficult for almost everyone to fathom. This is why many regulatory agencies are so concerned with informing and educating the public, even construing their role in terms of these activities (Raab 1993). But if they do not have sufficient resources to be very proactive in reaching out to those who are underpowered in terms of seeking redress, and if there is a weak social infrastructure of supportive agencies, then disparities are not likely to be eroded.

What, if anything, lawmakers wish to do about these distributions of privacy protection might become a more serious issue of public policy if questions such as those posed earlier can be answered with reliable information. In turn, the approach taken by regulators in deploying their resources could be more knowledge-based as well. But how far can they do this with any confidence that the social-policy conception of privacy protection is both politically legitimate and comprehensible within the prevailing paradigm of privacy and the knowledge-categories by which privacy invasions are reckoned? They may be forced, instead, to abide by political expectations or to follow administrative and legal procedures, which only register certain "problems"—perhaps the ones that are pressed upon them by vocal or well-resourced interest and pressure groups—and to leave other ones alone.

This effect is achieved in part because the paradigmatic emphasis on procedural due process and on a purely individualist construct of the value of privacy militate against raising distributional and redistributional issues of privacy protection. It may also be achieved by the way in which the paradigm's procedural emphasis encourages regulators to strike balances between privacy and other policy objectives, including the administrative or commercial use of personal data. This is an approach that is evident in the drafting of legislation such as the

European Union Directive as well as of national laws. Where far more is known about the consequences of inhibiting the use of personal data in trade or government administration than about the effects of limiting privacy, this approach makes it more difficult for privacy to be defended in the face of competing values. There are strong political demands, expressed nationally and internationally and inscribed in laws and policy documents, that the aim of privacy protection should be to smooth commerce's and government's exploitation of personal information. Regulators may find that the climate is poor for any "activist" interpretation of their role, and they may be constrained to operate only within the framework of a balance-seeking, pragmatic conception—an approach that has been criticized elsewhere (Raab 1999a, see also chapter 1).

The conception of privacy as a right rather than as a preference provides a better basis on which to strengthen privacy's claim to be taken seriously in the "balance." But to the extent that little is understood about the distribution of privacy, it is all the more difficult for equity to enter into consideration as a further policy objective in given instances of reconciling the processing of data with the obligation to protect privacy. Comprehending privacy in terms of values such as equity, however, does not necessarily lead to the conclusion that more equal distributions—whether of opportunity or result—are mandatory if injustice is to be avoided. But it at least strengthens the need to argue the grounds on which an unequal distribution can be justified. In chapter 3, we explore whether a reframing of the issue in terms of the reduction of risk can help to overcome these conceptual and practical difficulties.

3

Privacy Protection as Trust Promotion and Risk Management

Trust, Risk, and the Privacy Paradigm

Our discussion, in chapter 1, of the conventional paradigm of privacy indicated that the conception of privacy as an individual right could be challenged by an emergent recognition of privacy as a social value. Chapter 2 elaborated this argument in terms of the implications of the social value of privacy for the question of the equitable distribution of privacy protection. But a further, and somewhat different, observation can be made about the contemporary status of the paradigm within the broader economic, social, and political processes. There has been an increase in the prominence of a more instrumental or functional approach in which privacy is seen as only one interest and one right among others, and not as entitled to protection beyond what is necessary to underpin important economic and administrative processes and the maintenance of public order. The shoe, it seems, is on the other foot: invasions of privacy are increasingly regarded as acceptable, and it is the case *for* privacy protection that must be argued. As we saw in chapter 1, the conception of privacy as a value to be balanced against competing values, or, indeed, balanced against more mundane "interests," has become securely entrenched in data-protection policy and its practical implementation over the past thirty years or more.

To the extent that privacy comes off worse in these balancing processes, as many would argue, so we can observe the decentering of privacy. One interpretation of this phenomenon is that privacy was never really fundamental as a human value in the first place, as the paradigm would have us believe. For example, Posner (1978, p. 19) sees privacy as an instrumental, not a final, value—as an input to the achievement of some other value, such as "the production of income or some other broad measure of utility or welfare." Indeed, Westin (1967) takes a related, functional view in investigating the value of privacy to the individual. For him, "privacy is neither a self-sufficient state nor an end in itself. . . . [I]t is basically an instrument for achieving individual goals of self-realization" (Westin 1967, p. 39) and for protecting the "inner domain" of "independent persons in a free society" (Westin 1967, p. 238). But a second view is that the decentering of privacy is part of the essence of postmodernism's challenge to the importance of self-hood and to the very definition of the "self" (Giddens 1991, Poster 1990). If postmodernism threatens the foundations of privacy, so too, do communitarian theorists' criticisms of the elevation of the value of individual privacy (Etzioni 1999).

A third interpretation is perhaps more pedestrian and down-to-earth. It is that privacy cannot be allowed to get in the way of the exploitation of modern technologies in administration and in the economy, or of the satisfaction of public-order objectives that include, principally, the security of the state and the personal security and safety of its citizens. We must somehow be reasonable in our expectation of privacy, and learn to live with less privacy than we might otherwise want. Although the articulation of this view of the place of privacy is largely confined to activity within the single state, as in the received paradigm, it also has an increasingly significant meaning within international and global processes.

Yet, even while privacy is contextualized in these ways, there is evidence, in certain quarters, of a reassertion of the primacy of privacy as a basic human right into which incursions must be justified. For example, the incorporation of the European Convention on Human Rights into UK law by the Human Rights Act 1998 has stimulated an expectation that the case for privacy protection may be put more confidently in the jurisprudence of the coming years, given the absence in UK law of a clear right to privacy as such. The Information Commissioner sees this Act as making a significant contribution to the framework within which the Data Protection Act 1998 is interpreted and applied (UK House of Commons 2001, p. 18). While this enhancement of privacy's weight as a right may to some extent redress the balance, it does not undo those functional or decentering understandings that put privacy in its place. One of the most interesting questions to be debated is whether economic or administrative and rights-based arguments over the limits of privacy are compatible or at odds with each other. In practice, states and businesses are sometimes inclined to see no actual or potential inconsistency, to seek compromises, and to interpret "balances" in ways that suit their interests, however benevolent these may be. On the other hand, civil libertarians and privacy advocates tend to criticize the transmutation of privacy from a right to a "mere" functional utility that facilitates commerce or the workings of the state. Privacy regulators tend to stand uncomfortably in the middle of the road, sometimes dodging the two-way traffic, and sometimes uncomfortably switching the traffic lights to yellow in both directions.

In this chapter, we explore these developments in terms of two principal concepts—trust and risk—that are prominent in much contemporary social and political analysis, and that have also become touchstones in discourses involving the use of personal data. We also look at some findings of survey research on public attitudes toward privacy.[1] Safeguarding privacy is said to be an essential component for promoting trusting relationships both in the electronic commerce "revolution" and in less dramatic and less heavily technologized business-to-customer transactions, and also in the evolution of the electronic delivery of public services. It is also seen as integral to the success of electronic democracy, whether in terms of interaction between citizens and the state or among citizens themselves. Unless customers or citizens can trust others with their personal details or their political opinions, so goes the argument, governmental efficiency, economic prosperity, and the renewal of democratic practices and institutions will suffer. Burkert (1994, p. 239) observes that "[u]sing computers and communicating electronically are dependent on trust: trust in people, in organizations, in technology." As stated, the proposition is unexceptionable, although it should be noted that the idiom of its typical expression in public policy arguments is utilitarian rather than rights-based: privacy protection enhances trust, oils the wheels of commerce and politics, and is therefore of value. The corollary is that, like a thin coating of oil, it is of value only to the extent needed to enhance trust and make the wheels go round. Moreover, if the wheels can go round with the bare minimum of privacy, the argument for raising the level of privacy protection is weaker.

So, too, with risk, with which discussions of trust are very closely involved. All uses of information and communications technologies in the service of modern business and government expose individuals to some degree of risk that their privacy will be invaded. As we saw in chapter 2, there is as yet no certain method of ascertaining whose privacy is most or least "at risk" from these incursions. In addition, the techniques of assessing the degree of risk are not yet well established, although privacy impact assessments are being developed as a tool for this purpose, as we show in chapter 9. Yet elements of risk discourse have entered the armory of data protection and can be found in its laws, policy instruments, and practices. There the emphasis is on managing risks, reducing them to levels that are "tolerable" or "acceptable." But some crucial questions are side-stepped, such as acceptable to whom? Moreover, how do we know that the risk is acceptable?

Trust and the Use of Personal Data

There are inherent complications with both trust and risk as conceptual underpinnings for judgments about the relationship between information processes or systems and the individual—or, indeed, social—value of privacy. There has been an outpouring of stimulating sociological and philosophical writings on trust in recent years.[2] While they provide some purchase on our question of trust in information processes, they do not address it directly in terms of its importance as an interactive social process with implications for privacy protection.

The relevance of trust to processes involving personal data is amply recognized in at least the rhetoric of policy. It is also pointed to in practical proposals for electronic commerce and public administration. Thus, elevating the level of the public's "trust and confidence" in business and government has become something of a mantra in this contemporary discourse and practice. The July 1997 EU ministerial conference on Global Information Networks, held in Bonn, clearly illustrates the place that privacy protection was expected to play in the creation of a trustworthy environment in the emerging world of e-commerce. German Economics Minister Günter Rexrodt and EU Commissioner Martin Bangemann wrote: "Building confidence by achieving efficient protection is essential to allow the positive development of these networks. Those who entrust their data to the networks wish to be sure that it is not altered and that it will not be disclosed to unauthorised recipients or otherwise infringe their right to privacy."[3]

An interesting distinction was drawn between "hard trust," in which technologies, laws, and regulation are involved, and "psychological trust," involving backing by public authorities and endorsement by trusted commercial brands. Cryptography was envisaged as a confidence-building device to ensure the security and confidentiality of data across networks. In related ways not strictly concerning privacy, digital signatures were expected to establish the authenticity and integrity of messages. Illegal content could be controlled through clarifying the legal responsibilities of host service providers, network operators, access providers, and content providers. The misuse of networks for criminal activities that include terrorism, malicious hacking, pedophilia, and incitement to racial hatred had to be dealt with in the interest of greater public confidence. In a broader sense, data protection laws, principles, and rules were seen to play a crucial part in the trustworthiness of these networks.

Similarly, the important OECD Conference in Ottawa in October 1998 emphasized the necessity of inspiring public confidence and trust in business-to-consumer e-commerce, including privacy protection as a crucial instrument toward this end (OECD 1998). OECD Ministers adopted a "Declaration on Protection of Privacy on Global Networks," including a reaffirmation of the 1981 OECD Guidelines, which we discuss in chapter 4. It also saw the aim of online privacy protection as being "to ensure the respect of important rights, build confidence in global networks, and to prevent unnecessary restrictions on transborder flows of personal data" (OECD 1998, Annex 1, p. 14). The theme of "trust and confidence," and the relevance of privacy protection, was ubiquitous in this conference. One of the background papers highlighted the issue of "building consumer trust" by saying that consumers wanted a safe and predictable environment free of unfair or deceptive practices, one that put them on a more even footing with merchants. As in the "real" world, the global electronic marketplace is required to be trustworthy. With particular reference to privacy, the paper drew attention to customer profiling and the tracking of online activities and transactions: "[a]s consumers become increasingly aware and concerned about the potential online threats to personal privacy, they need assurances about the fair collection and use of their personal data."[4]

In light of our later discussion of privacy instruments and regimes in Part III, it is interesting to note that the OECD Ottawa conference saw the means for increasing trust and protecting privacy as comprising a balanced and "seamless" combination of legal intervention and industry self-regulation, to be devised through the collaboration of government, business, and consumer representatives. It was also argued that "[t]he interactive characteristics of digital and computer network technologies can help consumers to develop skills to protect themselves and exercise choice with respect to privacy protection online. However, technology alone will not provide consumers with sufficient online privacy protection."[5]

In both the public and the private sector—and, indeed, in the increasingly important interchange between them—there is an emerging international consensus on the importance of trust and confidence in modern information and communication technologies and their application to online transactions. There is a particularly prevalent concern for creating trustworthy conditions for electronic transactions among businesses, in which the authenticity of contractual documents, the validity of electronic signatures, and the confidentiality of business-to-business information exchanges have been seen as crucial. These issues played a leading part in the policy debates over the availability of strong cryptographic tools and over the part that "trusted third parties" might play in the management of cryptographic keys; we discuss this topic in chapter 7.

More broadly, the idea of the "networked organization" has brought questions of trust to the fore. Rockart and Short's (1991) discussion of this sees the consequences of technology-enabled networks—defined as interrelationships within or between firms to accomplish work—in terms of the sharing of a number of elements, including responsibility and accountability. Whereas face-to-face interactions have been the usual vehicles for cementing trust among persons in firms, they argue that the increasing replacement of these interactions by electronic interfaces "raises serious questions about how trust will be established and developed in this kind of environment, or, conversely, the use of networks cannot be truly effective until a certain level of trust is established in the organisation" (Rockart and Short 1991, p. 192).

As for transactions between governments and citizens, plans for electronic service-delivery are held to rest on the creation of a climate of trust in which citizens can feel confident about the way personal data are processed and protected in and among the organs of the state that are involved. Examples are legion; in the UK, for instance, they include the proposals for "joining up" government services to the citizen in the "information age," using online facilities for which the maintenance of public confidence, including privacy protection, is considered essential (UK CITU 2000, UK Cm 3438 1996). The UK government recognizes that "[t]here is concern that information technology could lead to mistaken identity, inadvertent disclosure and inappropriate transfer of data. The Government will address these concerns and will demonstrate our belief that data protection is an objective of information age government, not an obstacle to it" (UK Cm 4310 1999, p. 51). How robust this affirmation of belief will remain in the implementation of policy for joined-up government and data-sharing is yet to be seen (UK Performance and Innovation Unit, Cabinet Office, 2002).

At bottom, the question of trust in the use of personal information is a more precise application of the primordial social-psychological question of how to relate to and trust others, who may be either strangers or familiar to us. Trust is more easily destroyed than created; it takes a long time to establish, and it may well collapse—perhaps never to be regained—through mistakes and errors. Research on shoppers' attitudes by Hine and Eve (1998, p. 262) leads them to conclude that "[t]rust in data-using organizations is a skeptical trust and is fragile." The complex dynamics of trust are indicated in a review and further development of the literature (6, 1994), in which four elements in the core concept of trust are identified: relationships, beliefs, behavior, and discretion. The first element refers to reciprocal relationships of trusting and trustworthiness between persons or organizations. The second is a cognitive dimension, relating to what one believes about how the other will act. Third is a behavioral dimension: a person acts in certain ways that demonstrate trust in another, thus showing some degree of reliance in which something is put at risk. The person's "risk threshold"—a line determining whether the other will or will not be relied upon—shapes decisions to put an interest at risk. This dimension clearly links trust decisions to risk perceptions, to be discussed later. In the case of privacy, the way individuals evaluate the possible gains they might make from taking risks by yielding their personal data to information systems, and the way in which data controllers seek to give reasons to be trusted, help to determine the level of the threshold. The fourth, and related, dimension refers to trustworthiness and to the discretion the other person or organization has. Such discretion—a lack of certainty—is what makes it risky for persons to trust them; without discretion, the question of trust does not really arise.

There are further ways to dissect the concept of trust. Thus it is important to understand the following: what others are trusted to do or to be, the information that a person requires about another in order to trust them, the characteristics of persons that influence the reasons why they trust others, and their personal thresholds of risk (6, 1998). What type of trust is placed by whom in what persons or organizations, and the part played by worries about privacy in the dynamics of trust, are empirical questions. Knowledge about these might be useful in companies' marketing and advertising strategies, where the aim is to reassure potential customers, even if the company does not actually change its personal-data practices. This perhaps explains why business firms have shown an interest in attitude research in recent years. But equally, such knowledge could influence thinking in various parts of a privacy regime about how the social patterning of trust attitudes might be altered through a refined use of privacy-protecting instruments and through less invasive information operations. Later in this chapter, we look briefly at what various surveys have already discovered about trust in relation to privacy.

Somewhat ironically, the trustworthiness of many institutions is perceived to be low just at a time when it needs to be high in order to provide a reputational underpinning for electronic commerce and electronic service delivery. Many of the privacy policy instruments that we examine in Part II play a part in promoting public trust in the information processes and systems to which they are applied by helping to create a trusted environment; that, at least, is an express aim of those who proffer them.

Sociological and psychological research could play an important part here. On what grounds do people trust organizations that say they can be trusted with personal data, especially when there is evidence—or folklore and rumors—that could undermine such claims? Do people trust the information technologies and systems, including privacy safeguards, that are used by governments whose reassurances about other technologies have been shown to be misleading? Why should one trust organizations that say they provide good privacy protection through codes of practice? But equally, why should one trust in the protection that laws are supposed to provide, and in the workings of the regulatory authorities that enforce it? These are some of the issues and questions that could elevate trust, as concept and process, in the academic and policy circles in which privacy protection is studied and arbitrated. At a time when a major issue in privacy protection is the relationship among statutory regulation, self-regulation, and technology-based privacy instruments, we need to know more about the dynamics of trust in all these contexts.

Risk and Privacy Invasion

Risk is an equivalently complex concept, with its own controversial and vast literature that stretches across many fields including the physical environment, transport, food and product safety, and the effects of modern technologies such as nuclear energy and genetic engineering.[6] Once again, information privacy has not been a prominent subject in these and other studies. Apart from discussions of possible attacks on computers by hackers or viruses and the disruptions that were expected to be caused in the year 2000 by the "millennium bug," analyses of the risks to information technologies and systems are far less prominent (but see Neumann 1995).

Even less common are attempts to assess carefully the risks of privacy invasions that are not the direct result of security breaches or equipment failures, but that have to do with the more routine exposure of individuals to the ubiquitous processes by which their data are collected and used for commercial and governmental purposes. These privacy risks are usefully classified by 6 (1998, pp. 39–42) as risks of injustice (significant inaccuracy, unjust inference, function creep, and reversal of the presumption of innocence), risks to personal control over collection of personal information (excessive or unjustified surveillance, and unconsented collection), and risks to dignity by exposure or embarrassment (absence of transparency, physical intrusion into space, absence of anonymity, and unnecessary, unjustified, or unconsented disclosure). Many of these risks map clearly onto familiar "fair information" principles of data protection, but there is a complex relationship among a number of risks that go beyond simple paradigmatic notions of the value of privacy. In practice, the world of data protection has become, in effect, an arena in which various policy instruments and their combinations are tuned to the management or prevention of risk.

Questions concerning exposures to risk are the counterpart to the equity question, "who gets what data protection?" that we looked at in chapter 2. In theory, we should be able to determine whether, for example, women's privacy is more often invaded than men's, whether there are different ways in which the privacy of members of ethnic minority groups are threatened as compared with the majority, or whether the old and the socially dependent poor risk more of their privacy as a result of their frequent contacts with public agencies than those who are better able to take care of themselves. Of course, the complexity of interactions between people and wider systems belies the simplicity of these basic comparisons, and most of what is "known" about these distributions is anecdotal. As the poor, for example, are in regular touch with welfare institutions, it is often conjectured that they, more than the rich, are more prone to misuses of personal data by the public sector. On the other hand, the middle classes' inclusion in the credit-card and online economies leads them to run other, and perhaps equivalent, risks from the data practices of the private sector, perhaps especially in countries in which privacy protection for that sector is weak or nonexistent. Because it is young, educated, middle-class males who use the Internet in greater proportions than other people, it is tempting to suppose that they run more risks to their privacy from abuses of electronic mail or from the surveillance to which they are subjected on global networks.

However, we doubt that the interaction of social, psychological, and technical factors is so straightforward that we can rely on a distinction between private-sector and public-sector risks to privacy, or between the affluent and others in respect of their differential exposures, in order to explain actual or perceived privacy risks. Much must remain in the realm of speculation in the absence of sufficient research that could tell us how individuals in various social groups or categories take part in the domains of consumption, healthcare, social services, employment, education, and so on in which their personal information is used. Generalization about the basis of people's perceptions of privacy risks is unsafe, although Hine and Eve (1998) identify some of the factors that seem to influence the variations in persons' feelings of trust and risk as they face different intrusive information practices in shopping. These factors are the visibility of the technology (for example, supermarket loyalty cards), the legitimacy of the motives for information requests, the intrusion or disruption of legitimate activity, power and control imbalances, and the social context.

Further understanding of such perceptions is difficult in the absence of a well-established knowledge base concerning risks of privacy invasion. However, at various times certain practices that are considered prone to privacy breaches have been highlighted for precautionary or remedial attention by legislators, regulators, and privacy advocates. Credit reporting and video rentals are relevant examples from the United States, the former not uniquely so, and the latter arguably a legislative response that was disproportionate to the risk. Enforced subject-access requests for criminal or medical records have been of concern in the UK, while the recording of information about certain diseases such as HIV/AIDS has been an issue in many places. To some extent at least, these categories of data probably relate to different segments of a population, and thus exemplify qualitatively different risks to which they are exposed.

A major attempt to differentiate among risks, although not directly among persons at risk, is inscribed in data-protection law. This is the notion of "sensitive data," for which special procedures must be followed by data controllers. Article 6 of the Council of Europe Convention, an important international instrument which is further discussed in chapter 4, says: "Personal data revealing racial origin, political opinions or religious or other beliefs, as well as personal data concerning health or sexual life, may not be processed automatically unless domestic law provides appropriate safeguards. The same shall apply to personal data relating to criminal convictions."

An explanatory note (Council of Europe 1981 p. 17) elaborating on the meaning and scope of this provision points out that, while risks are context-, not content-dependent, these are "exceptional cases" in which encroachments are likely, and that they pertain to all countries in the Council. But any state would be free to add other categories according to the "legal or sociological context of the country concerned." The note further indicates that one's membership in a trade union could be sensitive in one country, whereas in others it might only be so to the extent that it is closely associated with political or religious views. Trade-union membership, indeed, is specified in the EU Data Protection Directive (see chapter 4) as falling within a "special category" under Article 8, which requires either the individual's explicit consent or other conditions for processing to be legitimate. The UK Data Protection Act 1998, Section 2 and Schedule 3, transposes these requirements in terms of "sensitive personal data," including a range of conditions that must be satisfied for processing to take place.[7] For certain categories of sensitive data, processing requires, in addition, "appropriate safeguards for the rights and freedoms of data subjects." Canada's federal privacy legislation for the private sector, enacted in 2000, requires express, opt-in consent for the collection and release of sensitive data. Thus, it seems, powerful legal instruments recognize that unusual risks can be run under certain circumstances and within specified legal constraints.

A major conceptual issue in investigating risk and its distribution concerns whether it is meaningful to consider that there are objective risks that may or may not differ from risk perception. This conceptual problem is well aired in the general literature on risk in other fields, and it poses difficulties for regulatory regimes (Baldwin and Cave 1999, chap. 11). It is increasingly considered to be facile to distinguish between "real" risks and "erroneous" perceptions, and foolish to assume that the former are subject to expert scientific determination on the basis of which the latter can be ignored as the unfounded fears of mere laypersons. For example, the risk that one's credit card details might be intercepted and misused in Internet transactions might be exceedingly low, yet one's perception and fears might amplify this into a major deterrent to engaging in e-commerce. Those concerned to promote e-commerce, and e-government as well, can ill afford to dismiss these worries, for some of the "trust and confidence" reasons that were noted earlier. As we shall see in chapter 7, the array of "trust" devices and technologies that are proffered on the Internet address this issue as part of an effort to boost public confidence in electronic markets, and to reduce risks by encouraging better data practices by sellers. In fields such as information processes, people's perceptions are potent factors that affect the collection and communication of personal information, and regulatory policy and practice must prudently cater to people's fears and impressions as much as, and perhaps more than, to any "objective" discernment of risk, even if calculations of the latter prove to be possible.

Some have tried to develop methods of "privacy impact assessment" for analyzing the effects of proposed innovations in information practices and systems; we reserve a fuller description of this for chapter 9. This approach would encourage systems designers and their clients to do what they otherwise might not do: to think systematically about the risk implications and to try to cope with them. There may well be limits to this technique, however, for the reasons we have indicated: the problematic nature of "risk" as a concept and as a factor to be measured. But as a way of managing and reducing risk, such methods may well be an improvement upon the one-dimensional notion that there are, a priori, qualitatively and quantitatively undifferentiated "risks" involving certain types of data, certain types of people, or certain types of practices. It should be possible to be more precise than to say, merely, that data-matching, online transactions, or excessive record collection "puts people at risk" of privacy invasion.

Such assessments are in keeping with risk analysts' "precautionary principle," which is strongly emphasized by the environmental protection movement.[8] One interpretation of this principle is that there should be anticipatory action to prevent harm, and that the burden of proof of the harmlessness of a new technology, process, or product should be placed upon its promoters, rather than the general public. Promoters should also search for alternatives, and decision-making should be open and involve affected parties.[9] Taken seriously, and applied to privacy protection, this could mean that information processes are regarded as (relatively) dangerous until shown to be (relatively) safe, rather than the other way round. Generally speaking, the first has been more favored in Europe and in countries where data protection laws and systems can be seen as anticipatory safeguarding measures. The other way round is rather more characteristic of the US approach, in which the emphasis is less on reducing or managing risk as on providing for litigation, redress, and compensation for damage shown to be done to individuals by privacy-invasive misuse of their personal information. To be sure, these are not starkly opposed alternatives, and no data protection regime is wholly predicated on the one or the other. But broad distinctions along this dimension could be drawn between, on the one hand, approaches to privacy protection that rely heavily on legal sanctions and penalties and, on the other, approaches that encourage risk prevention and risk management through public policy initiatives, codes of practice, informing the public of hazards and the means of self-protection, building protections into technologies, or licensing the processing of data.

There is a further issue, which concerns the allocation of responsibilities within a system of risk management. If we assume that we could know more about the risks, then whose responsibility is it to publicize them, reduce them, handle their consequences, or—indeed—ascertain them in the first place? Should these be the responsibility, singly or together, of official regulatory bodies, data controllers, technology designers, the media, or data subjects? This matter is germane to the developing consensus that privacy protection is a "mixed strategy" of tools and the agents who wield them, as we will see in chapter 8.

Survey Evidence about Trust and Risk

A government document about plans for the Canadian "information highway" asked a pertinent question: "Do we understand exactly what information privacy means to various users of the network, and agree on what level of privacy is required for different tasks?" (Industry Canada 1994, pp. 28–29). An answer would probably be that we do not know exactly, but that some headway has been made towards a more finely grained understanding of these patterns of meaning, attitudes towards trust, and perception of risk. Such policy-related knowledge, gained through surveys and focus-group research, is highly important for informing the protection of privacy in electronic and other transactions. However, as we suggest in chapter 2 with regard to the question of equality, the way is not yet clear for using our knowledge of social attitudes to shape a handy and consensual method of matching privacy "levels" to tasks. Observing the state of research in this area, 6 (1998, p. 82) remarks:

We have few specific data on the questions of who worries about which privacy risks and why, and we have still less on how the pattern has changed over time. Most of the data . . . is concerned with trust, confidence or the dampening of worry and risk perception. This means that we have few general rankings by the public of the seriousness of the harms caused by different kinds of violations of privacy by comparison with other kinds of risk, nor clear estimates of relative probability or unacceptability.

Yet investigations have been conducted in a number of countries, and some of them provide time-series for analysis of trends and changes in public belief and attitudes about the capture, use, and communication of their personal details, mainly in private-sector activities.[10] Many surveys to date cast light on who fears what invasions or who trusts what organizations and protective devices, allowing a better understanding of public perceptions of risk and attitudes toward particular aspects of data protection. Surveys have also indicated how far privacy is valued and to what extent its protection is seen as desirable. However, bearing in mind our concern to gain a purchase on the social distribution of privacy protection, who actually loses or gains what privacy can only be inferred from these studies.

Even with these limitations in mind, there is some value to be gained from survey findings, even though caution in interpreting them and in comparing their results is important. This is not least because of ambiguous definitions of *privacy*, but also because of the way surveys have been conducted, the wording of the questions asked, and the variable, but often unknown, context of public events and personal experiences that conditions answers. The quality of surveying varies considerably. While some surveys report findings according to age, gender, racial, and other categories, thus yielding a more finely grained picture, many do not. Surveys have often made for dramatic press headlines, and have been used by consumer groups, business organizations, privacy advocates, and other interested parties to advance or oppose policy causes.

In broad-brush terms, the most common finding in survey after survey is that privacy is regarded as a very important personal value, and is felt to be strongly threatened by new information and communication practices and technologies used in commerce and government. Levels of public trust in organizations that process personal data are variable but sometimes very low, as is confidence in existing protective instruments. There are more specific fears that privacy is at risk in the online environment, but worries persist about the protection afforded to personal data in more traditional, offline, transactions. Levels of knowledge about what happens to one's data, and about the ways in which they can be misused in the various technologies and sectors, are not high, testifying to a lack of transparency and candor among data controllers, and to large deficiencies in consumer and citizen education.

An international European survey (International Research Associates 1997) showed that more than 90 percent in all countries attached a great deal of importance to privacy protection and thought the EU should ensure it, although public awareness of data protection laws varied and was often low. It found that more women than men were concerned about leaving electronic tracks on information networks, and that levels of concern were linked with age and education levels in all countries. Most surveys have employed conventional variables to differentiate data subjects in terms of attitudes toward privacy. Thus a Dutch study considered religious and political affiliation and several categories of employment, among others (Holvast et al. 1989).

Among the most prominent surveys are the series carried out by the Louis Harris polling organization and conducted under Westin's direction. Most of these have been produced under the auspices of Equifax, a leading credit-referencing company based in the United States.

Although these surveys, like many others, can be faulted, one of their virtues is that they break the data down into numerous socioeconomic, demographic, and other variables, and that some of them concentrate upon particular sectors. In addition, they sometimes seek to explain variations in attitudes in terms of the contexts in which different categories of people engage in transactions involving their personal details, thus moving us closer to understanding something more than perceptions.

For example, the Harris-Equifax (1993) survey about health information in the United States revealed differences in levels of concern for privacy according to age, geographical area, education level, gender, and other factors. Westin (Harris-Equifax 1993, p. 13) interprets the findings of this and previous surveys in a way that suggests that certain groups are, or feel, less well protected than others. One example is that members of racial minorities who have low income and low levels of education scored highly on concern about "general privacy threats, violations of employee and consumer privacy rights, and government invasions of citizen privacy in law enforcement and social-program administration," and on medical privacy issues as well. To the extent that these concerns relate to actual experiences of privacy protection or violation, we can plausibly infer inequities in the distribution of the latter by virtue of the greater involvement of such persons in those information systems that have low levels of protection.

In general, the variables of race, income, and level of education—which are likely to vary together—seem to explain some of the differences in attitudes toward the use of personal data across many, although not all, contexts and issues, including the use of social security numbers, the idea of a national identification system, medical research, and utility services. Some previous surveys revealed that people at the higher end of the education and income scale were not very concerned about privacy in general, but they too scored high on some questions concerning health-related personal data. Westin's interpretation is interesting, as it again suggests something about actual patterns and means of protection. He argues that these people are heavy users of services for mental health and report high levels of the improper disclosure of their data. Westin (Harris-Equifax 1993, p. 15) writes:

It may be that such respondents feel capable of defending their informational interests quite well in the employment and consumer contexts, and feel a part of the governing elite as far as general privacy concerns are involved. But, their use of mental health services and their adverse medical confidentiality experiences make them feel sensitive—and vulnerable—when medical and health information is involved.

However, findings from the United States, within a health context, may not hold elsewhere or in other domains. Thus a somewhat different interpretation is given to variations in concerns about privacy breaches in a privacy survey conducted in Canada (Ekos Research Associates 1993), in which the findings are viewed more in terms of social and power structures than the extent to which certain groups are included in invasive information systems. Women, older persons, those with less education, and Francophones were most worried about privacy, according to the authors. They therefore discern a "class cleavage in the nature and impact of privacy issues" (Ekos Research Associates 1993, p. iii):

For those in the less powerful and less privileged classes, . . . powerlessness may be combining with a growing disillusionment with Government and other institutions, to produce a generalized fear. . . . At the same time, their economically marginal positions render them least capable of identifying and responding to these problems. For example, they are least capable of affording some of the new technologies designed to minimize privacy threats. They are also least likely to be subject to the irritants of marketing intrusions, since they are not attractive marketing opportunities. . . . More privileged members of society, on the other hand, understand and experience privacy issues in a fundamentally different way. As consumers, they are the more likely users of the new information technologies . . . [and] they endure the majority of telemarketing and charitable agency intrusions. Finally, they are also more interested in and capable of affording new privacy protection services.

For this survey, then, the most important data are those that speak to the specific privacy "trade-offs" that different groups make about the provision or concealment of different forms of personal information in different contexts.

The Ekos interpretation is particularly germane to our query about unequal access to privacy protection. It also reveals interesting complexities in the relationship between inclusion in intrusive data-gathering systems and social positions, and also between such inclusion and the ability to safeguard one's privacy. A study conducted in Hungary (Székely 1991) is similarly relevant. It took into account a range of sociodemographic variables and found, for instance, a relationship between age and individuals' sensitivity about medical and social-service information. Young people were most apprehensive, but people over sixty-six were less insistent on privacy. Székely (1991, p. 19) offers this explanation:

Elderly people, especially single ones, have to rely on other people's help and on medical and social services more intensively. . . . For all of this they have to give more information about themselves and to disclose an increasing number of dimensions of their private lives. To this is added their generally reduced incomes, and beyond a certain degree they are compelled to draw attention to this fact.

Unlike the findings elsewhere, those with less education were also not very sensitive, possibly because, he argues, they experience less privacy at home and have fewer contacts with bureaucracies in situations in which they might disclose their personal data. The most sensitive were the young, who are believed to feel a greater need for "informational self-determination" for many kinds of information. Less well-educated people were less sensitive; this is explained in terms of the lower levels of privacy experienced in their families and communities, the lower frequency of their data-disclosing contacts with officials, and their relative lack of knowledge about the processing and use of information (Székely 1991, p. 19).

Clearly, a host of cultural and social factors that are particular to nations and societies have to be taken into account in explaining cross-cultural differences such as those that are pointed out by these findings. So, too, may the dimensions of risk and trust relate to historical experiences across systems with democratic or authoritarian legacies. An objective of the Hungarian study was to identify and explain the circumstances of a group who demanded information privacy and autonomy, and who were highly aware of the need for protection. Thus a subsample were

somewhat better informed, . . . are more interested in the fate of their data, pay more attention to the differences between named and anonymous data processing, are bothered more by compulsory provision of data, and more strongly oppose the establishment of interconnection among registrations. . . . They place safety before comfort, prefer decentralised to centralised registration, and are suspicious about the computerised processing of personal data. Accordingly, they more strongly oppose an expansion of [State Office for Population Registering] activities, call for more information about their data, and almost 100 percent of them oppose the selling of their personal data for various information services. (Székely 1991, p. 37)

Conventional wisdom would assume that these persons were young, politically active, and technologically sophisticated Budapest intellectuals, but the findings showed that their sociodemographic characteristics did not differ greatly from that of the entire sample. This is thought to reflect the nature of Hungarian life at the time of the survey. The opportunity for information privacy had not been available, and consciousness of data protection could be traced to "familial, religious, cultural and other traditions" (Székely 1991, p. 37) rather than directly to the other variables. This pattern of high privacy awareness and desire is said to constitute a new development in Hungarian society. Perhaps it testifies to a risk aversion that has its roots in the recent political history of countries, like Hungary, in which the apparatuses of state surveillance were highly developed.

Other survey work, however, is less concerned to explain attitudes and perceptions in terms of social structures, processes, experiences, or other factors than it is to report them. Such surveys often do contain relevant findings about social distributions of attitudes towards the provision of personal information. For example, in the UK, a Henley Centre (1995) survey disaggregated findings by age, social class, and sector of industry, identifying what consumers feared about exclusion, inaccuracy, the passing-on of information, and technology. The fear of being labeled by firms was a majority feeling in all categories of respondent, but was strongest among older and poorer persons. The vast majority were apprehensive about inaccuracy, and also opposed the passage of information to other companies. There was also fear of technology's capability of linking data and compiling dossiers (The Henley Centre 1995, chap. 4).[11] Another Ekos study, conducted in 2001 on behalf of the Public Interest Advisory Centre in Canada (Ekos Research Associates 2001), concerned the use of consumer information in direct marketing, and broke the data down by education, age, income, and region within Canada. The less educated and less affluent were less aware of the information practices used in loyalty programs. Older people and the less educated were less likely to mind that businesses keep track of their purchases, while respondents in Atlantic Canada, the Prairies, and Ontario were far less likely to object than were those in Québec.

Also in 2001, the Australian Office of the Federal Privacy Commissioner produced a comprehensive set of privacy surveys of business organizations, government privacy contact officers, and the general public about a host of privacy matters (Australia, FPC, 2001). In line with many other studies, the community survey of some 1,500 people showed that privacy was highly valued although popular levels of knowledge were low. Some of the results bear upon the question of trust. Overall, the sample rated health service providers as overwhelmingly the most trustworthy; Internet and other retailers and real estate agents as the least; and financial organizations, government, and charities somewhere in the middle. There were, of course, some variations according to geographical location within Australia, age, gender, and income. By way of comparison, according to some UK research (UK House of Commons 1994, Appendix 5), organizations varied in their perceived trustworthiness as far as personal data are concerned. Thus doctors and the National Health Service were trusted most (88 percent), and mail-order firms the least (22 percent)—the same rank-ordering as was found in Australia in 1995 (Australia, FPC, 1995, p. 12) as well as more recently, and in Canada (Ekos Research Associates 1993, p. 20). But, as we argued earlier, the complexity of people's judgments concerning whom to trust, why, and for what tasks, must be taken into account, as they are in the UK research reported by 6 et al. (1998, pp. 51–54 and Appendix 3).

The recent Australian study enables attitudes towards risk to be inferred from the fact that over 40 percent of respondents reported their refusal to deal with organizations because of their concern with how their data would be used and protected. Although variations need to be explained, younger persons were somewhat less fearful, while those aged 40 to 49 were the most. Those respondents living in Western and Southern Australia were much more likely than those elsewhere to have refused; the better-off and more highly educated more likely than those lower down these scales. Those with more awareness of privacy laws were somewhat more likely to refuse than those who were not aware of privacy laws, although 38 percent of the latter had refused (Australia, FPC, 2001, pp. 7–8).

When people were asked what would increase their trust in organizations, 59 percent wanted to be allowed more control over their own data, and 55 percent mentioned the organization's having a privacy policy. For 47 percent, past experience or the organization's reputation was important, and 40 percent wanted to be treated with respect for one's privacy by the staff. Once again, there was some variation across the sociodemographic and other categories (Australia, FPC, 2001, pp. 18–20). These findings can be juxtaposed with the findings of a study published by the UK's Direct Marketing Association (n.d., chart 2.1) in the late 1990s. When asked what would make them trust a company with their personal information, some 80 percent wanted to be treated with respect and to be told what is done with the data; nearly as many looked for open and honest treatment, and relied on the company's reputation for quality. A company's membership in a trade association encouraged about 73 percent, and about 68 percent would want their information to remain within one department.

The UK Data Protection Registrar (now the Information Commissioner) has published survey findings since 1986. These investigations are of "members of the public"; the statistics are not reported in a sufficiently disaggregated form that would reveal important demographic variations. Yet some of the figures nevertheless may have some value in tracking trends. Survey results have fluctuated from year to year, sometimes reflecting the effects of advertising campaigns. In 1994 (UK House of Commons 1994, Appendix 5), 66 percent of a sample of 1,000 said that protecting people's rights to privacy was a "very important" issue.[12] Seventy-two percent were "very" or "quite" concerned about the amount of personal information that various organizations keep. When it came to information about financial matters, medical data, court judgments, and one's visitors that is kept without the individual's knowledge, a similar high proportion were concerned, although smaller proportions—far fewer than half—were disturbed about the gathering of data on education, job history, purchases, club membership, media consumption, and age. Unfortunately, the survey did not ascertain attitudes toward the collection of information of the kind that is becoming particularly controversial; these would include driving habits, video-surveillance data, and records of telephone calls.

Harris-Equifax (1994) research tends to bear out the assumption that trust plays an important part in perceptions of risk. In similar proportions as were found in the UK, doctors and nurses were trusted with personal data much more than were mail-order companies. But the level of individuals' distrust in technology and in government, which is especially high and increasing in the United States, correlated with attitudes on privacy issues. An interesting general theory about the relationship between trust and privacy fears is broached by the observation that "[t]he higher a respondent's distrust, the more he or she is concerned about threats to privacy, opposed to new uses of personal information (especially through information-technology applications), and in favor of legal and regulatory bans or controls on uses of personal information by business or government" (Harris-Equifax 1994, p. xii).

Equivalent correlations are found in Canadian data, going against the conventional assumption that Canadians hold government in greater trust than Americans do (Harris-Equifax 1992, p. ix). Some of the US findings interestingly suggest that perceived levels of risk are not necessarily a given prior condition, but may interact with the availability of privacy protection. Thus, even some highly distrustful persons were among those who were ready to have their data used so long as there were laws, remedies, and data controllers' compliance with fair information practices. Such persons included persons aged 40 to 49, African Americans, and those with low levels of education (Harris-Equifax 1994, p. xix).

Whether typical sociodemographic population categories are the ones most relevant to gaining a purchase on trust and risk remains an important question. So, too, is whether groups identified in other ways, incorporating individuals' self-identification, would better inform analysis. More information about the actual patterns of the sectoral involvement of different data subjects would be useful, as in the comparisons made by Harris-Equifax (1996, pp. 15–22) among credit-card holders, direct-mail purchasers, and users of the Internet. Other information could also help to relate attitudes to experiences, as in surveys that inquire whether the respondent has or has not been a victim of a privacy invasion, and that assess how consumers' attitudes are influenced by their own personal experiences with companies.

Some researchers have tried to express their data in terms of categories derived from responses to questions about individuals' levels of fear, and about their attitude to the way their personal data are used. For example, in the 1991 Harris-Equifax survey, Westin distinguished among three categories: "privacy fundamentalists" (25 percent), "the unconcerned" (18 percent), and "the pragmatic majority" (57 percent). This distinction's use of somewhat tendentious labels has been controversial, especially in a world that has become wary of "fundamentalism" and in which "pragmatism" has come to mean "sensible." Yet it has become an influential standard in such attitude research. Fundamentalists are the most distrustful and concerned about how data are used, whereas, at the other end of the scale, the unconcerned value consumption benefits and public order more than privacy. In the middle, the pragmatic majority hold subtle views, discriminating among organizations, practices and values in forming their stance on privacy (Harris-Equifax 1991, pp. 6–7).[13]

In contrast to this threefold distinction, a Canadian survey used factor analysis to develop a dramatically labeled fivefold typology of "fearful regulators," "extroverted technophobes," "guarded individualists," "open pragmatists," and "the indifferent" (Ekos Research Associates 1993, pp. 34–38). The way these categories relate to sociodemographic characteristics indicates the complexity of privacy as a socially distributed value, such that no confident generalizations can be made about women, the poorly educated, the young, or other groups as such. The study plotted the five typological categories against seven sociodemographic variables, but did not indicate the statistical significance of the differences that emerged (Ekos Research Associates 1993, p. 64). Looking overall, it appears that the majority of Canadians do not know how to deal with privacy problems. Sixty-one percent do not know whom to turn to, although there are age and regional variations: the older were more knowledgeable, and Francophones felt more competent as well as knowing more about the possibilities for redress.

Understandably, attitudes towards engaging in Internet activity have occupied the focus of attention in an increasing number of surveys in the 1990s and after. The advent of electronic commerce and electronic transactions with government and, more recently, anxiety over the collapse of the "dot.com" economy following exaggerated expectations, have drawn attention to the importance of confidence and trust in the security and privacy protection afforded by the online environment. It is not surprising that survey research into attitudes and behavior with regard to online transactions have been strongly policy-oriented in terms of the alternative instruments available, within and across countries, for providing a privacy-protective electronic environment. Public opinion research has played its part in alerting business and government to the necessity of allaying fears with substantive measures of protection.

The Harris organization, with Westin, has been prominent in this focus of attention. In their survey of computer users in the United States (Privacy & American Business 1997), Westin's interpretive essay dramatized the importance of understanding online activity and of addressing the privacy issues: "The Internet should be recognized as an explosive new medium where the full array of human conduct plays out, and all the traditional tensions in democratic society over individual privacy, public disclosure, and society-protecting surveillance will have to be confronted in new settings" (Privacy & American Business 1997, p. xvi).[14] Some four-fifths of computer and Internet users, similar to proportions found in previous studies of consumers, feel that they have lost all control over their data. However, they are less fearful of technology than are others, and are more trusting of institutions. Very few have experienced online privacy invasions, yet most are concerned about a variety of threats to their privacy. They are deeply worried about childrens' privacy online, and favor legislation to protect it.[15]

Some 70 percent of consumers, online and offline, would prefer voluntary self-regulation by business to regulatory legislation, according to this research. Yet it is also reported that 58 percent support the immediate passage of laws governing the collection and use of personal data on the Internet, although Westin argues that this finding may have been prompted by the sequence of questions asked in the survey (Privacy &

American Business 1997, p. xix). Nonetheless, while most people, including Internet users, are found to oppose the creation of a US federal regulatory agency for the private sector, there is majority support for sector-specific legislation—including the Internet as a "sector"—when voluntarism is ineffective or lagging.

Another survey of trust and privacy online (Pew Internet & American Life Project 2000, p. 2) found that "American Internet users overwhelmingly want the presumption of privacy when they go online." They reject the monitoring of their web browsing, want to see privacy violators punished, but are willing to provide personal information in order to engage in transactions. Going against the grain of US policy and business' preferred solution, most Internet users would prefer an "opt-in," rather than an "opt-out," if Internet companies want to use their data. Despite their apprehension about privacy invasions and other confidence-reducing characteristics of operating in an online environment, few have experienced privacy problems and other problems—a finding shared by other studies—and large proportions actively use the Internet for transactions and communication. There are variations in privacy concerns: for example, 72 percent of African Americans, 62 percent of Hispanics, and 57 percent of whites are concerned about keeping their information private; and 67 percent of those aged 50 to 64 as against 46 percent of those aged 18 to 29 (Pew Internet & American Life Project 2000, p. 5). Interestingly, a sizeable, though minority, proportion of people resort to "guerrilla tactics" to protect their own privacy online, such as providing false names to a website or using encryption. However, most users do not sufficiently understand how websites work or how they can use protective technologies to safeguard their privacy.

A rare cross-national survey (IBM-Harris 2000), again involving Westin in the research process, throws light on the concerns of Internet users in the UK and Germany as well. Considering the UK, while 78 percent are concerned about the possible misuse of their information, as compared with 94 percent in the United States, 23 percent of UK users and 29 percent of US users believe they have been a victim of business invasion of their consumer privacy. The latter are larger proportions than had been reported in earlier work; it is difficult to say whether this reflects the technical noncomparability of survey findings, or actual changes in attitudes and perceptions within a very few years. Nonetheless, Westin offers several reasons why privacy concerns and actions are less in the UK than in the United States: in the UK, there is less distrust of institutions, less direct marketing, fewer "alarmist" stories about privacy in the media, and fewer privacy-advocacy groups. In addition, the UK has a national legal framework for data protection and more US consumers are "activist."

Finally, research into electronic commerce and consumer protection conducted by the UK's National Consumer Council (2000) revealed that security of personal data is one of the main trust issues, more so for Internet shoppers but for other consumers as well, especially in conducting any transactions that are not face-to-face. Consumers are confused about the use and effectiveness of online security devices such as encryption and icons such as padlocks. The report states that "[t]rust, known name, reputable company are phrases that occur repeatedly in the discussion groups. . . . Consumers trust companies they are familiar with" (National Consumer Council 2000, p. 68). Consumers tend not to be well informed about the existence of regulations for offline or online trading. Some are skeptical about voluntary self-regulation by traders, and think that legislation is needed despite the complexity of the online environment; they understand that it would have to be international in scope (National Consumer Council 2000, chap. 12). In the long run, people expect security measures to improve, and that self-regulation or coregulation, including a role for government, will be likely to develop.

Conclusion: Trust, Risk, and Policy

We have canvassed a range of conceptual and empirical matters in this chapter, and in Part I generally, that indicate the kind of issues with which policy must contend in fashioning the means for privacy protection, especially when the rationale for privacy protection is one that is shaped by utilitarian concerns about risk and trust. Where have the discussion and the research findings brought us, in terms of getting closer to understanding the relationship between privacy protection and the management of risk or the promotion of trust? Arguably, not very far, partly because mapping the distribution of social attitudes towards these matters as well as patterns of protection in relation to population characteristics is not highly developed, and partly because of the conceptual complexities that we have described. In particular, the question of risk is beset by the difficulties in constructing the relationship between the objective and the subjective sides of the issue. Although public perceptions of risks and of the trustworthiness of data controllers might not be founded on what some might deem "objective" reality—even if, in the case of privacy risks, we could determine what that was—it remains true that policy and its implementation must be responsive to them.

Individuals are often unable to understand that their personal details are being collected and processed every day in a wide variety of mundane activities, much less being able to control the situation. This is an important reason for promoting transparency and better information for the customer, so that they can gain greater comprehension of the risks. Survey responses may only be registering rumor and fear, bred of media horror stories about invasions of privacy and the misuse of information, reinforced by worst-case scenarios about surveillance technologies, that might not indicate with any accuracy the privacy risks to which people are exposed.[16] Saloon-bar accounts may underestimate or overestimate them, or emphasize some invasive practices while ignoring others. The "problem" of privacy is socially and politically constructed, and the protection of privacy is therefore built upon that edifice. This point will be of importance to our subsequent discussion of privacy instruments and regimes. For the moment, however, we are still left in some doubt as to whether policies are over- or under-protective in their attempt to meet functional objectives concerning risk and trust.

The investigation of trust and risk concerning privacy is not uniquely tortuous. It is worth considering a wider canvas, and recalling that contemporary policy-related debate about risk analysis in other fields confronts similar conundrums. The relationship between scientific "objectivity" and lay "subjectivity" has come to be reformulated by some in terms of recognizing that "expert" knowledge is also in many ways subjective and value-laden. Therefore popular perceptions need not automatically defer to science in the evaluation and management of risk (The Royal Society 1992, chap. 5). As Beck (1992, p. 30) pertinently remarks: "The scientific concern . . . relies on social expectations and value judgements, just as the social discussion and perception of risks depend on scientific arguments. . . . Scientific rationality without social rationality remains empty, but social rationality without scientific rationality remains blind."

Moreover, the acceptability of any risk must be addressed in terms of "to whom, . . . when, and under what circumstances?" (The Royal Society 1992, p. 92). The dilemma facing public policy is "how, in the face of such plurality, societal decisions about risks may be made that are both equitable, and in some way in the interests of all" (The Royal Society 1992, p. 124). Differences in risk perception seem generally to be associated with individuals' membership of different sociocultural categories or groups and therefore with their subscription to different collective norms and beliefs (The Royal Society 1992, p. 108), and some of the privacy surveys suggest this. The individualist perspective of data protection, which we discuss in chapter 1, and of some existing surveys that are framed within it may lead us to forget that "purely psychological, individual-based analysis can account for only a part of risk perception and risk behaviour" (The Royal Society 1992, p. 112).

We cannot conclude that it is useless to search for patterns of actual privacy risk, or to estimate probabilities, magnitudes, and distributions of risk in terms of sociodemographic variables. After all, this would make explicit what is mainly implicit in data protection regimes concerning the dangers of "sensitive" data, or of transfers of data to "inadequate" countries, as we have seen. Nor is it futile to analyze the privacy implications and impacts of policies, information systems, and activities in business and government. But it would be unrealistic to hold out hope that there will be definitive results resolving the issues, ending the conflicts between data controllers and data subjects, and furnishing regulators with precise strategies. As Adams (1995, p. 194) argues, disagreements about risk cannot be scientifically resolved. This is because "people are constantly responding to their circumstances, and thereby constantly altering each other's risk-taking environments. . . . The future is constantly being reshaped by people's perceptions of it. Science has no firm ground on which to stand."

The typologies of privacy stances devised by Westin (Harris-Equifax 1991) and in the Canadian survey (Ekos Research Associates 1993) are echoed in the distinctions that Adams (1995) draws among risk perspectives.[17] His "individualists" de-emphasize risks, dislike regulation, and prefer to leave decisions about risk to the market and to the individual. They are contrasted with "hierarchists," who want risks to be scientifically and authoritatively managed from the top down and based on research that would ascertain "the facts." Then there are the "egalitarians": they perceive risks but are cautious and prudent. They sometimes support regulation, but they also sometimes reject it because it would inhibit other behavior held to be desirable. Egalitarians look for cooperation to reduce risk. "Fatalists" are those who see the world as unpredictable and unmanageable; they therefore take no part in discussions about risk.

A consequence of this model for our argument concerning privacy is that the hierarchists have no privileged position in the way in which privacy risks are socially constructed. If privacy rights are becoming less of a trump card in privacy policy and discourse, scientific research is not a candidate for that role, because knowledge concerning risks—the agreed facts—is still deficient as a basis for regulatory policy. If science cannot indicate how to regulate in situations of little consensus on the facts of privacy risks, we are then left with a continually contestable regulatory terrain, on which "balancing"—however unsatisfactory as a decision procedure—and the assumptions built into laws and regulatory practice win by default. Either that, or they are challenged in political arenas.

Yet we contend that some science may be better than having no science at all, and that a better understanding of exposures to privacy dangers, the distribution of risks, and the patterning of trusting may be worth seeking. This may only be because discourse based on possible evidence might more clearly delineate the areas of agreement and disagreement between protagonists whose outlooks differ, and what could be accepted as facts upon which a consensus for action could rest. Such discourse might also show the likely range of probabilities and magnitudes of risk, and might establish the plausibility or absurdity of claims in regard to who enjoys, and who does not enjoy, what privacy.

Debates about the findings of survey or other research might well generate strategies for coping better with the risks and fears surrounding information technology and practices, and with social disparities in privacy protection. Such strategies could be employed not only by regulatory agencies as hierarchists but, in their own way, by pragmatists and egalitarians. Even the feasibility of the positions of individualists or of those who are unconcerned might be tested by research that showed the effect of technological or market-based privacy solutions. As Adams (1995) shows, fatalists take themselves out of contention in arguments about risk; but better knowledge could indicate how their privacy, too, can be protected, as of right.

In Part II, we turn from these issues to consider the range of policy instruments that have been developed as part of regimes that aim to protect the privacy of personal data, and thus implicitly or explicitly come to grips with issues of risk and trust.

II

Policy Instruments

4

Transnational Policy Instruments

Introduction

In the second part of this book, we analyze the various policy instruments that now occupy the data protection landscape. Our analysis is organized according to an obvious, but imperfect, distinction between transnational, legal, self-regulatory, and technological policy instruments. We will see, however, that these categories obscure some common functions and characteristics that will be considered more systematically in chapter 8. In keeping with our larger theme concerning globalization, this initial chapter analyzes those instruments that have been negotiated at the international level with a view to addressing the transnational dimensions of the privacy problem. This starting point is in recognition that much of the domestic policy activity (described in chapters 5, 6, and 7) has arisen in response to initiatives at the transnational level.

A large number of international organizations have been involved with the privacy issue (Bygrave 2004). Some have confined their activities to the declaration of statements of principle. Others have negotiated more formal guidelines, and yet others have established more legally binding conventions. Rather than focus on the roles of different international organizations, we instead organize our analysis according to the most important international privacy regimes, with their different histories, functional concerns, and levels of compulsion. Historically, these regimes have centered on three separate international arenas, the Council of Europe, the Organisation for Economic Co-operation and Development (OECD) and the European Union (EU). An emergent Asia-Pacific regime also deserves attention. Many of the policy actors within the international policy community have floated effortlessly from one arena to another over the past twenty years. In more recent years, two further arenas have begun to play an important role in personal data protection policy—one relating to standards-setting and certification, the other relating to the wider process of international trade negotiation. We will see that each of these arenas has a separate policy role and identity, and each has addressed the international aspects of the privacy problem in some distinctive ways.

The Council of Europe Arena

The Council of Europe was established in 1949 by ten European countries with the task of strengthening democracy, human rights, and the rule of law throughout its member states. For the first forty years it remained a West European institution. Since 1989, however, it has assumed the role of encouraging democracy and human rights in Eastern and Central Europe with the result that its membership by the end of 2005 had grown to forty-six. From the outset the organization has recognized that the defense and promotion of fundamental democratic values is not simply an internal matter for governments, but a shared and collective responsibility of all the countries concerned that now embraces a range of political, economic, and social issues.[1]

The institutions of the Council of Europe first became interested in privacy and data protection in the late 1960s, when a Committee of Experts was established to advise on how best to protect privacy in the face of modern computing advances (Hondius 1975). The members of this committee served a critical role in disseminating expertise and advice, as they were key actors in domestic data protection efforts at the time. Two resolutions in the 1970s[2] led to the preparation of the *Convention for the Protection of Individuals with Regard to the Automatic Processing of Personal Data* (Treaty 108), which was duly adopted in 1980, and opened for ratification in January 1981. The Council explains that "European Conventions and Agreements, however, are not statutory acts of the organization; they owe their legal existence simply to the expression of the will of those states that may become parties thereto, as manifested by their signature and ratification of the treaty."[3]

Ratification means that a state consents to be bound by the treaty. In practice, this has meant the incorporation of the Convention signifies that the principles of the Convention have been incorporated into domestic law, and that—theoretically, at any rate—the citizen of one ratifying country can seek redress in another for the mistreatment of his or her personal information. As of mid-2005, thirty-eight of the Council's forty-six members had signed the Convention, and thirty-two had ratified it. The treaty is also open to accession by nonmember states, although none has done so.[4]

The Convention for the first time set out in an international legal text the basic information privacy principles that we outline in chapter 1. In this respect, the Convention has acted as a template for those countries without data protection legislation. Although it did not refer to them as "principles," the Convention stipulated in Article 5 that automatically processed personal data be

a. obtained and processed fairly and lawfully;

b. stored for specified and legitimate purposes and not used in a way incompatible with those purposes;

c. adequate, relevant, and not excessive in relation to the purposes for which they are stored;

d. accurate and, where necessary, kept up to date;

e. preserved in a form that permits identification of the data subjects for no longer than is required for the purpose for which those data are stored.

Article 7 went on to require appropriate security measures, and Article 8 enabled individuals to find out who holds what information about them, to see what is held, to correct or erase it if it has been unlawfully processed, and to obtain remedies if these access and correction rights have not been complied with.

The Convention also introduced the idea, in contrast to previous thinking, that certain special categories of data (racial origin, political opinions, religious or other beliefs, data related to health or sex life, criminal convictions) should not be processed at all unless appropriate safeguards are provided for in domestic law (Article 6). However, the Convention only applies to personal data that are "automatically processed." Moreover, the Council of Europe possesses no supranational legal structure to ensure that the principles within the Convention are enforced in practice. It cannot, therefore, be assumed that ratification of the Convention signifies the actual implementation of a common minimum standard of data protection (Bainbridge 1996, p. 9).

The Convention addressed the burgeoning issue of "transborder data flow" in Article 12. It contains the general rule that "a party shall not, for the sole purpose of the protection of privacy, prohibit or subject to special authorization transborder data flows of personal data to the territory of another party." The "exporter may, however, control such flow if its legislation includes specific regulations for certain categories of personal data or of automated data files" and if the other party does not offer an equivalent level of protection. The Convention also permits prohibitions where the personal data are transferred through intermediary and noncontracting states (Bennett 1992, pp. 135–136).

Thus, the Convention seeks to establish an equivalent level of protection among contracting parties and therefore to assure the free movement of such data among those parties. However, the question of data transfers to noncontracting states is left up to national law. This means that the ratifiers' mutual confidence in one another as safe destinations for personal data is undermined. As Bainbridge remarks: "If country A transfers data to country B, the fact that both are parties to the Convention doesn't help if country B is free to allow a further transfer to country C which has no data protection law" (Bainbridge 1996, p. 10).

As an instrument to regulate the international flow of personal data, therefore, the Convention is limited, and has since been overshadowed by the 1995 European Data Protection Directive, discussed below. This does not mean that the Convention has become redundant; it still serves as a model for newly democratizing states, and it was invoked as an underpinning document for protecting personal data within European interstate arrangements such as Europol. Also pursuant to the Convention, the Council has adopted a number of influential recommendations, as a wide range of governmental, social, and economic practices and technologies, including the Internet, have been developed and applied.[5] The Council has also developed a Model Contract, outlining the obligations of both licensor and licensee, to ensure equivalent data protection in the context of international data flows. This is in recognition of the fact that these flows are more complicated and multilateral than those that were contemplated when the Convention was drawn up. The contractual instrument has also been superseded in some respects by actions within the European Union.

The Convention has historically been very influential, but it has operated more as a template than as a binding instrument of international law. It continues to have an impact in formerly communist countries in Eastern and Central Europe, as ten of these countries have ratified it up to 2005. The work concluded on new technologies is also of great assistance to the data protection policy community (for example, Council of Europe 1989). As other international policy instruments have entered the data protection scene, however, the Council of Europe has had continually to reassess its role with respect to international data protection issues. Thus it adopted an amendment in 1999 allowing the European Communities as such to accede to the Convention,[6] and, as Treaty 181, formulated an Additional Protocol to the Convention regarding supervisory authorities and transborder data flows.[7] The latter opened for signature and ratification from November 2001; it came into force in July 2004 and, up to mid-2005, had been signed by nineteen countries and ratified by nine. It constitutes a significant response to the burgeoning of international traffic in personal data through new technologies, and remedies the original Convention's failure to require the establishment of regulatory machinery in the ratifying countries. The new Protocol also aims to harmonize and improve cooperation among supervisory authorities in order to provide more effective protection for individuals.

The Organisation for Economic Cooperation and Development Arena

The OECD comprises thirty of the world's most affluent countries. It "provides a setting where governments can compare policy experiences, seek answers to common problems, identify good practice and work to coordinate domestic and international policies."[8] The primary role of the OECD is to promote trade and economic cooperation and to negotiate agreements that will foster those goals. It serves therefore as an important forum for the negotiation of mainly voluntary instruments among countries that are committed to a market economy and pluralistic democracy. It also operates as the major international arena through which countries outside Europe, and especially the United States, can influence international information policy.

It was within the OECD arena in the late 1970s that the world witnessed the first transatlantic conflicts over privacy protection policy. To many Europeans, the American espousal of the principle that information flows should rarely be impeded was a veiled attempt to protect US hegemony in the global marketplace. Some Americans, on the other hand, saw ulterior trade-protectionist motivations behind the data protection label (Eger 1978, Bigelow 1979). The negotiation of the *Guidelines on the Protection of Personal Privacy and Transborder Flows of Personal Data* (OECD 1981) was, therefore, difficult and contentious (see Bennett 1992, p. 137).

The Guidelines were based on a number of assumptions, stated in the preface,

that, although national laws and policies may differ, Member countries have a common interest in protecting privacy and individual liberties, and in reconciling fundamental but competing values such as privacy and the free flow of information;

that automatic processing and transborder flows of personal data create new forms of relationships among countries and require the development of compatible rules and practices;

that transborder flows of personal data contribute to economic and social development;

that domestic legislation concerning privacy protection and transborder flows of personal data may hinder such transborder flows[.]

Applying to personal data in the public and private sectors, these Guidelines were thus intended to help harmonize national privacy legislation and provide a framework for facilitating international flows of data. They represented an important consensus on eight basic principles: collection limitation, data quality, purpose specification, use limitation, security safeguards, openness, individual participation, and accountability.

On the issue of transborder data flows, Section 17 states that

A Member country should refrain from restricting transborder flows of personal data between itself and another Member country except where the latter does not yet substantially observe these Guidelines or where the re-export of such data would circumvent its domestic privacy legislation. A Member country may also impose restrictions in respect of certain categories of personal data for which its domestic privacy legislation includes specific regulations in view of the nature of those data and for which the other Member country provides no equivalent protection.

However,

Member countries should avoid developing laws, policies and practices in the name of the protection of privacy and individual liberties, which would create obstacles to transborder flows of personal data that would exceed requirements for such protection. (Section 18)

In 1985, the Ministers of the OECD countries adopted a *Declaration on Transborder Data Flows* (OECD 1985), which addressed the policy issues arising out of trading activities, intracorporate flows, computerized information services, and scientific and technological exchanges. The governments recognized the diversity of participants involved in transborder data flows, and their growing importance and benefits to the international economy. These flows were acknowledged to play an increasingly important role in the economies of Member countries and in international trade and services. In adopting this *Declaration*, the governments of OECD Member countries expressed their intention to

1. *Promote* access to data and information and related services, and avoid the creation of unjustified barriers to the international exchange of data and information.
2. *Seek* transparency in regulations and policies relating to information, computer and communications services affecting transborder data flows.
3. *Develop* common approaches for dealing with issues related to transborder data flows and, when appropriate, develop harmonized solutions.
4. *Consider* possible implications for other countries when dealing with issues related to transborder data flows.

Efforts were also made to avoid unnecessary divergences between the OECD and Council of Europe agreements, although the former was driven more by economics than was the latter. They both encompass the basic principles of data protection, although in slightly different wording and with varying degrees of elaboration. However, there are some important differences that are worth noting. First, the Guidelines are explicitly voluntary: there is no penalty imposed for nonadoption (either by a country or an organization), and no penalty for noncompliance once adopted. In contrast, the Convention is legally binding, at least for those countries that have ratified it, although countries can meet the general requirements by adopting enforcement and oversight methods appropriate to their political, administrative, and legal systems. Second, the Convention applies solely to automated data processing, whereas the Guidelines apply to personal data regardless of the processing medium.

By the beginning of the 1980s, these two international instruments were used as models for national legislation (in Europe) and for voluntary codes of practice outside. The American and Canadian governments both tried to monitor the extent to which the OECD Guidelines were adopted within their respective societies, without any clear indication of what "adoption" entailed, nor any serious commitment (Gellman 1993, p. 230). The Committee on Information, Computer, and Communications Policy of the OECD has also monitored the effectiveness of these guidelines and tried to ascertain their relevance in the light of technological advances.

By the 1990s, however, attention shifted to the question of computer security and the negotiation of a set of guidelines on the *Security of Information Systems* (OECD 1992). These guidelines, replaced in 2002 by a less detailed set that promoted "a culture of security" (OECD 2002), were intended to provide the required framework for the protection of the availability, integrity, and confidentiality of information systems. They are addressed to the public and private sectors and apply to all information systems: computers, communication facilities, computer and communication networks, and the information that they process. The 1992 guidelines advise a range of policies, laws, codes of conduct, technical measures, management and user practices, and public education and awareness activities at both national and international levels. The security guidelines are also relevant for the safety of cross-border electronic commerce, including electronic money transactions and Internet payments.

The third element in the OECD's package is the *Guidelines for Cryptography Policy* published on 27 March 1997, following several years of heated international controversy concerning the export of cryptographic products for civilian use (OECD 1997). This is a nonbinding agreement that identifies the basic issues that countries should consider in drawing up cryptography policies at the national and international level. These Guidelines set out principles to guide countries in formulating their own policies relating to the use of cryptography. They provide internationally comparable criteria for encryption of computerized information, which governments would adopt and which businesses, individuals, and law enforcement officials would apply in safeguarding electronic transactions, communications, and data storage. They focus on the rights of users to choose cryptographic methods, the freedom of the market to develop them, interoperability, consequences for the protection of personal data and privacy, lawful access to encrypted data, and reducing the barriers to international trade, but they do not endorse any specific cryptographic system.

Each of these elements (privacy, security, cryptography) converged in the mid-1990s when the subject of electronic commerce surfaced as an OECD priority. An initial conference in 1997 in Finland on "Dismantling the Barriers to Global Electronic Commerce" and a number of studies led to a high-profile October 1998 Ministerial conference in Ottawa titled "A Borderless World: Realising the Potential for Electronic Commerce." The conference produced a Ministerial Declaration that reaffirmed "their commitment to the protection of privacy on global networks in order to ensure the respect of important rights, build confidence in global networks, and to prevent unnecessary restrictions on transborder flows of personal data." They also promised to "work to build bridges between the different approaches adopted by Member countries to ensure privacy protection on global networks based on the OECD Guidelines."[9]

The current emphasis on the promotion of electronic commerce has caused a number of shifts in OECD rhetoric and policy. First, the discourse tends to reflect the more interactive, dynamic, and networked nature of contemporary data transmissions. Second, the concentration on

legislation in the 1970s and 1980s has now given way to a recognition
—in keeping with what has become a widespread consensus—that
a multiplicity of solutions are needed in addition to law, including self-
regulation, privacy-enhancing technologies, contractual approaches, and
consumer education. The Working Party on Information Security
and Privacy has published a study of the "Inventory of Instruments
and Mechanisms" for the protection of privacy (OECD 1999, updated as
OECD 2003). The OECD has also attracted much attention by
developing a "privacy statement generator" for creating privacy policies
and statements on websites.[10] Thirdly, privacy protection is advanced
in these debates, not as a barrier to international communications
and trade, but as a necessary condition without which individuals will
not use the public networks for commercial transactions. According
to a background report for the Ottawa conference (OECD 1998,
p. 20):

One of the hallmarks of electronic commerce is that, by drastically reducing
transaction and search costs, it reduces the distance between buyer and seller,
enabling businesses to target very small niches, develop individual customer
profiles, and essentially provide a means of marketing on a one-to-one basis.
The ability to realise this goal will largely hinge on the climate of confidence
and trust that businesses are able to create in their relations with their business
partners and customers. Assurances about protection of consumer privacy and
personal information play an important role in building that confidence.

This report and the action plans inherent within it signal the insepa-
rability of privacy protection from other consumer-related questions, as
well as the profound faith in the marketplace to develop e-commerce in
a privacy-friendly manner. This view, too, is very widely shared in the
electronic commerce and privacy regulatory communities. These assumptions also reinforce the arguments made in chapter 3 about the shifting
discourse surrounding the privacy protection issue. However, we can
also note that the relationship between the protection of privacy, the
enhancement of consumer trust, and the use of public online networks
is perhaps a tenuous one, which has yet to be established with any
empirical confidence. Meanwhile, the "consumer-confidence" theory is
just that: a theory. Although many people say that the lack of privacy
is a crucial barrier to participation in cyberspace,[11] there is no clear
indication that significant numbers of individuals actually do perform

their transactions online as soon as better privacy statements and rules are offered. As we saw in chapter 3, that relationship may be reflected in attitudes more than in behavior (Swire and Litan 1998, pp. 79–80).

The European Union Arena

By the late 1980s, it was readily apparent that the Council of Europe Convention was not serving to harmonize European data protection law; there was no rush to ratify the Convention, and there remained significant legal differences among the legislation of those that had ratified. The OECD Guidelines were serving more as a way to justify self-regulatory approaches than as a method to promote good data protection practices throughout the advanced industrial world. Despite the fact that, since the 1970s, the European Parliament had been making repeated calls on the European Commission to propose a directive to harmonize data protection law, the Commission preferred to sit on the sidelines.

In the late 1980s, however, it was becoming increasingly clear that discrepancies in data protection could impede the free flow of personal information throughout the EU and obstruct the creation of the Internal Market, due to be completed by 1992. Data protection had ceased to be merely a human rights issue; it was also intrinsically linked to the operation of international trade. The Commission was therefore confident that it was justified in proposing a Directive on the basis of Article 100a of the EC Treaty, that is "to ensure the establishment and functioning of the Internal Market."

The result was by far the most influential international policy instrument to date: the *Directive on the Protection of Personal Data with Regard to the Processing of Personal Data and on the Free Movement of Such Data* (EU 1995).[12] This approval was the culmination of five years of drafting and redrafting as the document passed through the complicated and lengthy EU decision-making process.[13] It was finally assented to by all member states with the exception of the UK (which abstained). The goals expressed in directives are supposed to be binding, but Member States are granted some latitude in deciding the actual form of implementation and the more detailed content of their legislation.

The detailed story of how the Directive came into being is complex and has been described elsewhere (Simitis 1995, Bainbridge 1996, Bennett and Raab 1997). The initial draft Directive was issued, quite unexpectedly, in September 1990 (European Commission 1990), and was widely regarded by many private interests in Europe and North America as overly restrictive. It was substantially amended by the European Parliament in March 1992, after which the Commission issued a revised draft later that year (European Commission 1992). The added reference to the "Free Movement of Such Data" in the title of the second draft reflects the influence of private sector lobbying, but is also consistent with the economic motivations that permeated OECD thinking, as we have seen. After all, the Directive was developed and its processes steered by the then Directorate-General XV of the European Commission, which held the Internal Market portfolio.

The next two years were taken up with intensive bargaining within the Council of Ministers (Simitis 1995, p. 445). A "common position" was reached in April 1995, to which minor amendments were then made by the Parliament. The final version was published in October 1995 (EU 1995).[14] The bargaining over this text can be considered at two levels. Within the Council of Ministers (or more accurately the Working Party that prepared the text for the Council of Ministers), the interests were on a national level. Simitis (1995, p. 456) concludes that the "long debates in the Council have certainly left deep marks," and attributes many of these compromises to the primary interest of Member States "to preserve their own familiar rules" (Simitis 1995, p. 449). The protracted nature of the process can be explained, to some extent, by the reservations of Britain's Conservative government about the necessity of a directive on data protection, given the existing Convention—reservations informed also by wider suspicions of a gradual centralization of power in Brussels.

On another level, however, the substance of the Directive can be understood as the reflection of negotiated bargains among a range of public and private sector stakeholders. As the necessity for data protection came to be felt more widely in most public and private organizations, it began to generate a wider, more fragmented and complex network, expert in the particular data protection problems of their sector of industry, or area of government. Many of these interests forged international linkages to influence European policy. The European Direct Marketing Association, for instance, spent millions of dollars lobbying primarily against the "positive consent" option within the 1990 draft. American interests, particularly in direct marketing and credit reporting, also found natural allies in their European counterparts and were happy to offer political and financial support to help these lobbying efforts (Regan 1999). On the other side of the debate, data protection authorities themselves also institutionalized cooperation, especially through the Annual Conference of Privacy and Data Protection Commissioners and in frequent interchanges among Commissioners of the European states. The relatively confined group of experts that negotiated earlier instruments through the Council of Europe and the OECD therefore gave way, in the 1990s, to a complex range of cross-cutting and cross-national networks.

During the long emergence of the Directive, and thereafter, many countries and organizations were also promoting "information super-highway" policies, replete with action plans, exhortations to develop the infrastructures of electronic commerce and the interchange of data, and encouragement of consumers and citizens to engage in online transactions (Raab 1995). Central to these efforts was a perception, enunciated from the highest circles of governmental and intergovernmental policy-making, that trust and trustworthiness were key elements of the climate within which these initiatives would flourish.[15] The Directive played a major part in helping to achieve the legal and psychological conditions, and was seen in European circles as a major asset. However, it played to a somewhat different reception abroad.

The aim of the Directive, Single Market Commissioner Mario Monti said, is to "ensure a high level of protection for the privacy of individuals in all Member States . . . [and] also to help ensure the free flow of Information Society services in the Single Market by fostering consumer confidence and minimising differences between Member States' rules" (EC 1995). This reflects the underlying assumption that harmonized data protection legislation and the free flow of data are complementary rather than conflicting values, and that the single European market relies not only on the free flow of capital, goods, and labor, but also of information. The hope is that "any person whose data are processed in the Community will be afforded an equivalent level of protection of his rights, in particular his right to privacy, irrespective of the Member State where the processing is carried out" (EC 1995).

That the Directive is a complicated instrument is mainly attributable to its continuous revision as compromises were struck and restruck within the Commission, the Parliament, and the Council. As is the case with Directives, which are addressed to Member States, it is not meant to be a user-friendly document by which individuals can ascertain and exercise their privacy rights. In the Directive, the reader is initially confronted with a series of recitals in the form of seventy-two "whereas" statements that state intentions, that place this Directive in the context of other values and policies that help interpretation, and that reflect the variety of interests that shaped its content. The familiar set of fair information principles, around which previous national laws and international agreements have converged, do not appear in any one easily accessible place. The principles of consent, access, notification, security, and so on are certainly reflected in particular Articles, but the document is very much a legal text whose main purpose is to give guidance to drafters of national data protection legislation.

Despite the complexity, the Directive does make some real innovations in data protection policy. Most notably, the final version abandoned certain artificial and outdated concepts. For instance, there is now little distinction made between public and private sector data processing; the first draft differentiated between the sectors in regard to the fair obtaining, and legitimacy of processing, of personal data. Some laws only covered "automated" data processing, whereas the Directive applies to "any structured set of personal data which are accessible according to specific criteria, whether centralized, decentralized or dispersed on a functional or geographical basis" (Art. 2 (c)). Thus "structured" manual files are also covered, a provision that was resisted by, and has caused headaches for, the British whose 1984 law only regulated computerized personal information. Like the Convention, the Directive also includes specific provisions for "sensitive" forms of data. It also tries to avoid artificial distinctions between information collection, use, and disclosure, preferring to define "processing" as embracing all these phases as well as other operations.

Unlike the Convention, the Directive also specifies the nature and function of a Member State's "supervisory authority." Each country must provide that one or more public authorities are responsible for monitoring the application within its territory of the national provisions adopted pursuant to the Directive (Art. 28 (1)). These authorities must act with complete independence and must be endowed with investigative powers, effective powers of intervention (especially *before* processing operations begin), powers to engage in legal proceedings, and powers to hear claims concerning the protection of rights and freedoms and regarding the lawfulness of data processing under the Directive. In addition, Member States should provide that the supervisory authorities are consulted when administrative measures are being developed that might have privacy implications. In total, these provisions require a greater range of powers and responsibilities than had existed within many European data protection regimes.

Articles 29 and 30 establish an advisory Working Party composed of a representative from the data protection authority in each Member State, joined by representatives of the European Commission, and of other Community institutions. The Working Party is expected to give the Commission advice on divergences among national laws, on the level of protection in third countries, on codes of conduct, and on proposed amendments to the Directive. Executive decision-making power over the Directive is granted to a body simply called "The Committee" (Art. 31), comprised of representatives from the Member States, and chaired by someone from the Commission. This is a mechanism by which the Commission can adopt decisions and regulations pursuant to the Directive, and in particular with regard to the determination of the adequacy of protection within non-EU third countries. Thus, the Working Party will report its advice and opinions to the Commission, which are referred to the Committee, which then reports back to the Commission on the measures to be taken. If the Commission adopts the measures, then Member States have no choice but to implement them.

An Adequate Level of Protection

For some countries outside the EU, the extraterritorial implications of the Directive have caused considerable anxiety. Article 25(1 and 2) stipulate that "Member States shall provide that the transfer to a third country of personal data which are undergoing processing or are intended for processing after transfer may take place only if . . . the third country in question ensures an adequate level of protection." The "adequacy" of protection shall be assessed "in the light of all the circumstances surrounding a data transfer operation or set of data transfer operations." Particular consideration is to be given to the nature and purpose of the data and "the rules of law, both general and sectoral" and "the professional rules and security measures which are complied with." Article 26(1) lists a number of derogations from this provision. Personal data may be transferred to a country with "inadequate" protection when

• the data subject has given his consent "unambiguously";
• the transfer is necessary to fulfil a contract between the data subject and the controller, or between the controller and a third party;
• the transfer is necessary on "important public interest grounds, or for the establishment, exercise or defence of legal claims";
• the transfer is necessary to protect "the vital interests of the data subject" or;
• the transfer is of data that are already in a public register.

Member States can also authorize transfer to a country with "inadequate" protection if the data controller enters into a contract that "adduces adequate safeguards with respect to the protection of the privacy and fundamental rights and freedoms of individuals" (Art. 26 (2)). In such cases, the country concerned shall inform the Commission and the other Member States of such authorizations, in order to allow for any objections. The Commission may also decide, through the Article 31 Committee, that certain "standard contractual clauses offer sufficient safeguards" (Art. 26 (4)). As a result of concerns about the development of a German Railway Card (*Bahnkarte*) and the associated processing of information about German citizens in the United States, one of the first contracts was negotiated by the German data protection authorities between the Germany railways and Citibank. While this contract is generally regarded as "adequate," the complexities and expense of these negotiations probably means that it will not offer a model for many other transborder data flow processes (Dix 1996). However, in June 2001 the European Commission finally adopted a

Decision that set standard contractual clauses to ensure adequate safe-guards for personal data transferred from the EU to third countries (EC 2001). An alternative set of clauses was promulgated in 2004 following negotiations with an international business coalition (EC 2004).

Where the Commission decides that a third country does not ensure adequate protection, Member States should "take the measures neces-sary to prevent any transfer of data of the same type to the third country in question" (Art. 25 (4)). Then the Commission "shall enter into nego-tiations with a view to remedying the situation" (Art. 25 (5)). Thus, if the Commission finds an inadequate level of protection, Member States are effectively mandated, rather than simply permitted, to prohibit the transfer. This represents a stronger approach than that embodied within either the OECD Guidelines or the Council of Europe Convention. Even though both these instruments contain a principle of "equivalence" (arguably stronger than "adequate"), neither of these instruments requires its signatories to block the transfer of data to countries that cannot ensure an equivalent level of protection. So, whereas the Direc-tive adopts a weaker standard, it also embodies a stronger method of enforcement (Greenleaf 1995, p. 16).

Enforcing Adequacy
The implementation of Articles 25 and 26 obviously poses a number of problems for international businesses that rely on the transborder flows of personal data. It has major implications for credit-granting and financial institutions, for hotel and airline reservations systems, for the direct-marketing sector, for life and property insurance, for the phar-maceutical industry, and for any online company that markets its prod-ucts and services worldwide. In essence, the EU's adequacy provisions have become the de facto rules of the road for the increasingly global character of personal data processing operations. They have also become a main focus of attention, debate, and controversy in international economic arenas.

From the outset, commentators have generally agreed that the Euro-peans were never going to tolerate the existence of "data havens"—juris-dictions in which data processing may take place because of the absence or weakness of data protection safeguards. The *Directive* would be seriously undermined if multinationals could instantaneously transmit their processing offshore in order to avoid the transaction costs of having to abide by the stronger measures in force in Europe. European private-sector data controllers would be justifiably aggrieved if they had to abide by strong data protection measures in Europe, while their overseas competitors could act with impunity. European citizens, and the public interest and consumer groups that represent them, would also not look kindly on the continual flouting of their privacy rights by overseas interests.

Subsequent to the passage of the Directive, the Article 29 Working Party issued a series of policy statements designed to clarify how Articles 25 and 26 of the Directive would be interpreted. An initial 1997 document titled "First Orientations on Transfers of Personal Data to Third Countries" (EU 1997) gave some initial indication of the Working Party's thinking on how adequacy would be judged. Where outside countries do not have comprehensive data protection legislation on the European model, then judgments would need to be made on a case-by-case basis, a task that generally exceeds the resources not only of European data protection authorities, but also of data controllers contemplating the export of personal data to these countries. The Working Party, therefore, floated the idea of "white lists" of countries whose systems of data protection display prima facie the requirements of the Directive. This evaluation would not be based on the analysis of abstract legal text or of the mere existence of other instruments, but on the consideration of "several representative cases of transfers to a particular third country." The Working Party was quick to point out, however, that "[w]here a country is not included in such a white list, this need not imply that the country is implicitly 'black-listed,' but rather that no general guidance regarding that particular country is yet available. The establishment of an explicit black-list of countries, even if for the purposes of guidance, would be politically very sensitive" (EU 1997, p. 4).

"Adequate protection" requires both content and enforcement. The content principles should include purpose limitation, data quality and proportionality, transparency, security, rights of access, rectification and opposition, and restrictions on onward transfers to further third countries. Rather than specifying certain structural requirements, however, the Working Group detailed the essential functions that a data protection system should perform:

1) to deliver a *good level of compliance* with the rules. (No system can guarantee 100% compliance, but some are better than others.) A good system is generally characterised by a high degree of awareness among data controllers of their obligations, and among data subjects of their rights and the means of exercising them. The existence of effective and dissuasive sanctions is important in ensuring respect for rules, as of course are systems of direct verification by authorities, auditors, or independent data protection officials.

2) to provide *support and help to individual data subjects* in the exercise of their rights. The individual must be able to enforce his/her rights rapidly and effectively, and without prohibitive cost. To do so there must be some sort of institutional mechanism allowing independent investigation of complaints.

3) to provide *appropriate redress* to the injured party where rules are not complied with. This is a key element which must involve a system of independent arbitration which allows compensation to be paid and sanctions imposed where appropriate. (EU 1997, p. 7; emphasis in original)

In later documents, this functional approach was applied to other self-regulatory instruments of data protection. Thus, in January 1998, the Working Party turned its attention to the adequacy of measures for industry self-regulation, including codes of practice, concluding the following:

For a self-regulatory instrument to be considered as a valid ingredient of "adequate protection" it must be binding on all the members to whom personal data are transferred and provide with adequate safeguards if data are passed on to non-members. The instrument must be transparent and include the basic content of core data protection principles. The instrument must have mechanisms, which effectively ensure a good level of general compliance. A system of dissuasive and punitive sanctions is one way of achieving this. Mandatory external audits are another. The instrument must provide support and help to individual data subjects who are faced with a problem involving the processing of their personal data. An easily accessible, impartial and independent body to hear complaints from data subjects and adjudicate on breaches of the code must therefore be in place. The instrument must guarantee appropriate redress in cases of non-compliance. A data subject must be able to obtain a remedy for his/her problem and compensation as appropriate.[16] (EU 1998)

The Working Party also applied these same criteria to the use of contractual provisions in the context of transfers of personal data to third countries.[17] The standard contractual clauses that the Commission agreed to in June 2001 can be used voluntarily by any organization that operates within a country not already on the "white list" or that has not signed up to the "Safe Harbor Agreement" with the United States; that Agreement is discussed further in chapter 6.

Throughout this process, the standard of data protection within the United States posed an intractable dilemma. If the United States was found to meet the adequacy test under the Directive, despite the fact that many areas of the American economy are not obliged to maintain data protection standards, then the credibility of the EU Directive would be undermined. If, on the other hand, the Directive were enforced to the letter, then the broad bans on data flows would seriously disrupt international trade and travel, and would almost certainly lead to a transatlantic trade dispute (Gellman 1996, p. 158). In recognition of this, a high-level dialogue between John Mogg, the then director-general of DG XV and the US undersecretary for commerce, David Aaron (Charlesworth 2000, Farrell 2002) resulted in the Safe Harbor Agreement. The intent of this proposal, however, is to bind those companies that subscribe to Safe Harbor to a set of privacy principles overseen and enforced by the Federal Trade Commission. As of May 2005, some 710 US companies had committed themselves to the privacy principles inherent in the Safe Harbor Agreement, which, if they were to be breached, would open these companies to challenge under the Federal Trade Commission's power to regulate "unfair and deceptive" trade practices.[18]

The Safe Harbor proposal aside, a number of concerns remain about the implementation of Articles 25 and 26. The Directive provides for the Commission (with the Article 31 Committee's approval) to set an EU-wide standard for acceptance of transfers to specific third countries. There is at least the danger that judgments about adequacy will be susceptible to the vagaries of the European policy process and are likely to be enmeshed with the resolution of issues that have nothing to do with information privacy. Log-rolling may therefore override the more predictable and rational pursuit of a data protection standard (Pounder and Kosten 1995, p. 33).

Another lingering concern is that neither the supervisory authority nor the data controller has the capacity to scrutinize the processing of personal data in another jurisdiction, nor can they be fully satisfied that data subjects can exercise their privacy rights. The Directive establishes a more centralized and institutionalized process to make judgments about adequacy. Yet those determinations will probably continue to be made on the assumption that the wording of contracts, laws, and professional codes is reflected in practice. The Directive does not get round the central dilemma inherent in former attempts to regulate international data transmissions by the Convention, or through model contracts. In the absence of an audit mechanism that ensures that personal data are *actually* processed fairly and legally in a third country, judgments about adequacy will probably continue to made in a nonempirical way, and according to the analysis of the "black letter of the law" or of other formal indicators.

A report produced under the Commission's auspices in 1998 highlighted many of these difficulties (Raab et al. 1998). The report studied five different transfers of personal information (airline reservations, human resources data, subcontracted outsourcing of data processing, electronic commerce, and medical data) in six different jurisdictions (United States, Canada, Hong Kong, Japan, New Zealand, and Australia). In analyzing real transfers of personal data (with the collaboration of some key institutions), the practical difficulties of assessing adequacy became very apparent. In particular, contemporary data transfers are not discrete and time-bound transmissions of data from one organization to another. In a highly networked and dynamic information economy, a number of intermediaries can complicate the process of discovering who is responsible for the processing of what data, when, where, and how. These and other empirical difficulties can only be resolved when cases are brought before the Commission under the Article 25 and 26 standards.

There continue to be serious questions, therefore, about the ability of international data protection agreements to deliver a "good level of compliance with the rules," as is stated in the first of the Article 29 Working Party's adequacy tests. The other two tests—whether a system "provides support and help to data subjects," and whether there are appropriate and independent redress mechanisms for the injured party—are relatively easy to assess. These last two tests are largely procedural, and can be assessed from afar and with reference to documentary evidence concerning the qualities of regulatory, or indeed self-regulatory, provisions. But how does one observe whether the system actually delivers a "good level of compliance with the rules" without detailed and onsite inspection of a data controller's practices, and, indeed, of a regulatory authority's efficacy?

The necessity for onsite auditing programs has been a theme in several independent evaluations of data protection systems (for example, Flaherty 1989, p. 400), but it is also a function that tends to be relegated in the priorities of the busy, understaffed, and underresourced privacy protection agency. Thus, it is difficult to understand how the existing mechanisms for measuring "adequacy" in non-EU countries seriously can take compliance questions into account. Moreover, there is the distinct possibility that the level of compliance by an organization in a country without a regime for data protection might be just as high, if not higher, than that of a similar organization within a European country with a supposedly "adequate" level of data protection.

That said, up to mid-2005, the Commission had recognized the adequacy of the protection afforded by Switzerland, Canada, Argentina, Guernsey, the Isle of Man, the Safe Harbor Privacy Principles, and the transfer of air passenger records to the US Bureau of Customs and Border Protection.[19]

The Asia-Pacific Arena

It is worth looking briefly at the efforts to concert data protection beyond national boundaries in the Asia-Pacific region.[20] In that region, many countries have created privacy statutes that, in some cases, are deemed to have surpassed the requirements of the OECD Guidelines, which are the foundational touchstone for Asia-Pacific countries (Greenleaf 2003). An Australian-inspired step was taken by Asia-Pacific Economic Cooperation (APEC), a group of twenty-one countries, to fashion a regional privacy standard based on revised OECD principles and addressing the issue of transborder data flows. Its method of determining compliance with principles relied on national self-certification. This initiative was seen by critics, on balance, as a retrograde step if it were to lead to a lower level of protection based on guidelines that were being criticized as outdated and ineffectual, and that had been overtaken by several countries' national laws. Thus the Asia-Pacific Privacy Charter Council (APPCC), an independent group of privacy experts that included former regulatory officials, was established late in 2003 to draft a higher-standard privacy charter,[21] one with stronger principles and more rigorous implementation requirements.

Work on the APEC Privacy Framework, with further amendments and revisions, proceeded within the APEC e-commerce steering group at meetings during 2004. There was much at stake in the outcome: the United States and Canada, which are both Atlantic- and Pacific-facing countries, are APEC members, and the United States, with its leaning towards less exacting data protection, plays an active and influential part in the work of the steering groups. Anticipating a possible formal Asia-Pacific treaty or convention, the APPCC critics sought to influence the process by promoting a high-level charter; the explicit models for that future were envisaged as the Council of Europe Convention and the EU Directive. Nevertheless, the APEC went ahead and adopted its Privacy Framework in November 2004. It received the endorsement of the US secretary of state, but also the condemnation of the APPCC as "a new low standard" (Greenleaf 2005). But it would not be correct to view the EU and the Asia-Pacific region as tectonic plates on a collision course, especially as the APEC Framework remained incomplete through its deferment of specifying cross-border provisions.

The International Standards Arena

The perceived gap in the enforcement process for data protection has led some to contend that the data protection question should be taken up by the world's standards-setting and certification bodies, institutions with many years of experience of observing and measuring "levels of compliance" with various international norms.[22] Information security standards have played a peripheral but important role in privacy protection for some years, with the adoption, in December 2000, of ISO 17799 as the security standard.[23] In the 1990s, however, the idea of a more general management standard for the complete set of privacy principles emerged onto the international agenda. In large measure, the idea has stemmed from the negotiation in Canada of the "Model Code for the Protection of Personal Information" under the auspices of the Canadian Standards Association (CSA 1996), an instrument that is discussed in more detail in chapter 6. The publication of this standard prompted a series of attempts to produce a similar instrument at the international level, with the idea that privacy protection could be regarded as an element of "quality management," similar to that of the ISO 9000 series of quality management standards.

The process first began within the institutions of the International Organization for Standardization (ISO). In September 1996, as a result of some initial pressure from the consumer associations' committee (COPOLCO) of ISO, the General Council of ISO recommended that work should begin on the development of an international standard for the protection of privacy. The twelve-member Technical Management Board (TMB) of ISO then met in January 1997 and decided to refer the issue to an Ad Hoc Advisory Group (AHAG), which was to pave the way for a positive TMB resolution in 1998. The expected resolution, however, did not materialize mainly as a result of some very intensive lobbying by certain US multinational business interests. The AHAG was maintained for another year in order to study the issue further, but was disbanded in June 1999. A meeting in Hong Kong in September 1999 hosted by the Standards Council of Canada concluded that some other useful instruments, short of a full-fledged standard, could be negotiated. By mid-2003, however, privacy was not listed among COPOLCO's fourteen priority areas for international standardization.[24]

From there, the idea migrated to specifically European standards bodies. The Comité Européen de Normalisation/Information Society Standardization System (CEN/ISSS), responsible for the negotiation of standards within Europe, began to study the feasibility of an international privacy standard, supported by the Article 29 Working Party.[25] At an open seminar in Brussels in March 2000, it was proposed to begin standardization activities along three paths: a general data protection standard that would set out practical operational steps to be taken by an organization in order to comply with relevant data protection legislation, principally the EU Directive; a series of sector-specific initiatives in key areas such as health information and human resources management; and task-specific initiatives mainly related to the online environment (Dumortier and Goemans 2000). A formal resolution gave three standards bodies (CEN, CENELEC, and ETSI) a mandate to study the potential for further standardization work in support of the European Directive. From then, the reins were taken up under the auspices of the "Initiative on Privacy Standardization in Europe" (IPSE).[26] IPSE's final report, in 2002, surveyed a wide canvas of regulatory techniques and instruments for privacy protection before identifying a number of issues where further standardization work could be pursued. However, it shied away from any aim to produce a specific privacy management standard.[27] The approach therefore gravitated toward standardizing or harmonizing voluntary, contractual, auditing, technological, and educational tools. The Article 29 Working Party gave a brief opinion welcoming the CEN/ISSS initiative for its practical and awareness-raising recommendations.[28] At the end of 2004, a CEN/ISSS workshop proposed a business plan for further work along the lines of its recommendations two years earlier.[29]

Proponents contend that an international standard would hold a number of advantages over national models. It would carry far greater weight and credibility in both Europe and the United States. It would attract attention and international certification efforts from different national standards bodies. It would give business outside Europe a more reliable and consistent method by which to demonstrate their conformity to international data protection standards. It would also provide a more reliable mechanism for the implementation of Article 25 of the Directive. As mentioned earlier, the scrutiny of laws and contracts provides no assurances to European data protection agencies that data protection rules are complied with in the receiving jurisdiction. Required registration to a standard, which would oblige independent and regular auditing, would provide a greater certainty that "adequate" data protection is being practiced by the receiving organization, wherever it is located. This does, of course, require concomitant efforts to harmonize systems of conformity assessment and auditor certification. At the end of the day, bilateral and multilateral mutual recognition agreements would also have to be negotiated to ensure that domestic conformity assessment programs are commonly respected (Bennett 1997b).

These initiatives have, however, been met with very high levels of resistance from businesses in information-intensive sectors (Bennett 2000).

However, there was further development within the ISO during 2004, with the formation of a privacy technology study group that soon received, for fast-track approval, a draft international standard for a privacy framework that had been developed by the International Security, Trust and Privacy Alliance (ISTPA), a grouping of companies, technology providers, and other organizations. At their annual meeting in Wroclaw in September 2004, the world's privacy and information commissioners, in their "Wroclaw Resolution," welcomed and strongly supported the ISO initiative, including institutional machinery for testing privacy technologies, which linked the commissioners with the ISO. However, they urged the ISO not to consider the ISTPA framework because of its weakness on the question of limiting the collection of personal data. The commissioners pressed, instead, for further and fuller discussion of privacy standards. The Resolution also declared that a technology standard, however valuable it might be, must be seen as a tool for assisting in compliance with legal requirements for data protection. The Wroclaw Resolution followed upon the adoption of a working paper on a future ISO privacy standard by the commissioners' International Working Group on Data Protection in Telecommunications, meeting in Buenos Aires earlier in the year, which warned of the dangers of undue haste in the approval of a global privacy technology standard.[30]

The World Trade Arena

The final international arena is one in which the issue is more likely to be addressed in the future. When privacy protection became a trade-related question, it was inevitable that it would, sooner or later, be injected into the wider panoply of issues negotiated and arbitrated within the World Trade Organization (WTO). It is fitting, therefore, to conclude this chapter with some speculation about how data protection might relate to the wider politics of international trade.

From the outset of the European data protection movement in the 1970s, American commentators have been concerned that the extraterritorial provisions within these laws could be used as a nontariff trade barrier to protect what was considered the less-developed and less-innovative information technology industries within Europe. In 1978, an American official commented that "those countries constraining the transnational flow of information may be constructing a whole body of contradictory international law that will cause worldwide confusion in communications, perhaps ultimately blocking information flow altogether" (Eger 1978, p. 1066). Of course, back in the 1970s the focus of American criticism was a relatively small number of national statutes each with quite weak provisions for the control of transborder data flows.

As the harmonization efforts of the Council of Europe, the OECD, and the EU have progressed, and as data protection has become of central importance to international electronic commerce, so rhetoric about European motives has been ratcheted up. For instance, Ira Magaziner, the senior Clinton Administration official responsible for e-commerce issues, asserted: "In general, we [in the United States] don't recognize an extra-territorial attempt to shut down the flow of data between countries. . . . According to principles of international trade, I think that's a violation of WTO rules" (quoted in Shaffer 2000, p. 47). Similar statements were made throughout the negotiation of the Safe Harbor agreement between the United States and Europe.

Regardless of European motives, which are obviously diverse and complex, the very prospect that the Directive might have the effect of protecting European business interests against American competition raises a series of fascinating questions about whether or not these European regulations violate the existing rules of the world trading system. Swire and Litan (1998, p. 145) argue that, at the very least, European data protection law will force US businesses that wish to operate within Europe to comply with those rules, and to be constrained in the ways in which they use personal information. They also maintain that European firms would be more inclined to contract with domestic information processing companies with whom they can freely exchange personal data under the umbrella protection of the Directive.

Any action by the United States, or any other non-European state, against the trade-protectionist effects of data protection law would most likely be covered by the General Agreement on Trade in Services (GATS) (Shaffer 2000, p. 48), under which states make "market access commitments" for various sectors and activities. If a personal data transfer is covered under one of these commitments, then the EU is obliged to treat US companies no less favorably than European ones. According to Article VI(1) of GATS: "In sectors where specific commitments are undertaken, each Member shall ensure that all measures of general application affecting trade in services are administered in a reasonable, objective and impartial manner." Any challenge to the operation of the Directive would then hinge on the meaning of the word *reasonable* (Shaffer 2000, p. 49). In addition, and perhaps more importantly, any ban on data transfers under the provisions in Articles 25 and 26 of the Directive must be applied in an even-handed manner. Thus, if the EU were to ban data exports to one country, but not to another with equally inadequate data protection, then it could fall foul of the "most favoured nation" clause of the GATS. Article II(1) states: "With respect to any measure covered by this Agreement, each Member shall accord immediately and unconditionally to services and service suppliers of any other Member treatment no less favourable than that it accords to like services and service suppliers of any other country."

The requirement for impartiality helps to explain the careful attempts by the Directive's Article 29 and 31 committees to develop a clear methodology for the assessment of adequacy, as well as their attempts to gain a more comprehensive and empirical understanding of aspects of data protection in third countries (see Schwartz and Reidenberg 1996, Raab et al. 1998). Moreover, both committees adopted formal commitments to nondiscrimination in 2000. Citing provisions from the European Convention on Human Rights, the Article 31 committee affirmed its commitment to the principle of nondiscrimination and to the "general principle of equality, of which the prohibition of discrimination on grounds of nationality is a specific enunciation, is one of the fundamental principles of Community law." It also went on to explain that it is "important to be able to judge different situations on their merits and not to regard the equal treatment principle as imposing a single model on third countries."[31] Thus, the policy appears to rest on the questionable assumption that different and flexible methods for assessing adequacy can be applied in an even-handed manner.

Notwithstanding these difficulties, Shaffer (2000) has concluded that any third-country attempt to challenge EU data protection rules before the WTO would probably not succeed for three reasons. First, it can be argued that any ban on data transfers would harm EU-owned and -registered companies as much as it would those companies outside the EU. Second, the EU's action is directed toward a legitimate public policy objective that is explicitly mentioned in Article XIV(c)(2) of the GATS as a general exception:

Subject to the requirement that such measures are not applied in a manner which would constitute a means of arbitrary or unjustifiable discrimination between countries where like conditions prevail, or a disguised restriction on trade in services, nothing in this Agreement shall be construed to prevent the adoption or enforcement by any Member of measures . . . necessary to secure compliance with laws or regulations which are not inconsistent with the provisions of this Agreement including those relating to . . . (ii) the protection of the privacy of individuals in relation to the processing and dissemination of personal data and the protection of confidentiality of individual records and accounts.

Third, he contends that any WTO dispute settlement panel would be reluctant to rule on the substantive policy interests, but would prefer to focus instead on procedural questions. This deference is, Shaffer argues, supported by recent WTO jurisprudence.[32]

We have no way of judging whether these predictions are correct. It is possible, however, that at some point, and in some context, international data protection rules will be tested within the WTO. Much prior analysis understandably has considered these scenarios in the context of an American challenge to European rules. But we should bear in mind that transborder data flow provisions appear in most national legislation. Potential disputes could arise between any number of trading partners in almost any area of the world.[33] For this reason, the complicated, and for data protection experts somewhat unfamiliar, world of international trade policy may arise as a significant arena in which data protection rules are negotiated in the future.

Conclusion

We have described the activities on data protection within four international regimes, and speculated on the possible involvement of two
further arenas of transnational cooperation, one relating to standards-
setting, the other concerned with world trade. There is no doubt that
other less-important international activity could have been discussed.
There is, for instance, a set of data protection guidelines issued by the
United Nations (UN 1990). It is also important to note that both consumer and business groups have developed parallel international bodies
to shadow—and sometimes to lobby or counterpoise—the activities
within these international regimes.[34] The world's data protection commissioners also cooperate in a number of forums, including their annual
conference.

As we view the effect of this intense international activity at the beginning of the twenty-first century, there can be no doubt that it has had
a profound and widespread impact on the ways in which the policies
and practices of public and private organizations have developed. Bennett
(1992, 1997a) has contended that these efforts have produced a continuing process of policy convergence, as both the principles and instruments of privacy protection have grown increasingly alike and have been
adopted by a greater number of countries. But this convergence has
stemmed from rather some different, though interrelated, processes
throughout the history of data protection. For the pioneering states, the
convergence resulted largely from independent and indigenous analysis
of the problem. As the experts then coalesced at international levels, an
elite network developed, sharing ideas and emulating each other's experiences. This elite networking then became formalized first within the
Council of Europe and the OECD, and later within the EU. The agreements that resulted served to harmonize data protection policy, which
then had a penetrative impact on those states that legislated later on.
Thus, every country that has adopted data protection law since the mid-
1980s has been virtually forced to take into account the relevant policy
activity at the international level. For the European states, the operative
instruments have been the Council of Europe Convention, and later
the EU Data Protection Directive. For others, the more influential

instrument has been the OECD Privacy Guidelines. Yet, by the turn of the century, the shortcomings of the Guidelines and their relevance to modern information-processing conditions were being seriously questioned (Clarke 2000a, Kirby 1999).

One can debate the level and extent of convergence. Bennett (1992) has argued that there was a notable convergence on the question of statutory principles, but (at least in the 1980s) a considerable divergence in terms of the policy instruments that had been designed to oversee their implementation. From the 1990s, however, it has become apparent that the EU Directive's stipulations about the appropriate functions for "supervisory authorities" has instigated a greater similarity in the powers of the agencies through which data protection law is enforced. A supervisory authority with a specific set of powers and responsibilities is now considered a necessary condition for effective data protection and an obligation under European law (Bennett 1997a, p. 108).

The point about convergence should not, however, be overstated. The EU Directive contains many derogations, qualifications, and alternatives available to Member States in transposing and implementing the Directive in their own countries, giving rise to fears that important aspects of privacy protection may be weakened rather than elevated to the "high and common level" envisaged by its progenitors. Furthermore, Reidenberg (2000, p. 1340) contends that this policy convergence continues to obscure some profound differences that are deeply rooted in "distinct visions of democratic governance" and in profound cultural perspectives on the "role of the state in protecting the rights of citizens and the ability of the market to assure the fair treatment of citizens." We return to these issues in chapter 10.

These transnational instruments have played three overlapping functions over time. They have acted as instruments of harmonization, as templates that any state or organization might use in order to fashion its own data protection policy. They have acted as exemplars, producing a progressive and inexorable desire to be within the community of nations that has adopted data protection legislation; the more states that adopt, the higher the pressure on the nonadopters. More recently, the European Directive has acted as a penetrative force, with significant economic consequences for those businesses that rely upon the unimpeded international flow of personal information, and that cannot claim to protect those data in ways that meet the adequacy test. By extension, the Directive has had an influence on those governments who see a need to protect their domestic industries from the possible consequences of noncompliance.

These instruments have built upon each other. They represent a logical progression reflecting an increasing policy interdependence of different countries. The Directive was only possible because of prior agreement on data protection principles within the OECD and the Council of Europe. It attempts to rectify some of the perceived weaknesses within these instruments, especially with regard to the enforceability of data protection rules in a global economy. The prospective standardization initiatives in the ISO and the CEN/ISSS can be seen in a similar light.

It is also worth noting that the principal exporter of data protection policy has been Europe. Historically, it has been non-Americans who have been concerned about the extraterritorial impact of US domestic policy. The hegemonic position of the United States in the international economy has typically created externalities requiring a range of policy responses in economic, trade, environmental, and other areas by other states. In human rights policy, there is also a perception that influence has historically flowed from the United States to Europe. The reversal of this pattern has not gone unnoticed. Trubow, for instance, remarks: "It will be ironic, indeed, if Europe's insistence on the protection of human rights causes this country to pay some real attention to informational privacy in both the public and private sectors. Usually we are in the position of lecturing other nations about the sanctity of fundamental human rights; in the informational privacy dimension we are the ones who must be lectured" (Trubow 1992, p. 175). In testifying on the effects of the adequacy standard, Westin comments that "we deliberately chose to break with European institutions in 1776, and it would be remarkable if we thought that a return to deference *without agreement* was the right course in 1996" (Westin 1996, emphasis in original).

Increasingly, therefore, the domestic policy instruments to be discussed and compared in chapters 5, 6, and 7 have been designed with one firm eye on the international context. This growing policy interdependence has caused a proliferation in the number of transnational actors, and a progressive frequency and regularity of networking opportunities. It might be assumed that this transnational policy-making has caused a concomitant reduction in state sovereignty. It is quite obvious that the latitude of state policy-makers in fashioning a distinctive national data protection policy is more limited than it was thirty years ago. But this challenge to state autonomy does not stem, as the US commentators quoted above believe, from the actions of other states. Rather the challenge comes from within each country, as "economic networks . . . increasingly operate in a nonterritorial functional space that defies individual territorialities and thus internal sovereignties" (Reinicke 1998, p. 69). The question is not, anymore, whether data protection policy should be made at the international or the national governmental levels. It is, and must be, made at both. Rather, the question is how national and international regimes interact to respond to an inherently transnational policy problem caused by a global economy, which "is not located in another place or at a different level; it *is* another place" (Reinicke 1998, p. 70; emphasis in original). Privacy is a global problem, and it is being addressed through a repertoire of policy instruments that also know few attachments to traditional conceptions of legal and territorial sovereignties.

We return to these larger questions about forces behind, and effects of, policy interdependence in chapter 10. At the moment, the actions by these international regimes constitute an important backdrop for our discussion of the variety of legal, self-regulatory, and technological policy instruments that now appear in the global armory of approaches to the privacy problem. We investigate this repertoire of instruments in the next three chapters.

5

Legal Instruments and Regulatory Agencies

Introduction: What Is "Regulation"?

We have already addressed the question of international and global regulation through a legal instrument, the EU Data Protection Directive, and through other transnational measures. These had a significant effect not only on EU Member States, but also—through the "adequacy" requirement—on the development of data protection in East and Central European countries that have acceded to membership of the EU. Consequences have also been felt elsewhere. In North America, the Directive contributed to the eventual passage in 2000 of Canadian federal privacy legislation affecting the private sector, to the "Safe Harbor" episode in US–EU relations, and to a flurry of electorally motivated legislative proposals in the American Congress. In the Asia-Pacific region, more and more countries have been developing comprehensive data protection law on the European model.

This chapter draws on the previous discussion to investigate the embodiment of the principles of data protection in legal instruments and implementation machinery. We take these instruments to be *regulatory* in one way or another, in that they apply rules to the processing of personal data—defining the limits of, but also facilitating, that processing, and establishing controls over what could otherwise be a far more extensive and intensive set of activities. But legal provisions and mechanisms do not exhaust the repertory of ways in which information privacy can be protected. The difference among these ways lies principally in the kind of agent that is *necessarily* involved in each of them as its distinguishing feature, although, as we will argue in chapter 8, the interdependence of all of these instruments is what characterizes a privacy-protection regime as a whole.

The meaning of "processing" needs first to be explained briefly, for it has had both specific and general reference to information-handling phenomena. In some interpretations, processing refers to only one of many stages in the activity that takes place concerning data—the stage where data, having been collected, are manipulated in various ways in order to derive information about persons for subsequent use by the organization, or for communication to other entities. For our purposes, however, it seems useful to adopt a wider definition covering an entire trajectory of data "events" rather than only one section or phase of it. We therefore adopt the definition given in Article 2(b) of the EU Data Protection Directive:

> any operation or set of operations which is performed upon personal data, whether or not by automatic means, such as collection, recording, organization, storage, adaptation or alteration, retrieval, consultation, use, disclosure by transmission, dissemination or otherwise making available, alignment or combination, blocking, erasure or destruction.

This definition has the merit of being appropriately all-encompassing, so that it covers the range of actions or events to which information-privacy regulation is typically addressed. Moreover, it is a politically potent definition, in that it applies to all the Member States of the EU as well as to prospective new Member States, and in that it serves as a benchmark for non-EU countries involved in the flow of personal data to and from the EU.

The term *regulation*, too, requires some clarification. Here again, we use it in a broad sense to embrace a variety of instruments that aim to control the processing of personal data and its consequences, and not only in the more specific sense of state or governmental activity involving laws and their enforcement by government agencies. Hood et al. (1999, p. 3) observe that the term *regulatory State* suggests that "modern states are placing more emphasis on the use of authority, rules and standard-setting, partly displacing an earlier emphasis on public ownership, public subsidies, and directly provided services." In that context, regulation—"broadly denoting the use of public authority (often in the hands of specialized agencies) to set and apply rules and standards"

(Hood et al. 1999, p. 3)—involves state activity vis-à-vis outside organizations or processes. Baldwin and Cave (1999, p. 2) refer to Selznick's (1985; quoted in Ogus 1994, p. 1) idea of regulation having to do with "sustained and focused control exercised by a public agency over activities that are valued by a community." However, they also point to other usages. These include regulation as a specific set of commands (the promulgation of binding rules by a specific agency), deliberate state influence (actions designed to influence industry or society, but employing a repertory of instruments, not only commands), and all forms of social control or influence (whether by the state or the market) (Baldwin and Cave 1999, p. 2).

Regulation, therefore, does not only, or even principally, connote government command and control, involving legal requirements and their direct application, but embraces other tools as well. Thus Majone (1996, pp. 23–26) takes self-regulation to be a mode of regulation, while Priest (1997) systematically elaborates several models of "self-regulation" as forms of regulation in which government's direct role varies. Vogel's (1986) analysis of national regulatory styles of environmental regulation examines different patterns even within statutory regimes, contrasting the centralized, legalistic enforcement of rules with a more informal and flexible style of relations between the state and business in which self-regulation plays an important part.

In all these related senses, data protection may be taken, in part, as an example of regulation by the state. Conventionally, the object of regulation is construed as activity "out there" in society or the economy. But it is equally so, and perhaps more complex in some ways, when public authority is exerted *within* the state; that is, when rules and standards are applied to parts of the state itself, or to public-sector activities. As Hood et al. (1999, pp. 3–4) note, "[w]e are not normally accustomed to think of government as 'regulating' itself. The word regulation is not generally used to denote the various ways in which public organizations are shaped by rules and standards emanating from arm's-length authorities."

Hood et al.'s (1999) study of regulation *within* government aims at bringing to light this neglected side of the regulatory state. Data protection has only a walk-on part in that study, but in much current activity concerning the modernization of states in the direction of citizen-orientation, "joined-up" and "information-age government," and the electronic provision of services, this side of the regulatory state is of increasing interest (Raab 2001). In particular, the protection of personal data in the "informatized" state looms large as an issue. This is because a state that is organized in this manner relies on much more extensive exploitation of citizens' information to achieve the objectives of efficiency, effectiveness, and economy, and the application of privacy rules to these processes is part and parcel of developments in many countries.

In many respects, however, it is proving to be no less difficult and contentious for the state to apply the law to itself than it is to enjoin legal restrictions on the private sector's processing of personal data. In countries such as Canada, Australia, and the United States, data protection was in the first instance an area of legal regulation of the public sector itself. Where data protection policy sets the conditions under which *public* activity should be undertaken, there is no external target group that is rewarded or deprived by the policy, although successful implementation is still dependent on public sector bodies changing their behavior in conformity with the programmatic goals. The target group is thus the public sector itself. Policy impact takes place within, and not external to, the agencies of government.

However, matters are complicated by the erosion of the distinction between private and public sectors, in part owing to the shift from government to "governance"—which may be seen as a pattern of state-society relations or networks that may span different jurisdictional levels, and through which functions are jointly performed (Kooiman 1993, 2003; Rhodes 1997; Pierre 2000). Indeed, some of the incentive for countries like Canada and Australia to apply similar privacy protection rules to the private sector as had applied to the public is attributable to practices that were blurring the distinction between the two. In many countries, the contemporary governmental affection for privatization, outsourcing, public-private partnerships, and so on has increased the flows of personal data across the public-private divide, rendered old sectoral distinctions obsolete, and has motivated persuasive arguments for policy harmonization within such countries.[1] The EU Directive also overcame the distinction.

In this context, what does it mean to bring the instruments of the state to bear upon the privacy problem? What does it mean for the state both to regulate not only its own personal data processing activities, but increasingly those of nonstate organizations?

From Privacy Principles to Privacy Laws

We have shown how transnational policy instruments have played a crucial part in establishing a repertoire of principles and rules governing the use of data. These instruments were themselves a reflection of conventional wisdom and legal activity in several countries in the 1970s, and they powerfully influenced policy and legislation from the 1980s to the present time. In large part, their influence was felt in terms of the establishment in good currency, and as a guide to legislation, of one version or another of the data protection or "fair information" principles that we see in chapter 1. An indication of their potency to the present time can be seen in their universal embodiment in national and subnational laws, in the EU Directive, and then in legislation passed subsequent to that.

Baldwin and Cave (1999, p. 2) note that regulation may be seen as both an enabling and facilitating activity, as well as one that constrains actions; it can empower as well as prevent. This is an important observation with regard to privacy protection. The traditional roster of fair information principles can also be divided into those that empower individuals (data subjects), and those that constrain organizations (data controllers). The distinction is not clear-cut, but it will serve to organize the following discussion.

Privacy Principles that Empower
Among the most important of the rights created by statutes that embody the principles is that of *subject access*, whereby data subjects may inspect the data that controllers hold on them. This right embodies four separate processes: to know that an organization is indeed processing information about one; to see that information; to correct or delete it if it is inaccurate, obsolete, or incomplete; and to have some means of redress if the organization is not sufficiently forthcoming or compliant. The precise terms and conditions of access and correction procedures

are matters for laws to stipulate; time limits and costs for applications vary across jurisdictions. The circumstances under which one can bring legal action for redress in case of damages or distress suffered through the misuse of data are also shaped by national administrative rules. Nevertheless, from the outset of the debate, the principle of subject access has appeared in national and international policy instruments.

Thus, for example, Section 7 of the UK Data Protection Act 1998 provides that the individual "data subject" is entitled (upon application in writing and payment of a fee) to be informed by a "data controller" whether the latter is processing the former's personal data. If so, the person has a right to be given a description of the data, why it is being processed, and to whom the data may be disclosed. In addition, if the processing uses automatic means as the sole basis for making evaluative decisions about certain important matters concerning the data subject, the individual is entitled to be informed of the logic involved in the decision process. Section 14 provides that a data subject may seek judicial means to require the correction or destruction of inaccurate data, to have various adverse consequences of the inaccuracy rectified by means of a court order, to have an expression of opinion based on the inaccurate data rectified, and to require the data controller to inform third parties of the action taken against the inaccurate data. Furthermore, under the UK Act the data subject has a right to prevent processing that is likely to cause damage or distress, and to prevent processing for purposes of direct marketing; the latter right was a controversial innovation brought about through the EU Directive. Thus Article 14(b) of the Directive, as one of the alternative ways of giving effect to this right, requires data controllers to inform persons that their data will be disclosed to third parties or used on their behalf for direct marketing, and to offer the right to object without charge.

The provision that personal data must be collected and disclosed with the consent of data subjects is also an important empowering principle. This may be a precondition for processing, although it may not be necessary where laws stipulate other legitimate grounds: protecting the vital interests of the data subject, adherence to other legal requirements, contractual reasons, and so on. What constitutes *consent*, whether it needs to be *informed* and *explicit*, how it should be obtained, and how long it is deemed to last, are matters that are often not laid down, or not clearly specified, in data protection laws. While the EU Directive defines *consent*, the UK Act, for instance, does not, although Schedule 2 includes it as one of the many legitimate grounds for processing and Schedule 3 adds the term *explicit*—not defined in the Directive—where sensitive personal data are involved. Although Canada's Personal Information Protection and Electronic Documents Act (PIPEDA) 2000 does not define it, Section 7 and Schedule 1 include elaborate rules and explanations concerning when consent is or is not required, how it may be obtained, and related points. In many jurisdictions, the scope of an exemption from consent requirements where data are used for journalistic, artistic, and literary purposes has also been a contentious issue, not least because it impinges on the question of free speech and freedom of the press, which can be seen as limitations on the consent obligation.

Principles that Impose Obligations

Legal principles that empower individuals also, of course, impose concomitant obligations upon data controllers. Data protection laws not only establish rights; they also assign responsibilities, impose penalties for those who fail to comply, and provide rules for conduct and behavior.[2]

A first condition for effective data protection is that of transparency. Data protection statutes enjoin data controllers to be open about their processing activities. This obligation may include the requirement to notify the state's supervisory authority of their processing activities. The maintenance of national registers of data controllers is far from a universal feature of information privacy laws, and there are many exemptions from such notification requirements where registers do exist. Over the years, there has been an attempt to reduce the onerous burden placed on data controllers by the obligation to notify or register their activities, whether through the simplification or automation of the process, or through broadening the range of exemptions; the UK and Germany are examples (Lloyd 1998, pp. 29–36). Ireland, which passed its first legislation somewhat later than many other countries, established lighter notification responsibilities from the start. Registration, however, has never been seriously considered in data protection regimes in North America or Australasia. As an alternative, some laws stipulate an explicit principle of accountability, and mandate that every organization should appoint a person responsible for the implementation of data protection rules within that organization.[3]

Beyond this, data controllers are expected to adhere to basic rules of fair information practice at every stage of personal data processing. At the point of first collection, they are expected to identify, in clear and understandable terms, the purposes for which the information is to be used. They must only collect that information through fair and lawful means, and ensure that collection is not excessive. As a corollary, organizations are then obliged to use and disclose that information only in ways that are consistent with the original purpose of collection. In most jurisdictions, the circumstances under which other uses and disclosures are permitted are defined in the legislation and subject to judicial interpretation. This is the so-called principle of "finality" that is supposed to prevent new and unrelated uses and disclosures about which data subjects are unaware, and to which they have never consented.

Most data protection laws include a principle of data quality, stipulating that information should be accurate, up-to-date, and complete. Most laws also stipulate that it should not be retained for longer than is required to accomplish the necessary tasks. Personal information should also be kept secure against inappropriate or unauthorized access. For example, the seventh principle of the UK Act has to do with the technical and organizational measures that must be taken against unauthorized or unlawful processing and against the data's accidental loss, destruction, or damage. The interpretation of this says that the data controller must match the level of security to the level of harm that might result, must take reasonable steps to ensure the reliability of employees who have access, must ensure that any outsourced data processor provides sufficient security guarantees, and so on.

Of course, the constraints indicated by the do's and don'ts of the principles written into laws are also intended to have an effect on organizations' learning and change of practice in regard to their information systems and managerial routines. In many companies and public bodies, the need to comply with these legal provisions triggers off a reconsideration of the ways in which personal data are dealt with in all phases of processing. As we will see, however, the question of how, and under what external regulatory pressures, laws are to be implemented may be all-important.

In all, data protection laws are expected to establish a climate of certainty for the data controller and the data subject, who need to know their responsibilities and their rights. That depends, however, on the clarity of legal definitions. One severe problem with existing data protection laws is that many terms are ambiguous, thus leaving participants and stakeholders unsure of what is permissible and what is proscribed, what is acceptable and what is actionable. For example, the requirement that data be obtained and processed fairly has given rise to debates and arguments in the UK that have only been settled—provisionally— through judicial interpretation of this term. Likewise, the meaning of *reasonable* in regard to the provision of subject access, and of *consent* in regard to permissions to process data, is not self-evident. Other terms also are not self-explanatory: *relevance* and *adequate* in terms of the quality of the data, for example. There are also problems about describing, registering and verifying the *purpose* for which data are processed. Nevertheless, the legal context and interpretative procedures within which such terms are arbitrated help to channel discourse about these terms into common avenues in which powerful precedents may be established for the enforceable rights that data protection laws provide for data subjects.

An Overview of Data Protection Legislation

In essence, data protection legislation is an exercise of the power of the state in regulating the processing of personal data. As such, it is a manifestation of a political process that could lead to nonlegislative outcomes as well, or that could leave it to nonstatutory administrative action to provide protection. The political process also determines the scope of data protection—for instance, confining it mainly to the public sector (as in the United States) or to automatically processed data (as in the UK before 1998). The enactment of data protection laws, whether general or sector-specific, is not the only legal route to regulating privacy.

In various countries, constitutional provisions (for example, the Fourth Amendment in the United States), privacy torts (Prosser 1960), contract-law remedies and privacy-protective restrictions in other laws (for example, for the control of wiretapping) are among the relevant tools (Gellman 1997).

Nevertheless, over the past thirty or more years, comprehensive and general data protection laws have been regarded as essential tools for regulating the use of personal data through the law itself and as a basis for the work of the organizational instruments they bring into being. What trajectory have these laws followed from the 1970s to the present time? Since at least the "computer age" of the 1960s, there has been an accumulation of experience with data protection laws and systems in successive "ages" of information and communication technology. These stretch from the mainframe to the PC, from paper mail to e-mail, and from faxes to the current stages of mobile, multimedia telephony, electronic households, "smart" transportation systems, and the like. This experience has left a still-potent and practical residue of assumptions and procedures about how to protect privacy when personal data are implicated, about the possibilities and limitations of protection, and about who should do what. Table 5.1 shows the world-wide diffusion of data protection legislation.[4]

Can any pattern be discerned? For Europe, a sequence of phases of data protection law up to the mid-1990s has been identified by Mayer-Schönberger (1997). The first responded to the rise of government and business data processing in the early 1970s and aimed at countering the centralization of large scale data banks. The exemplars of these laws or proposals were in Hesse, Sweden, Rheinland-Pfalz, Federal Germany, and Austria. They focused on the computer and data processing, sought to establish rules and norms, favored registration or licensing, and established regulatory bodies. This approach was overtaken by a second wave in the late 1970s, in closer relation to the trend away from the centralized "data-bank society" of Big Brother, and as data-processing capabilities proliferated in the decentralized environments of the state and business. Protecting the citizen's privacy rights came to the fore as an objective of law, as seen in France, Norway, Austria, Denmark, and some other German *Länder*: "Data protection as an attempt to regulate

Table 5.1
The diffusion of data protection legislation by region

	1970s	1980s	1990s	2000s
W. Europe	Sweden (1973) W. Germany (1978) Denmark (1978) Austria (1978) France (1978) Norway (1978) Luxembourg (1978)	Iceland (1981) UK (1984) Finland (1987) Ireland (1988) Netherlands (1988)	Portugal (1991) Spain (1992) Switzerland (1992) Belgium (1992) Monaco (1993) Italy (1996) Greece (1997)	
East and Central Europe			Slovenia (1990) Hungary (1992) Czech Republic (1992) Russia (1995) Estonia (1996) Lithuania (1996) Poland (1997) Slovak Republic (1998) Latvia (2000)	
N. America	United States (1974)	Canada (1982)		Canada (2000)
S. America			Chile (1999)	Argentina (2000)
Australasia		New Zealand (1982) Australia (1988)	Australia (1997)	
Middle East and Asia		Israel (1981) Japan (1988)	South Korea (1994) Hong Kong (1995) Taiwan (1995) Thailand (1998)	Japan (2004)

technology was transformed into an individual liberty of the citizens" (Mayer-Schönberger 1997, p. 227). Commissioners oriented their tasks toward helping citizens to exercise their rights, and to adjudicate.

The normative theme was that of negative liberty, but this was scarcely possible in modern society and the welfare state; thus there was a shift to a third, more participatory phase, in which the right to informational self-determination was emphasized. As Mayer-Schönberger (1997, p. 229) points out, the German Constitutional Court's decision of 1983, attacking the constitutionality of the census, signaled this change. It was reflected in amendments to German and Austrian laws, and to other legal measures in Norway, the Netherlands, and Finland. But the expense of exercising one's rights, plus the hollowness of the concept of individual self-determination in practice, contributed to the development of a fourth generation of laws in which the individual's arm was strengthened against data controllers in the assertion of rights—for example, with regard to compensation. At the same time, some areas of privacy were removed from the realm of self-determination and placed under legal protection, such as sensitive data and the assertion of rights of access, correction, and deletion. Examples of the latter are found in the 1980s and later legislation of the UK and Belgium. Advocacy as well as adjudication became the twin roles played within the regimes of some countries (for example, Finland and Switzerland), as individual rights-based solutions—reflecting the dominant paradigm—were supplemented by state action. Moreover, a sectoral approach came to be developed alongside comprehensive legislation; we will discuss this later in this chapter.

Up to a point, this is a cogent account of change, pointing us toward salient aspects of the legislative history that provides a backdrop for our further analysis. On the other hand, it is perhaps too tidy to capture the reality of change, and its generational distinctions can be exaggerated, as Bygrave (2002, p. 88) argues. Moreover, it does not attempt to explain why some European countries legislated when they did, while others delayed their laws or failed to act until the middle or the end of the 1990s in the shadow of the EU Directive, as was the case in Italy and Greece. The forces of international economic competition must play a large part in that story, as well as the effect of the international instruments that were canvassed in chapter 4, in particular, the Council of Europe Convention. Moreover, the availability of alternative privacy instruments besides law in the more recent stages, and their virtual absence earlier on, shaped aspects of the law and altered expectations about its role in safeguarding the various norms.

This account does not address experience in the advanced industrial world outside Europe, where the technological and philosophical factors that drove European responses were also present. The scope of analysis therefore needs to be widened to the world as well as narrowed to look at more particular developments. Although he does not examine the nuances of shifts in normative emphases in the content of the laws, Bennett (1997c) attempts to explain the spread of data protection since the 1970s around the world. There are prerequisite factors, such as the growth of big government and consequent public perceptions of the decline of accountability and the increase of state intrusiveness in private lives. But, he shows, these are insufficient to explain the passage of legislation. For that, other factors seem important as well, including patterns of diffusion and policy-learning through the interactions of a policy community or "network or policy experts that enjoyed constant communication through informal personal meetings, international organizations, conferences, articles, and books" (Bennett 1997c, p. 227). There have also been powerful effects of the penetration of domestic policy agenda by external sources and the obligations they incur in many countries. The Council of Europe Convention and, more recently, the EU Directive have been the most prominent sources of this kind. The latter has exerted a strong influence not only on national decisions to legislate, but to legislate according to some quite specific requirements or else face potential difficulties in the global economy of information flows.

In terms of legislation, among the main events of recent years has been the renewal of data protection law in Europe in those countries that legislated from the 1970s to the 1990s, and the passage of legislation for the first time in those countries that lagged behind. These activities have occurred not only among the Member States of the EU and the European Economic Area, but in several countries in Eastern and Central Europe—some of which have joined the EU—as they have undergone "democratization" and experienced greater contact with Western economic and technological currents. Legislative developments, or at least the elevation of data protection laws more prominently on political agendas, have also taken place in the 1990s in the Asia-Pacific region and in North and South America.[5]

In the countries of the EU, however, the new laws have to conform to a more detailed and stringent legislated form of the data protection principles, as embodied in the EU Directive. The UK's experience highlights some of the difficulties involved for countries with older legislation, which had to be extended to cover data that are not automatically processed. Transition periods were provided for different types of processing activities, and a host of private, commercial consultancy organizations and law firms were salient in helping data controllers to make the change. Some new national laws of the 1990s—for instance, in Greece and Italy—in fact anticipated many of the Directive's requirements. As table 5.1 shows, there has been a spate of activity in the 1990s and after in many countries of East and Central Europe, where new legislation has been passed with an eye on Directive requirements in view of the expected enlargement of the EU to include countries from that area. Hungary's law, for example, enacted in 1992 but subsequently altered, was deemed by the European Commission in 1999 to satisfy the requirements of adequacy.

In some non-European countries, laws have been written *ab initio*; a relatively blank slate has allowed comprehensive legislation to be introduced in both public and private sectors. Other countries, for example, Canada and Australia, have had a long experience of public sector data protection statutes overseen by independent Privacy Commissioners. The policy developments in both Canada and Australia have, therefore, followed quite parallel paths during the 1990s. In both countries, similar forces have produced simultaneous efforts to extend data protection standards to the private sector in ways that are consistent with each country's distinctive federal constitutional systems. In both, the observed weaknesses of existing forms of self-regulation, the pressures to harmonize the standards of the public and private sectors, as well as concerns about the extraterritorial effect of the EU Data Protection Directive have produced innovative data protection statutes.

Not so in the United States. The United States is now the only advanced industrial state that has not passed, or is not in the process of passing, a data protection law covering private sector activities. Although the Privacy Act of 1974 set an example for later legislation elsewhere, it applies only to the Federal Government and its implementation has been very limited. In the Federal executive branch, the Office of Management and Budget is supposed to have oversight of the compliance of government agencies and bureaus with the Act. However, it is not a "dedicated" authority, in contrast to privacy protection agencies in other countries, and its impact has been both sporadic and blunt (Gellman 1997). In the United States, the adoption of general legislation for the private sector has been strongly resisted, and although there are many sectoral privacy laws, privacy is protected in a very incomplete manner (Reidenberg 1995). This is also made worse by the circumstances of two levels of government, federal and state, both of which have legislated within the privacy sphere. But large areas of data processing go unregulated, resulting in a confusing patchwork of provisions that reveals large gaps. Data protection has become "fragmented, incomplete, and discontinuous" (Gellman 1993, p. 238). Under these circumstances, individuals' rights are difficult and costly to pursue.

Sectoral Data Protection Laws

Influential business and governmental interests in North America, and frequently in other places, have tended to argue that comprehensive, general privacy laws are unnecessary, and that privacy can be better protected at the *sectoral* level, when and if necessary, or through self-regulation.[6] In this approach, policy-making for privacy is mainly reactive: it responds to specific problems with a piece of legislation here, a few rules there, and some enhancement of the powers and the responsibilities of sectoral managers, rather than providing comprehensive, full coverage. The latter would include enforcement machinery devoted to the tasks we have outlined, and applied to the spectrum of industries and fields, including government itself.

In addition to comprehensive laws, many countries have passed legislation applying privacy rules to specific sectors of activity, or to particular industries and technologies. The usefulness of sectoral legislation has been claimed by Flaherty (1989, pp. 404–405), who praises the ability of these laws to deal with special problems and to grant specific individual rights. A sectoral approach can also involve the inclusion of privacy regulations in other policies or laws where the main aim is to empower public agencies or to legalize certain functions for which personal data are processed, but for which, it is felt, there should also be some privacy safeguards. Sometimes, sectoral laws clarify rights and responsibilities, but also restrict the application of privacy principles in order to accommodate policies that are considered more important. The field of social security and welfare is an example, especially where there is public and political concern about fraud. In practice, data protection laws seldom interfere very much with the activities of policing and state security, and laws in those sectors may weaken privacy protection, sometimes for understandable reasons. Switzerland is only one instance: the passage of its general law in 1993 was followed by the creation of sectoral laws restricting subject access in the fields of internal security, organized crime, and antidrug activities.

The United States provides several examples of sectoral legislation being enacted without a comprehensive law. The "patchwork" coverage of these measures includes fair credit reporting, education records, video-rental records, polygraph tests, electronic funds transfer, financial privacy, telephone consumer protection, children's privacy online, cable communications, health information, and many more areas at Federal or state levels, and in many or few states (Plesser and Cividanes 1991). The United States's sectoral approach, chosen as a deliberate policy in the 1970s (US Privacy Protection Study Commission 1977) is sometimes contrasted with Europe's more comprehensive approach. This distinction is too simple, as the "European approach" itself also includes many sectoral laws. Belgium, for instance, provides an example of specific laws preceding the national adoption of general data protection legislation by about ten years. The first law involved safeguards for a databank concerning public sector employees, but the most important protection was provided in the 1983 law forming the national register of persons. Later on, there was one for a central social security database, one for drivers who violated the law, and one for consumer-credit information.[7]

Sectoral provisions were retained but amended by the 1992 Data Protection Act.

The Netherlands, Germany, Austria, Finland, Norway, Sweden, and Denmark provide further illustrations of the combination of general laws with sectoral legislation, including laws passed after general legislation came into force.[8] Taken together, these cover a wide range of data-processing fields, including the census, public service "one-stop-shops," public order, telecommunications, video surveillance, sensitive data registers, credit cards, public archives, the media, data matching in the field of taxation, and the collection of personal data for payroll wage-deduction. Increasing concern over the use of genetic data has given rise to laws or proposals in a number of places, including Denmark and Austria.

In the future, countries with comprehensive laws may well find that more specific laws covering sectors or particular information practices, such as data matching and data sharing, offer a flexible as well as a targeted approach to protecting privacy. But as with comprehensive statutes, their oversight and implementation will remain the key to their effectiveness.

The Oversight and Enforcement of Data Protection Law

Normative information privacy principles are not self-enforcing. By and large, three broad sets of public agencies play a role in the enforcement and oversight of data protection legislation: supervisory authorities (data protection and privacy commissioners), central coordinating agencies, and tribunals or courts. But the most important are the "supervisory bodies," required under the EU Directive, and now in existence in most advanced industrial states. Bennett (1992, pp. 153–192) distinguishes between several models for data protection implementation: *licensing*, as with Sweden's Data Inspection Board under their initial legislation of 1973; *registration*, as with the UK's Registrar under the 1984 Act, but exemplified in many other countries as well; the *commissioner* model, as with Federal Germany's *Bundesbeauftragte*; and the *self-help* model, exemplified by the American reliance on the assertion of individual privacy rights through the courts. Although one or another model may be dominant in different countries, in practice hybrids are typically found in most regimes (Bennett 1992, p. 192). For example, the UK's Information Commissioner under the 1998 Act, and even the Registrar under the 1984 Act, performed many *commissioner* roles (Bennett 1992, pp. 179–185), albeit armed with different powers and greater constitutional independence: advising, investigating, mediating, and educating.

Over time, therefore, it has become more and more difficult to classify data protection agencies according to any one model. They each perform an intricate blend of functions that appear in various mixes and with different emphases in different regimes. Through these activities, the framework laid down in statute, reflecting the data protection principles, is fleshed out, bringing the regulatory body into contact with a large number of public and private bodies, and with the public as well (Raab 1996). Table 5.2 provides a list of the current personal data protection agencies in all OECD countries.[9]

The existence of vigorous supervisory authorities has been regarded as a *sine qua non* of good privacy protection inasmuch as laws are not self-implementing and the culture of privacy cannot securely establish itself without an authoritative champion. Flaherty says that "data protection commissioners or agencies are an alarm system for the protection of privacy," (Flaherty 1989, p. 383) whose tools include "oversight, auditing, monitoring, evaluation, expert knowledge, mediation, dispute resolution, and the balancing of competing interests" (Flaherty 1997, p. 175). The EU Directive, in requiring the establishment of supervisory authorities, underscored many of these roles and powers, and also enjoined these organizations to cooperate with one another in the performance of their duties.

The following discussion is organized according to seven interrelated roles played by privacy and data protection commissioners, in which we highlight the main points and give some examples. Commissioners act, variously, as ombudsmen, auditors, consultants, educators, negotiators, policy advisers, and enforcers. Not every role is played with equal weight by every commissioner. Nor are these functions the exclusive responsibility of the data protection agency; other central coordinating ministries and departments have important responsibilities for data protection policy in different states. Nevertheless, the head of any independent data protection authority needs to consider how the following roles ought to be performed.

Data Protectors as Ombudsmen

First, all data supervisory authorities are responsible for the receipt, investigation, and resolution of complaints from data subjects. A traditional role of the ombudsman, the resolution of complaints, is central to any effective oversight of personal data protection, even though it can also be time-consuming and a significant drain on resources. The system for complaints-handling needs careful consideration and the specification of what powers should be granted to allow this function to be performed. Although subject to variations across countries, these powers normally include the power to enter premises, to require records to be produced, and to summon the appearance of responsible persons. One difficult question is whether or not the commissioner should be expressly empowered to conduct investigations in the absence of a complaint. Some offices have the power to initiate an investigation on their own initiative.

The resolution of complaints about privacy may take a number of different forms and may culminate in a binding enforcement order, such as in the UK, or in less mandatory recommendations, such as in Canada, New Zealand, and Australia. Agencies that have to rely on conciliation and mediation also have to rely on the hope that an organization's desire to avoid bad publicity will encourage a satisfactory settlement of the complaint.

Data Protectors as Auditors

Complaint investigation and resolution are inherently reactive processes. But commissioners may have suspicions about the personal information practices of a particular organization that arise from a number of sources, leading to the conduct of more general audits of the organization or of a particular technology. Audits are not only more systematic, but they may be less confrontational than an investigation into the circumstances of a specific complaint. The German federal data protection authority has conducted audits of personal information systems almost

Table 5.2
Data protection supervisory authorities in OECD countries

Australia	Office of the Federal Privacy Commissioner
	http://www.privacy.gov.au/
Austria	Büro der Datenschutzkommission
	(Data Protection Commission)
	http://www.dsk.gv.at/
Belgium	Commissie Voor De Bescherming van de Persoonlijke
	Levenssfeer
	(Consultative Commission for the Protection of Private
	Life)
	http://www.privacy.fgov.be/
Canada	Privacy Commissioner of Canada
	http://www.privcom.gc.ca/
Czech Republic	Office for Personal Data Protection
	http://www.uoou.cz/
Denmark	Datatilsynet
	(Danish Data Protection Agency)
	http://www.datatilsynet.dk/
Finland	Office of the Data Protection Ombudsman
	http://www.tietosuoja.fi/
France	Commission Nationale de L'Informatique et des Libertés
	http://www.cnil.fr/
Germany	Der Bundesbeauftragte für den Datenschutz
	(Federal Data Protection Commission)
	http://www.bfd.bund.de/
Greece	Hellenic Data Protection Authority
	http://www.dpa.gr/
Hungary	Parliamentary Commissioner for Data Protection and
	Freedom of Information
	http://abiweb.obh.hu/dpc/index.htm
Iceland	Persónuvernd
	(Icelandic Data Protection Commission)
	http://www.personuvernd.is/
Italy	Garante per la Protezione dei dati Personali
	(Data Protection Commission)
	http://www.garanteprivacy.it/
Japan	No Authority
Korea	Korea Information Security Agency
	http://www.kisa.or.kr/
Luxembourg	Commission à la Protection des Données Nominatives
	(Data Protection Commission)
	http://www.cnpd.lu/
Mexico	No Authority

Table 5.2
(continued)

Netherlands	College Bescherming Persoonsgegevens (Dutch Data Protection Authority) http://www.cbpweb.nl/
New Zealand	Privacy Commissioner http://www.privacy.org.nz/
Norway	Datatilsynet (The Data Inspectorate) http://www.datatilsynet.no/
Poland	Bureau of the Inspector General for the Protection of Personal Data http://www.giodo.gov.pl/
Portugal	Comissão Nacional de Proteção de Dados (National Data Protection Commission) http://www.cnpd.pt/
Slovak Republic	Commissioner for the Protection of Personal Data http://www.dataprotection.gov.sk/
Spain	Agencia de Protección de Datos (Data Protection Agency) https://www.agpd.es/index.php
Sweden	Datainspektionen (Data Inspection Board) http://www.datainspektionen.se/
Switzerland	Federal Data Protection Commissioner http://www.edsb.ch/
Turkey	No Authority
United Kingdom	Information Commissioner http://www.informationcommissioner.gov.uk/
United States	No Authority

from the outset (Flaherty 1989, p. 77), and has, over the years, developed a methodology for the examination of all phases of personal data usage within an organization (Bennett 1992, p. 182). Audits obviously vary in terms of their frequency and rigor. In other countries, such as Canada, an audit program has been a constant, if underresourced, component of the Privacy Commissioner's agenda from the start, even though the word is not used in the federal Privacy Act. In other Canadian jurisdictions, more informal "site visits" of premises might be conducted.[10]

Some legislation also explicitly empowers the commissioner to delegate the auditing function. The Canadian PIPED Act, for instance, contemplates that audits might be delegated to provincial commissioners, to accounting firms, to standards certification bodies, and so on. The innovation of including a certifiable standard within the body of the statute was deliberately intended to provide a built-in auditing mechanism. A standard is more than a code of practice, because it also embraces a common conformity assessment methodology, by which compliance can be independently and regularly tested. Other commissioners, such as the president of the Dutch Data Protection Authority, have also required audits to be performed by accredited auditors under certain circumstances.

Data Protectors as Consultants

With or without audit powers, data protection authorities also constantly give advice to individual data users on how to comply with data protection norms. The implementation of data protection law can be as much a consultative effort as a regulatory one, regardless of legal powers. Much can be achieved in anticipation of policy and system development if privacy protection is *built in* at the outset, rather than *bolted on* afterward. Consultation and advice are highly regarded as preferable to adversarial relationships between the regulator and the regulated, where conflicts can be expensive and unproductive, given commissioners' mission to encourage privacy cultures in organizations, and to educate data controllers, as much as to ensure their formal compliance.

Thus data protection authorities expect to be consulted when new systems are being developed that have privacy-invasive implications. Organizations will often want to know, in advance of significant resource commitment, whether proposals are in compliance with applicable law. This consultative function tends to occur outside of public scrutiny, as often quite sensitive issues have to be addressed. Commissioners will also need to be quite careful that their advice does not prejudice their independence if subsequent complaints were to arise about the organization concerned.

Data Protectors as Educators

There is, of course, a fine line between the advisory responsibilities—generally conducted in confidence—and the performance of broader educational and research roles. The analysis of wider privacy and surveillance questions and the continuous education of data users and data subjects can do much to anticipate problems and encourage citizens to protect their own privacy. Most commissioners are given this role, the interpretation of which varies from office to office.

To an increasing extent, many regulatory agencies see their roles not only in relation to public policy, big issues, and big events, but also in encouraging a culture of privacy protection throughout society, the economy, and government in an era of widespread adoption of new and privacy-invasive information technologies. Thus resources may be invested in instilling an understanding of the rules and a privacy culture in more accessible ways than can be done through the interpretation and application of legal rules in particular cases. There have been many interesting developments in this vein. The Office of the Privacy Commissioner of Canada provides an example in the form of a plain-language *Guide for Businesses and Organizations*[11] for compliance with PIPEDA 2000. The *Guide* reviews the ten principles that the Act adopted from the Canadian Standards Association's *Model Code for the Protection of Personal Information* (CSA 1996). Ways of meeting organizations' obligations under these principles are given, including useful tips; the aim of these is to shape the behavior of data controllers. The commissioner's Ontario counterpart has also issued a Privacy Diagnostic Tool, developed in conjunction with some major accounting firms and designed to permit a self-assessment of compliance with privacy principles (Ontario OIPC 2001).

Other regulatory authorities devote considerable resources to producing guidelines and advice on paper and in electronic form, from public platforms, and through the mass media. For example, in 2000 the Office of the Privacy Commissioner of Hong Kong launched a kit titled *Privacy. SAFE: Guidance Notes for Self-Assessment*, printed in Chinese and English and including a CD-ROM, to assist organizations in assessing their compliance with the Privacy Ordinance. For the general public, in the 1990s the Dutch authority made explanatory booklets and leaflets available in main post offices. These included simple information about the Data Protection Act, the rights of the citizen and the duties of the data controller, how to exercise the rights, and where to go for further information—including the addresses of the consumers' association and the leading watchdog committee of privacy activists. From the late 1980s on, the Berlin authority disseminated a checkbook (*"Datens-checkheft"*) of printed subject-access forms that were pre-addressed to a range of public and private organizations. The citizen could fill in these forms in order to make subject-access requests, ask for inaccurate data to be corrected, obtain further information about data protection, and so on.

In addition, of course, commissioners are expected to give frequent speeches and presentations concerning the importance of privacy. Furthermore, some agencies commission special studies relating to special privacy problems[12]; others produce shorter and more frequent research publications on new technologies such as smart cards, electronic mail systems, and intelligent transport systems[13]; and others occasionally sponsor public opinion surveys (for example, Australia Office of the Federal Privacy Commissioner 2001). Reports are extremely useful ways of alerting public, government, and business opinion to the privacy risks inherent in new technologies.

Data Protectors as Policy Advisers

Most legislation grants responsibilities to commissioners to comment on the privacy implications of proposed legislation or on new automated personal record systems. The Canadian Federal Privacy Commissioner, for example, is empowered to "make a special report to Parliament referring to and commenting on any matter within the scope of the powers, duties, and functions of the commissioner."[14] High-profile legislative changes that involve radical implications for the processing of personal information are often the circumstances under which consultation is the most serious; recent examples from Canada would be proposals for DNA databanks (OPC 1995, p. 19), a permanent voters' register, the firearms registry (OPC 1996, p. 47), or an organ donor registry (OPC 1999). As in many countries, the census process invariably brings the Canadian Privacy Commissioner into conflict with the government of Canada (OPC 2000), and is normally attended by significant media interest. Some commissioners, such as New Zealand's, now expect the preparation of a "privacy impact statement" whenever a new technology is introduced (see chapter 9). A UK example of policy involvement is the Information Commissioner's advisory role concerning the privacy implications of a governmental proposal for more extensive data-sharing in the delivery of public services and in the reduction of fraud (UK Performance and Innovation Unit, Cabinet Office, 2002).

Commissioners also frequently give testimony on issues at hearings of legislatures, and publish their responses to government policy documents where privacy interests are affected. A well-publicized case in point was the apprehensive response of the UK Registrar (the Information Commissioner's previous title) to the Home Office's Green Paper on identity cards in 1995 (UK Home Office 1995); the Registrar conducted her own survey of public attitudes, published separately from the Home Office's findings. Her successor expressed his deep misgivings about the Labour government's proposed identity card scheme when the issue resurfaced in 2004.[15] Another was the Canadian Privacy Commissioner's reaction to the Longitudinal Labour Force Survey in 2000, discussed below. Television and radio interviews also provide vehicles for giving responses to issues as they arise.

Data Protectors as Negotiators

Some commissioners have explicit responsibilities to negotiate privacy codes of practice. Codes of practice are primarily instruments of self-regulation, and are discussed in chapter 6. But they may also offer some clear advantages even within a legislated data protection regime. The procedure of negotiating codes may enhance the understanding of the privacy problem within different sectors. Codes are quite flexible instruments and once negotiated can be adapted to changing economic and technological developments. They also allow organizations to publicize their privacy policies and to remove suspicions about the improper collection, processing, and dissemination of personal data. They facilitate an "enhanced measure of understanding on both sides" (Hustinx 1994).

There is, however, a difficult problem concerning the relationship between privacy codes of practice and the privacy law. There are three subtly different models that have evolved in those countries that use or countenance privacy codes. The first, and in many ways most stringent, is represented by the system under the New Zealand and Australian Privacy Acts.[16] The crucial aspect of this New Zealand approach is that codes of practice negotiated under these Privacy Acts have the force of law. A breach of a ratified code of practice is as serious as a breach of the information privacy principles expressed in the law, which would then trigger the complaints and enforcement procedures in the legislation. The second, slightly more flexible regime, exists in the Netherlands. Although the Dutch system is similar in most respects to those in New Zealand and Australia, and includes a lengthy and careful process of code negotiation, at the end of the day the codes are not formally binding on the courts. Certainly if an organization can prove that it has met the requirements of its code, it will have a strong case. Conversely, a complainant's demonstration that the provisions of the code have been breached constitutes *prima facie* evidence of liability under the law. Codes, therefore, have indirect, rather than direct, legal effect. In other countries, such as the UK and Canada, the law simply empowers the commissioner concerned to encourage the development of codes as a further instrument of compliance with the law. Indeed, this is all that is expected by the EU Directive.[17]

There seems to be a central dilemma with the use of codes of practice within systems that have a comprehensive data protection law. If a commissioner does not formally endorse them, they may contain language that conflicts with the wording of the law, giving rise to possible confusion about applicability and enforcement. If a more formal ratification process is laid out, as in New Zealand, Australia, and the Netherlands, this can bureaucratize a process that, in theory, is supposed to allow the flexibility of self-regulation. The advantages of codes of practice are mitigated by some other problems. Submission of codes in some sectors is often hindered by competition within the sector, and by unclear boundaries and overlaps that weaken the claim that the association submitting the code is sufficiently "representative."

Data Protectors as Enforcers

In the final analysis, the central question concerns the powers that a commissioner has to order compliance with the privacy protection principles. Here there is a clear distinction between those authorities whose powers are limited to those of investigation and recommendation, and those that can mandate changes in behavior. The more advisory approach is often preferred because it avoids the adversarial relationships that arise when enforcement powers are used or threatened. Besides, it may be argued that adverse publicity for poor privacy protection can be an effective sanction. In contrast, others contend that the ability to negotiate with data users is facilitated by the existence of enforcement powers, even if those powers are rarely used. Moreover, government and business organizations need certainty and consistency in the application of data protection rules. The provision of a formal order-making process assures a greater level of consistency, transparency, and accountability over time in the implementation of the law.[18]

Ultimate redress in most countries is vested in the courts, and each law outlines the circumstances under which disputes might be reviewed at the judicial level. Looking at the EU once again, Recital 55 of the Directive says that "if the controller fails to respect the rights of data subjects, national legislation must provide for a judicial remedy. . . . [A]ny damage which a person may suffer as a result of unlawful processing must be compensated for by the controller. . . . [S]anctions must be imposed on any person, whether governed by private or public law, who fails to comply with the national measures taken under this Directive."

In the belief that the courts are not necessarily the most suitable institutions to deal with comparatively specialized and technical issues, some countries have established small tribunals, ad hoc groups of experts that perform a quasi-judicial function. In Britain, for example, the 1998 Data Protection Act establishes a Data Protection Tribunal to which individuals or data users may appeal a decision of the Information Commissioner; this body is constituted from a panel of experts as necessary. In New Zealand, an aggrieved individual may appeal a finding of the Privacy Commissioner to the Complaints Review Tribunal established under the Human Rights Commission Act of 1977.[19]

The International Data Protection Network

Data protection agencies are creatures of the law. However, the functional approach adopted above demonstrates that the letter of the law does not tell the whole story about regulation in practice. It also shows that legislative rules only give very partial guidance to the activities of data protection agencies in different societies. In addition, the agencies have developed very important relationships and activities among themselves on the international level and in smaller regional groupings. Over the years, these agencies have learned a good deal from each other about the most effective ways to advance data protection. The world's "privacy commissioners," under whatever title, have evolved into an intricate network that meets annually as well as more frequently in smaller regional, functionally specific, or less formal contexts. These include, for instance, the commissioners of the EU meeting in the Working Party established under Article 29 of the Directive.

In Europe, the field of police and justice cooperation (Anderson et al. 1995) has given rise to various organizations in which national data protection officials come together. The work of the European Police Office is supervised with regard to information systems by a Joint Supervisory Body, established under the Europol Convention, in which two data protection experts from each country monitor the use and content of Europol's personal data holdings. A Data Protection Common Control Authority oversees arrangements for the sharing of police data under the Schengen Convention. Eurojust—the framework for cooperation by judicial and prosecution authorities—has developed data protection rules for its database, and its Joint Supervisory Body includes national data protection regulators. Eurodac (shared fingerprint data relating to asylum seekers and illegal immigrants) also has such a body, made up of national data protection representatives. The Customs Information System, run by the European Anti-Fraud Office is another one that has a supervisory authority of similar composition. Information systems of these various European organizations are also overseen by a newly established European Data Protection Supervisor. In sum, the importance of these involvements of national data protection regulators—who are the supervisory authorities in their own countries for the functions of these EU bodies—in EU supervisory work can be seen in two ways. First, they extend and enhance the networks of relationships between state regulation and supranational regulation, and among the national systems. Second, they indicate the increasing significance of privacy protection in myriad specific functions of great importance to the operations of the EU and its Member States.

A telecommunications privacy grouping has been active in Europe as well, and an important international collaboration took place between the Dutch and Ontario commissioners concerning the development of research and appraisal of technologies for protecting privacy (Ontario and The Netherlands Registratiekamer 1995). Links have also been forged in the Asia-Pacific area, where an emergent Forum on Privacy and Data Protection was jointly organized by the Australia and New Zealand commissioners and hosted in Hong Kong in 1998 and 1999 (Wilson 1999); the third meeting was held in New Zealand in 2002.

All these departures testify to—as well as contribute to, in terms of bureaucratic expansion and issue-promotion—the increasing salience of privacy and privacy protection as phenomena of the "information age." Not only does policy learning take place in these networks, but also a good deal of debate and attempted concertation of policy positions over specific issues such as the regulation of the Internet, cybercrime, and the use of cryptography. However, the question whether the world's commissioners can and should take a stand on public issues on the agendas of political and governmental forums has itself been contentious. Thus, at the 2001 annual conference, held in Paris only two weeks after the terrorist attack on the United States on 11 September, there was some reluctance about concerting a collective public stance on the likely infringement of privacy by states that was expected to follow, involving intensified surveillance and the interception of communications. However, individual commissioners did express their foreboding and the need to find a proper balance between privacy and security in any "war on terrorism."

Some privacy commissioners have often complained that, in an era when government and business are adopting new and privacy-invasive information technologies, their policy-related role has been inhibited by their more routine roles, including registration and compliance, and by the lack of staff resources to keep abreast of the latest technological developments. Some have felt themselves ignored in the policy process. Yet opportunities have been seized by some commissioners to take a public stance on privacy-intrusive developments. There are many examples of this, but a particularly striking one is Canadian. Todd (2001, pp. 58–86) shows how, in 2000, the Canadian Federal Privacy Commissioner dramatically brought to public attention the existence of the government's Longitudinal Labour Force File. This massive, permanent collection of up to 2,000 pieces of information on about 34 million Canadians amounted to a centralized, invisible profile of virtually the entire population, and was judged to pose severe threats to privacy. The ensuing events led to the dismantling of the File in its existing form, greater transparency and accountability, and the application of privacy-protection rules for the use of such information.

Data protection agencies have undoubtedly played a crucial part in enforcing the law, and in advising and stimulating greater awareness and better compliance. However, their task has become more difficult in the face of the proliferation of business practices and government policies in which personal data are more intensively processed or are seen as a key resource. Data protectors often see themselves as struggling uphill with few resources (including an often ambiguous or weak law) against more powerful interests in the commercial and technological worlds, in governmental and nongovernmental public organizations, and in the interrelationships among these bodies in the changing business processes of the state and industry.

Conclusion: If Not Data Protection Laws, What?

The proliferation of statutory protection for information privacy over the past thirty or more years, the development of infrastructures of implementation through regulatory agencies, and the evolution of a jurisprudence growing out of cases brought to courts or tribunals all give some comfort to the cause of privacy. Yet in many countries and sectors of the policy community there has always been considerable skepticism about the efficacy and relevance of legal instruments of data protection, especially concerning the private sector. Gellman (1997,

p. 212) concludes that "[I]t is difficult to say whether the law is really an effective device for protecting privacy. Different attempts have produced a mixed bag of results." We may observe that the laws have typically provided *procedural* rules and devices without greatly tackling many *substantive* issues concerning the processing of personal data in contemporary society, especially if the latter is conceived of as a "surveillance society" (Lyon 2001). In other words, laws may enforce appropriate methods of the processing and storage of personal data, once collected. But they are only sometimes able to prevent the collection of personal information in the first place, or to effect the dismantling of existing systems.

This is why some critics see the whole panoply of law as legitimizing privacy invasion rather than preventing it or providing sufficient remedies. Flaherty (1989, p. 384) concluded his comparative study by stating that "at present, data protection agencies are in many ways functioning as legitimators of new technology. For the most part, their licensing and advisory functions have not prevented the introduction of threatening new technologies." More recently, Rule and Hunter (1999, p. 169) conclude that "a generation's perspective yields an ironic juxtaposition. More formal legislation and policy aimed at protecting privacy, yet at the same time, apparently, more unchecked appropriation of personal data." The efficacy and, indeed, the appropriateness and misleading nature of procedural due-process guarantees against privacy invasion have been questioned by many (for example, Rule et al. 1980, pp. 69–82). Laperrière (1999, p. 190) similarly argues that, in the "brave new world of global information law may seem to be a solution of the past. . . . Privacy legislation does not contribute significantly to reducing the collection and flow of personal data. . . . Law is essentially reactive or curative, . . . designed to punish abuse, not to restrain initiatives."

Perhaps the latter is too broad a generalization, but his claim, based on observation of experiences in Québec, rings true elsewhere in the world. This is that laws provide no criteria to determine what kinds of information systems are legitimate, and that their exemptions provide too many loopholes. Resembling our argument in chapter 2, that laws do not recognize the collective nature of privacy, their presumption of the formal equality of citizens also ignores the social problems of groups

(Laperrière 1999, pp. 190–191). Another diagnosis is that the *implementation* of laws has lagged far behind the valuable symbolic and black-letter rules and sanctions that they provide; that is, "effective fair-information practices laws require active, regular oversight and enforcement if they are to be effective" (Gellman 1997, p. 213). This may be particularly germane to the United States, but Gellman's (1997) further remarks are more generalizable. He holds that the privacy-protection target is too broad—personal privacy is affected by a host of institutions of all kinds—so that a stiff regulatory challenge is posed. In addition, this target keeps changing as new records and record keepers constantly emerge. Finally, the incentives for compliance are weak: "Few existing legal devices have proved effective in pressuring record keepers to take affirmative steps to meet privacy objectives. . . . Statutes, torts, and contracts could be more effective if there were either an especially attractive carrot or a realistically threatening stick" (Gellman 1997, pp. 213–214).

Some critics have sought alternatives to data protection statutes in solutions that are themselves still part of the legal armory. Thus a property right over the commercial exploitation of one's own information is proposed by Rule and Hunter (1999), not as a panacea for all legal or policy problems, but as a way of giving individuals choice over how and whether their personal data is to be used commercially, and to gain recompense in the form of royalties for these releases. They advocate legislation that would create a property right over commercial exploitation of personal information by which "no information could legally be sold or traded from any personal data file, for any commercial purpose, without express permission from the person concerned" (Rule and Hunter 1999, p. 170). This system would arguably generate a new kind of business: information brokers who would represent individuals' interests in the treatment of their personal information.

In a similar vein, Laudon believes that the conceptual foundations of the fair information principles doctrine are entirely outdated due to changes in the nature of the market economy, facilitated by changes in the capacity and speed of modern information technologies. According to Laudon, the fair information practices regime was developed to deal with the privacy problems inherent in a relatively small number of large-scale mainframe databanks, rather than in a fluid, decentralized, and networked computing environment. He therefore contends that personal information should be regarded as a form of property, in which the individual has not only a "mere juridical or administrative interest" but a stronger property interest (Laudon 1996, p. 92). He goes on to suggest that we should consider mechanisms based upon individual ownership of personal information and a National Information Market (NIM) where individuals can receive fair compensation for information about themselves. Yet Laudon still sees regulatory mechanisms as having a role to play alongside the market: "There is indeed a proper role for government, namely ensuring that the NIM operates fairly" (Laudon 1996, p. 102).

A related but somewhat different proposal for a property solution is Lessig's (1999, p. 160) suggestion for a "machine-to-machine protocol for negotiating privacy protections." A property regime, he argues, is very different from a liability regime, because "a property regime requires negotiation before taking; a liability regime allows a taking, and payment later. . . . Property protects choice; liability protects transfer" (Lessig 1999, pp. 160–161). He attempts to combine a particular configuration of the architecture of the World Wide Web, using a privacy-preference tool called P3P (analyzed in chapter 7) that enables individuals to discriminate among websites offering different levels of privacy protection, with a property right that requires the web merchant to negotiate for the use of the individual's data. The role of the law in such a scheme is to establish that such a negotiation must occur.[20]

Schwartz's (2000) trenchant criticism of this approach faults it for not taking account of the structural failure of such a privacy market and its consequences. His preferred solution relies on fair information practices that combine mandatory rules with some negotiable default rules; this brings action by democratic institutions—legislatures—into the task of fashioning the rules for Internet privacy. He further objects to the market-choice solution's reinforcement of a "personal control" conception of privacy, which under current conditions has deleterious, socially suboptimal effects on privacy. But, in particular, that solution ignores what Schwartz (2000, pp. 759–762) calls "constitutive privacy," protecting participation and association in a free society: "Democratic social systems therefore require information privacy because each of us, in one or more of our social roles, requires some insulation from observation and influence. . . . Information privacy does not derive from the state of nature or an inborn capacity of autonomy, but depends on its essential relation to the health of a democratic society" (Schwartz 2000, p. 761).

This argument recalls Regan's (1995) and our discussion of the collective value of privacy in chapter 2, and brings us back to the necessity, but insufficiency, of legal instruments for its defense. However, the heated controversy over the "Safe Harbor" solution to the question of transborder flows of data from the EU to the United States, discussed in chapter 4, as well as the Internet context more generally, point to a further erosion of confidence within the policy community that the established, heavily law-based assumptions that have been built into the systems of regulation since the 1970s can remain effective in the face of new threats to privacy. These threats are perceived to come from the way in which technologies that allow ever more intensive and extensive processing of personal data interact with governmental and commercial applications that are facilitated by, but which also shape, these new technologies. But the threats are particularly posed by the fluid, global environment of international telecommunications networks and the lack of transparency of the flow of personal data through these channels and systems. In subsequent chapters, we see how this changing climate for regulation has given rise to concerted attempts to protect privacy through other devices that complement or substitute for legal solutions.

6

Self-Regulatory Instruments

Introduction

The last chapter considered the legal instruments developed over the past thirty years to protect personal data. Law is generally based on a model of command and sanction. It tries to set a clear line for acceptable behavior. Organizations whose practices fall below that line are susceptible to a variety of penalties, dependent on the context and seriousness of the offense. Laws are necessary in order to frame a system of rights and responsibilities, to provide a degree of certainty for all participants in information processes, and to redress the imbalance between data controllers and data subjects.

However, an examination of laws is only one part of the evaluation of the kind and quality of data protection that is available to the public in a particular country. This is not to deny that the profusion of legal commentary on data protection statutes is very important. So, too, is a desire to strengthen and clarify the laws. However, this may divert attention from looking at data protection in wider dimensions—as a social, organizational, political, and technological practice, and as an increasingly international and global problem for which imaginative solutions must be found at all levels.

This chapter considers instruments that are inherently *voluntary* in nature. The term *voluntary* is often used in a number of different senses, but it does capture the simple point that the instruments discussed here lack any statutory force. Thus, we focus our attention on those instruments that have been developed, and have largely operated, outside the legal context. "Self-regulation" can play a key role in legal regimes, as we show in chapter 5. However, we argue that these instruments perform fundamentally different functions when a statutory standard is already in place. Peter Hustinx, the head of the Netherlands Data Protection Authority has argued that privacy codes of practice have been developed for four different purposes: to avoid legislation, to anticipate legislation, to implement legislation, and to supplement legislation (Hustinx 1991). Privacy codes, as we see in chapter 5, may perform the latter two functions within the framework of statutory data protection regimes, such as those of the Netherlands, New Zealand, Australia, Ireland, and the UK. They will also play a role in the determination of "adequacy" under Article 25 of the EU Data Protection Directive. Furthermore, Article 27 of the Directive requires the European Commission and Member States to "encourage the drawing up of codes of conduct intended to contribute to the proper implementation of . . . national provisions . . . taking account of the specific features of various sectors."

For the purposes of this chapter, we are more interested in those codes that have been produced according to Hustinx's first two motivations: to avoid and to anticipate legislation. These motivations lead us to ask, "What role do privacy codes of practice play when no legal requirements are in place?" The interesting questions for this chapter relate to those mechanisms that operate to encourage compliance with data protection norms where no legal standards exist. For these purposes, our examples are drawn mainly from the United States, as well as from countries such as Canada, Japan, and Australia, the governments of which experimented with various schemes for self-regulation before deciding to introduce legislation.

Self-regulatory instruments for privacy protection have been called codes, guidelines, standards, and so on, and there is generally no correlation between name and function. But they do operate almost exclusively to influence, shape, or set benchmarks for behavior in the marketplace; very few operate to provide guidance in the public sector, except where laws already provide that benchmark and the codes exist to tailor general legal provisions to specific functions and processes. However, voluntary instruments of self-regulation do not suggest a freedom from compulsion of any kind, because the possible incentives for compliance fall along a continuum, where a complicated and fluctuating range of incentives and sanctions might be continuously in play. As there is no absolute distinction between regulation and self-regulation, it is therefore more important to make sense of this range of incentives than to argue about the correct labels. The ultimate purpose of this chapter, then, is to provide a functional analysis of these various self-regulatory policy instruments, to give illustrations of how they have been applied and to determine the conditions under which they are more likely to be successful in encouraging compliance with the basic privacy principles.

We organize our analysis according to four interrelated policy instruments: *privacy commitments, privacy codes, privacy standards,* and *privacy seals.* These different instruments are not mutually exclusive, but each has some distinctive features. We then consider how these instruments have come together within the Safe Harbor Agreement between the United States and the EU. That agreement is intended to provide a mechanism by which US firms might comply with the EU Data Protection Directive. The initial experience of the Safe Harbor policy also provides an interesting barometer of which kinds of firms are more likely to embrace self-regulation in the absence of any legal compulsion. Our conclusion attempts to generalize from these experiences by outlining the conditions under which these self-regulatory instruments are more likely to be adopted by different organizations within the private sector.

Privacy Commitments

The very first examples of self-regulatory action by businesses tended to take the form of brief statements of commitment to the set of privacy principles. The most typical examples emerged in North America in the 1980s as private sector companies and associations were encouraged to "adopt" the 1981 OECD Guidelines (Privacy & American Business 1994). Neither in Canada nor the United States was there any serious monitoring of the adoption of those guidelines, nor any clear idea of what "adoption" entailed. Thus companies were able to declare their compliance without either internal analysis or external verification. The resulting instruments were generally, therefore, no more than indicators that the business had considered privacy protection at the highest levels and believed that it would be good public relations to state a set of public commitments about what is, and is not, done with personal information. Examples of privacy commitments (often designated by a link to a "Privacy Policy") also appear in the privacy statements found on the websites of online traders.

Privacy commitments tend to be relatively brief pledges, often more public-relations in tone than substantive, and they are often designed more for external consumption than to affect the internal functioning of the organization. They also have probably not been produced as a result of a careful and thorough analysis of the organization's personal information holdings. They tend to be statements of what top management believes is happening (and ought to happen) rather than a comprehensive instrument of self-regulation that binds employees and reflects a deep understanding of organizational practices. Privacy commitments may inform data subjects about certain rights—to access and correct, to opt-out of disclosures, and so on. But they may also tend to finesse crucial questions about how those rights might be exercised.

Quite often privacy commitments are produced in a reactive way as a result of some bad publicity. There are several recent examples where public scrutiny of a company's or industry's practices have led to a rushed attempt to save face. Smith (1994) demonstrates how "drifting and reacting" can be a quite typical response of major American companies to the privacy issue. Unless the organization finds itself the subject of front-page articles or frenzied discussion on the privacy newsgroups, there is often little incentive to make privacy a priority. According to Smith, it tends to be one of those issues that can always be placed below something else in a corporation's priorities.

However, privacy commitments need not be merely symbolic. Indeed, a clear and public statement of organizational policy is a necessary, but not sufficient, condition for effective self-regulation. Frequently, a privacy commitment is quite useful for a company to state its policies in a brief, open, and user-friendly manner, provided that is not the only instrument of self-regulation. Privacy commitments can supplement more detailed and thorough codes of practice that are based on a realistic and comprehensive analysis of how the organization collects, uses, stores, and processes personal information.

Privacy Codes of Practice

A crucial distinction should be made between privacy commitments and privacy codes. Privacy codes of practice differ from privacy commitments in the simple fact that they embody a set of rules for employees, members, or member organizations to follow. They state more than a simple claim; they provide important guidance about correct procedure and behavior based on a version of the information privacy principles. We can make a distinction between five kinds of privacy code: the organizational code, the sectoral code, the functional code, the technological code, and the professional code (Bennett 1995, pp. 18–21).

The simplest instrument is the *organizational code* that applies to one corporation or agency that is bounded by a clear organizational structure. Typically these codes have been developed by large, high-profile organizations whose practices have come under scrutiny from the media or from privacy advocates, or who may have received a volume of consumer complaint. Many of the early examples came from large multinational companies such as American Express and Reader's Digest. Others, such as the consumer credit company, Equifax, have developed policies as a result of consumer surveys (Harris-Equifax 1992). Some organizational codes, typically within the telecommunications industry, have been adopted to an indeterminate extent to gain a competitive advantage within their respective sectors.[1]

A second, and perhaps more important category is that of the *sectoral code* developed by industry associations for adoption by their member organizations. Perhaps Canada is the country in which these instruments were developed most extensively, in the absence of a privacy law for the private sector. The model codes of the Canadian Bankers Association (CBA 1996), the Canadian Life and Health Insurance Association (CLHIA 1993), the Insurance Bureau of Canada (Canada IBC 1996), the former telecommunications alliance Stentor (Canada Stentor 1992), and the Canadian Cable Television Standards Council (CTSC 1991) fall within this category. In each of these sectors, a "model code" was adapted from the OECD Guidelines, or later from the Canadian Standards Association (CSA) Model Code, and promulgated within the member companies, some of whom then distributed their own separate publicity and privacy commitments. On the international plane, sectoral codes have begun to emerge within industries that operate on a global scale, such as those of the International Air Traffic Association (IATA), the Federation of European Direct Marketing Associations (FEDMA), and the global information processing industry, represented by the International Commerce Exchange (ICX).[2]

The defining feature of the sectoral code is that there is a broad consonance of economic interest and function among organizations in the sector, and by extension a similarity in the kinds of personal information processed. Sectoral codes permit, therefore, a more refined set of rules tailored to the issues within each industry. Sectors also tend to operate within an already defined set of regulatory institutions and rules, which in turn have established a relatively cohesive policy community that is engaged on a continuous basis in the negotiation and implementation of policies for the industry. However, trade associations vary in the extent to which they might represent a sector. Some, such as the Canadian examples above, may be relatively inclusive. For others, such as a number of US trade associations, there are clearly players (perhaps "free-riders") that operate by choice outside an association's membership and oversight. The membership of some trade associations may be dominated by one or two large players that exercise disproportionate influence in the market.

Trade or industry associations also differ in their structure and thus in the balance they strike between lobbying and policy development activities. A continuous tension exists for trade association officials between representing interests to government and encouraging new policies and better practices. At one extreme, the leadership can simply reflect the views of members and offer no leadership role. At the other, they can act more authoritatively, and try to convince members to pursue practices they would not otherwise follow, and that "doing the right thing" is in their economic self-interest. The leadership in successful associations needs to locate itself at the correct place along this continuum. Their assessment of where this position should be clearly influences the processes through which privacy codes of practice have been negotiated and developed.

The idea of the sectoral code was taken one step further in Japan when the Ministry of International Trade and Industry (MITI) published guidelines in 1997 on the content and substance of industry codes of practice, and on procedures for development, implementation, and oversight. As a result, different trade associations, such as the Electronic Commerce Promotion Council of Japan (ECOM), the Cyber Business Association (CBA), the Electronic Network Consortium (ENC), and the Japan Information Technology Industry Services Association (JISA) prepared codes, tailored to the conditions of individual Japanese industries. In 1998, MITI extended its guidelines to electronic commerce.[3] This form of oversight is possible in Japan because of very close ties between industry associations and MITI, and relatively established understandings about the boundaries between industry sectors. This process of standardization also helped pave the way for the introduction of a general Japanese data protection law in 2004.

The final three types of code clearly span these more traditional sectoral boundaries. What we call *functional codes* are defined less by economic sector and more by the practice in which the organization is engaged. The most obvious example is direct-mail and telemarketing. The direct marketing associations in the United States, Canada, Australia, and many other countries represent businesses in a wide and growing number of types of economic activity. They have responded to long-standing concerns about direct marketing by developing privacy codes of practice that have tried to regulate members and keep pace with evolving technologies. The direct marketing associations in the United States, the UK, Canada, and Australia all operate a mail preference service and telephone preference service to allow consumers to remove their names from the marketing lists of member organizations.[4] In the United States, a Do-Not-Call registry was set up by 2003 legislation and is now operated by the Federal Trade Commission (FTC).[5] Direct-marketing associations have also extended this service to electronic mail, through a web-based e-mail preference service, and to the collection of *clickstream data*. The Canadian Marketing Association even claims that its code is "compulsory" because members are expected to sign a commitment to its provisions and may be expelled from the association if found in violation of its provisions. The International Labour Organization's code of practice on workers' privacy is an example of a general code applicable across sectors and organizations (ILO 1997).

A fourth set of codes can be defined not by function, but by technology. As new, potentially intrusive technologies have emerged, so codes have developed to deal with the specific privacy problems associated with their application and distribution. *Technological codes* typically apply to very new applications. In 1992, for instance, the Canadian banks developed a code for the governance of electronic funds transfers (EFT), regulating the issuance of debit cards and personal identification numbers, the content of agreements between the issuer of the card and the cardholder, the nature of transaction records and statements, and security issues. Smart card technology is also amenable to specific regulation through privacy codes of practice. Smart cards have a range of commercial, transportation, health, telecommunications, and governmental applications that overlap traditional sectoral boundaries within and between the public and the private sectors. In some countries, specific trade associations have emerged to promote research into, and applications of, smart card technology. Such associations can also play a self-regulatory role, in the same way as more established trade associations.[6] Of course, the distinction between functional and technological codes is not clearcut, as the example of electronic mail guidelines from various marketing associations attests.[7]

A final category of privacy codes includes those that have been developed by professional societies. Typically, these codes apply to those directly engaged in information-processing activities. Thus *professional codes* have been developed for information processing professionals, for survey researchers, for market researchers, for librarians,[8] and for a range of health and welfare-related professionals.[9] They are created by professional, rather than trade, associations and can be reinforced by some significant disciplinary measures entailing a loss of professional reputation. They may also be incorporated into larger sets of ethical guidelines and codes of conduct.

Privacy codes of all kinds have been formulated with varying amounts of care and analysis, and have no consistent format (Bennett 1995). Procedures for implementation, complaints resolution, and communication vary substantially. This lack of consistency was one reason why the Canadian government decided, from 1996 to 1998, to analyze codes of practice in a variety of fields, including privacy, and to issue a brief primer on how best to develop and implement codes of practice in the marketplace (Canada 1998, Webb 2004). The success of codes of practice, however, is unpredictable and variable. Obviously privacy codes work if strong privacy protection is consistent with the profit interests of business, but that is not always the case. As we will see at the end of this chapter, privacy codes of practice operate within a complicated and fluctuating set of political, organizational, cultural, technological, and economic incentives that vary between and even within business sectors. Without a regulatory framework, which can impose sanctions for noncompliance, they generally suffer from the reasonable public perception that the individual's privacy rights are arbitrated by those who have the most to gain from the processing of personal data.

Code development in countries without private sector data protection law seems to have followed a common pattern. Codes are initially prompted by the powerful defensive motivation that "if we don't regulate ourselves, government will." There then follows a process of code development that attempts to do enough to satisfy potential regulators and advocates, but not so much that the burdens of compliance are as onerous as if there were legislation. For some businesses, the benefits of self-regulation might not outweigh the costs of regulation, especially where governments provide quite explicit stipulations about the expected content of the code and the process by which it should be produced (Government of Canada 1998). Over time, therefore, codes of practice that have been developed to avoid regulation evolve into instruments that might anticipate it. This seems to have been the dominant pattern in Canada, Australia, and Japan.

Privacy Standards

The phenomenon of privacy standards extends the self-regulatory code of practice in some important ways. Standards imply not only a common yardstick of measurement, but also a process through which organizational claims about adherence to a set of norms can be more objectively tested. We use the term *standardization* to mean not only a common code, but also a conformity assessment procedure that might more effectively determine that an organization "says what it does, and does what it says."

Technical standards have played an important role in computer security for many years. One example is the certification system established under the British Standard, BS7799. This standard comprises a code of practice for computer security, as well as a standard specification for security management systems that includes a risk analysis for the different categories of information stored by the organization. There is also a certification scheme, called "c-cure" that can operate in conjunction with the ISO 9000 range of generic quality management standards.[10] More recently, the wireless industry has negotiated a series of standards for the security of cellular communications.[11]

However, the idea of a more general privacy, rather than security, standard that would incorporate the entire range of privacy protection principles is a rather different innovation. The first comprehensive privacy standard was negotiated in Canada. In 1992, representatives of the major trade associations joined with key government officials and consumer representatives ostensibly to harmonize existing codes of practice developed under the OECD Guidelines. Later that year, it was decided to formalize the process by using the more institutionalized process of standard development within the CSA, which then acted as facilitator and secretariat. The *Model Code for the Protection of Personal Information* was finally passed without dissent on 20 September 1995, was subsequently approved as a "National Standard of Canada" by the Standards Council of Canada, and was published in March 1996 (CSA 1996).

The standard is constructed around ten principles, each of which is accompanied by an interpretive commentary. Organizations have been advised that all principles must be adopted in their entirety, and are also expected to reproduce the CSA principles in their codes although they may adapt the accompanying commentary to their own personal information practices. The standard may be adopted by any public or private organization that processes personal data. An accompanying workbook, giving more practical advice about the development and implementation of a privacy policy, was also released (CSA 1997).

Although the standard uses certain prescriptive language ("shall" and "must") it is clearly described as a voluntary instrument in the sense that there is no external compulsion upon any organization to adopt the principles. Once adopted, however, the code would operate like any other standard in that it would carry certain obligations to follow through on organizational claims.

Within CSA, the Quality Management Institute (QMI) registers companies to the series of "quality assurance" standards, principally those within the ISO 9000 series. There are some interesting parallels between the goals of "total quality management" and the implementation of fair information principles. In September 1996, the QMI announced a three-tier recognition program designed to be sensitive to the needs of both large and small businesses. Thus, unlike under the OECD Guidelines, what it means to "adopt" the CSA Model Code is clearly specified. At the very least, a business would have to develop its own privacy code consistent with the CSA model and produce a set of operational guidelines for its employees to follow. The CSA, or another accredited registrar, would then check these, register the company to the privacy standard, and, under certain conditions, conduct regular audits of personal information practices.

Although very few businesses in Canada have so far gone through this process, the privacy standard is potentially a different type of instrument from the typical "voluntary" code of practice. Privacy certification to a common standard can encourage a greater consistency of policy, higher levels of consumer awareness of privacy rights, a better yardstick for the measurement of the adoption of data protection, and an enhanced responsibility for the collection, storage, and disclosure of personal data (Bennett 1995). If, as many claim, good privacy protection is also good business, then there should be a desire to allay consumer and client fears by adopting the standard, proclaiming that the standard has been adopted, and thus being subject to audit. Furthermore unlike a code of practice, a standard can be referenced in contract either between private enterprises or between government and a private contractor. For instance, if a private contractor processed personal data under government contract, a simple way for the government agency to ensure adherence to the same data protection standards as apply in government would be to require the contractor to register with the standard. The same would apply to international contracts and the transborder flow of data. It is certainly possible for European data protection agencies to enforce Article 25 of the EU Data Protection Directive by requiring any recipient of European data in Canada to be registered to the CSA Model Code.

However, adoption of the code would always be incremental and piecemeal even though pressures can be exerted by government, international data protection authorities, and by market forces. Partly for this reason, the Canadian government decided that legislation should be introduced to apply the principles within the CSA standard in a mandatory way. *The Personal Information Protection and Electronic Documents Act* (PIPEDA) came into effect in 2001 for many private sector companies operating in Canada, and a mandated phased introduction thereafter. As a result of PIPEDA, there has never been a pure test of whether the standard could be adopted in the absence of legislation. Companies in most sectors decided that they would wait to see what the law said before committing resources to the implementation of the standard. On the other hand, other organizations have subsequently seized on the idea. The International Association of Privacy Professionals (IAPP), for example, now offers a certification program for government and business privacy managers.[12] Several accounting firms now also offer such services. In 2004, the Dutch Data Protection Authority took the initiative to provide a Privacy Audit Framework for any certified auditor to follow.[13]

General standards, similar to that of the CSA, have also been negotiated in Australia and Japan. In 1999 the Japanese Standards Association released JIS Q15001, which adapts the environmental management standard, ISO 14001, to personal data protection (Dumortier and Goemans 2000). The JIS code establishes a standard similar in structure and content to the CSA Model Code. It complies with MITI's 1997 privacy guidelines, provides a minimum privacy standard for Japanese enterprises, and applies to online as well as offline activities. As with the CSA Code, it may be adapted to particular business needs. Other standards have been developed by ECOM, the Japanese Information Processing Development Centre (JIPDEC), and the CBA.[14] As in Canada, however, this self-regulatory activity was considered necessary, but not sufficient. The Japanese government decided, therefore, to introduce a private sector data protection legislation, which came into force in 2005.

In Australia, a set of National Privacy Principles, similar to those of the CSA, were issued in February 1998 by the Privacy Commissioner. Although there was no explicit certification scheme offered, the overall aim was to get Australian businesses to adopt these National Principles in a formal manner, and thus to produce greater consistency in the Australian marketplace. In December 1998, the Commonwealth Government announced its intention to legislate to support these Privacy Principles. The Privacy Amendment (Private Sector) Act was passed in December 2000, and came into force a year later. The Privacy Commissioner has written a series of guidelines to the National Privacy Principles to assist businesses in meeting their obligations.[15] Thus, as in Canada, the broad acceptance by business of a set of national standards eased the process by which data protection law could be introduced. Unlike in Canada, however, the Australian approach is explicitly described as "co-regulation," and it is obvious from initial experiences that existing industry codes of practice will play a far more central role in the Australian scheme than they will in Canada.

As we see in chapter 4, these national efforts have led to initiatives for developing an international standards instrument that might operate as a more reliable and consistent method by which to demonstrate conformity to data protection norms. The initiative proceeded with little success through the International Organization for Standardization (ISO), and now through the Comité Européen de Normalisation (CEN), which is now in the process of finalizing deliverables in the following areas: a Generic set of contract clauses (Sponsored by the European Commission), a Common European voluntary best practices for data controllers and data processors, an Assessment of data protection audit practice (Sponsored by the European Commission), and Technology impact analysis.[16]

This CEN initiative is somewhat less than the general management standard initially contemplated, indicating that the added-value of privacy standards has yet to be convincingly demonstrated to those key stakeholders within the private sector whose participation is necessary if a standard, with a credible conformity assessment process, is to be negotiated. There also comes a point when the rational actor in the business world might decide that costs of compliance with standards far outweigh the costs of compliance with the kinds of "flexible" and "light-touch" legislation introduced in Canada, Japan, and Australia.

Privacy Seals

One logical corollary of any standard is a commonly understood mark, symbol, or cachet that can be awarded to any organization that is successfully certified or registered. The CSA's *mark* is generally regarded as a symbol of quality within the Canadian marketplace, and its use is jealously guarded and restricted to those companies that have followed an appropriate registration or certification process. The claim that an organization might make about its compliance is also carefully monitored. But the CSA has never developed a special cachet for "privacy friendliness." The development of a specific mark or *seal* for privacy protection has, however, proliferated on the Internet. Several schemes can be mentioned. The most notable have been developed by the TRUSTe organization, by the Better Business Bureau (BBB) Online, by Webtrust, and by JIPDEC.[17]

In 1996, TRUSTe was founded as a nonprofit organization dedicated to building public confidence in the online environment. It developed a program built upon the privacy guidelines established by the Online Privacy Alliance (OPA), a consortium of corporations and associations devoted to promoting privacy-friendly practices online.[18] The program was built on the premise that consumers should be able to have consistent disclosure of privacy practices from all sites with which they interact. To build this consistency, TRUSTe's licensing program requires participating websites to post a privacy policy disclosing their online information-gathering and dissemination practices, to complete a privacy assessment, and to participate in web site audit and review. The basis of the program is the TRUSTe "trustmark," an online branded seal displayed by member websites, awarded only to sites that adhere to the privacy principles and agree to comply with ongoing TRUSTe oversight and dispute-resolution procedures. All TRUSTe licensees display the resulting trustmark either on their website with a link to their site's privacy policy or directly on the privacy statement. The full list of licensees is also published on the Internet.[19]

TRUSTe monitors its licensees' sites through a process called "seeding," whereby personal information is submitted to member sites to ascertain whether or not they adhere to stated policies. Currently, there is no provision in the TRUSTe program for an onsite examination of a site's privacy practices as a precondition for receiving the TRUSTe mark. In the case of a privacy violation, licensee sites are contractually liable to a more comprehensive examination of its privacy practices. A TRUSTe-designated public accounting firm will then investigate the alleged violations. However, this comprehensive examination is only performed "for cause" at TRUSTe's request in response to formally stated concerns about a licensed site's compliance with the TRUSTe requirements.[20] TRUSTe has more recently added additional certification programs: a Children's Seal Program, an E-Health Seal Program, and a Safe-Harbor Seal Program. These are designed for those businesses that wish to import data from Europe.

In March 1999, the Council of Better Business Bureaus (CBBB)—an organization representing America's 135 Better Business Bureaus—released a privacy seal program called BBBOnLine.[21] Within the BBBOn-Line program there are three types of seals available to participating companies: "Reliability," "Privacy," and "Kids' Privacy," each seal indicating the company's agreement to abide by a set of principles outlined by the CBBB. They also offer a compliance program for the EU Safe Harbor Agreement. BBBOnLine claims that participants can take advantage of the longstanding expertise that the better business network holds in self-regulation and dispute resolution. Like the TRUSTe licensees, websites displaying the BBBOnLine Privacy seal have established a privacy policy to protect consumer information that meets all the program's standards. As part of the privacy policy, businesses must include notification to consumers of how information is collected, used, and shared. They must provide adequate data security, opt-outs for third-party information transfers, and reasonable access to information, and they must use encryption for the receipt and transfer of sensitive information. Websites or online services displaying a BBBOnLine Privacy seal must also commit themselves to the BBBOnLine dispute resolution process.

Perhaps the most stringent program is that offered by WebTrust. This seal was developed jointly by the American Institute of Certified Public Accountants (AICPA) and the Canadian Institute of Chartered Accountants (CICA). It is offered by specially trained and licensed Certified Public Accountants (CPAs) in the United States, Canada, Hong Kong, Australia, and a growing number of European countries. WebTrust claims to be part of a global effort by the accounting profession to bring effective e-commerce solutions to the Internet to protect businesses and consumers when shopping online. It is, therefore, more broadly concerned with issues of security, confidentiality, and business integrity.[22]

To obtain the WebTrust seal of assurance, the website must meet all the WebTrust Principles. The management of the website will make such assertions by filling in a self-assessment questionnaire. In addition, and in distinction to the other two programs, the organization must engage a CPA or Chartered Accountant practitioner who has a WebTrust business license from AICPA, CICA, or another authorized national accounting institute. The organization must obtain an unqualified report from such a practitioner. In 2000, the Office of the Information and Privacy Commissioner of Ontario and the Privacy Commissioner of Australia issued a joint evaluation of these three seal programs. Among their conclusions was the finding that, whereas BBBOnLine probably offered the most customer-friendly dispute-resolution system, WebTrust probably offered the most rigorous compliance regime (Ontario IPC and Privacy Commissioner of Australia 2000). This rigor probably explains why relatively few businesses have subscribed to WebTrust in comparison with the other two programs.

The final example of a seal program is the "Privacy Protection Mark" (PPM) system that was devised in Japan in 1998.[23] This system was conceived to apply to any organization, not just those operating on the Internet. JIPDEC serves as the granting body and is responsible for examining private enterprises' applications for the privacy mark, certifying them, and operating the system appropriately. A Privacy Mark System Committee, consisting of representatives of business groups, consumers, and lawyers, is responsible for overseeing the regime. The system also allows for a designated organization, such as a trade association, to implement the PPM within its own sphere of competence. Besides the above requirement, an enterprise must have a compliance program complying with MITI's "Guidelines for Protection of Personal Information Related to Computer Processing in the Private Sector" (Japan MITI 1997) or with industry guidelines that are based on the Guidelines by the business group to which the enterprise belongs. It must also demonstrate that personal information is appropriately managed based on the compliance program, or that a feasible structure has been established. The certification is then in existence for two years. Front-end audits are not a precondition of certification, but they may be required during the application process or as a result of consumer complaints. In 2000, JIPDEC announced a partnership with BBBOnLine that will allow BBBOnLine Privacy Program participants to take part in the Japanese privacy seal program and vice-versa.

Privacy protection marks or seals are certainly a necessary corollary of the code of practice and the standard. Ideally, privacy seals should operate to distinguish the compliant from the noncompliant and present consumers with clear and visible information by which to make informed choices in the marketplace, and particularly in the online marketplace. None of these systems, however, has yet achieved general recognition and credibility. Ironically, the more privacy seal programs in existence, the more the consumer will be confused, and the more difficult it will be for any one system to achieve a reputation as the methodology by which privacy-protective practices can be claimed and assured. Moreover, each organization operates in a competitive marketplace. The more stringent the registration requirements, the higher the likely consumer confidence, but the lower the likelihood that businesses will sign up.

The Safe Harbor Agreement

In many ways, the above instruments have come together on a global scale in the negotiation of a Safe Harbor Agreement between the European Commission and the US Department of Commerce. As the United States has no comprehensive laws protecting personal information processing in the private sector, the Safe Harbor Agreement was designed to give US companies that import data from Europe a more predictable and "adequate" framework of privacy protection, thus meeting the requirements of Article 25 of the EU Directive.

Attempts to devise the Safe Harbor Agreement produced some protracted and conflictual negotiations in 1999 and 2000. Earlier drafts of the Safe Harbor Principles were strongly criticized by the TransAtlantic Consumer Dialogue (TACD), a coalition of EU and US consumer groups; by the Article 29 Working Party; and by the European Parliament. The final draft was eventually approved by the EU in July 2000. The Agreement states seven basic privacy principles concerning notice, choice, onward transfer, security, data integrity, access, and enforcement. The benefits of entering the "safe harbor" are assured from the date on which an organization self-certifies to the Department of Commerce, or to a designated body, its adherence to these principles. Self-certification comprises a letter, signed by a responsible corporate officer, that contains all contact details; a description of the activities of the organization with respect to personal information received from the EU; and a description of the organization's privacy policy for such information, including its date of implementation, the contact person, the specific statutory body that has jurisdiction over the organization, the method of verification (whether in-house or third-party), and the independent recourse mechanism that is available to investigate unresolved complaints. These letters should be updated annually. The Department maintains and publishes a list of all organizations filing such letters.[24]

The crucial enforcement mechanism is embodied in the requirement that any public misrepresentation concerning adherence to the Safe Harbor principles may be actionable by the Federal Trade Commission, which has statutory responsibility to monitor "unfair and deceptive" trade practices. Thus the act of self-declaration to the Safe Harbor principles, while voluntary, also binds the organization to a set of legal requirements. It should be noted, however, that the Safe Harbor only applies to data about EU individuals transmitted to the United States; data on American citizens are therefore not covered, an irony that has not been lost on US privacy advocates.

According to the Department of Commerce, there are significant incentives for US companies to participate in the Safe Harbor. Those who do will be deemed adequate and data flows to those companies will continue. All fifteen Member States of the EU will be bound by the European Commission's finding of adequacy. Member State requirements for prior approval of data transfers either will be waived or approval will be automatically granted. Finally, any claims brought by European citizens against US companies will be heard in the United States subject to limited exceptions.[25]

Here we have an interesting test of the incentives for self-regulation. With only sporadic legal protections for personal data in the US private sector, and little immediate prospect of comprehensive data protection legislation, the market incentives to be privacy-friendly can operate, and be observed, in a manner that is less affected by the prospects of regulatory intervention. Unlike the CSA Model Code or the Australian National Privacy Principles, which were ostensibly preparatory instruments for law, the Safe Harbor process provides a more objective test of the success of self-regulation in the US marketplace.

The Department of Commerce has presented a rough tabulation of the industrial sectors represented by the companies that have signed up to Safe Harbor in the first year of operation. By far the most frequently represented are those categorized as "Information Services," "Computer Services," and "Computer Software." A fair number of businesses in "Advertising Services" and "Biotechnology" are also represented. This rough profile is more revealing for the businesses that are absent, than about those that are present. Very few of the major American banks, insurance companies, or consumer credit companies have so far self-certified. It is also surprising that no more than a handful of companies in the travel and tourism sector are represented. The overall list is perhaps also inflated by the presence of companies, like TRUSTe, which offer privacy-related services. The entire Safe Harbor process has been subjected to a good deal of critical scrutiny (Dhont et al. 2004). Nevertheless, this initial experience allows us to reach some more general conclusions about the conditions that seem to be associated with compliance with data protection norms, both in the United States and elsewhere.

Conclusion: The Conditions for Effective Self-Regulation

We can reach three broad conclusions as a result of the analysis of self-regulatory instruments sketched above. First, the range of incentives for the adoption of self-regulatory instruments is far broader than in the past. *Moral suasion*, stemming from government, information and privacy commissioners, some trade associations, and consumer groups, is an incentive that has operated for a long time. The desire to avoid adverse publicity is often the related sanction if moral suasion is insufficient. Increasingly, we see self-regulation used, especially on the Internet, as a method to gain competitive advantage. Pressures also stem from government through the contracting-out of government services; self-regulation is often a condition specified in contract when, for example, government data processing services are performed in the private sector.[26] Finally, international pressures, principally from the EU, have mandated "adequate" levels of data protection for which effective self-regulation is a crucial component in countries without comprehensive legal regimes. Thus, more incentives now operate to self-regulate properly, and these incentives flow from a wider range of sources.

Second, the scope of self-regulatory activity has expanded. The application of these instruments varies by sector and by jurisdiction. However, in Australia, Canada, and Japan—those countries that were relatively late in passing comprehensive data protection law for the private sector—there seems to be a discernible pattern; symbolic commitments gave way to more serious codes of practice, which in turn produced efforts at standardization, which in turn meant a system for publicly identifying the compliant from the noncompliant. This process was accompanied by a steady expansion of the understanding of what it means for an organization to "adopt" a privacy protection policy.

The scope of application for these instruments has also broadened. Privacy commitments and the early privacy codes were largely based upon a defined organization. Codes of practice then spread to sectors, to functions, to professions, and to specific technologies. The process of standardization then pushed these instruments up to the national level, in the case of the CSA and Japanese privacy marks, and even to the international levels, in the case of the Safe Harbor Agreement, and the US-based privacy seal programs. Perhaps the final step in this process is represented by the drafting of a "Global Code of Conduct" by the ICX, directed primarily to organizations engaged in international data flows.[27]

Third, it would be tempting to conclude that there is a progressive logic behind this pattern of adoption, and that each form of self-regulation is a prerequisite for the next. The reality is obviously less tidy, because the process of adoption of these instruments is rarely a linear one. Ideally, the adoption of these four instruments (commitments, codes, standards, and seals) should be cumulative. The self-regulatory process should involve: 1) an agreement and commitment to an organizational policy, 2) a codification of that policy throughout the organization or sector, 3) a verification of those practices through some external and independent conformity assessment process, and 4) the assignment of a "seal of good house-keeping." More often than not, however, public claims are made without adequate internal analysis or external auditing, and privacy seals are invariably awarded without a proper codification and verification of organizational practices. Therefore, the number of organizations that have engaged in privacy self-regulation in this cumulative and logical manner is very small.

For these reasons, critics remain skeptical that codes and other self-regulatory rules will be applied forcefully. Self-regulation will always suffer from the perception that it is more symbolic than real because those who are responsible for implementation are those who have a vested interest in the processing of personal data. Perhaps the appetite for the collection and processing of greater quantities and increasingly more refined types of personal information is inherent in the logic of the capitalist enterprise (Gandy 1993, Lyon 1994), or in bureaucratic organization more generally (Rule et al. 1980). Therefore, the incentive to breach privacy rules and, in particular, to collect, process, and disclose personal information without consent will tend to overwhelm the desire to be privacy-friendly.

Other commentators have argued the opposite, on the grounds that the protection of privacy fosters greater trust among consumers and is therefore a relatively inexpensive way to promote the image of corporate social responsibility (Cavoukian and Hamilton 2002, Ontario IPC

1994). There is some empirical evidence that privacy protection may well be linked to higher levels of consumer trust (Culnan and Bies 1999), and that this is a powerful motive for serious self-regulation. On the other hand, the analysis in this chapter suggests, inevitably, that the truth is more complicated and contingent. Sometimes the conditions for self-regulation are present; sometimes they are not. To grapple with this larger question, therefore, we need to suggest in a more systematic manner the various conditions that might promote an organization to self-regulate at a contemporary privacy protection standard, in the absence of comprehensive data protection legislation. These conditions might be related to the international environment, the level of techno-logical complexity, the amount of publicity and the industrial structure.

On an *international* dimension, we might first hypothesize that in those enterprises in which there is a greater need for the free interna-tional flow of personal data the exposure to international privacy stan-dards will be greater and the motivation to self-regulate will be higher. The global impact of the EU Directive, in particular, is the main force behind the development of privacy standards and seal programs in North America and Japan, as well as the Safe Harbor dialogue. If one scans the list of licensees to TRUSTe, for example, it is obvious that those companies with an actual, or intended, global reach are those that have tended to sign on, although there are very many others in that category that have not.

A second set of factors that can be mentioned are *technological*. New technologies tend to raise privacy fears more so than old ones. To the extent that new information technologies with publicly perceived privacy implications are continually introduced, the motive to self-regulate will be higher. Most notably, as electronic commerce has penetrated the activities of every sector, there has been a corresponding need to antici-pate privacy problems before they arise, and to assure consumers that their privacy is not at risk. Quite often the same practices as are con-ducted in the offline world can raise far greater fears when they are conducted online. The provision of credit-card information, for example, is generally less secure when a card is physically handed over the counter in a traditional retail store, than when it is transmitted via a secure server with strong encryption over the Internet. Nevertheless, the subjective perception of risk associated with a new technology can be a powerful motivation for companies to anticipate concerns and produce higher levels of self-regulation.

A third set of factors stem from the *level of publicity*. A strong motivation for self-regulation is the extent to which the enterprise or sector is the subject of negative publicity in both the traditional media and over the Internet. Represented within the list of Safe Harbor subscribers are several companies whose practices have motivated some highly publicized disputes. Thus Doubleclick, Inc. was the center of attention in 1999 to 2000 for its attempts to link anonymized clickstream data with a database of identifiable personal information owned by Abacus; Intel Corporation was forced to withdraw a personal identification system when it introduced its Pentium III chip in 1998; and Microsoft has been under constant scrutiny for the privacy-invasiveness of many of its products. The 2005 controversies over the practices of the commercial data brokerage firm, Choicepoint, have renewed calls for US data protection legislation.

A final set of conditions relates to the *structure of the industry* in question. The incentive to self-regulate will be higher the more the sector is controlled by a broadly representative trade association, which can self-regulate to minimize the influence of "free-riders." The more numerous the actors within a "sector" who abide by any standard, the more will the noncompliant be exposed.[28] In this respect, trade associations tend to be far more inclusive in Canada, Japan, and Australia than they are in the United States. The self-regulatory dynamic in the former three countries, therefore, produced a quite defined critical mass of associations representative of some of the biggest and most important companies in the service sectors. This inclusiveness facilitated the process whereby governments in these three societies could build a consensus around data protection principles, and then argue convincingly that if the membership can comply with these principles voluntarily, then there was no reason not to give them the greater public benefit of having statutory force.

However, the world is not neatly divided into sectors in which laws and codes of practice can be devised. The stability, over time, of sectors is questionable in the light of rapid changes in technology and in the way government and the economy are structured (Bennett 1995, pp. 19–22). Indeed, the very characterization of sectors as "public" or "private" is rapidly becoming doubtful as organizations on both sides connect their operations and systems and exchange personal data. In practice, there is a rather incoherent categorization of sectors or industries in which privacy protection codes are established. An exposition of the confusion that may arise in sectoral approaches is given in this hypothetical example (Gellman 1997, p. 260):

[A]ssume that there are privacy codes for the banking, direct marketing, and insurance industries. Assume further that a bank is a member of all three industry associations that promulgated the codes. Which code applies when the bank sells insurance through direct mail? Which code applies to corporate activities of the bank holding company that operates banking, insurance, and marketing subsidiaries, each of which has promised to comply with the applicable industry codes? If all codes are general or identical, then there may be no problem. But if the codes have different standards or procedures, then jurisdictional conflicts will occur.

As organizations diversify their business, they change the field on which sectoral codes, and perhaps even sectoral laws, may have an effect. The financial sector is being transformed and its subdivisions are becoming obsolete, as supermarkets and other retail outlets are developing significant banking functions. Moreover, many sectors that were previously thought of as discrete can now travel down the multimedia "information superhighway" in the same vehicle, as part of the "multimedia content industry." Information industries, entertainment industries, broadcasting industries, and communication industries are in the midst of a dramatic restructuring that poses serious questions for privacy regulators and self-regulators.

Furthermore, as the boundaries between sectors break down, the potential for the reputation of any business to be negatively affected by the actions of others increases. In an electronic commerce environment, old roles and functions are being radically redefined, with the result that bad actors might have a more widespread effect, far beyond the traditional sector in which they operate. We would suggest that this is one further explanation for the proliferation of instruments of self-regulation, and particularly trans-sectoral ones.

Whether these instruments are indeed effective is a more complex question that is addressed in Part III. The measurement of the level of privacy protection is fraught with many intricate conceptual and empirical difficulties. Before we tackle these issues, however, we need to complete the picture of the inventory of policy instruments for the protection of privacy by analyzing those that are more centrally located in the technology itself. The analysis of technological instruments is the subject of chapter 7.

7

Technological Instruments

Introduction: Designing Privacy In

It has been generally assumed that the contemporary privacy and data protection movement would not have arisen had it not been for the spread of increasingly sophisticated information and communications technologies. The policy instruments discussed in the previous chapters have been designed, in large measure, to control the worst effects of technologies. As Garfinkel asserts, "today's war on privacy is intimately related to the dramatic advances in technology we've seen in recent years" (Garfinkel 2000, p. 5). But this statement asserts a truism, which begs a number of deeper conceptual and theoretical questions.

Theories about the relationship between technology and politics generally center on the extent to which technology operates as an autonomous or deterministic force. Once technologies are set in motion, one argument goes, they tend to follow their own course independent of human direction. This idea has always been a powerful theme in political and social thought (Winner 1977). A kind of organic growth has been observed in the implementation of technology in whatever field of operation. Social and political factors may determine the initial application of a technology. However, once a system is in place, it is rare for its continual growth ever to be reversed once the strategic potential of the technology becomes more obvious to those who use it. Winner (1977, p. 208) states the principle as follows: "once underway, the technological reconstruction of the world tends to continue." In other terms, this view of technology produces the phenomenon of "function creep," the tendency for new uses and applications to be found over time unrelated to the purposes for which the technology was originally designed.

Against the deterministic view, there is also a range of writings that believe that technology cannot be understood outside its social and political context, and therefore cannot be regarded as an independent force (MacKenzie and Wajcman 1999). Most commentators see outcomes as shaped by a complex dynamic interaction between technology and society. The outcomes of information technology usage will reflect "the interactive relationship between technological developments, political decisions and existent organizational norms and practices. Technology sets boundaries to achievements, but within those limits, human choice and conflict have considerable latitude" (Bennett 1991, p. 64). Whether technology is shaped by the conscious and autonomous decisions of political agents, or existent organizational norms or standard operating procedures, it is clear, as Pool puts it, that "technology shapes the structure of the battle but not every outcome" (Pool 1983, p. 251).

These theoretical debates rest heavily, of course, on the prior conceptualization of the terms *technology* and *information technology*. To be sure, there is no clear distinction between the technology (or apparatus) of the computer, and the organizational structures and processes that support and surround it. Most social scientists would agree that, for meaningful analysis of social issues like privacy, it is necessary to have a broader conception of technology that comprises not just the apparatus, but the whole variety of social and organizational techniques that support them (Winner 1977, pp. 11–12). Danziger and his colleagues, for instance, in their study of the use of computers in local government, talk of a "computer package" to denote an interdependence of people, equipment, and machines (Danziger et al. 1982, pp. 4–5). The significant unit of analysis is the *technology practice*, or the behaviors, rules, conditions, etc. that surround the hardware and the software.

Thus it is inappropriate to think of technology as having an "impact" on society, as if the two were conceptually and empirically separable. Rather, the more important task of the social scientist is to try to understand the extent to which technologies themselves are imbued with social and political values. In this interpretation artifacts actually "contain" political and social biases (Winner 1989). Their very structure and architecture may be inextricably linked to particular patterns of power. In the terms of this book, information technologies may carry, intentionally or unintentionally, a valence that may be pro-privacy, or pro-surveillance.

Those who would reject this argument would probably view the privacy problem as stemming from the inherent tendencies of bureaucratic organization, or the imperatives of the marketplace. Thus the problem is the acquisition and aggrandizement of power or the competition for profit or market share. These assumptions underpin, to some extent, the bureaucratic theories at the heart of Rule's (1974, Rule et al. 1980) work. If the root of the privacy problem is political and bureaucratic power or economic behavior, then these factors can only be stemmed through countervailing regulatory action, and the introduction of technologies that might be privacy-enhancing, rather than privacy-invasive, is likely always to be a secondary and derivative consideration. If one accepts, however, that at least part of the privacy problem is caused by the properties inherent in the design of certain information technologies, then it follows that the same technologies can be effectively shaped to protect privacy, rather than to invade it.

Thus, the privacy policy community over the past twenty years has gradually embraced this notion that technologies can also be part of the solution, as well as part of the problem. Chaum (1992), for example, claims that the traditional data protection model, based on the fair information principles doctrine, can be radically altered if technologies can be designed in such a way that the default is the zero-collection of personal information. With the revolutionary discovery of "public-key" or "asymmetric" cryptography in the late 1970s, privacy or, perhaps more accurately, anonymity can be built into information systems in ways that do not compromise the ability of public and private organizations to verify identity (Diffie and Landau 1998). If this goal is achieved, then the technology itself becomes a policy instrument and perhaps the panoply of procedural rights and guarantees that form the basis of the legal and self-regulatory instruments discussed in chapters 5 and 6 is rendered less relevant.

In this chapter, our interest is not in the technology itself, but how it has emerged as a policy instrument, becoming the subject of considerable attention and arousing much enthusiasm in policy and regulatory networks. The relevant questions concern how those technology tools can, and do, operate as policy instruments, and what roles they have played in relation to other more traditional privacy policy instruments.

Privacy-enhancing technologies (PETs) obviously come in a variety of forms. Burkert (1997) makes an important distinction between privacy-enhancing technologies and data security technologies. The latter are clearly technologies that have played a necessary, if not a sufficient, role in the implementation of privacy protection policy. Data security measures, ranging from the sophisticated use of computer passwords to the more mundane requirement of filing cabinet locks, seek to "render data processing safe regardless of the legitimacy of processing. . . . PETs, on the other hand, seek to eliminate the use of personal data altogether or to give direct control over revelation of personal information to the person concerned" (Burkert 1997, p. 125). Thus, an organization can keep highly intrusive and sensitive personal information extremely secure. But this fact does not mean that the organization should be collecting that information in the first place, passing it to whomever they wish, storing it forever, or ignoring any inaccuracies it may contain. Yet it is important to point out that many organizations' belief that "data protection just means data security" has been a common misunderstanding over the years. This chapter does not address the kinds of data security measures that have formed a necessary part of any data protection regime since the beginning.

Burkert goes on to develop a useful typology of different PETs based on whether the subject, the object, the transaction, or the system forms the target of any privacy-enhancing technology. Thus "subject-oriented" concepts seek to "eliminate or substantially reduce the capability to personally identify the acting subject." "Object-oriented concepts" try to eliminate or minimize the traces left by the objects of interpersonal transactions, such as electronic cash. "Transaction-oriented concepts" seek to hide the transaction process without directly addressing the objects being exchanged. "System-oriented" concepts seek to integrate some or all of the above (Burkert 1997, pp. 126–128).

As a conceptual device, Burkert's classification is insightful, but it is pitched at a high level of abstraction. These distinctions, as he admits, are not necessarily reflected in empirical examples of applied technologies. Our discussion, therefore, is structured somewhat differently to highlight the different agents involved in the construction of these technologies, and thus their different features as policy instruments. Three overlapping types of privacy-enhancing technologies are discussed. *Systemic instruments* are those that arise from the decisions (intended or unintended) of the hardware and software engineers who design networks or machinery and who write computer code, and from the technical standards and protocols that are then negotiated to enhance network efficiency. These instruments correlate with Reidenberg's (1998) conception of "Lex Informatica" and Lessig's (1999) arguments about the regulatory effects of computer code. *Collective instruments* are created as a result of government policy. They are top-down policy applications where government or business makes explicit decisions to "build privacy into" new applications and forms of the provision of services and goods. The most notable examples are the attempts to develop public-key infrastructures for government service-delivery. *Instruments of individual empowerment*, of which we provide a further classificatory breakdown, require explicit choices by end-users—the consumer or citizen. In this instance, the PET is only activated when individuals make an explicit choice to select privacy-enhancement in their transactions with private and public sector institutions. This categorization, therefore, correlates more with the level at which technological instruments are applied, and the agents who apply them, than with specific types of technology. Our discussion will reveal other key differences, and will lead to general conclusions about the role of PETs as policy instruments.

Systemic Instruments: Code and "Lex Informatica"

Lessig (1999, pp. 26–27) recounts an interesting comparison between two American universities. At the University of Chicago, it is possible for students, staff, and administrators to communicate anonymously. If one wants access to the Internet, one can simply connect one's computer to any Ethernet connection jack located throughout the university. At Harvard, however, a machine cannot be connected unless it is registered, so that all interactions with the network can be monitored and identified with a particular machine, and probably with a user.

These two network designs carry significant policy implications for free speech, privacy, and other important values. Lessig's point is that the design of these networks "differ in the extent to which they make behavior within each network regulable. This difference is simply a matter of code—a difference in the software. Regulability is not determined by the essential nature of these networks. It is determined instead by their architecture" (Lessig 1999, pp. 26–27).

The argument that computer code is tantamount to legal code is not particularly surprising to those that have followed debates over US encryption policy in recent years, and the attempts by US law enforcement to try to achieve by technical standards and protocols what could not be obtained through the legislative process (Rotenberg 2000). But if Lessig is correct, and computer code can regulate, then this raises profoundly important questions about accountability for, and participation in, the decision-making that produces these technical designs, standards, and instruments. It also points out the significance of recent debates within the circles of computer professionals and innovators concerning the way in which ethical and political awareness can be incorporated into their training and careers.[1]

Reidenberg introduces the concept of "Lex Informatica" to explore the various ways that choices over systems design and capabilities can act as policy devices: "The creation and implementation of information policy are embedded in network designs and standards as well as in system configurations. Even user preferences and technical choices create overarching local default rules" (Reidenberg 1998, p. 555). Lex Informatica performs very similar functions to more traditional legal regulation. It has a framework (the architecture standards), a jurisdiction (the network), an expression of content (the technical capabilities), a source agency (the technologists), a set of customized rules and processes (the configuration), and an enforcement mechanism (automated self-execution) (Reidenberg 1998, p. 569).

Reidenberg goes on to argue that Lex Informatica possesses some characteristics that are particularly useful for information policy-making. First, there is a set of jurisdictional advantages because networks are not bounded by artificial state boundaries, with all the attendant difficulties of delineating legal sovereignty claims. Second, there are customization advantages in that Lex Informatica can allow for flexibility in the adoption of standard configurations and for empowering individuals to make their own policy decisions. Third, it has enforcement advantages: technologies can be developed to monitor compliance with information policy rules and this enforcement tends to be anticipatory, rather than reactive (Reidenberg 1998, pp. 579–581).

Reidenberg explicitly refers to Lex Informatica as a policy instrument. Whereas technologies may always be used in order to implement existing policy decisions, Lex Informatica, however, may actually substitute for law, and may constrain the ability of the law to deal with a problem. Conversely, legal rules may encourage the development of Lex Informatica, or may sanction its evasion (Reidenberg 1998, p. 583). Reidenberg explores how the two forms of rule parallel and overlap one another.

Illustrations of Systemic Instruments

The importance of this form of technological rule-making has been recognized for some time, and certainly before the advent of the Internet. In the mid-1990s, Samarajiva (1996) analyzed evolving communications networks and new call-management features to highlight the dangers of "surveillance by design." In the telecommunications environment, the default settings for practices such as itemized billing, and calling-number identification can operate as de facto policy instruments. More recent examples of Internet standards and protocols offer more graphic and immediate evidence of the policy implications of default settings and protocols.

Lessig (1999, pp. 32–33) provides the example of the Internet Protocol (IP) address. When the basic TCP/IP protocols were being developed for the exchange of packets of data between computers on the Internet, the IP address was developed simply to identify the machines to and from which the packets should be carried. The IP address in and of itself reveals nothing about the users, very little about the data being exchanged, and nothing about the geographical location of the sender and the receiver. When an individual accesses a webpage, the server delivering that page also knows nothing about that individual—at least, nothing from the IP address alone. Lessig argues that this minimalism in design was intentional because the designers were far more interested in network speed and efficiency than they were in advancing social and political control. Although Lessig goes on to contend that the "invisible hand" of commerce is building an architecture that is very different from this initial vision, it can be argued that the basic IP address design has acted as a privacy-enhancing technology.

The effects of this invisible hand have been revealed in conflicts about identification on the Internet. Considerable concern continues to be directed towards the *cookies* that have been a feature of Internet browsers ever since Netscape introduced its new version of Netscape 2.0 in late 1995. A *cookie* is a record stored on a user's machine, as a result of a web-server instructing a web-browser to do so. Cookies allow a web-server to remember its conversation with a particular web-browser, and thus to implement what computer engineers call "state-maintenance." Cookies can be highly beneficial to organizations and their clients. However, because cookies also provide marketers with the ability to maintain and profile data, and to do so on the user's own machine, they have aroused the suspicion and opposition of privacy advocates and others who are concerned that they constitute a powerful form of surveillance. The issue of less intrusive mechanisms and standards for "state-maintenance" continues to be debated in the Internet Engineering Task Force (IETF) (Clarke 2001). Late in 2001, a European Parliament amendment to an EU draft directive on electronic data collection and privacy would have required explicit and positive consent before a cookie was served to a client machine.[2]

Several further controversies illustrate the power of Lex Informatica. The first example occurred in 1999 when the Intel Corporation announced its new generation of Pentium III processors. Intel thought it would be a good idea to have a unique code in each processor—a processor serial number—to help the company identify the over-clocking of cpus (for example, when a 500 MHz chip is sold as a 700 MHz chip), and also to help large organizations track machines as they move around. But privacy advocates claimed that it was also possible for websites to use special software to read the processor serial number of their customers' computers over the Internet. Linked to a computer's IP address, this could serve as a valuable tracking device and surveillance tool. Intel quickly dropped its plans (Garfinkel 2000, p. 78).

A second example concerns "WebBugs," a very small code that is embedded in Microsoft Word Documents, and any other application capable of displaying HTML-based content. The WebBug can notify a server when a document is transferred over the Internet, and literally "phones home." The technology allows organizations to track stolen documents, or authors to track illicit copying of copyrighted materials. As companies blend desktop applications into the Internet, more of this tracking capability has been seen. Privacy advocates have offered warnings about the number and variety of new "spyware" software that is embedded in quite normal consumer applications.[3] This example, incidentally, points out the way in which other aims of information policy—in this case, intellectual property protection—may cut across the aim of privacy protection. Such conflicts of this kind are frequent, and cast doubt on the problem-solving or problem-avoiding potential of technologies by themselves when considered within wider contexts.

A further, and perhaps more general example, relates to the move from HTML (Hyper-Text Markup) to XML (Extensible Markup) Language, the standards for which were released by the World Wide Web Consortium in 1998. XML is designed to improve the functionality of the web by providing more flexible and adaptable information identification. It is called "extensible" because it is not a fixed format like HTML (a single, predefined markup language), but a kind of "metalanguage" that lets the user design his or her own customized markup languages for limitless types of applications, including the exchange of personal information. The more adaptable XML tags can thus be used to link information from disparate sources in ways that the more static HTML language cannot. The implications for the analysis of personal information in commercial, educational, health, and other fields has not gone unnoticed.

The Smart Tags associated with XML are integral to the most recent Microsoft operating systems. One feature of these new systems is the Microsoft Passport, a centralized, cross-domain log-on–automation service. It is encountered as a mandatory element of many of Microsoft's bundled offerings such as MSN/Hotmail and Messenger and essentially allows participants to use their e-mail addresses and a single password to sign in securely to any Passport-participating website. The Passport is designed to allow the user to move easily among different sites without needing to remember a different password and sign-in for each site.[4] The central Passport site stores a limited amount of user data. By default, signing up for Passport authorizes Microsoft to share demographic data with its partners in nonidentifiable form; participants can opt-out of having their data shared in this manner. But critics have pointed out that Passport also associates a unique identifier with every Passport account at registration, which Microsoft sends to each participating site. This gives Passport-enabled sites a way to get around techniques used for anonymous surfing. Even if a Passport site does not initially know you by name, it may still know you by your Passport's numeric code and thus can build an ongoing profile of you and your surfing habits on that site. Moreover, there is no technical reason why Passport-enabled sites could not combine their information to build profiles. These and other troubling features of the Passport system were a subject of a complaint to the Federal Trade Commission and to the American States' Attorneys General.[5]

The default settings of these and other Internet-related technologies can range in their flexibility. Some, such as the IP address protocol, are quite immutable. Others, such as the cookie technology can be disabled, filtered, blocked, and so on, yet it is not in the interest of organizations prominently to inform users that they have the ability to make such choices. Moreover, some online services are not accessible unless users allow the placement of cookies. One implication of Lex Informatica is that it provides the potential for policy-makers to shape designers' technical choices and standards to allow for individual policy choices through customization of configurations (Reidenberg 1998, p. 587). On the other hand, if governments try to influence technical standards, then the institutional focus shifts toward technical arenas, such as the World Wide Web Consortium, the Internet Engineering Task Force, and traditional standards organizations like the ISO and the European Telecommunications Standards Institute (ETSI). These bodies are not necessarily democratically accountable, and they are not normally attuned to making decisions that have such broad governmental and policy consequences. We discuss these implications in chapter 8.

State-Directed Technological Policy Instruments

Governments can do far more than influence the setting of technical standards. They may develop policy strategies to build privacy protection into new service-delivery systems. Under these circumstances, key policy decisions are more visible and are more likely to be made by state policy-makers than by technological developers and standards bodies. Indeed, it may be important for governments to act in this way, as part of a state strategy for the promotion of electronic commerce. Without a legislative framework, sufficient assurances may be difficult to give to firms and customers alike—whether in business-to-business, business-to-consumer, or state-to-citizen transactions—that their dealings are secure.

The most notable example of these initiatives is the development of *public-key infrastructures* (PKI) for government service-delivery, and a range of business applications. It is first necessary to explain a little about the difference between new and conventional cryptographic techniques. Conventional symmetric-key cryptography consists of a single mathematical key used for both the encryption and decryption of the data. Traditionally, a person wanting to send a secure message to addressees would encrypt the message using a key known only to the sender and the recipient, and then would pass both the key and encrypted message to the recipient so that the message could only be decrypted by that person. Public key cryptography, in contrast, uses two keys: one key is kept private and the other key is made public. If the public key is used to encrypt a message, the private key can decrypt it. Thus, if one wants to send a message to addressees, one encrypts the message with the addressees' public keys and passes the message to them; they can then use the private keys to decrypt it (Diffie and Landau 1998).

Public key cryptography also allows the creation of a digital signature that provides proof—known as authentication—that a person is the originator of the message. If the person wants to sign a message sent to an addressee, one passes the message through a mathematical function (or a "hash code"), which provides a summary of that message. This summary is unique for every message, operating much like a fingerprint. The person then encrypts this hash code with the private key and attaches the code to the end of the message. This attached code is known as a digital signature. Using the public key, the addressee can then verify that that person sent the message by decrypting the digital signature, to get the hash code. The addressee then passes the received message through the same hash function. If the two hash codes are the same, then the message was sent by the person in question and was not altered in the process.

Public key cryptography, on its own, is not enough to create the conditions for secure communication, at least not for complex transactions between individuals and public or private organizations. It also requires a package of other measures: security policies to set the rules under which the cryptographic systems should operate; products to generate, store, and manage the keys; organizational procedures to define how the keys and certificates should be generated, distributed, and used; and technical standards to ensure interoperability, the most common of which is the X509 standard. PKI, therefore, is the package of policies and products that attempts to provide the framework for a wide variety of applications and to achieve the four principal security functions for informational transactions. These are *confidentiality*—to keep information private, *integrity*—to prove that information has not been altered, *authentication*—to prove the identity of an individual, and *nonrepudiation*—to ensure that information was sent by the originator.

In more detail, a PKI should consist of a number of separate components. First, a *security policy* should lay out an organization's policy on information security, as well as its processes and principles for the use of cryptography. Typically this policy will include statements on how the organization will handle keys and other confidential information, and will set the levels of control required to match the levels of risk. Second, some PKI systems are operated by commercial *certificate authorities* (CAs) or *trusted third parties* (TTPs), and therefore require a detailed document containing the operational procedures for how the

CAs are constructed and operated; how certificates are issued, accepted, and revoked; how keys will be generated, registered, and certified; where they will be stored; and how they will be made available to users. The CA is therefore the institutional foundation for any PKI, as it manages the public key certificates for their whole life cycle. The CA will issue certificates by tying the identity of a user to a public key with a digital signature, scheduling expiration dates for certificates, and ensuring that certificates are revoked as soon as they are no longer necessary. When implementing a PKI, an organization can either operate its own CA system, or use the services of a commercial CA or TTP.

Third, there is the need for some kind of registration authority to provide the interface between the user and the CA. This authority would capture and authenticate the identity of the user and submit the certificate request to the CA. Finally, the system must have a certificate distribution system. Certificates can be distributed in a number of ways depending on the structure of the PKI environment either by the users themselves, or through a directory service. A directory server may already exist within an organization or one may be supplied as part of the PKI solution.[6]

For about a decade, several governments have been putting these frameworks in place to provide uniform and trusted key management systems. Details will obviously differ from jurisdiction to jurisdiction. The Canadian federal PKI, for example, is designed to be the infrastructure that integrates other technologies into a more seamless solution for secure departmental information management and electronic commerce. A number of federal departments and agencies are involved in this development. Potential applications include electronic cash, electronic postage, legal contract management, health care information storage, electronic voting, and the delivery of a range of social services.[7]

In the UK, the Electronic Communications Act 2000 aims to put in place a secure infrastructure for electronic transactions in order to strengthen confidence in electronic commerce and its underlying technology. It lays down the regulations for the legal recognition of electronic signatures and the process under which they are verified, generated, or communicated, and a scheme of approvals for organizations that provide cryptography services, such as electronic signature and confidentiality services. The Act is consistent with, and implements, important provisions of the 1999 EU Electronic Signatures Directive,[8] and was passed following long and heated controversy in and outside Parliament concerning issues such as "key escrow" and the effects of law-enforcement requirements upon confidentiality.[9]

Instruments for Individual Empowerment

A final range of privacy-enhancing policy instruments is dependent on the decisions by individuals to take steps to protect their privacy. Responsibility to apply the technology lies with the end users, who may have a range of choices about the extent to which they wish to take responsibility for personal information.

A wide range of tools might fall into this category of instrument. Defined broadly, PETs in this category might encompass an entire spectrum of measures and initiatives, including some very basic common-sense, nontechnological procedures that were readily available before computers entered our lives, such as locking filing cabinets and closing doors. More recently, the term has tended to denote the range of products and applications that individuals might use to protect their privacy in the online environment. We confine our analysis, therefore, to those technologies that operate within this environment and that are currently available to the privacy-conscious individual.

The inventory of Internet privacy tools is extensive and continually changing. The Electronic Privacy Information Center (EPIC) has developed an interesting and useful typology of instruments currently in the marketplace in its "Online Guide to Practical Privacy Tools."[10] They offer a cornucopia of examples: snoop-proof e-mail programs, anonymous remailers, anonymous web-browsing tools, html filters, cookie busters, voice privacy tools, e-mail encryption tools, web encryption tools, telnet encryption tools, disk encryption, disk-file erasing programs, privacy-policy generators, password generators, spyware detectors, and firewalls. A 2001 report by the OECD analyzed 83 different websites that offered privacy-enhancing tools (OECD 2001). The report revealed that the vast majority of these products come from American sources; many have now fallen by the wayside. The presence of large financial and telecommunications companies in their list shows that the provision of these services has moved from a fringe interest of a few cyberactivists to a big-business concern.

Thus a bewildering and highly dynamic variety of products has entered the online privacy marketplace over the past ten years, eluding an adequate or stable typology. For simplification, let us make a distinction among encryption instruments, which encrypt the content of any message or transaction; anonymity and pseudonymity instruments, which shield the identity of the user; filters, which attempt to block the transmission of cookies and the deployment of other privacy-invasive techniques; and privacy-management instruments, which attempt to negotiate a consumer's privacy preferences with a website.[11]

Encryption Instruments

According to the Office of the Information and Privacy Commissioner in Ontario, there were no fewer than 800 different encryption programs available in the marketplace in 1999 (Ontario IPC 1999). These obviously vary in quality; some have been independently tested and verified, while others have not. Some, the less secure, are based on traditional symmetric-key encryption. Others are based on the principle of asymmetric encryption using a pair of keys (public and private). The basic function of an encryption program is to generate at random the algorithms in the background; digital signatures can then be added in order to assure the intended recipient that nobody has interfered with the message, and that the authors are indeed who they say they are.

In addition to the PKI model, in which a framework is established centrally in order to manage secure communications, e-mail encryption programs can further be classified into two types. The first are web-based, in which the website concerned acts as a kind of traffic controller for the user's e-mail and the encryption software is resident at that website. The second, and more common, types are computer-based applications where the necessary programs are installed on the user's computer.[12] Most e-mail encryption products also fall into two main standards or protocols: S/MIME (Secure Multipurpose Internet Mail Extension) and Open PGP (Open Pretty Good Privacy).

The encryption of e-mail was the earliest application offered to individuals on the Internet. Since then, encryption products have been offered for the full range of Internet activities. For example, many products now exist for encryption of the customer information sent to online merchants. When the customer is ready to make a purchase, the merchant's web server redirects the customer to a separate web server, dedicated to the collection and protection (that is, encryption) of the consumer's personal information. This server then sends the encrypted packets of the buyer's information to the merchant's e-commerce server, where it is stored in the order-processing system. The software then protects the buyer's information with strong encryption before the merchant ever sees it. For instance, the credit card information is encrypted so that only the bank and credit card company can see the credit card number; the shipping address is encrypted so that only the delivery firm knows where to bring the package, and so on.

Other encryption applications allow one to browse the Internet and send e-mail through encrypted network connections. When one normally connects to the Internet, the transactions are relayed through several servers before reaching their final destination. Since these requests are not encrypted, any server between the sender and the final destination, including that of the Internet Service Provider, can potentially "see" the content of what is being sent. Some products use a method known as "port forwarding" to allow one to encrypt incoming and outgoing e-mail, browsing activity, and newsgroup postings. Specific types of Internet traffic are assigned to specific "ports" on computers connected to the Internet. Web-surfing or e-mail requests are then sent to the secure ports on the remote site's machine. Using such software, the user can transfer all web, news, and e-mail traffic to the secure port connection.

Instruments for Anonymity and Pseudonymity

Many of the most creative tools have been developed to allow anonymous Internet browsing. Fearful of the consequences of malicious hacking and of the potential for online profiling by marketers, the privacy-conscious Internet user now has available a plethora of different products. The market is very fluid, and there have been a number of ingenious and subtly different models upon which these applications are based.

The simplest model relies on an intermediary that acts as a proxy between the user and the end server. Some of the first anonymizing applications, such as the anonymous remailer, anon.penet.fi, were based on this model. The main company that offers this service for web-browsing is anonymizer.com; it was initially introduced in 1996 and seems to have enjoyed the greatest customer loyalty. Several similar products have been introduced with less success, and most are now obsolete.[13] Most of these products have free services, offering to block banner ads, as well as more enhanced subscription features, such as cookie filtering techniques, firewalls, form-filling devices, and disk-cleaning services.

The problem with each of these concepts is that at some point the end users have to identify and authenticate themselves to the intermediary, either by the purchase of software or through registration. Under certain circumstances, the intermediary then becomes susceptible to requests for one's identity by, for instance, law enforcement agencies. Therefore, the "anonymizing" entity still requires a policy for the secure collection, use, and disclosure of its clients' personal information. Moreover, the level of privacy afforded may depend upon the laws in force in the jurisdiction regarding the steps that law enforcement agencies must follow to gain access (for example, warrants). A final model tries to get around this problem by employing the concept of a "pseudonymous identity." One company has tried to market the concept of pseudonymous nicknames called *nyms* to disguise one's true identity, even from the company itself. These *nyms* are randomly generated and allow the user to create completely separate online identities, each with its own randomly generated personal information. The network then automatically re-routes data through a series of globally distributed servers, acting like a cloak to provide completely anonymous connections to the Internet.[14]

Filtering Instruments

Many applications simply try to filter out the most intrusive forms of Internet monitoring. Most of these attempt to block or filter the transmission of cookies. As noted earlier, cookies have beneficial purposes. They allow a website to monitor traffic, and they are used to re-identify the user when one returns to a website, so one does not have to remember passwords or other identifiers. But they can also be used to profile the browsing habits of Internet users, as the "clickstream data" can then be linked to the personal information that may originate from a number of different sources. These data may then be used by online advertisers to target banner advertisements to consumers.

One of the earliest online privacy tools were the very basic programs to block and delete cookies; examples are "Cookie Crusher," "Cookie Cruncher," "Junkbuster," and "Cookie Monster."[15] These allow the blocking of cookies in real-time, before they appear on the hard drive, or the deletion of cookies from the hard drive. Some also allow the blocking of banner advertisements. To some extent these applications have been rendered less necessary because of the decisions by Microsoft and Netscape to allow enhanced cookie-management features in the latest versions of their respective browsers, permitting users to accept all cookies, to permit only "session cookies," or to disable them completely. Also in this category fall the variety of products designed to detect and remove *spyware*—a broad term to encompass a range of deceptive programs that may be logged deep within the registry keys of a user's system. Many such programs are motivated by aggressive advertising. Some install malicious dialers or can capture the homepage and "favorites" settings on one's Internet browser. There are a number of ways deceptive software can get onto a computer system. A common trick is to install covertly the software during the installation of other software, notably music or video file sharing programs.[16]

Other filtering software has been developed in order to protect children's activities online. Mainly directed at the filtering of sexual and violent content, some websites also offer tools for parents to block the collection of information on their children. New child privacy protection legislation in the United States has heightened the importance of controlling how websites access data about children.[17] Educational awareness programs and filtering software that blocks the transmission of certain information via e-mail, chat rooms, or web forums when a child is using a computer have arisen as a consequence.[18]

Privacy-Management Protocols
On the assumption that the average consumer is likely to be extremely confused by the wide variety of privacy-enhancing devices on the marketplace, more recent applications have attempted to create a more

user-friendly set of privacy choices for individuals. Back in 1998, Reidenberg argued that the Platform for Internet Content Selection (PICS), a set of technical specifications for rating and distributing labels that describe the content of websites, may have applications to privacy protection as well. He foresaw that filter configurations using the PICS protocol, or something similar, could allow users to make choices about the use of their personal information and to assure the implementation of those decisions on the Net. Users would express their privacy preferences, similar to the level of obscenity that the user wants to tolerate, and websites would be rated for their treatment of personal information. He pointed out, however, that unlike content-rating systems where the label can be assigned without the cooperation of the website concerned, with regard to privacy, the organization actually processing the data must assist third-party labelers if accurate ratings are to be assigned (Reidenberg 1998, pp. 563–564). Privacy rating requires knowledge, not just of the information on the website, but also of organizational practices and policies.

In a similar vein, Lessig argued that "[w]hat is needed is a way for the machine to negotiate our privacy concerns for us, a way to delegate the negotiating process to a smart agent—an electronic butler—who, like the butler, knows well what we like and what we do not like" (Lessig 1999, p. 160). Others have called these devices "intelligent software agent technologies" (ISATs), which would create profiles of a user's preferences, habits, contact information, transactional history, and so on, and would then inform the user about products and services and about actions that might be taken, such as renewing a subscription (Ontario IPC and The Netherlands IPC 1999). These agents help individuals manage their online identity.

A number of commercial products claim to be able to offer these functions.[19] By far the most significant initiative is the Platform for Privacy Preferences (P3P) constructed by the World Wide Web Consortium (W3C). Website operators use the P3P language to make a machine-readable version of their privacy policy. Consumers can use their browsers (enabled with P3P readers) or other software tools to read a site's privacy policy, and these tools automatically provide notifications about whether the policy matches the user's privacy preferences.

Arguably, consumers are able to make better judgments about whether to patronize a website. The P3P technology was incorporated into the latest generation of Microsoft's Internet browsers. Subsequently other browser technologies followed suit. Users are able to set their browser to one of six levels of privacy. When that user enters a website, the browser interacts with the site's privacy policy and alerts the user if their privacy expectations are not met.[20]

It is difficult to generalize about the potential for a "privacy-industry" on the Internet from such a short and volatile history. But there are some notable trends. First, no company can afford simply to offer one product; most offer a bundling of different services: anonymized browsing, personal firewalls, antispam filters, encrypted e-mails, methods to remove spyware and traces of browsing behavior ("window-washers"), or an entire package of applications for "personal information management." Second, it is obvious that few companies can survive by just targeting the consumer market; most have been forced to offer a variety of "business solutions" for a secure e-commerce environment, so it is now impossible to distinguish the Internet privacy industry from the Internet security industry. Security is, of course, a necessary condition for the implementation of a privacy protection policy, but it is not sufficient. But the two terms are sometimes elided, in the effort to gain market share in this highly dynamic market. Third, PETs that involve the cooperation of intermediaries, and particularly distributed intermediaries, have been far more difficult to market than those where the software can be downloaded from a single party to reside on the user's own machine.[21] Finally, the development of de facto privacy standards has obviously driven some of the smaller products from the marketplace; when Microsoft decided that it would incorporate the P3P software into its more recent browsers (Internet Explorer 6.0), this decision virtually forced many e-businesses to become P3P-compliant.[22]

A calculation about the strength of the privacy market is difficult in another sense. The existence of a product on a website does not indicate an active consumer base. Once the initial start-up costs (such as software development) have been overcome, some could conceivably coast because operating and labor costs are low, and a small amount of revenue would be forthcoming from advertising. In this regard, it is worth noting that all but two of the websites listed in the 2001 OECD survey, cited above, were still active in 2005. Moreover, the alluring world of the computer laboratory in which new PETs are developed has not been that conducive to the less glamorous market research that is needed to identify real-life problems that users need to solve. While much attention has been devoted to the "user-interface," less work has been conducted on the needs and behavior of ordinary individuals, and on the amount of inconvenience that they will tolerate in order to protect their privacy while online.[23]

Many of the examples cited in this chapter are North American in origin. But we should also note a Dutch-led initiative, funded by the European Commission's Fifth Framework Program of research on information society technologies, and with technical and governmental partners in several other countries, to develop a "Privacy Incorporated Software Agent" (PISA).[24] In PISA, government, users, service providers, research institutes, and universities have cooperated to specify, validate, and promote an open and secure solution for the security of privacy in e-commerce. PISA provides a filter, termed the "identity protector," which prevents the collection of personal data without the user's knowledge or consent, as well as preventing the disclosure of data unless required to do so in the context of a specific transaction or task. The user's identity can be converted into a pseudo-identity, as the "real" identity is not necessary in many transactional circumstances. PISA's proposers see it as working "contrary to systems like P3P where an asymmetric situation exists to the benefit of the web site owner?" (Borking 2001, p. 4). PISA is being developed as a better technology-based intermediary instrument, which, in its first pilot projects, aims to protect privacy in the context of matching supply and demand in labor markets, and bringing together buyers and sellers of vehicles and real estate. Privacy protection is thus provided by a PET instrument in which the specifications are informed by legal requirements for privacy (such as the EU Data Protection Directive), rather than consumer preferences alone.

Conclusion: Technological Instruments and the Roles for Government

Different technologies for privacy enhancement will come and go as the Internet and other technologies mature. Our concluding discussion focuses on the different roles that privacy-enhancing technologies have so far assumed. Government agents, including privacy commissioners, consider these various instruments in a number of different lights.

The first, and most, general role is for PETs to be regarded as a useful complement to existing regulatory and self-regulatory approaches. This is certainly one of the justifications of the PISA project. Similarly, the 2001 OECD report on PETs concluded that "an examination of the characteristics of these tools and an assessment of their limitations confirms that they can be of value in helping users to protect their privacy, but also that they are necessarily complementary to other tools (educational, contractual, regulatory, etc.)" (OECD 2001, p. 6). In the same vein, the OECD also concludes that "PETs should be seen, . . . by both governments and consumers, as a secondary tool for privacy protection. Consumer engagement—namely checking privacy policies and establishing one's own privacy preferences—are crucial elements without which PETs are largely ineffective. In addition to national law . . . and proactive consumers, PETs can be beneficial" (OECD 2002b, p. 25).

There are several strategies that governmental organizations can pursue to encourage the development of PETs. They might sponsor research as, for example, the EU's Fifth Framework Program of research and development has done in the case of PISA. They might also use their purchasing power to encourage some applications over others, or to mandate that PETs be built into the information systems they procure and to specify the details of their use, as the following Ontario example illustrates. As the OECD (2002b, p. 26) argues, governments can also protect encryption-using persons against civil or criminal investigations where they might be suspected of "hiding something." They can also shape legislation to encourage the use of PETs, and be sympathetic to websites that use PETs or make them available to customers.

The complementarity of PETs to other approaches is illustrated in the policy debates of the late 1990s and later, in which PETs have been regarded as a necessary, but not sufficient, condition for effective privacy protection in the digital economy. PETs are thus regarded as just one tool in a toolbox that also contains legislation, codes of practice, and public education. The Canadian Government's privacy protection policy is heavily influenced by this "toolbox" approach (Industry Canada

1998, p. 13). Article 13 of the new Dutch data protection legislation of 2000 (Wet Bescherming Persoongegevens/WBP) also contains language about PETs, alongside "organizational measures."

The person responsible shall ensure suitable technical and organizational measures to protect personal data against loss or any form of unlawful processing. Taking into account the technical status and enforcement expenses, these measures shall guarantee suitable protection given the risks that accompany the processing and the nature of the data to be protected. The measures should also avoid unnecessary collection and the further processing of personal data.[25]

A second role for PETs is as a condition or standard for service delivery. Hypothetically, the application of a sufficient level of encryption could be incorporated, by law or regulation, into the provision of a particular service or product. Privacy-protecting configurations of smart cards and of the specific way in which they are to be used for access to services might serve as an illustration of this approach. A different example of this role is found in Ontario, where the Office of the Information and Privacy Commissioner succeeded in obtaining a very high level of encryption when it became clear that the city of Toronto was considering the introduction of a biometric measure in its efforts to control welfare fraud.[26] As a starting point, the Commissioner developed a list of procedural and technical safeguards that she believed should be present when biometric technology is used. Further, the Commissioner's office recommended that these safeguards be enshrined in legislation.

The Ontario government then passed a Social Assistance Reform Act in 1997 which embodied a number of provisions about the level of encryption of the biometric, and the procedures for destruction and storage of both the original and the encrypted biometric. Typical data protection regulations of access by third parties (such as law enforcement) to individually identifiable information are therefore rendered redundant as a result of the technical specifications included in the Act. The claimed ingenuity of this solution is described as follows:

Neither the director nor an administrator shall implement a system that can reconstruct or retain the original biometric sample from encrypted biometric information, or that can compare it to a copy or reproduction of biometric information not obtained directly from the individual. Therefore, the biometric technology selected must not be capable of either reconstructing or recreating an original biometric pattern from the encrypted biometric nor having it matched to a copy or reproduction of a biometric not obtained directly from the individual (that is, a latent fingerprint taken from a crime scene). As a result, the database containing the encrypted biometrics of welfare recipients would be of little interest to the police. However, should they or any other third party want to access the biometric information, they only could do so through the production of a court order or a warrant. Otherwise, they would not be permitted access to the data.[27]

Third, as privacy-enhancing technologies have proliferated, they have sometimes been encouraged as an alternative, rather than a complement, to legislation. In the United States, where no national and comprehensive data protection legislation exists, the promise of these instruments has been held out as a possible way to avoid what is often regarded as more onerous alternatives. In 2000, the Senate Judiciary Committee presented an overview of the many privacy-enhancing tools available, particularly those that could assist consumers to protect their privacy online. In the preface to the report, the Chairman, Senator Orrin Hatch, remarked:

It is my hope that with greater awareness of how their personal information can be collected online and used, along with an understanding of the resources and technological tools available to them, consumers will be empowered to protect the privacy of their personal information in accordance with their individual needs. I also hope that once informed about this issue, consumers can begin to demand the level of privacy protection they desire from Internet businesses. This would enable the marketplace, rather than burdensome government regulation to address privacy concerns. (US Senate Committee on Judiciary 2000, p. 2)

Some privacy advocates have been very sensitive to the ways that advocacy for privacy-enhancing technologies can turn into opposition to other instruments. In the context of the debate about the P3P technology, Jason Catlett of "Junkbusters" has contended that the program should in fact be disbanded, partly because

it has come to be used by some as an excuse to delay the progress of genuine enforceable privacy rights in the US. . . . But there is currently a widespread expectation that P3P will before long solve the privacy problem that makes Jane Doe of Main St. hesitate to buy online from a major US cataloger. I don't believe it will; on the contrary I believe that the solution to that problem lies elsewhere and is being delayed by the unrealistic expectations that have accreted around the P3P project. Unjustly, it has been marketers and lobbyists, not the P3P researchers, who have portrayed P3P as the golden pot of consumer privacy just waiting at the end of the technology rainbow.[28]

In response, proponents of P3P and others have reiterated the argument about complementarity, pointing out that this tool was never intended to replace other instruments and should not be "trotted out as a reason to discourage regulatory or self-regulatory efforts to protect privacy" (Center for Democracy and Technology 2000). One of the German data protection officials remarks that "technology is however no panacea for privacy risks in cyberspace; it cannot replace a regulatory framework or legislation, contracts or codes of conduct. Rather it may only operate within such a framework. Privacy by negotiation is therefore no alternative to regulation but a necessary additional tool" (Dix 2000). We discuss in the next chapter whether the "toolbox" metaphor is, in fact, adequate to describe the desired relationship between technological and other instruments.

We should conclude by noting the attempts by governments to restrict the development of privacy-enhancing technologies, and strong encryption techniques in particular. In this regard, some privacy-enhancing technologies in the public's hands might be regarded as a threat to the state. This issue was hotly debated and contested in the 1990s in many countries and in policy-making organizations like the OECD. Civil libertarians often found themselves aligned, to some extent, with business-sector developers of electronic commerce, as for instance in the UK during the legislative passage of the Electronic Communications Act 2000, mentioned earlier. They shared a hostility to restrictions on the availability of strong cryptography, given the importance of the latter in protecting the confidentiality of communications, which in turn was seen as a prerequisite to public confidence and trust in online transactions, both business-to-business and state-to-citizen. Various strategies have been used by US law enforcement and security agencies to restrict the availability of free encryption (Diffie and Landau 1998, Levy 2001). These strategies range from mandatory key-escrow programs, to export restrictions. The level and extent of control over cryptographic products varies internationally. The OECD Guidelines on cryptography, discussed in chapter 4, have been developed to attempt to add a measure of international harmonization.

Conclusions about the role for privacy-enhancing technologies as policy instruments are probably elusive at the moment. The wide variety of applications available, and the variable quality of those applications, will continue to militate against neat generalizations concerning impact. Governments will continue, however, to play a range of roles along a continuum from restriction to promotion. They will fund research, legislate frameworks for their use and recognition, and influence the market place through procurement and design decisions.

Having completed the inventory, it is now time to attempt a more general synthesis and comparison. In chapter 8, we ask the question, what goals do each of these various regulatory, self-regulatory, and technological instruments strive to attain? How do they, and can they, operate in conjunction with one another to address privacy-related problems?

III

Policy Impacts

8

Privacy Regimes

Introduction

The discussion in the previous four chapters can be seen as an examination, in outline, of the main individual instruments of data protection that are current in contemporary practice, and in legal and technological discourse. But much more can be said about them, especially if they are seen as components of *regimes* of privacy protection, as we argue they should be. For one thing, comparisons can be drawn among them as components, according to several criteria. For another, they can be analyzed in terms of their *interaction*. Only in these ways can we properly evaluate the effectiveness of data protection regimes, which is the subject of chapter 9, and speculate about the likely future of these regimes, which we undertake in chapter 10.

A conventional wisdom emerged in the 1990s that data protection required something more than a monotechnic, one-size-fits-all solution, especially if the key instrument in that approach were legislation. To put it in terms used by Kooiman (1993) in his general approach to governance, the complexity, dynamics, and diversity of the processing of personal data entailed a migration to new relationships between state regulation and societal forms of privacy protection.[1] According to this new consensual view, good privacy protection involves the application of several instruments, considered as a "privacy toolbox," a "mosaic of solutions," or a "regulatory mix." An example is Industry Canada's policy paper concerning the Canadian Information Highway, which said that "[p]ossible approaches" for protecting the privacy of Canadians "include legislation, the advancement of a national voluntary privacy standard, the promotion of privacy protective technologies such as encryption and smart cards, and consumer education" (Industry Canada 1994, p. 15). This was a relatively early enunciation of the "polytechnic" approach, and its further significance lay in the fact that the Internet environment was the context for the envisaged flexible strategy. However, beyond the description of each of these types of instruments and questions about where the balance of responsibilities should lie as between government and the individual, the paper gave no further analysis of how these approaches would aggregate to a comprehensive regime. As in many other discussions, it was left unclear whether the various solutions were alternatives to each other, or compatible ingredients of something more comprehensive.

Other sources (for example, 6 and Briscoe 1996, Swire 1997) have gone further than this in discussing various privacy solutions. But there still remained a tendency in the literature, and in policy discourse, to consider each policy instrument as a supplement, complement, or substitute for others, without investigating their relationships in any depth. For some time, however, it has been apparent that each country's system of data protection relies on a more integrated combination of different instruments. Bennett (1992) made an analytical distinction among these: licensing data users, registering their holdings, establishing a data commissioner, voluntary control through self-regulation by organizations that use personal data, and subject control or individual self-help. Yet these distinctions have always been blurred in practice, as many regimes employ several tools together. One effect of the EU Directive has been to establish a common set of criteria for the powers of a "supervisory authority" to produce an even greater blending of instruments in each country (Bennett 1997a). Perhaps the ultimate recognition of this pluralism has emerged in the Australian regime, where the practical discourse on privacy protection for the private sector has centred on a "coregulatory" approach, promoted by the Attorney-General's Department. This involves a legislative context for flexible industry codes of practice, developed in conjunction with the Privacy Commissioner.[2]

These academic and practical approaches have thus moved a bit nearer to comprehending mutually supportive relationships between instruments and between those who wield them. Reidenberg (1997) came closer still to an understanding of holistic privacy regimes by identifying specific *interactions* among state, business, technical, and citizen mechanisms for regulating privacy, both online and offline. Raab's (1997a) attempt to give a fuller exposition of how privacy strategies relate to, and mutually affect, each other within an implementation system moved the analysis on but remained underdeveloped. Referring to the welter of approaches and instruments, Bennett and Grant (1999, pp. 7–8) stated the issue thus:

> The . . . approaches are not mutually exclusive, even though the existing literature generally treats them as if they were. There is a certain amount of rhetoric about the need for a "mosaic of solutions." On the other hand, there has yet to be a serious treatment of how these approaches relate to one another and of the extent to which incompatibilities of interests and resources might turn the mosaic into a confusing and irreconcilable set of strategies.

Chapter 7 concluded by pointing out government's roles in relation to technological instruments. This chapter takes a further step by more systematically discussing the relationships that do, or could, exist among all the parts of a privacy protection regime.

Misleading Metaphors?

"Toolbox," "mix," and "mosaic" are suggestive metaphors for combined approaches to data protection. Each has a somewhat different implication, but they are misleading. In a toolbox, each instrument is suited to a different purpose and has a specific use. But most of the tools are used separately, not in conjunction with each other, and there is no overall single purpose for their use. Throw away the screwdriver, the drill, and the saw, yet the hammer remains, still capable of doing its job and driving the nail home. But it cannot do what the other tools can do, and its efficacy as a nail-driver may depend, in part, on factors to do with the person who wields it. Among these is the ability to recognize what is a nail, and what is not.

Cavoukian and Tapscott (1995, p. 180) argue for the need for a "mosaic of solutions." The tiles in a mosaic, similarly, stand alone, although they all contribute to a total effect. Each has its place in the picture, adding its specific color and shape. But the tiles do not affect one another, except in the subtle sense that the juxtaposition of different colors affects color perception. Yet without all the tiles, the picture is incomplete. It is debatable how many tiles are necessary to make a picture, and with what quality of result. The idea of a "mix" better approximates what happens in many situations where individual instruments combine to produce a result that would be substantially different, or even impossible, without the combination: a whole that is greater than the sum of its parts. But the conventional use of this metaphor in the data protection context has been as a synonym for "inventory," "roster," or "repertory," or sometimes similar to a cake recipe. How the instruments, or ingredients, actually mix or combine is obscure; what kinds of combination are best, which one must be added before another one can be added, and whether the "mix" can be designed from the start as a comprehensive privacy protection regime, are questions that are rarely asked.

However, we can observe, in practice, that true combinations of privacy protection instruments do occur, and that their combination is more than incidental to their effective operation. To varying degrees, these instruments are *interdependent*. The users of these instruments often know this, and sometimes emphasize it. Privacy commissioners, for example, acknowledge the importance to their own work of a public that is educated about data protection. Privacy advocates want laws to provide sanctions against those who breach self-regulatory codes. Resisting laws, self-regulating organizations may think that the market will work effectively, alongside codes or commitments, to help give people the privacy they want. We will take up further illustrations later in the chapter.

These observations suggest that attempts to design a regime should be alert to synergy, but also to conflict, in talking about coregulation or "co-production" (Raab 1997a), involving broader and multiple relations within and across jurisdictions, organizations, and instruments. For this approach, there is also both analytical and prescriptive value in acknowledging the relevance of more actors than those who appeared prominently in previous chapters. They include consumer organizations, the media, academics, and data subjects; Bennett and Grant (1999,

p. 7) note the trend toward "a greater role for social movements and privacy advocacy" in the emerging armory of privacy protection. To prepare the ground for understanding privacy regimes in this holistic sense, we must first outline some common criteria against which to consider each of the policy instruments, and then revisit the latter to describe, compare, and appraise their salient characteristics in terms of these categories.

Instruments of Privacy Protection: Points of Comparison

We identify four criteria for investigating the common aspects and differences among the main types of instruments. For each of the latter, these are: its *scope of application*, its *enforceability*, the *accountability* of its users, and the nature of the *policy community* that relates to it.[3] A systematic interrogation of the instruments in terms of the four factors is likely to give sufficient insights into the way they work, their advantages, and their limitations.

The Scope of Application

Each policy instrument applies to a range of situations or arenas in which personal data are implicated. Among the types of instruments discussed earlier, we can distinguish among transnational, national, public or private sectoral, industrial-sectoral, and organizational arenas to which they apply. At the broadest, transnational instruments could apply, by definition, globally, although currently there is no such instrument. They may encompass both automated and nonautomated forms of data processing, and both the public and private sectors are conventionally defined. The Council of Europe Convention is, however, restricted to automated processing in the countries that are its members, although the OECD Guidelines and the European Union Directive—for their respective member countries—cover all forms. Although the latter two are geographically restricted in one sense, their external influence is great. For example, the Directive applies only to EU Member States, but its effect has been powerfully felt much further afield, as evidenced by the Safe Harbor episode, by the Directive's influence on policy in

Australia and Canada, and by the orientation of the data protection policies of prospective new EU Member States.

National laws apply to data processing where the data controller is established within the jurisdiction in question, although the impact of these laws may be felt abroad where the actual activities are contracted out to foreign processors under the instructions of the controller. However, whereas some national laws cover both the public and private sectors, some only affect the public sector, although the current trend for most countries is to encompass both. Within these broad sectors, some laws are more specific in their scope, dealing with, for example, census or health records on the public side, or with particular industries—financial instruments or video rentals—on the private side. Some of the specific laws focus on particular processes or practices, such as data-matching or subject access, whereas others cover the wider range of activities engaged in by the actors within that sector. Laws may also vary in the extent that they exempt certain kinds of data from some or all of the rules, or impose specific rules for these data—for example, sensitive personal data or data that relate to policing or national security.[4]

Self-regulation through commitments, codes, standards, and seals is typically restricted to the processing of data by organizations within the private sector. There has been something of an evolutionary widening of institutional and territorial scope with regard to self-regulatory instruments. They may also apply to technologies, functions, or activities that cut across institutional sectors; video surveillance and Internet transactions are examples. More rarely, self-regulatory instruments may also appear across very large swathes of the public sector, for example in health care and policing. The framing, in 2001, of a proposed "e-Trust Charter" for electronic service delivery covering all of UK central government illustrates this.[5] Such instruments play a rather different self-regulatory function, however, when an overarching legislative framework is already in place. They serve to clarify and elaborate the legislative rules, and to apply them to specific contexts.

Finally, whereas transnational, national, sectoral, and organizational instruments are defined by a particular arena of application, technological instruments span all four and are not institutionally or geographically specific. Yet some distinctions can be drawn in terms of their scope. As P3P illustrates, technological privacy instruments may relate only to online activities, but some others may cover broader areas of daily life. Thus smart cards and biometric devices can be incorporated into a variety of transactions between citizens and public or private organizations, where goods and services are provided. Through the anonymity that they could provide, technological devices may also be used to limit the amount of personal data that are captured when people move through space or between places. Some tools may be confined to particular aims, such as data security, or they may be more deeply "designed in" to afford a wider protective cover through cryptography, for example. But cost considerations and the way in which technological instruments are configured may limit them to a narrower range of privacy principles, perhaps ignoring issues of subject access, data relevance, and accuracy, or the period of data retention.

In summary, the scope of data protection instruments has become progressively less determinate. Traditional legal instruments embody an understanding of sovereignty and jurisdiction, and it is at least relatively clear to whom they are designed to apply. The scope of application of self-regulatory and technological instruments is determined not by any preconceived conception of legal sovereignty but by the myriad and unpredictable choices of data controllers and data subjects the world over.

Enforceability

We argued in chapter 6 that voluntary instruments of self-regulation do not suggest freedom from compulsion, for an intricate and fluctuating range of incentives and sanctions are in play along a continuum, thus blurring the boundary between legal regulation and self-regulation. To an extent, this is also true even of international instruments that have an aura of legal prescription, or even the quality of binding rules. Some of these create obligations for countries: a Member State of the EU has no choice but to implement the Directive in its own laws, although there are variations in how they do this, and the deadline for transposition was breached by some countries. The mechanism for other instruments is different: the Convention requires signature and ratification but became binding on all countries within the Council of Europe when five countries ratified it, whereas there is no legal mechanism to enforce the OECD Guidelines.

Of course, the reality is that pressures to comply or else to suffer potential economic consequences may be very considerable even in the absence of legal prescription. But whereas the Convention and the Directive apply directly only to countries, it is open to any data controller to follow the Guidelines, perhaps reproducing them in a self-regulatory instrument. More generally, the Guidelines have served as a basis for the formulation of codes of practice and standards for firms and industries and within national jurisdictions, as in the CSA Model Code or Japan's MITI Guidelines.

The enforceability of laws varies with the powers given to the regulatory agency to enforce them, and with the way these are used. An agency may only have very limited powers to enter the premises of a data controller and inspect its processes and equipment. As in the UK, tribunal proceedings and court cases for adjudicating disputes and handling prosecutions are expensive and infrequent, although the prospect of legal proceedings may be a strong inducement for data controllers to comply with the law. A distinction can be drawn between a "deterrence" approach to regulation, which employs prosecutions and penal sanctions in order to prevent future breaches of the law, and a less adversarial "compliance" style (Baldwin and Cave 1999, p. 97). Even where their powers are considerable, privacy commissioners and the like are constrained in their enforcement work not only by the normal administrative problems of limited financial and staff resources, and by lack of time, but by knowledge or intelligence about what is going on in the world of the regulated. A mandatory registration system for data controllers may fall far short of gaining the compliance of all who should register—small and medium-sized enterprises are a particular problem here—so that the regulator is deprived of information about whose activities to investigate. Formal enforcement must normally wait upon complaints from the public about particular organizations.

Although these factors also affect compliance work, it is not surprising that regulators frequently resort to the less adversarial and punitive approach, seeking compliance through discussion, persuasion, encouragement of good practice, awareness-raising among data controllers, resolving conflicts amicably, and the like, thus keeping their powder dry. The existence of an enforcement body is no guarantee that laws will be complied with at a high level, but where there is no such independent regulatory body, as in the US federal government under public-sector privacy legislation, enforceability is more spasmodic and weaker still (Gellman 1997).

Privacy commitments are pledges that by themselves are not enforceable, although companies might abide by them for fear of bad publicity and loss of consumer confidence. Codes of practice, like laws, also vary in their enforceability: firms that are members of an industry association may be required to implement its code or else face possible financial penalties, loss of reputation, or expulsion. Yet, as they are not required to belong to the association, their compliance is closer to the voluntary end of the scale. Thus, sanctions apart, self-regulating organizations may realize that there are beneficial incentives to comply: improved public trust, competitive advantage, and the other market-related factors canvassed in chapter 6. Other codes may be of a more compulsory nature, and may even have a legal framework. For example, the Canadian Model Code is incorporated into the terms of PIPEDA 2000, and in varying ways Dutch, Irish, British, Japanese, and New Zealand codes come within the purview of the law and of the activities of regulatory agencies. Self-certification to the US–EU Safe Harbor Agreement, as we saw, occurs under the aegis of administrative enforcement by the United States's FTC, thus concentrating attention on the extent to which that body is willing or able to take action.

The enforceability of technological instruments has its own share of problems. In a sense, systemic and state-mandated technological instruments are self-enforcing once they form part of information and communications technologies (ICTs) that are put into practice. But prior to that, they may either be mandated as part of the procurement specifications for systems of ICT, or else left as optional devices to be grafted onto existing systems. Then, too, they may be relatively weak or relatively strong; for example, the number of "bits" in encryption may be greater or smaller, and the maximal number may be controlled by law. The third category, instruments of individual empowerment are by their nature less enforceable, as they are dependent for their effectiveness on the choices of data users whose technical competence varies enormously.

The enforceability of each policy instrument operates in complex and contingent ways, such that it is impossible to draw a unidimensional continuum from weak to strong enforcement and to place each of the instruments at some specified and stable point. It is commonplace to assume that law carries the highest level of compulsion, in the sense that data controllers have no formal choice but to comply, and in the sense that there are clear penalties for noncompliance. But, as a large body of literature on policy implementation has demonstrated (for example, Pressman and Wildavsky 1973), there are many obstacles between legal fiat and practical effect. In this sense, it is conceivable that some self-regulatory and technological instruments, being in closer proximity to the organizational practices that require modification, embody higher levels of effective compulsion. Proponents of self-regulation, in fact, often point to this factor as a major advantage, in principle; skeptics look more deeply for actual evidence of effectiveness where self-regulation is in place.

A further important distinction should also be kept in mind. For some of these instruments, there is a difference between adoption and implementation. The adoption of some instruments, such as commitments and codes of practice, may be quite voluntary in a legal sense. Moreover, the implementation of such instruments may also largely be voluntary, in the sense that no legal or regulatory body can force an organization to abide by its own rules, in the absence of law. But there is also a growing range of instruments—standards and the Safe Harbor Principles are examples—of which the adoption is still voluntary; there may be market and consumer pressures, but no legal sanction attends refusal to "sign up." Yet such instruments, once adopted, do carry a higher level of compulsion for implementation; under Safe Harbor, for instance, regulatory action can be taken by the FTC. It is also plausible that, because of the quite focused and self-selecting nature of this process, the behavior of the firms that have adopted Safe Harbor is likely to come under closer scrutiny than it would under a comprehensive legal regime. Figure 8.1 attempts to depict these relationships.

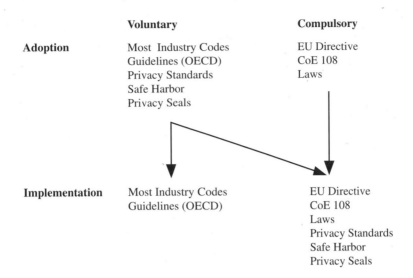

	Voluntary	**Compulsory**
Adoption	Most Industry Codes Guidelines (OECD) Privacy Standards Safe Harbor Privacy Seals	EU Directive CoE 108 Laws
Implementation	Most Industry Codes Guidelines (OECD)	EU Directive CoE 108 Laws Privacy Standards Safe Harbor Privacy Seals

Figure 8.1
An enforceability framework

Accountability

Although related to the issue of enforceability, we also need to address the question of accountability. If an instrument is adopted, who is accountable for its success or failure, how, and to whom? There is a continuum of interested parties to whom data controllers and even countries may be accountable, ranging from international bodies to national government and its machinery, to the public at large within a country, and to the individual consumer of a product or a service. Moreover, these are not mutually exclusive. Under international instruments, governments may be accountable to the bodies that promulgate them. Data controllers are only indirectly accountable for their compliance with these instruments insofar as the latter are incorporated into domestic legislation. These laws and their implementation mechanisms may make public-sector data controllers accountable both within the bureaucracy and to regulators for adherence to the rules. Those who are bound by laws covering the private sector are answerable to the regulator for compliance, and ultimately perhaps to the courts.

Self-regulators who make privacy commitments are seemingly answerable only to their customers in the marketplace, whereas subscribers to codes of practice or standards are accountable to their industry associations as well; through audit procedures, there may be a wider public accountability. Where privacy marks or seals play a role in self-regulation, the data controllers are open to monitoring and accountability procedures applied by the program or scheme organization. We have seen how the Japanese PPM scheme has developed an elaborate accountability system within a coregulatory arrangement that gives oversight roles to the state and to trade associations. Finally, in an online environment, those who use privacy technologies are involved in marketplace accountability, but if these are coupled with privacy marks, they incur obligations to organizations like TRUSTe and BBBOnline for the proper working of those devices.

The lines of accountability are clearly more defined and hierarchical, the fewer the policy instruments in play. In the early years of data protection policy, before self-regulatory and technological instruments entered the landscape, data controllers were deemed to be accountable to data subjects for the personal information they processed. The law alone established expectations. Regulatory instruments then mediated that relationship through enforcement, advisory, and educational powers.

The entrance of other instruments complicates these lines of accountability. Where data protection policy has been built upon pre-existing self-regulatory instruments, as in Canada, Japan, and Australia, practical tensions exist between those instruments and the new statutory provisions. Other bodies, including trade associations and standards bodies, play a role in the implementation of law, and in an indirect sense are accountable to data subjects. Arguments by data controllers that they have implemented a code of practice may have much persuasive impact in the marketplace. But what legal force do such arguments possess? Moreover, should consumers avail themselves of the complaints procedures offered by private sector organizations before invoking legal rights? Do the official data protection agencies then become an avenue of last resort when other mechanisms have failed?

The advent of PETs can also complicate lines of accountability. Does the fact that a website displays a privacy seal have any bearing on a later investigation of a complaint by the data protection authority? Do complaints by consumers that their e-mails have been hacked carry less force if they do not use encryption? Should consumers expect a lower level of privacy protection simply because they have not, or cannot, manipulate the privacy settings on the latest Internet browsers? Formally the providers of PETs, especially those that rely on a user interface, are only accountable to the users. But where technological instruments have been held up as alternatives to legislation, as in the United States, then in many senses they also bear a responsibility to work effectively as policy instruments. Thus the P3P technology is currently under considerable scrutiny from data protection authorities in many countries.

The "mosaic of solutions" rhetoric, therefore, has not been accompanied by a clear sense of who is accountable to whom, and how, for the operation of the different instruments within the mosaic. In states where the legal tradition of data protection has a long history, self-regulatory and technological instruments are clearly regarded as secondary to law; their role is to assist in the implementation of law and nothing more. In other countries, however, the picture is more complicated. How accountability and legal liability operate in practice is only now being worked out under the newly formed privacy regimes in countries such as Canada, Japan, and Australia.

The Policy Community

The fourth factor is the policy community or participants in the development and application of each of the privacy instruments. International privacy instruments have been the work of international legal experts, administrators, and policy elites in and around the international forums through which the Guidelines, the Convention, the Directive, and other outputs were devised. Let us consider the case of the Directive: the relevant community for its formulation included national data protection regulatory officials who, by the 1990s, had emerged as a significant set of proponents of the cause of privacy protection. But it also included politicians within the institutions of the EU and in Member States. Industrial interest groups also participated prominently: for example, national and European associations of direct marketers, the financial industry, and charitable organizations who all had a stake in designing the rules concerning what would be permitted or proscribed in terms of the phases of data processing. Yet these pressures were not all on the side of business interests: privacy advocates and consumer groups also made their voices heard, not least through parliamentary bodies. Moreover, the European Commission itself maintained a firm hold upon the process and content of the emergent Directive. Its officials had to deal not only with the constellation of pressures within Europe, but with representations originating from national and industrial interests in "third" countries that stood to be affected by the Directive's external implications. The implementation of the Directive has involved EU officials and new constellations of participants in the central machinery created by it under Articles 29 and 31. It also encompasses a wide array of groups and players within the Member States during the transposition into domestic law. This is not unlike the pluralistic set of interests that were involved in the preceding rounds of data protection legislation before the Directive was created, except that, in the earlier periods, there were, of course, no privacy regulatory officials to take part in the process.

The configuration of the policy community for these national and sectoral laws cannot be investigated in all its global variety here, but the categories of "stakeholders" for each are similar. They include politicians, a wide variety of public officials with a stake in the outcome as data controllers, regulators, and a multiplicity of different industry associations and individual firms representing data controllers' interests. They also include legal and academic specialists, associations and firms in the fields of information and communication technologies, groups acting on behalf of consumers or data subjects' interests, privacy advocates, and the media. Not all have been equally influential, but there have been shifting coalitions and sometimes "strange bedfellows" brought together on one side of the debate or another. Data controllers —the "regulated"—have often been particularly active, either in opposition to legislation as a whole, or in terms of shaping specific aspects such as the rules concerning consent for processing ("opt in" or "opt out") or exemptions for certain public sector processing activities (for example, in law enforcement). Although many national laws have been considered to be relatively weak, the fact that they have been brought into the statute book at all, along with regulatory machinery, testifies to the influence of proponents of privacy protection, albeit with a mixture of goals and incentives that were analyzed in Part I.

The policy community for self-regulation includes those operating in specific industries or sectors, sometimes along with regulatory bodies that are involved in coregulatory modes. Other participants may also be present—consumer organizations and certain governmental interests that favor self-regulation rather than legislative approaches. For example, the US Department of Commerce has been an advocate of self-regulation (US Department of Commerce 1997), and was the lead department responsible for carrying on the Safe Harbor negotiations with the European Commission. Government agencies in other countries have acted to monitor the effectiveness of self-regulatory initiatives.

Elsewhere, standards organizations have been heavily involved in developing self-regulation, as in the example described in chapter 6, in which the CSA brought together consumer representatives and government officials along with business organizations in formal processes for this purpose. In Europe, CEN's work towards a privacy standard has also included a similar range of participants. Specialists from the academic world as well as providers of privacy technologies have also been important in standards work. The development of these technologies themselves takes place through a community of technical specialists along with business interests, including Internet service providers, and have also involved regulatory officials who are particularly interested in the promotion of PETs; the Dutch and Ontario contributions (chapter 7) are leading examples. Individual academics and privacy advocates have been influential in promoting and developing technological tools as well as the theoretical rationale for their place in the array of instruments for privacy protection.

Exploring Privacy Policy Communities

The players involved in these policy communities, and their relationships, are depicted in very general and abstract terms in figure 8.2.

There are two ways of looking at this figure. First, it describes players and their interdependence in a *policy and implementation system* or

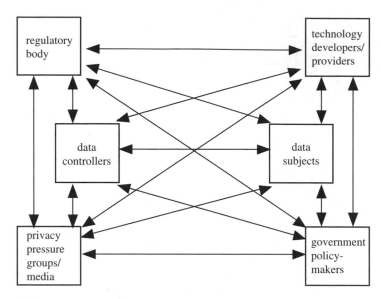

Figure 8.2
Privacy participants and their relationships

network for privacy protection: that is, a system that shapes the quality of privacy as an outcome. In this sense, the arrows represent mutual support, as the participants act in concert to protect privacy by developing and implementing policy instruments. Of course, some links are stronger than others—more support may be evident in some relationships than in others, and the relationships, roles, and strength of ties may change over a period of time. Therefore, the figure could be redrawn to reflect this empirical reality by varying the thickness of the connecting lines, by indicating uneven reciprocities of support, by indicating temporal change, and by relating it to specific cases or issues. The figure could also be redrawn for each tool, showing perhaps fewer participants and a different pattern of connections.

In a second sense, however, the figure depicts not simply a purpose-built mechanism for protection, but a *political system* in which the *distribution of power* determines outcomes—again, different and more nuanced pictures would apply to each instrument, issue, or phase. Moreover, relationships may vary along a continuum between consensus and conflict. Privacy protection must be negotiated through the system described in the figure, and is not necessarily commanded "from the top down," especially as, in the view of some governance and network theories (and as the figure implies) there may be no identifiable "top" except in formal procedural terms. The role of the state or government cannot be overlooked, but the exercise of constitutional authority may not be prevalent in particular situations. In the political system thus portrayed, the attitudes and actions of participants contribute to the outcome as they use resources of various kinds—formal powers, money, technical expertise, publicity, and others—in complex exchanges, influences, compromises, sanctions, and shifting alliances.

In the next subsections, we give a brief commentary on these issues along with some examples of functions and interactions for every category of participant; the discussion of each naturally includes some comment on other types of participants involved in relationships. This discussion allows us to bring together and recapitulate some of the material from previous chapters in order to illustrate the point that a regime is something more than a kit of individual tools.

Government

Government is involved in two ways: it is authoritatively concerned with legislation and can be a crucial player in the formation of other privacy instruments, and it is also a major user of personal data. Thus the "government" box in the figure does not signify a uniform interest, and would be subdivided in a more realistic and disaggregated elaboration of the picture. For example, government encompasses both elected and unelected officials. The former only infrequently take up the question of information privacy and the use of personal data, and typically only when a growing public concern about intrusive practices force closer political attention. Thus workplace surveillance, the use of health and other sensitive personal information beyond the purpose for which it has been collected, and online privacy are among the issues that are growing in public concern, forcing closer political attention in many countries. Thus, government may be more a target for pressure-group activity than an instigator of data protection policy.

Beyond its role in privacy law and policy, government's activities in framing other policies that either embody privacy protection or ignore it are extremely important. Building data protection into policy initiatives such as road-charging, health care administration, identity documents, data sharing, and anticrime campaigns can make a significant difference. On the other hand, these add to the policy conflicts, often across a range of agencies that may see privacy protection as an obstacle rather than an asset. Figure 8.2 does not reflect the fact that government is actually a large collection of agencies and departments with divergent interests and separate policy agendas. Their collaboration for privacy protection may depend upon the leverage exerted by privacy "champions" in the executive on the various parts, given an overall political will to protect privacy. The requirement that policy initiatives be accompanied by privacy impact assessments, for example, might be an exercise of leverage, but this is less likely without the support of outside constituencies of players, perhaps including the regulatory body. Much the same could also be said about the self-regulation of parts of government and the state machine, broadly defined, by means of codes of practice.

On the other hand, government can also resist legislating for privacy protection, and inhibit the issue's trajectory through stages of the policy process. Many parts of government wish to ensure that privacy considerations do not unduly constrain their intensive use and sharing of databases, whether for law-enforcement purposes, better delivery of services, or statistical analyses of administrative data. Such issues give rise to further engagement with other participants and provide occasions for regulators to develop positions and affect others' attitudes. The implicit dilemma posed in recent UK policy efforts to modernize and "join up" government is how to make personal data usage more efficient by rationalizing the delivery of public services while maintaining public confidence in government's use of data.[6] In developments of this nature, trust must be re-engineered alongside the re-engineering of administrative processes, for trust is indispensable to informatized transactions (Raab 1998a, 6 1998). This may require the assistance of other participants, including the privacy regulator, technology developers, the media, consumer groups, and perhaps "trusted third parties" for electronic transactions. How government deploys carrots and sticks to gain this kind of collaboration depends on a host of political and economic factors.

The Regulatory Body

Considering the figure in terms of the privacy *regulatory body* casts light on a great deal of interaction, much of it in terms of the roles discussed in chapter 5. The regulatory organization's independence of government is held to be a crucial resource for its effectiveness. For example, the UK Information Commissioner reports to Parliament and not to a government minister, and is generally regarded as well insulated from direct political interference. In Italy, the *Garante*'s members are elected by Parliament and in turn elect their chairman, an arrangement that is stated to ensure independence from the Government (Italy, Garante, 1997, p. 5). Elsewhere, the requirement of parliamentary ratification of appointments may result in a failure to continue an existing regulator in office, as occurred in Hungary in 2001.

In other countries, the regulators have closer ties with government. In Germany, the federal Data Protection Commissioner is selected by the government and is subject to the supervision of the minister of the Interior, who provides the personnel and resources of his office (Flaherty 1989, p. 40). In France, the nominal independence of the CNIL is circumscribed by the stipulation that one of the commissioners shall be appointed by the Prime Minister. Moreover, the CNIL is embedded within a highly politicized administrative culture that makes it extremely difficult to operate with true independence (Flaherty 1989, p. 184). In Canada, although the Privacy Commissioner is an independent officer of the legislature and needs to be ratified by the House of Commons, the candidate selected by the Prime Minister's office has never been refused. The independence of privacy and data protection regulators is therefore a complex variable that is affected as much by processes of appointment and financing as by the formal lines of authority stipulated in law.

Regulators' powers and duties notwithstanding, the enforcement of the law against violators may only be an infrequent occurrence as a last resort when "compliance" modes of regulation fail. Both enforcement and compliance-seeking exhibit a combination of power and opportunity, and in some cases opportunities can be created; more will be said about this later. Whatever the strength of their formal powers, regulators must know what is going on among the regulated; they need good "tools for detection" (Hood 1983). But this is difficult as information systems and applications of technology become more diverse and sophisticated, thus severely challenging the "intelligence capability" of regulators, and revealing the depth of their dependence on others. Their own detection resources are typically relatively slender, so they need the cooperation and compliance of data controllers, and of pressure groups, the media, and the public as "whistle-blowers" and complainants about specific data controllers. More generally, regulatory officials take the frequency and content of complaints as an indicator of practices that need closer scrutiny.

In a global online environment, intelligence and the power to act upon it are particularly problematic. This suggests that figure 8.2 should be extended from a single-country focus to an international one, to encompass a larger policy community. This would take account of the increasing frequency of contacts among, and interdependence of, regulators for intelligence-sharing, policy concertation, and practical mutual assistance. In fact, the Directive as well as national laws in the EU empower or require regulatory authorities to assist each other, to share information, and to work together, thus reinforcing a transnational approach to policy formulation and implementation.

Where data controllers are required to register or notify the regulator of their activities, the details of the reporting requirements are a negotiated outcome, devised through interactions among the regulator, government, data controllers, and others. For compliance beyond this, regulators must encourage, enable, and exhort, and not simply impose penalties. Promoting good practice, they must convey an understanding of the key elements of data protection as they affect controllers. Education and publicity are important, as they are in the regulators' relationship with data subjects. Where budgets allow little scope for these campaigns, a premium is placed on ingenuity in amplifying messages. This may make the regulator dependent upon influential media channels, pressure groups, consultancy firms, and others who can fulfill their own interests while serving the regulator's as well.

Because many government policies have privacy implications, regulators seek to influence policy at an early stage. Law and order, public services, telecommunications, and high-tech industries are among the most prominent policy areas attracting the intervention of regulators, and in which they therefore engage in policy networks at high levels of government and industry. "Electronic government" agendas in many countries provide examples of interactions between regulators and government agencies that are developing systems in which the safeguarding of privacy in transactions between individuals and the state is considered important. These policy roles may indicate a proactive rather than a reactive philosophy of regulation. The laws establishing regulatory bodies, and international legal instruments like the Directive, may be permissive to the extent of allowing such an expansive view of the role. Some proactivity is envisaged in the 1999 Italian Data Protection Act's specification of the *Garante*'s duty of "informing the Government of the need for introducing legislative measures as required by ... developments" (Article 31(1)(m)). In any event, regulators in many countries seek some policy influence, and public expectation may endorse this.

Regulatory bodies need sufficient resources, including expertise— whether in-house or "on tap"—to keep abreast of technical developments and to influence them, and to shape thinking in business and government about potentially privacy-invasive practices. Partly traced by figure 8.2, but certainly in its external context, are factors that affect the degree of influence wielded by regulators. Among these is the availability of public issues that provide opportunities for creativity in raising the profile of privacy concerns in public arenas. The political and regulatory culture, the available resources, and the regulatory body's "style" all shape the extent to which supervisory authorities create opportunities, merely respond to issues, or ignore them. In the UK, for example, identity cards have been among the prominent issues that have provided opportunities. Media and parliamentary attention, as well as debate between civil libertarians and proponents of identity cards, are important in such issues, and illustrate the participation of wider groups in the system.

Data Controllers

Data controllers, including business firms, trade organizations that represent them, and public-sector organizations that process personal data, are among those who are affected by government legislation and the regulatory body. The regulatory system is predicated on the adversarial assumption that data controllers' interests cut across those of data subjects, and that their activities must be controlled. Data controllers and their organizations in certain industries seek to minimize the effects of data protection rules and policies, and have lobbied hard against legislative proposals, as for example with regard to the EU Directive, and in the United States, Australia, and Canada with regard to private-sector privacy legislation.

Data controllers may seek to gain a reputation for good privacy practice in some competitive industries, such as banking, in which security and confidentiality are important and marketable qualities, although the evidence is not strong that proclaiming one's "good privacy housekeeping" has become normal business practice. This is becoming a prominent motivation in the online environment, which is difficult to regulate by law, and where controls are more likely to be self-regulatory through the international adoption of common codes and standards (Gellman 1997). The role of national and international privacy regimes in assisting, or requiring, industry to develop policy instruments for regulating transborder flows of personal data further illustrates the modalities of the relationship between data controllers and others.

Controllers interact frequently with regulatory officials and are consulted over many issues. Actual instances of this relationship range between the adversarial and the accommodating. Whether because of its limited powers and resources, style, or regulatory culture, a regulatory body's desire to resolve issues amicably and to reach mutually helpful solutions with data controllers may invite a more subtle understanding of the efficacy of its performance in achieving better data protection. Privacy advocates and civil liberties groups, for example, are often suspicious of agreements and settlements made between the regulators and the regulated. Regulators, on the other hand, rely on the doctrine of "balance" to describe their aims and role-requirements.

Industry associations are central to the development of codes of practice, but they do this in contact with regulators and other participants. As we have seen, these have been important instruments in a number of countries lacking comprehensive data protection laws, but even where such laws exist, voluntary self-regulation is an alternative preferred by many business sectors and other players, despite the lack of clear evidence that self-regulation works. The EU Directive (Article 27) encourages sectoral codes of practice ("conduct") to help implement national laws, and this provision is transposed into laws in Member States. In the UK, the regulator may take the initiative to consult and then promulgate a code, and must also give an opinion, when asked by a trade association, on whether its draft code promotes good practice; the representatives of data subjects may also be consulted. The Italian law includes a similar provision. In one sense, these arrangements may only indicate that legislators have recognized the futility of legal regulation on its own. On the other hand, an increased emphasis on codes of practice is consistent with political desires to deregulate industry.

Part of these interactions between regulators and data controllers over voluntary codes is the implicit neocorporatist expectation that trade bodies will enjoin compliance upon their members in exchange for the association's privileged place in the policy process, and as the price of keeping regulators at bay.[7] But the internal affairs of these self-regulating sectors are likely to be of interest to regulators, who may have to increase their knowledge concerning the extent to which codes are actually adhered to, and are not just symbolic statements.

Interaction among three participants is illustrated where, as envisaged in the new UK legislation, the supervisory authority issues a sectoral code, perhaps at the behest of a minister. Interactions between privacy advocates or consumers' associations and data controllers are likely to be antagonistic, given these groups' wariness of controllers' professed concern to protect privacy. Finally, technology developers have an interest in getting data controllers to adopt technological instruments for data protection, whether in conjunction with voluntary codes or not; devices that comply with security standards are an illustration.

Data Subjects

To the extent that data controllers' commitments and codes give some form of guarantee to data subjects, the latter are brought into a direct relationship with the former. The issue here is *trust*: the data controller's accountability is offered in exchange for the data subject's consent to transactions involving personal data. Consent as well as the transparency of processing are key principles that may pervade exchanges between data subjects and others in promoting privacy protection. Data subjects may therefore play multiple roles in the protection of their personal data, entering into a variety of relationships depending upon the prevailing philosophy and approach to data protection. Proponents of more libertarian positions argue that market incentives should be constructed to allow individuals to negotiate the privacy they desire. This, however, is scarcely possible in public-sector transactions, for individuals are obliged to part with their information by law or in order to receive their entitlements as citizens to social benefits, health care, licenses, passports, and the like. However, there is increasing talk of allowing individuals greater choice and control over the data involved in smart cards used for public-sector transactions.

Yet in commercial transactions, and even where the state is involved, individuals themselves can develop greater sensitivity to potential privacy risks and become "intelligent customers," clients or consumers, aware of their rights and how to implement them. As the "coproduction" interpretation of figure 8.2 suggests, this might require help from other participants: government itself, regulators, data controllers, technologists, consumer groups, and the media. Knowledgeable individuals who demand and expect privacy in transactions are less likely to exchange it for questionable benefits. Collectively, they can influence policy; there are rare but nonetheless instructive examples of this, especially where opinion is mobilized by pressure groups (Davies 1999). But generally, consumer or citizen awareness, education, and empowerment are poorly developed, although surveys show that there are signs of growing anxiety over the nontransparent, nonconsented data processing.

It is difficult to achieve improved public education, and this is a low priority for some participants. Given the resources, regulators play an important role here, if it is part of their mission or mandate. In order to encourage trust, enlightened, self-interested data controllers could also do this. However, few of them have come to see it as in their interest, although the posting of privacy policies on websites can have an effect on education and awareness. A coproduced contribution to data protection is made by individual data subjects when they seek redress from controllers or complain to the regulatory authority. Complaints, singly or aggregated, are useful as a "detection tool," helping the regulator to enforce the law, to monitor data controllers, and to become alerted to sectors or practices that need closer supervision. The regulatory agency can also use them to indicate something of the efficacy of their own regulatory, enforcement, and educational work.

In certain philosophies of privacy protection, it is the framework of laws, as promulgated by government and implemented by regulators, that has the most powerful effect in protecting individuals and in enabling individuals to protect themselves. The protection that laws afford are manifestations of the interplay of individuals' rights and obligations, bringing individuals into direct relationship with the state. In addition, laws and policies in areas that pose privacy questions—for example, the conduct of electronic commerce and electronic government, or the use of personal data in law enforcement and social control— give individuals as data subjects a stake in the outcome of legislation and thus an enhanced interest in the politics and legislative enactment of data protection. They may be better able to protect themselves if more subject-friendly legislation is framed, owing to the increased prominence of privacy on policy agendas. The claim that individual self-help on its own is efficacious is therefore suspect. Even privacy-conscious consumers are likely to be underpowered in the "market." They are unlikely to refuse to trade with firms who offer weak protection or who subscribe to no codes although, as we have seen, this may become an issue in online commerce. Worries about privacy play only a small part in most individuals' consumption behavior, although this should not necessarily be taken to signify implied consent to privacy-invasive practices. Therefore, majoritarian market norms may make it difficult for others who are more concerned to negotiate higher levels of privacy for themselves.

Technology Developers and Providers

Market solutions may involve technologies that can be used by individuals in their transactions for commercial goods or public services. As PETs are increasingly prominent as privacy instruments, the role of technology developers and providers, along with those who devise the systems and services within which they work, are key participants in the system. As we have seen, the provision of anonymity and pseudo-nymity through encryption, greater individual control over the contents and use of smart cards, biometric devices, digital signatures and "trusted third parties" for transactions, and the like, may contribute greatly to privacy protection. But achieving these goals depends not only on the technology itself but on the laws, organizational systems, business processes, and economic and social relations that provide its context. How these tools are used must become part of knowledge and action in the domains of state enforcement and corporate self-regulation. This underlines the connections among many kinds of participants shown in figure 8.2. The involvement of law, policy, and regulators might become more important, with government requiring or encouraging PETs when information systems are designed (6 and Briscoe 1996). The UK regulator, for example, has invited providers "to design privacy into systems and to be part of the solution rather than the problem" (UK House of Commons 1999, p. 46).

Conversely, PETs in other societies have also been positioned as an alternative to regulatory intervention, and as tools that can be directly wielded by the individual. In the United States, at least in the early years, the libertarian culture that permeated debates about the emerging cyber-space environment also produced a good deal of the early privacy-enhancing and anonymization practices. For some groups, such as the "Cyberpunks," the ability to communicate in total privacy over the Internet was fully consistent with, and reinforcing of, libertarian views about freedom of speech. Thus, some proponents of PETs, deeply suspicious of government intervention, were producing their technologies as alternatives, rather than complements, to other policy instruments. Some of these arguments were embraced by many US business interests in their desire to avoid regulatory intervention by Congress.

In other countries, closer relationships exist between policy-makers, implementers, and the world of technology users, suppliers, and designers. Governments recognize the value of new technologies in their own agendas, for example, in "modernizing government." They thus create liaisons that give scope for mutual influences that might determine how far data protection is accommodated through the use of technology tools. In turn, technologists have begun to take privacy more seriously.

Organizations such as the Association for Computing Machinery in the United States and the British Computing Society have been engaged in self-regulatory code-making, and privacy issues are arguably making more of a mark than before in education and training.

Privacy Groups and the Media

These participants are among those who are most aware of developments that may invade privacy. Organizations of privacy advocates play the most prominent role, especially in countries such as the United States where business and other groups have resisted the passage of privacy legislation. But even where laws are on the statute books, privacy advocates engage in prominent educational activities, and mount public campaigns over specific issues such as identity cards and the public availability of cryptography products. Perhaps the most prominent activity are the "Big Brother Awards" presented to organizations whose practices are deemed excessively intrusive and worthy of public exposure. These events began in the United States, and are now held in a number of European countries as well. But privacy groups also insert themselves into consultations with government over policies on behalf of the public at large.

Most groups maintain a website presence that helps to inform general and specialized publics, and that assists in campaigning activities.[8] Often allied with civil-liberties groups, they have in some countries been almost alone in raising privacy issues on policy agendas and in public consciousness. They have been particularly visible in this role in some newly democratizing states, such as Argentina, Thailand, and Ukraine. The orientation of human rights organizations, whose concern is particularly with public-sector, and specifically law-enforcement and invasions of rights, lends support to pressures for better privacy protection. Although privacy activists' influence may be limited by government's distrust, they do gain greater respectability when their knowledge is seen to be useful to regulators.

Trade unions, on the other hand, have played a much less prominent part in advocating privacy to the extent of acting decisively against employers' workplace surveillance of their members, although this is becoming a significant issue. If such surveillance practices become more pervasive, unions may get further involved in raising awareness of the implications of new technologies and practices for privacy in the everyday milieux of consumption, services, and employment. To some extent, consumer groups may find themselves cross-pressured against adopting a clear position over new privacy-invasive technologies, since they advocate consumer convenience as well as consumer protection. Yet they sometimes have the ear of government insofar as "consumer-orientation" has become a fashionable approach in public administration, and politicians may seek some electoral advantage in heeding their call for better privacy protection. In addition, consumer organizations have used resources to conduct and publish surveys about public attitudes toward privacy in the marketplace. These have contributed to raising the privacy-awareness of the public, and consumer groups also assist individual citizens.

The development and coalescence of a strong privacy lobby, both in individual nations and internationally, is impeded by four central constraints. First, as hinted, privacy protection can contradict other issues of interest to an established public-interest or consumer movement. Thus any privacy campaign tends to need to build a fresh coalition for each issue. The constellation of groups that might oppose national identity cards is not necessarily the same as that which would have an interest in opposing Internet surveillance, or health records linkage, for example. The interests, and particularly the expertise needed, may well be divergent. Second, the privacy lobby is hindered by the somewhat abstract and hypothetical nature of many privacy issues. Whereas it is possible to observe and measure the direct results of much environmental pollution, arguments against excessive levels of surveillance often have to be pitched in terms of abstract rights and fears of hypothetical consequences. To be sure, many horror stories about the inappropriate collection and use of personal information can be marshalled to the cause (Smith 1993). But still, after more than thirty years of advocacy, the privacy movement in every country hears the familiar and quite bogus argument: "If you have nothing to hide, you have nothing to fear."

Third, the definition of a privacy *advocate* or *activist* is inherently difficult. The number of advocates who are funded solely to promote the cause of personal privacy is quite small. Many therefore play other roles. Some, for instance, are journalists; we have already seen how press freedom issues can cut across privacy values. Others are academics and are therefore constrained by an imperative to remain more objective and aloof from the day-to-day conflicts. Still others are consultants, taking money from government and the private sector in exchange for confidential advice, and in some instances, lobbying services. The lure of consultancy income can then temper the zeal and forthrightness of the advocate.

Finally, and like other public interest issues, the lobby is hampered by the familiar "free-rider" dilemma. The goal pursued, enhanced privacy protection, is for the most part enjoyed by all members of the society. Like clean air, privacy in this sense is an indivisible public good, as the argument in chapter 2 indicates. Any individual may benefit from privacy protection law whether or not he or she actively participates in the movement or, indeed, cares about the issue at all. The inherent logic of collective action (Olson 1971), therefore, produces an inescapable dilemma about how to bring together a larger social movement for an issue that everyone might potentially benefit from at some point in the future, but for which few can see any direct, visible, and personal gain. In combination, these three factors perhaps explain why the dominant pressures for privacy protection legislation in many countries have been driven by organized elites rather than by the general public.[9]

Conclusion

This excursion through the criteria for analyzing policy instruments, and through the categories of participants and their relationships, has shown how an analysis of interactions, interdependence, and conflict in data protection systems might be conducted. This moves toward an analysis of the governance of data protection in terms of complex regimes, which include multiple actors and structures and many tools, and which help us to understand the intricate processes through which privacy protection is provided, going beyond simple "toolbox" conceptions. Although systematic investigation would involve further differentiation related to the various instruments, our general discussion has pointed out certain kinds of relationships, and has hinted that such interaction may be cultivated, relationships designed, and tools created, rather than simply waited for. This is most important if, beyond empirical description, one considers the privacy instruments, and the roles or structures that relate to them, in terms of strategies and regimes. In a sense, this is the management or policy dimension of privacy protection. On the other hand, it can also be argued that, within this dimension, privacy protection has to be negotiated through the various "stakeholders," rather than decreed: there is a politics of data protection, not just a blueprint.

These questions of power and its distribution—the direction and density of figure 8.2's lines and arrows, what is exchanged, accountability, coalition-formation, and the time dimension—have been left on one side here, but would have to be explored before privacy protection as a system of governance can be properly understood, or shaped in terms of public policy.[10] Moreover, it is plain that no analysis that confines its frame of reference to only one country or jurisdiction as the field of play for policy actors and privacy instruments can be adequate. The information processes that shape privacy as a policy issue are emphatically global; the development of instruments for protecting privacy transcends individual countries' institutions, processes, and political systems. As the experience of thirty or more years has shown, and perhaps increasingly now, the governance of privacy is not only a matter for many instruments and many actors, but is also multilevel, ranging from that of individual jurisdictions to that of the world. Understanding what happens at and across these levels overwhelms the capacity of simple diagrams. In chapter 10, we will look at issues related to this growing globalization of the governance of privacy, with an eye to the future. Whether that will mean better privacy protection is a crucial question. But before we can address the factors that influence such an outcome, a prior question is whether it is at all possible to assess the quality and level of protection for personal data. This is the subject of chapter 9.

9

The Evaluation of Impact

Introduction

It is one thing to describe and analyze the international instruments, laws, codes, commitments, technologies, and other elements that compose what we have called regimes of privacy protection. It is quite another thing to evaluate any or all of these in terms of the effect they may have—singly or together—upon protecting individual privacy. There is a conventional wisdom about the effects of privacy strategies, which includes comparisons across regimes and instruments. For example, it has often been said that the German and French data protection regimes are "strong" in relation to those of other countries; conversely, that the instruments available in the United States provide only "weak" protection. It is also considered that data protection laws are better at protecting privacy than, say, the market.

We do not necessarily dissent from either specific judgments of this type, or from the tendency to make comparative statements of the kind involved in them. Nevertheless, it is not very satisfactory that such evaluative pronouncements are made at a very general level, without explicit criteria or evidence. Summary statements about effectiveness owe more to the discourse of engaged policy debate and advocacy than to that of reasonably detached analysis. It remains a major problem that there exists no satisfactory way of evaluating or measuring the approximation of regulatory laws and mechanisms to the goal of protecting privacy. Yet evaluating the quality of data protection is a matter of increasing importance for data controllers, individuals, regulatory officials, and a variety of interest groups who have a stake in the control of information systems. Our discussion of equity in chapter 2 touched on the question of what kinds of performance criteria could be used to evaluate the ability of privacy protection systems to achieve certain objectives. Inevitably, such evaluation is politically and conceptually controversial, and there is no obvious, well-founded route to its achievement. Does this mean that nothing more can be said about this until such a method is found, and that policy must grope its way from one fashionable handhold to another?

We do not think so. Although we do not formulate a definitive evaluative framework or method, in this chapter we mark out some lines for it by identifying the issues that must first be considered.[1] The main purpose is to assess the possibility of "measuring" the effectiveness of data protection systems in order to assist policy-making and implementation. The key question concerns the extent to which certain standards of data protection can be objectively identified and molded into a reliable instrument for measuring the performance of these systems, both over time and comparatively.

In striking a skeptical note about policy debate, we do not mean to denigrate it. After all, the vague and subjective nature of privacy as a human value may well mean that evaluations of these systems should be left to the workings of the "real world" policy process, and can only misleadingly be framed in the strict terms of performance criteria as used elsewhere in the public service. Therefore, any attempt to construct a hard-nosed evaluation of the performance of a data protection system should be seized of the likely naivety of approaches that use numerical indicators and quantitative measures. Numbers may misleadingly drive out other forms of evaluation. It may be, as Bennett (1988, p. 441) argues, that the methods of moral and social philosophy are more useful than systematic policy analysis in answering the question whether privacy can be protected in the "information society." Nevertheless, some systematic exploration is overdue in the literature as well as in the world of administrative practice. Only by taking these steps can we both identify the possibilities of moving closer to a usable instrument for practice, and also gain a better purchase on how knowledge of aspects of data protection systems and their components could be improved.

As we point out in chapter 1, privacy embodies a range of values that are only partially advanced by data protection. We need first, then, to limit the task to an evaluation of the fair information principles that are central to all national data protection statutes and international conventions. The achievement of privacy in its wider and more "human rights" aspects, embodying a range of rights to intimacy, seclusion, reserve, autonomy, and so on (Westin 1967), is not under investigation here. Even with this restriction, the task remains difficult. Yet, analogously, administrators, policy-makers, and the public seek and use performance indicators in the field of health policy despite controversies over the definition of health and the values measured. For privacy protection, as in other fields, it is always possible to propose new criteria to be taken into account, as Pollitt (1988) has done, for example, with regard to health "consumers," or as others have done in arguing that quality should be distinguished from productivity and measured (see Bouckaert 1990). Data protection is no less intricate, conceptually and empirically, than health protection, and its characteristics that are amenable to evaluation are no less debatable. Civil liberties organizations, for example, often invoke standards that reflect different or more absolutist values than those embraced by regulators and policy-makers.

To begin this exploration, we address the following questions: Why evaluate data protection? What are the fundamental goals of data protection policy? By what criteria should these processes be evaluated? On what functions and actors should evaluation focus, and with what measures? And what facilitates and obstructs evaluation?

Why Evaluate Data Protection?

Four purposes can be identified as the main aims of evaluation.

Public Accountability
Democratic theory sees the rendering of accounts as a response to the public's interest in the performance of their representatives or of government institutions. Public confidence in government may be at stake in such accountability. In the new "evaluative state" (Henkel 1991), public

bodies are under increased pressure not only to explain what they do and how they do it, but also to provide evidence of their achievements in terms of the policies that they carry out. Inside government, accountability opens the activities of state organs to scrutiny in terms of managerial criteria such as effectiveness, efficiency, and economy.

With regard to data protection, accountability relates to both public and private sectors. Citizens who are required to exchange their personal details for state benefits may seek reassurance, via procedures of accountability, that government is a trustworthy controller of their personal data. This is becoming particularly important where governments are seeking new uses for the data they hold, sharing it across conventional organizational boundaries in order to accomplish a number of policy purposes such as better delivery of public services or the reduction of welfare fraud. We note, in passing, the relevance of government transparency, or freedom of information, to these accountability procedures. In the private sector, evaluating a company's performance in data protection may also be seen as both an internal managerial check on information processes, and as an external effort of public relations aimed at maintaining good will and confidence among customers that the personal information that forms part of their transactions is being properly safeguarded. In an environment of online business-to-customer marketing, the ability to evaluate a company's website in terms of privacy protection is an important element. Some of the technological instruments discussed in chapter 7 are relevant to this objective, and regulators have become interested in gaining systematic knowledge of marketers' privacy policies as stated on their websites as well as whether or not they adhere to them in practice. Generally speaking, a good account should go beyond public relations "spin" to convey an explanation of achievements and shortcomings, based on evidence that is open to independent scrutiny and interrogation using explicit, albeit debatable, criteria of judgment.

Making Comparisons

Evaluation is part of systematic comparisons made at various levels. The development of an EU data protection regime illustrates the importance of international comparisons, for the establishment of common standards presupposes some way of judging the "adequacy" or "equiva-lence" of national data protection systems (Raab et al. 1998). Article 25 of·the 1995 EU Data Protection Directive is clear that comparing the black letter of the law in various countries is an insufficient method of arriving at such conclusions. Even if it were sufficient, evaluating these laws would require explicit and defensible categories of analysis, and considering a wider set of factors for comparison across countries only multiplies the problem of evaluation. Only by making more explicit the evaluative criteria that underpin the conventional wisdom of the field—"strong" and "weak" laws, for example—can these assessments be made and used as a reasoned basis for making decisions about the permissibility of data transfer to third countries.

Comparisons are also essential at other levels. Domestically, they may be made across the various sectors in which personal data are used, such as direct marketing or credit referencing, or across firms within a sector, or across government agencies such as those concerned with social security benefits, driver and vehicle licensing, and policing. Comparative indicators of the quality of data protection afforded by these organiza-tions is a prerequisite for assessing the differential privacy risks run by consumers, customers, or citizens.

A Tool for Management and Policy

Evaluations of all kinds are important to those who are most closely involved with implementing data protection and with general public administration. As we noted, performance measurements are increas-ingly employed in monitoring the effectiveness, efficiency, and economy of public-sector activities. In data protection, evaluations form the basis for diagnosing problems and for criticizing and improving official regu-latory action, and are therefore potentially usable by regulatory officials or by data controllers, politicians, and interest groups. For privacy com-missioners and the like, performance measurement may provide a clearer rationale for changing regulatory strategies and tactics, for re-allocating resources, and for training staff. Organizations that actually process personal data may evaluate their own practices in order to improve the quality of protection that they provide to their customers' or clients' data. They may be able to maintain essential public confidence or trust by being seen to be taking pains over monitoring and publicizing their own performance, and to be acting on their findings. For all the relevant participants in privacy protection, evaluations may be useful in assessing how far the risks of privacy invasion have been prevented or remedied.

In terms of general theories of public policy, evaluations of achievement may also lead to major changes of direction in steering toward goals, or to the selection of new goals. Such formative evaluation may be particularly important in the case of data-protection policy, where the goals of government policy, and even the objectives of legislation embodying it, are ambiguous and multiple, and where the full articulation of policy can only come about during implementation. Unlike discrete programs with stable, singular, or clear-cut goals, the looseness of the distinction between policy-making and policy-implementation (Barrett and Fudge 1981, Hill 1997) is an important feature to be taken into consideration when data protection is evaluated. The categories for such reporting may be fluid and charged with political significance, and the evaluative accounts that are rendered can assist debate about the aims and objectives of policy.

A Tool for Policy Analysis and Formation

A more subtle purpose served by evaluations concerns the extent to which policies and practices throughout the public or private sector may have implications for individual privacy. There is an analogy here with the environmental effects of industrial practices where, for example, new manufacturing processes may increase the level of air or water pollution and thus activate regulatory systems that are designed to prevent or penalize such effects. With regard to personal data, if there were a reliable method of evaluating the risk that new commercial or administrative practices pose to privacy, it might be possible to devise better strategies for building in data protection at an early stage of these innovations, or at least of attaching privacy impact statements or privacy price tags to policies.

Privacy impact assessment and other diagnostic tools are indeed being developed as techniques that rest implicitly or explicitly on evaluative measures of privacy *invasion*—the reverse side of the coin of measures of privacy *protection* (Stewart 1996; Perrin et al. 2001, pp. 265–73; White 2001). Neither are possible without better ways of assessing more precisely the likely effect of certain kinds of data protection techniques on the level of risk, which we touch on in chapter 3 (Douglas and Wildavsky 1982; 6 1998, chap. 2). Once again, the advent of increased data-sharing in the public sector, and the concomitant desire to reassure the public that their personal information is being well protected, may provide a stimulus for the center to improve and promulgate the evaluative criteria and implementation tools for privacy protection across public management sites. This approach seems likely to emerge in the UK, for example, although it is more closely connected to the assessment of the impact that data sharing may have on privacy (UK Performance and Innovation Unit 2002).

Related to this fourth purpose, evaluations may clarify the extent to which the usual array of criteria of policy "success" is adequate by suggesting new ones for incorporation in the design or redesign of policies. In chapter 2, for example, we speculate about the importance of a social-policy interpretation of privacy that might have consequences by generating novel criteria for practice and evaluation.

In Terms of What Goals Should Data Protection Be Evaluated?

The articulation of goals for policies, laws, and systems of data protection provide important reference points for evaluations of practice. While these articulations are not straightforward, and while the goals exist in a state of some tension with others, they can be seen in terms of three primary analytical categories.

Protecting Privacy

Individual privacy is the goal of data protection laws and other instruments, but they also aim to facilitate the processing of personal data while reducing the harm to individuals. It is true that the political reality has often been that legislation has been prompted more by the desire to reap the commercial and administrative benefits that stem from information technology and data usage than to protect privacy. Nonetheless, insofar as privacy is the main legitimizing aim of data protection laws, it is appropriate to take privacy as the goal against which to evaluate data protection. However, as already mentioned, evaluation is complicated by the vagueness and contestability of the definition of privacy. It is not easy to select criteria that could be used unambiguously and objectively. Moreover, while useful attitude surveys are frequently conducted by regulatory and other organizations, measures of people's feelings about the extent to which their privacy is ensured or invaded cannot assume that those surveyed had the same concept of privacy in mind. In addition, while privacy is never regarded as an all-or-nothing concept, and degrees of privacy protection that fall short of some hypothetical total protection are not to be denigrated, it is not easy to construct a scale along which partial achievements can be measured or compared.

Promoting Good Computing Practice

Improving the practices of data controllers—the second goal of data protection—might provide an easier objective against which to make an assessment of achievements, one that would surpass impressionistic judgments. The data protection principles enjoin many elaborate obligations upon the data controller, some of which go with the grain of existing organizational interests. Although it is but one of the principles of data protection, data security is probably the first question that comes to mind in a large number of organizations when they consider privacy protection. Adequate security is obviously in the interests of all organizations, perhaps especially those that process large quantities of highly sensitive financial, health, or criminal information. This is a fairly uncontroversial example of "good computing practice," although it only addresses one of the requirements of laws and codes of practice.

Another crucial principle is subject access, by which data controllers are required to enable data subjects to access their information. If more rationalized internal information storage and retrieval systems are developed for this purpose, the efficiency savings over the range of the organization's information-management practices are likely to be measurable. As with security, adherence to this and other data protection principles may generate efficiency gains for data controllers through the resulting improvement in records management. Similarly, data controllers should be able to judge the gains they make when they comply with accuracy, relevance, and time-limitation requirements. Adherence to good data practices may also make it possible for firms to compete in international markets where transfers of data are contingent upon privacy protection.

Looking at the public sector in measurable ways may also facilitate the activities of public administrators in their dealings with individuals whose willingness to trust government with their personal data depends on the implementation of data safeguards, consent requirements, and transparency. Where public-sector managers have targets to reach for the volume of transactions with the public that can be encouraged to move online, it may become possible to impute increases in volume to the attainment of levels of public trust and confidence that are reached through public perceptions of—and the reality of—better data protection. In both sectors, meeting privacy obligations, however, imposes costs, whether in terms of money, time, freedom, competitive advantage—especially internationally—or flexibility. For instance, the provision of viable procedures for securing individuals' consent, or for allowing access and correction to personal data, requires the continuous commitment of staff and financial resources. However, as has been suggested, some costs may be turned to advantage in commerce or government. Nonetheless, it is rather more likely that controllers of personal data will recognize the costs of data protection rather than the benefits, which, in particular operations, might only be hypothetical or realized far in the future. Data protection is in the interests of the data controller, but not always.

A "Balance" Between the Two

To reconcile these conflicting objectives of privacy and organizational benefits, the goal of data protection is often stated in terms of a balance between the two—a sufficient level of protection that would provide privacy for individuals while not interfering unduly with, and perhaps benefiting, the conduct of government or business. For evaluation purposes, the problem with formulation is that the concept of "balance" is misleading and rhetorical because the two sides of the equation are literally incommensurable (Raab 1999a). Moreover, as Reidenberg (1993) has observed, the balance in different phases and instruments of data protection over the past twenty years or so has shifted or varied, sometimes favoring the free flow of information, and sometimes favoring the protection of privacy. "Balance" is best seen as a political or bargaining outcome between conflicting objectives (Raab and Bennett 1994), or as a general exhortation not to forget one objective when pursuing the other. Insofar as it becomes a goal, measuring the extent to which it is reached would seem to be necessary but conceptually and operationally problematic. It is nonetheless important to consider how such balances, or at least balancing processes, can be evaluated. This is because the political or conflict-resolution objectives that "balancing" might achieve constitute very significant indicators of successful policy work amidst the powerful constellation of competing interests in the fields of information systems, public services, or commerce.

What Are the Operational Criteria for Evaluation?

Evaluators of the quality of data protection require some categorical criteria against which to measure practices of different systems or the same system over time. There are some commonly used general criteria in public administration and private business that may be considered useful for evaluating data protection, although they are not easily adaptable or rendered operational.

Economy, Efficiency, Effectiveness, and Equity

As we have seen, the promotion of privacy and good computing practice are familiar concepts within the dominant discourse of privacy experts and officials. The "three Es" of economy, efficiency, and effectiveness are less familiar values, derived from the more widely applicable language of policy analysis and evaluation, in which they are components of "value for money": "an analogue to profit as a measure of management success" (UK HM Treasury 1988). But an abiding problem in the public services is how "value" can be measured when the product is not marketed, and when other valid criteria besides the "three Es" could also be invoked. Yet these three might, in some respects, be made more precise for use as comparative measures within the same organization over time.

Economy typically refers to the cost of input resources. In data protection, these resources are chiefly the money and staff deployed by the data protection agencies, where such bodies exist, as well as by data controllers in regard to the activities they engage in for complying with data protection, codes, or laws. Examples would include regulatory agencies' administrative and publicity expenditure, firms' registration fees (where data controllers are required by law to register with a central authority), the cost of staff training and of developing expertise, fees for legal advice, and expenditure on systems of physical security for data collections and for complying with data subjects' access requests. Over the years, competitive markets have developed for supplying these goods and services, and new roles and career opportunities have opened for managerial and technical staff employed as data protection officers.

Efficiency refers to the relationship between inputs and outputs. That is much more difficult to assess: what, indeed, is obtained for a given outlay on salaries or equipment devoted to protecting privacy? From the standpoint of the regulatory agency, the outputs of implementation might include the advice and guidance they give to the public and to other policy-makers, the negotiation of codes of practice, publicity materials, enforcement decisions, and in some systems, such as the British, the maintenance of a register of data controllers. From the standpoint of data controllers, outputs might include a reduction in the volume of public complaints about breaches of information privacy, an increase in the speed with which subject-access requests are met, and improvements in data quality. Although businesses or government departments might regard their code of practice as an output, the code itself is more appropriately seen as an input—a resource for producing measurable outputs, whether these are increased public and staff awareness of privacy protection, better customer relations, better information systems, and so on.

Effectiveness refers to the relationship between outputs and ultimate objectives, requiring a clear statement and understanding of those objectives throughout the data protection system. This is the most problematical criterion, partly because of the ambiguity and multiplicity of goals. Ambiguity deprives us of a clear "target" against which to measure progress: "privacy," "better privacy," "good practice," "a balance," or whatever. Multiplicity of goals requires that evaluations of effectiveness be stated in more elaborate, less succinct terms, possibly straining public comprehension and reducing the practical or remedial value of such appraisals. Moreover, to reinforce an earlier point, unclear and multiple goals easily give rise to conflicting judgments of effectiveness: privacy advocates may well disagree with the conclusions reached by business or government, perhaps especially over the achievement of a "balance."

Effectiveness is also a problematic criterion because of the inherent difficulty of connecting goals to specific performances, inputs, or outputs of data protection authorities or of data controllers. Whether or not privacy is protected through, for example, the application of legal sanctions, or the mounting of publicity campaigns, may be debatable. One might only be left with such inputs and outputs as proxies for outcomes—rather like expenditure increases for health care are often taken as a proxy for better health.

Yet it is instructive to note the skepticism expressed by some commissioners. The UK Information Commissioner's Office, for example, has been considering the possibility of developing performance criteria for some time, and indeed the Commissioner is now required to have output measures and performance indicators. The Deputy has remarked that this means counting the activities that you can count, and that "[e]ven so it is not clear that [these measures and indicators] are measuring output in any useful way" (Aldhouse 1992). For instance, even a ratio that showed that the processing of complaints was highly efficient could not indicate how valuable this activity is to the goals of data protection.

Finally, a fourth "E" should be introduced: *equity*. As mentioned in chapter 2, this distributional criterion is normally ignored in conventional privacy analysis. It has yet to be constructed as part of the dominant discourse of privacy protection; much less has it emerged as an objective for regulatory policy or public policy more broadly considered. Yet some notion of equity (or equality) is already implicitly part of conventional data-protection wisdom across countries. Thus, up to the late 1990s, it was often said that Germans get among the best, and that Greeks and Italians received among the worst protection of the privacy of their personal data. Comparisons are essential in the attempt to implement international regulations for transborder data flow, although there are serious doubts about the reliability and conceptual rigor of such judgments (Raab and Bennett 1994).

But can one say anything more precisely about the social distribution of data protection? As we saw in chapter 2, here the simple question is "who gets data protection and whose data gets protected best?" Do urban dwellers, for example, who buy less from mail-order catalogs have less to worry about than do those from rural areas, who buy more? Does data protection help to reduce social disparities in the quality of privacy? Are some groups disadvantaged by race, gender, class, religion, occupation, geography, or age in preventing intrusions or in seeking remedies?

Speculations are worth entertaining. Thus it is probably untrue that the relatively poor will inevitably have less privacy; it is generally the better-off who are profiled and targeted by the direct-marketing industry. In addition, as personal data collection and processing become more prevalent through the application of new technologies, such as geographic information technologies used in vehicles, the characteristics of those who come into the purview of such systems is not likely to be a microcosm of society, and might well disproportionately expose the relatively better-off to further invasions. On the other hand, the poorer, who come into contact with state agencies more frequently and for a wider range of services and benefits, are arguably more threatened by these agencies' surveillance practices. Moreover, the advent of electronic commerce through multimedia infrastructures is likely to reach further down the social scale if these facilities become cheaper, providing new opportunities for the capture of personal data in systems whose use is difficult to regulate. A better grasp of the social distribution of privacy risks and safeguards is needed in order to evaluate the allocation of data protection within and across systems, and thus to judge the equitability of data protection systems in meeting different needs. Perhaps one way forward would be to consider the question of equity mainly on a disaggregated basis of sectors or types of transactions, rather than in terms of an overall summation for a society as a whole.

What Factors Facilitate Evaluation?

The relatively constant characteristics of policies in specific fields often override contextual variations of time and space. Data protection policy has some distinctive properties, owing to the similarity of problems and the use of technologies that span national boundaries. On the other hand, variations in the way data protection is implemented across these contexts may affect the prospect of judging the success of policy. We briefly consider four main factors that enhance the possibility of evaluation.

Dominant Policy and Legal Clarity

The first facilitating factor is the presence of a coherent, comprehensible body of law and policy that can be readily identified and that state the objectives with reasonable clarity. The emergence and construction of data protection as a discrete area of public policy in the 1970s produced a consensus that one law is the optimum way to define the "shalls, shoulds, mays and must nots" of personal data processing. This legal concentration can assist evaluation; to the extent that data protection policy is dispersed among a variety of statutory and nonstatutory instruments, as is often the case in coregulatory models, evaluation is significantly harder.

A Dominant Regulatory Agency

The second factor—also a product of the same consensus—is that implementation is facilitated by a data protection authority whose sole responsibility is the pursuit of the goals of the legislation. There are, however, several jurisdictions in which the regulatory body has a dual role in regard to both data protection and freedom of information. To the extent that information privacy policy is implemented and overseen by an authority with additional, and maybe competing responsibilities, the evaluation task is correspondingly more complex; this would be the case for Ontario, Québec, and British Columbia in Canada, and for

Hungary. These systems combine oversight of privacy with the implementation of access to information legislation, producing a continuous and institutionalized method to "balance" these competing values and therefore, in given situations and for good cause, to override privacy protection by public right-to-know considerations (Majtényi 2001). These circumstances would need to be reflected in the way the data protection role is evaluated. The lack of singular, coherent implementation machinery in the United States (Gellman 1993), by contrast, makes evaluation of data protection very difficult except in terms of blanket judgments about its regulatory insufficiency, or in terms of specific activities in specific sectors involved in transfers of data from third countries. At a lower level, within data-controlling organizations or among industrial or sectoral associations, the existence of an explicit, responsible privacy office may help evaluators to identify functions and to measure performance. This is because the routine collection of knowledge about implementation and compliance within the sector or organization is more likely to take place under such conditions, as is the production of internal advice and regulations. All these may give a purchase upon the performances or outputs to be evaluated, and upon their outcomes in terms of the quality of data protection.

Explicit Agency Activities

Data protection authorities, and sometimes organizational officers as well, have clearly defined though varying responsibilities for education, enforcement, investigation, registration, research, and so on. It is generally possible to enumerate these statutory duties and compare their conduct across time and space, using appropriate measures and criteria. Flaherty's (1989) comparison of the data protection systems within Canada, West Germany, France, the United States, and Sweden provides an illustration of the use of a fairly consistent analytical framework of regulatory and advisory responsibilities. This facilitates judgments of the efficacy of different systems, but is set in a context of national variations in public administration, legal cultures, and policy styles that is useful for explanation as well as evaluation, even if these variations mean that cross-jurisdictional comparisons need to be heavily qualified.

A Developing Tradition of Accountability

Finally, the production of an annual report by each data protection authority forces it to undertake regular internal analyses of its operations, as well as systematic conceptualization and discussion of problems, issues, strategies, and responses. These external reporting requirements, along with internal management procedures, mean that staff have to maintain a careful record of complaints resolution, advisory and educational activities, and regulatory and enforcement actions. Most reports are written in a fairly consistent format that permits internal and external analysts to compare activities over time and with counterparts in other countries. Not only do these routines of accountability promote organizational learning, they also facilitate evaluation and measurement. But there are variations in the extent to which the materials for reporting and accountability are detailed, well developed, and informative, and external evaluators would have to develop procedures for verifying the agency's self-reported information. Moreover, many kinds of qualitative and quantitative information about the implementation process are simply not collected or reported systematically by the agency itself, and require independent research to bring them to light; management-related information and external evaluative information may overlap, but are not identical.

What Factors Impede Evaluation?

Offsetting these facilitating factors are some inherent problems. We identify five of these.

Unclear and Multiple Policy Objectives

We have already noted the existence of vague and multiple policy objectives. Each of the goals outlined earlier is susceptible to alternative definitions. The ostensible primary goal, to protect personal privacy, is not only vague but also highly subjective; an invasion of privacy for one person may be an important social or economic benefit for another. One person may find direct mail highly intrusive, for instance; another may find it a convenient way to order goods and services. Closed-circuit television surveillance may raise fears of "Big Brother" for some, while others may regard it as contributing to their sense of physical security and peace of mind. Moreover, if the policy goal is to "balance" privacy protection against the facilitation of information systems and technologies used in commerce and government, the evaluation may have to be conceived and conducted differently.

Conflicting Interests

This leads to a second problem, raised by the question of whose objectives should be taken into consideration in measuring progress or quality. Data protection enjoins obligations upon data controllers, provides rights for data subjects and gives responsibilities to the data protection authority. It embodies a range of complicated principles for different actors and institutions. This complexity has led to a tendency for some organizations to emphasize some requirements above others and to claim that they are faithfully fulfilling their obligations according to a set of criteria that are defined in terms of their own interests and operating circumstances. Perhaps the most typical example is when data protection is confused with data security. Some institutions or sectors can thus subtly redefine policy objectives, demonstrate that they have implanted security measures, and claim that they comply with the law. Yet although data security is a necessary condition for data protection, it is not a sufficient condition. Thus an evaluator may well argue that the law is not "working" if the well-secured data are inaccurate, held for too long, and passed to third parties without an opportunity for consent to be obtained, even if these weaknesses and any resulting privacy violations only occur infrequently for the organization being scrutinized. These criteria reflect a different set of priorities in respect of fair information principles.

Unclear Time Frame and Targets

A third obstacle is an unclear time frame within which to measure the quality of protection. How long should one give for a data protection policy to work? What were the original expectations of policy-makers and regulators as to the length of time it would take for data users to recognize and act upon their responsibilities, or for members of the public to become aware of data protection and of their rights? Following the 1995 EU Data Protection Directive, the UK's 1998 Data Protection Act provided for several transitional periods for compliance with certain aspects, reflecting the anticipated difficulties for organizations to comply with the law in regard to manual files, for instance. Yet some responsibilities should be fairly easy and quick to implement, such as the provision of a system for access to and correction of personal data. But many observers have also underlined the importance of building a culture of data protection over time, such that the implementation of the law, in both letter and spirit, becomes an integral part of standard operating procedures. How long should one have to wait for this cultural change to happen, and does the rapidity of technological developments affect such change to the extent that the evaluation of success in data protection requires a more subtle approach?

Multiple Issues and Blurred Boundaries

Fourth, the information practices against which data protection operates are so varied and pervasive that it is likely that only some could be highlighted for evaluation. Annual reports of data protection agencies tend to emphasize big issues like data matching, direct marketing, credit referencing, access to criminal records, genetic databanks, and video surveillance. Giving priority to these may be praiseworthy as a necessary attempt to focus on more intrusive issues with public policy implications, and on new applications of technology, but there is a danger that doing so may marginalize mundane issues related to routine records management affecting large sections of the population. That said, however, the development of these technologies, including telecommunications and multimedia innovations, has blurred the boundaries of organizations and their "databanks." Thus, evaluations of organizational or national protective activity, or of responses to single issues, are often unrealistic or irrelevant, given such fluid interdependencies and the multiple levels at which protective action must take place.

Uncertainty About Who Should Do the Evaluation

The final obstacle is the absence of a tradition or expertise for external or relatively independent evaluation. The main institutions that have performed evaluations to date, namely the data protection authorities, are themselves part of the system itself. Evaluators from the business world are implicated by their roles as major controllers of personal data. Political and administrative bodies are also compromised by their interests in the development and use of personal information systems. Although they are more detached, official auditing agencies and the like—as we have seen—may only focus upon the work of the regulatory agency in brief, once-for-all reports, and cannot gain sufficient depth and breadth of experience of this complex field to pronounce upon the quality of the system as a whole. It is not to denigrate consultancy organizations or legal firms that undertake appraisals of information systems and privacy-protection compliance to say that they have a keen interest in selling their advice and services to improve systems. This perhaps involves them in diagnosing as deficient, and suggesting how to fix, things that do not really need to be fixed.

There are no agents that are totally external to the entire system. "Neutral competence" is difficult to locate and is not yet established as a facility in this controversial field, although some regulatory agencies may try to be even-handed in their approach to competing interests even while they also promote stronger privacy protection. We are all data subjects and a large proportion of us are data controllers in the work we do. On the other hand, in every country where data protection is public policy, there are consultants and observers drawn from academic life, public-interest groups, and business who have developed at least some degree of disinterested expertise in data protection law and practice. They are occasionally invited to develop codes, to audit organizations' information practices, to advise official regulators, and to comment upon issues and new developments. To the extent that self-regulatory codes and standards will play an increasing role in any data protection system, there will be a concomitant need for a more professional and consistent understanding among such experts about what a proper privacy audit should entail (Bennett 1995). Yet it should be borne in mind that risk perceptions and assessments are socially and culturally conditioned, and experts may well disagree among themselves, as Douglas and Wildavsky (1982) argue with regard to environmental policy. This is perforce likely to be so concerning privacy risks, as well as concerning judgments of the relative success of regulatory policies and regimes for data protection.

What or Who Should Be Evaluated?

The system of data protection affords a number of possible subjects for evaluation or measurement, and evaluators may differ in what they wish to scrutinize. At least five can be envisaged as plausible candidates. They relate to our canvass of a range of policy instruments in Part II, which leads us to consider how their impact on protecting privacy can be evaluated, whether singly or in combination. Ideally, the contribution of each should be assessed; in reality, however, it is empirically not possible to disentangle these tools sufficiently to enable such judgments to be made. The consequences of this indeterminacy for practice are substantial: for instance, how is it possible, on the basis of an evaluation, to identify which of the instruments is weak in promoting privacy and therefore in need of improvement? Or, on what evaluative evidence about efficacy should a specific technique, or combination, be borrowed from another system? Despite the difficulties of such questioning, insights can be gained about how to assess the effect of policy tools by the further indicative remarks given below, which we present as a general inventory of relevant subjects for evaluation, rather than as a substantive evaluation of any system's instruments.

The Law

Perhaps the most common subject of appraisal is the data protection or privacy law itself. Evaluations may take note of many aspects. One is the scope of the law—for example, whether it regulates the private as well as the public sector, and manual as well as computerized data. Another is the clarity and consistency of the law—whether its definitions and provisions leave too much to varied and contestable interpretations, thus impeding the realization of privacy, and whether its allocation of rights and responsibilities among data controllers, data subjects, and regulatory authorities is clear. Others include the scope of the law's exemptions, the remedies and sanctions that it provides, the kind of enforcement machinery that it establishes, and the extent to which the law is able to cover circumstances brought about by future technological change. Where a country has revised or replaced its original law, as for instance in many Member States of the EU for the purpose of implementing the 1995 Directive, comparisons of old and new legal provisions may facilitate the making of judgments within these categories. Where a country has extended its protection of data through a new enactment, such as the Canadian law of 2000 covering the private sector, it may be possible to say whether the legal framework as well as particular provisions have been strengthened or weakened in terms of their likelihood of protecting citizens' or customers' privacy.

However, it is misleading to examine data protection laws alone. In every society—including those, like the United States, without comprehensive data protection statutes—a range of other unrelated statutes may govern personal data processing for individual sectors. In addition, the common law must also be taken into account where courts have found remedies for intrusion, breach of confidence, and other torts. Then there are constitutional provisions, such as the protection against "unreasonable searches and seizures" in the American and Canadian Constitutions, which may also be relevant to an evaluation. Nonetheless, it is not enough simply to take laws and related documents into account, and misleading to base comparative judgments of the "level" of data protection in various jurisdictions upon legal texts themselves without considering the way law enters into practice.

The Performance of the Implementation Machinery

Most data protection laws establish a regulatory authority with responsibility for the implementation and enforcement of legislation. Where such an agency exists, it is appropriate to consider the authority as a key focus of evaluation because of the central part it plays in the wide range of processes that comprise data protection. Moreover, it is arguably the most prominent "target" for evaluation, not only when "value for money" appraisals are made within the institutional machinery of the state, but also in the wider public domain, among pressure groups, and in the media. In practice, however, there is more of the latter form of comment, arising from specific actions or omissions that attract the attention of the media or of other observers, than there is of the systematic or concentrated attempt to scrutinize and appraise the performance of the regulatory body. In the UK, for example, over a period of twenty years, there has only been one occasion on which a formal overview was produced and reported to Parliament by an organ of the central state—in this case, the influential Comptroller and Auditor General, the main independent scrutiny body that undertakes systematic investigations of this kind (UK National Audit Office 1993).

Some data protection authorities have made some initial strides in developing performance indicators. The Finnish Data Protection Ombudsman, for instance, has given considerable thought to the indicators that measure the "social impact" of their work.[2] The Data protection authority in the Swiss canton of Zurich has gone so far as to subject its own management processes to external audit and has been certified to the internationally recognized ISO 9001:2000 standard.[3] An indication of the seriousness with which performance measurement is on the agenda of data protection authorities is the emphasis spent on the subject at the 2004 Conference of the European Data Protection Commissioners in Rotterdam.

As mentioned in chapter 5, the world's data protection systems exhibit several different models for implementing the set of fair information principles, although empirical reality is, however, more complicated because all systems display a combination of approaches. Despite these complexities, certain activities in which regulatory bodies engage lend themselves to evaluation. Many data protection authorities already measure and report on their own activities when they render their accounts or annual reports to legislatures, administrative overseers, and the general public. The volume and style of advice they give to data controllers and to data subjects lend themselves to quantitative and qualitative appraisal. Statistics of inquiries and complaints handled by the office, prosecutions, information booklets, orders or rulings made, and the like, are standard features of annual reports in a number of countries. It may be difficult to transform these statistics into performance indicators, but they do give some purchase on an authority's "productivity," and they may provide feedback for steering purposes in terms, for example, of whether or not staff and financial resources should be redeployed.

Indicative information for an evaluation of a data protection system can thus be taken from administrative records that are generated by the activities themselves, or the information can be gathered explicitly for that purpose. For example, information about what proportion of the general public understand their rights under the legislation, or what proportion of large or small companies are aware of their obligations, can be used to assess the effectiveness of publicity campaigns. The UK's Information Commissioner, for example, has for many years commissioned surveys of public opinion and knowledge in order to give some measures of the success of public awareness efforts, to which the Office devoted considerable attention as part of the "learning aspects" of data protection (Raab 1993).

The danger is that numbers, charts, graphs, and the like might give a spurious sense that "hard" evaluation is at hand. Such data may be ambiguous indicators of the success of implementation policy, and may take inputs or outputs for actual achievement of goals. Consider, for instance, public complaints about data controllers' practices. If legislation is to improve data practices, public complaints are a key element in achieving that objective; the regulatory agency may constructively encourage the public to come forward with problems in order to fulfill part of their role. On the one hand, a rising number of complaints may indicate the regulatory body's success in informing citizens of their rights. If the agency can demonstrate its ability to handle rising levels of complaint over time, it can also claim a measure of effectiveness. On the other hand, is this evidence that the law is "working"? More complaints are evidence of greater awareness, but they could also indicate a growing lack of compliance among data controllers. Another possible indicator might be the number of sanctions applied by the authority, but this too is ambiguous, and many regulatory officials in fact hope that compliance can be induced through better understanding, negotiation, and amicable settlements, rather than through a confrontational approach that relies on sanctions.

Quantitative measures of actions taken by a data protection authority therefore face both ways. So it is important not to confuse *output* indicators with *outcome* measures of greater privacy protection. For these reasons, qualitative indicators may be more appropriate and less contradictory, although requiring more elaborate research. Where the regulatory authority is expected to play a broader role in public affairs, as is the case in many countries, evaluation of its activity and effectiveness in influencing government or business policy over issues that pose threats to privacy is particularly important. Proposals for national identity cards, new uses for criminal records, increased surveillance for combatting fraud or terrorism, road-use charging systems, RFID applications, calling-line identification, and closed-circuit television systems, for example, provide challenges to privacy protection. They also offer opportunities for regulators to exert influence in the corridors of power, or more widely to instigate public debate. More routinely, the extent of the authority's activity in encouraging or negotiating data controllers' codes of practice would be an essential part of evaluation in those data protection systems in which self-regulation plays a key role, as mentioned below.

The Performance of Data Controllers

Where data protection law exists, every controller of personal data, from single individuals to large commercial or governmental organizations, is legally required to comply with the law and with the fair information principles that support it. Because implementation is therefore widely dispersed in society, the overall quality of data protection depends upon controllers' compliance. As a German example shows (Weise 1992), organizations themselves can evaluate their own compliance activity, although, unlike internal financial accounting, for example, such "privacy auditing" is relatively rare and nonstandardized.

A possible focus for qualitative evaluation is the extent to which data-controlling organizations realize the relationship between their practices and the requirements of good data protection, and how they then use this awareness to modify what they do, to deploy their resources and train their staff, to audit their information systems, and to increase public trust. The establishment of a company or bureau official or department to preside over the organization's compliance may be a *prima facie* indicator. But obviously the actual performance of these individuals must provide the basis for appraisal, as it would in Germany, where company officers (*Beauftragte*) are a legal requirement. As mentioned earlier, data protection officers are rapidly becoming ubiquitous in private sector organizations' managerial structures, and many public sector agencies are increasing the centrality of data protection roles and functions.[4]

In chapter 6, we explain the range of self-regulatory instruments that included privacy commitments, codes, standards, and seals. Another focus for evaluation is therefore the adoption and further implementation of these devices. The proliferation of these self-regulatory instruments is a rough indication that self-regulation has shifted in meaning from mere symbolic value statements to instruments through which compliance might be more accurately gauged. Thus privacy commitments, while necessary, lack any methodology for external evaluation. Privacy codes should provide a more complete codification of the rules that employees should follow, but generally also lack an explicit method by which compliance can be measured.

When external conformity assessment organizations are brought into the picture, as they are with privacy standards and seals, the performance of data controllers can be more objectively measured. When data protection began to be considered in standards-setting and certification terms, one of the initial realizations was that it was necessary to have a graduated measurement system for compliance sensitive to the needs of the marketplace. Thus a distinction can be drawn between three levels of compliance: of policy, of procedure, and of practice (Bennett 1995). For some organizations, it may be quite sufficient to know that their *policy* (code of practice) is consistent with the standard. For others, external agencies might want to be assured that those policies are communicated effectively and regularly throughout the organization. When compliance of *procedure* is desired, therefore, evaluations would focus on the internal mechanisms that an organization has adopted to implement its code. The search for conformity of *practice*, by extension, attempts to assess whether the code is in fact being adhered to throughout the organization through a regular, independent and external auditing program. At this latter level, it is important to realize that only the data controller's behavior can be evaluated. Sectoral, technological, or professional codes obviously have a wider span, but one cannot audit a sector, a profession, or a technology.

One of the conclusions of chapter 6 is that these instruments have not progressed in a cumulative fashion, and therefore they can rarely be used to determine with any degree of certainty that an organization in fact says what it does, and does what it says. With regard to the compliance of data controllers in the private sector, there has been little evidence that the market itself will motivate an organization to engage in a serious audit program in the absence of some other external inducement. The experience of privacy standards and seals programs to date is that consumer demand itself is not sufficient to motivate the kind of expenditure that the more onerous programs require. Thus organizations prefer self-certification to external certification, and internal audits are preferred to external audits. For most companies, conformity of policy is all that can be claimed and observed.

Of course, privacy codes, standards, and seals can be used to measure the compliance of data controllers in the public sector as well. Even though government agencies are more likely to be governed by law, they may seek to gain public confidence by being seen to implement these other devices as well. For a policy as complicated and multifaceted as data protection, only a regular, independent, and external audit program can evaluate whether or not the privacy principles have affected the culture of decision-making throughout the hierarchy of a public organization. This was one important conclusion of Flaherty's (1989, p. 400) analysis: "Government officials who handle personal information have to fear a privacy audit as much as most of us dread a tax audit." Privacy auditing can be, however, an expensive and time-consuming process, and many data protection authorities do not have the financial and human resources to conduct an audit program on a regular basis.

The obvious weakness of privacy audit programs has led some privacy experts to shift attention away from these more reactive measures toward more anticipatory instruments in the belief in the rationale of an "ounce of prevention." In trying to prevent privacy abuses before they occur, the technique of the Privacy Impact Assessment (PIA) has become increasingly important in many countries. The development of thinking about PIAs dates from the mid-1990s and gathered pace in New Zealand and a few other countries (Stewart 1996). For example, in 1994, they were urged on a then-unregulated business sector by Tom Wright, Ontario's Information and Privacy Commissioner, who wrote: "The preparation of a privacy impact statement should be required prior to the introduction of any potentially privacy-intrusive technology, service or product. Approval of such activity should be contingent upon a demonstration that privacy will be adequately protected." More an inventory of good-practice guidelines, the privacy impact statement nonetheless asked for "an evaluation of the probable or potential effects that the proposed technology, service or product would have on the privacy of the customers" (Ontario IPC 1994, Appendix D).

More recently, White (2001, p. 2) sees PIAs as "a methodology that identifies privacy issues, privacy impacts and potential privacy risks that may be associated with proposals to develop new information technology applications." PIAs are supposed to raise alarms, to provide the necessary "early-warning systems" of where privacy-related problems are likely to emerge. Although the intent and definition varies, Flaherty's (2001, p. 265) idea is commonly accepted: "to require the preparation of privacy impact assessments for new products, practices, databases, and delivery systems involving personal information." He notes that "a privacy impact assessment seeks to set forth, in as much detail as required to promote necessary understanding, the essential components of any personal information system or any system that contains significant amounts of personal information" (Flaherty 2001, p. 266). In practice, PIAs are often used mainly to ascertain the compliance of existing personal information systems to applicable privacy standards. Thus PIAs over time may become indistinguishable from privacy audits, which can be applied as readily to existing systems as to new ones. Furthermore, it is often difficult to define a new system from the old, when personal information from existing applications are combined or matched to create new databases posing new privacy risks (White 2001, p. 2).

In recent years, a number of data protection authorities have extolled the virtues of PIAs and developed explicit methodologies.[5] In May 2002, the Canadian federal government became the first jurisdiction in the world to make PIAs mandatory for new programs and services; and the Treasury Board published some PIA guidelines that agencies are expected to follow.[6] They are important instruments that enhance the general awareness of privacy issues at the program level. They ensure accountability, and build the trust and confidence of citizens; this is especially crucial in an era of electronic government. They enhance the "due diligence" necessary for substantial investments in new technology, and they create a common language of evaluation.[7] PIA methodologies are driven by the requirements of the particular legal standard in operation, and they therefore read like standard audit checklists. But PIAs are also "a risk-assessment tool for decision makers to address not only the legal, but the moral and ethical, issues posed by whatever is being proposed" (Flaherty 2001, p. 266). Thus it is often difficult to capture the intangible and subjective quality of privacy risk assessment in standard checklists. PIAs are, nevertheless, now another established instrument in the toolkit of the data protector.

The Performance of Data Subjects

Data protection policy not only imposes obligations upon data controllers for the responsible processing of personal data, it also confers rights upon individuals as data subjects. Successful data protection may thus depend in part upon the degree to which the general public is aware of privacy dangers, and of the ways in which they may help to abate them in the wide variety of transactions in which their personal data are involved. Some avenues for the latter are available to individuals. They may bring complaints against data controllers either directly or through the enforcement authority, and they can exercise their rights of access and correction with respect to their own data. They can inform themselves about what they can do to safeguard their own privacy, such as keeping credit cards securely, carefully scrutinizing online traders' privacy policies, or restricting access to their data to those who need to know it. Therefore, focusing evaluation upon the extent of public learning and protective behavior may yield useful information for judgments of the actual level of data protection in a society. As shown in chapter 3, there is no shortage of surveys of public attitudes toward privacy, awareness of risks, and knowledge of remedies or means of redress.

Yet there is little systematic and comparative knowledge about the extent to which even well-informed data subjects actually take steps to protect their personal data. There are a number of important measures. What proportion of a population seek to sign up for the mailing preference services offered in their respective countries? What proportion of consumers actively "opt-out" of having their names subjected to secondary marketing practices? How many people actively exercise their rights of access and correction under data protection law? How many people refuse to transact online purchases with insecure or poorly compliant traders? Do responses vary in interesting ways according to jurisdiction, type of law, the nature of the organization, and so on?

The overall impression is that public awareness of its rights under privacy protection laws is low. A 1995 survey in Canada asked the question: "Were you to experience an invasion of your personal information, who would you go to?" Only 2 percent of respondents answered that they would complain to the Office of the Privacy Commissioner of Canada, and only 3 percent mentioned their provincial office. More than 30 percent of Canadians believe that a lawyer or legal clinic would be the best recourse. The same survey concluded that 73 percent of Canadians were unaware of any law or program related to the protection of personal information (Public Interest Advocacy Centre 1995, pp. 31–33). A more recent poll in Australia found that just 43 percent were aware that privacy protection laws existed, and only one in ten had any idea of whom these laws applied to. As in Canada, a very small number of people (5 percent) reported that they would complain to the Privacy Commissioner if there were a misuse of their personal information (Australia FPC 2001, pp. 30–32).

The Data Protection System as a Whole

It is fairly obvious that these identified items are not independent of each other, lending weight to the view that data protection might best be seen as a system of interacting parts, as discussed in chapter 8. For example, the level of public awareness may depend upon the efforts of the data protection authority in publicizing dangers and how to prevent or counteract them. The number or efficacy of codes of practice may similarly reflect the authority's exhortation of data controllers to adopt and abide by them. By the same token, data subjects are dependent upon the efforts of regulators and data controllers to enable the public to act upon their rights by, for instance, simplifying procedures for complaint or access.

Moreover, the quality of data protection overall reflects not only the actions of various actors, but the structural limits, requirements, and opportunities given in the law itself.

Therefore, evaluations and measurements of the data protection system as a whole should reflect these systemic properties, where data protection is seen as a collaborative endeavor in which it may be difficult to identify the "value added" by any one component. But holistic judgments of the system might provide only crude summary statements that are of little diagnostic value in improving performance. They may merely provide fuel for political debate rather than accounts of the system's merits, deficiencies, improvement, or deterioration over time that are capable of being interrogated in rational discourse. This is an endemic problem in measuring the quality of public systems generally, for it is difficult to draw robust empirical or conceptual distinctions among the roles or organizations when their performances are closely intertwined.

However, evaluators in practice should probably try to avoid entanglement in these complexities, even though they should be aware of them as well as of the ambiguities outlined above. Some acceptable and intellectually defensible boundaries may nonetheless be drawn around the various subjects of evaluation, and some useful measures seem possible. These may be guided by the consideration that a highly efficacious data protection system would comprise

- a strong and unambiguous law;
- an active and assertive regulatory authority;
- a strong commitment by data controllers, reflected at least in the establishment of the requisite procedures for compliance and, in particular, by an effort to collect as little data as possible for the carrying out of their legitimate activities;
- with respect to private sector compliance, a set of market incentives that drive companies to be pro-privacy and to implement those goals through strong self-regulatory mechanisms;
- a vigilant, concerned, and activist citizenry that is prepared to complain, to exercise access and correction rights, and to opt out of secondary uses of their data;
- the application, as far as possible at the outset of system development, of privacy-enhancing technologies to assist in the overall provision of privacy protection.

No a priori judgment can be made about the relative importance of each of these; all are necessary conditions for high quality data protection. None is a sufficient condition.

Conclusion

The discussion in this chapter suggests that further exploration of the potential for a more systematic evaluative framework for data protection should be fruitful. What conclusions can be reached from the preceding analysis that would point to the most promising avenues for future work? Four observations can be made.

First, any attempt to establish the criteria for assessing performance is beset by the central difficulty that the goals of data protection policy are not self-defining. Bearing in mind remarks made at the beginning of this chapter, we should note that most of the dilemmas of accountability stem from the very difficulty of making robust conceptual and empirical separations between ends and means. If one focuses on means or procedures, it is possible to develop measurable performance indicators, but these may only have a tenuous connection to wider policy goals. If, however, one focuses on the activities of the data protection agency, one can develop fairly convenient and relevant measures of performance that are at least comparable over time, if not across space.

Such indicators and measures are necessary, but they are not sufficient. They fall short of a holistic perspective on the data protection system and on the crucial interrelationships between data controllers and data subjects. Data protection should be seen not just as a system that produces outputs and outcomes, but as a process that involves organizational change and learning, and that involves an elaborate implementation network of persons and organizations engaged in the collaborative, albeit often conflictual, production of data protection. This process involves complex relationships among official regulators; organizations such as business, trade and professional associations, government departments, and interest groups; and individual decisions and actions constituting "informational self-determination." At all levels and among them, data protection is a political process. To evaluate that process would require analytical categories and frameworks derived from discourses other than the ones in which performance measurement normally takes place.

Thus, second, the only reliable subjects for evaluation seem to be procedural, involving rules, codes, sanctions, and decisions that may lead to the protection of privacy but that do not themselves represent privacy as such. How these outputs are produced is itself important in assessing how, and whether, the system "works," and in modifying these processes. It may well be that a data protection system can only be evaluated on the basis of whether it adequately puts the procedures in place for data subjects to exercise their own privacy rights if they so wish and are not otherwise hindered through structured patterns of disadvantage, limited access to knowledge of what happens to personal data, intimidation or lack of self-confidence in exercising rights, or other conditions. The criteria for evaluation, therefore, are the outputs of the system, rather than the outcomes.

Third, the difficulty of establishing criteria for evaluating ultimate outcomes should not, however, prevent regulatory authorities from devising their own systematic measures of procedural outputs, and it should not prevent "consumers" of such accounts—politicians, auditors, and the public—from taking these measures seriously and debating them, even if the result is only a small step towards comprehensive evaluation. Thus, in the context of one system, it might be very profitable to measure the relationship of inputs, in terms of staff and resources, to outputs, such as successful complaints resolution, the negotiation of codes of practice, the provision of advice and guidance, enforcement, and sanctions. That relationship may also be measured over time. But given the fallacy of taking indicators out of context, such measures can only be used for cross-national comparisons with extreme caution.

Fourth, a focus on procedural questions means, in practical terms, that it is often more important for a data controller to be asking the correct questions about privacy protection, than coming to the "correct" answers. The logic behind PIAs, for instance, merely insists that privacy interests be considered carefully when new products and services are being introduced. But PIAs are not based on the assumption that there are necessarily "correct" answers to the checklists of questions asked in the variety of public and private organizations that might use them. More significant is the fact that issues of personal information collection, retention, use, disclosure, and so on are considered and debated by those at the top level of the organization. The institution of the Chief Privacy Officer in many corporations is designed to achieve the same goal. Privacy problems and abuses more often arise when privacy issues are ignored, rather than conscientiously balanced against organizational interests. PIAs and Chief Privacy Officers are instruments that ensure that the correct privacy questions are asked, even if not always answered in clear and acceptable terms.

Finally, the interdependence of actions and organizations in a data protection system points to the merits of a "bottom-up" perspective on policy implementation. Although we do not see it as a stark and irrevocable contrast between quantitative and qualitative assessment, quantitative indicators generally assume a tidy world of policy-making and implementation, one that is amenable to a stepwise approach to evaluation. This involves an unambiguous definition of goals and a measurement of goal attainment through known implementation processes taking place across time, across organizations, across sectors, across technology, and ultimately across systems. Qualitative indicators, on the other hand, lend themselves more to a "bottom-up" approach to understanding the policy process, and are concerned with evaluation as diagnosis. This approach centers on an explanation of what happens through negotiation, bargaining, mutual influence, and the exercise of power. Although the measurement of performance and the use of indicators owe more to the "top-down" approach, the realism of the "bottom-up" perspective may have much to commend it because it opens up to analysis those situations in which the formulation and implementation of policy run together. The definition of goals does not necessarily precede the implementation of policy, and the decisions of those near the "top" of an organization are not necessarily more important than those lower down.

The ultimate evaluative criterion was perhaps best put by a British data protection official (UK House of Commons 1990): "One approach to getting data protection properly implemented is to say that we should work ourselves out of business if all data users were doing everything absolutely properly and complying with the data protection principles."

That outcome is obviously more likely to be brought about by political and organizational pressures in different states than by any abstract measurement and evaluation that purports to show that the goal has been achieved, and that the policy is a "success." It is also an outcome scenario that would have to take account of the migration of many privacy problems, issues, and solutions to the international or global arena. Evaluations of success, and measurement of the quality of privacy protection, are also problematic at that level. Our exploration of the problems of measurement and the appraisal of quality sets the stage for the final chapter's analysis of the likelihood of and pressures toward establishing an international regime for privacy protection, and of how the resultant quality of such a regime could be assessed.

10

International Privacy Protection: A Race to the Top, the Bottom, or Somewhere Else?

Introduction

The privacy paradigm outlined in chapter 1 was originally founded upon an assumption that the privacy value is rooted in a desired relationship between the individual and the state. The privacy policy instruments have been generally developed in order to protect that relationship. As these instruments have been extended to operate with regard to the private sector, they still provide rights of redress through the legal apparatus of the state. Thus, according to the traditional paradigm, privacy protection entails an exercise of rights by Citizen A of Country A against an organization that was geographically located within Country A. Those assumptions have obviously broken down, as personal information now knows fewer organizational and national attachments. Privacy regimes are no longer discrete, independent, and bounded by a traditional conception about where the state begins and ends.

What does privacy protection mean now that personal information flows more freely, knows fewer national attachments, and indeed represents one of the significant forces behind the processes of globalization? Let us recall how Held and his colleagues (Held et al. 1999, pp. 15–16; emphasis in original) characterize the globalization phenomenon. It implies, first, "a *stretching* of social, political and economic activities across frontiers such that events, decisions and activities in one region of the world can come to have significance for individuals and communities in distant regions of the globe." Second, globalization implies that these connections are not random or intermittent, but are regularized so that there is a "detectable *intensification*." Third,

globalization implies a *speeding up* of global interactions as new communications processes increase the "velocity of the global diffusion of
ideas, goods, information, capital and people." Fourth, each of these
processes contributes to the deepening enmeshment of local, national,
and regional institutions, such that local events can come to have global
impacts. The transnational transactions related to personal information
flows display each of these characteristics.

At the same time, we have witnessed an enormous and increasing
variety of policy activities for data protection. What explains this? Our
final chapter tries to situate the privacy protection issue within larger
debates about the impact of globalization on government regulation,
and on the autonomy of state institutions to fashion distinctive national
public policies. We therefore provide an overview of privacy protection
policy from the point of view of a high-flying aircraft in which much of
the detail might be lost, but which nevertheless tries to observe the main
contours and dynamics concerning the past, present, and future of this
issue.

The Impact of Globalization on Government Regulation: The Theories

There is a common consensus that the global economy necessitates
competition on a global level, as transnational corporations engage in
a competitive scramble for ever-wider markets, and as states compete
for inward investment by offering conditions favorable to these firms'
operations. Such regulatory competition has been defined as "the competitive adjustment of rules, processes, or enforcement regimes in order
to secure an advantage" (Baldwin and Cave 1999, p. 180). It takes place
under certain conditions that include firms' freedom of movement, the
access that they as well as regulators have to information about alternative regulatory regimes, and the degree of certainty about the enforcement of regulations. But, depending on a variety of conditions that may
be present in particular instances, this competition can result in a raising
as well as a lowering of regulatory standards.

Broadly, the theoretical literature can be divided into three camps.
First are those authors who contend that globalization will inevitably

produce a race to the bottom, a downward spiral of jurisdictional standards as corporations search for competitive advantage and as jurisdictions cater to their needs. Second, there are those authors who would accept the logic of the "race-to-the-bottom" theory, but who would insist that this process could be obstructed by important domestic variables. Finally, there are those who contend that the principal dynamic is a fashioning of policy according to the highest possible standard, a trading-up or a race to the top.[1] We review these theories and then, in the next section, address the evidence with respect to privacy protection.

The basic race-to-the-bottom theory is founded on very powerful logic. As corporations spread throughout the global economy, they engage in a constant search for competitive advantage. In so doing they will seek to situate themselves or to have their business processes performed in those jurisdictions that might offer the lowest short-term and long-term costs—those that offer lower tax rates, lower labor and environmental standards, and so on. For their part, governments might consider that a less regulatory climate would attract global businesses that would want to circumvent the higher standards at work elsewhere. This competitive deregulation would lead to a race to the bottom, as countries progressively weaken their standards to attract global investment (Collingsworth et al. 1994).

The race-to-the-bottom argument is based on the underlying premise that there might be competitive advantages for any state to have regulatory policies that are distinctly weaker than those elsewhere. Assuming that firms will seek the locations with lowest costs, states will need, despite their own preferences, to reduce or weaken their regulations to gain competitive advantage for these firms. States will purportedly value the higher investment and employment over and above the public good that their regulations aim to achieve, whether that be cleaner air, higher workplace standards, or indeed, a greater protection for the personal privacy of their citizens.

Beyond the policy consequences, critics of globalization have pointed to wider implications for the autonomy of nation states to fashion distinctive public policies to protect their citizens from environmental pollution, hazardous working conditions, discrimination, and so on.

Some paint a picture of the state being under siege from globalizing forces (Strange 1996). As Cerny (1995, p. 610) writes: "The capacity of industrial and financial sectors to whipsaw the state apparatus by pushing state agencies into a process of competitive deregulation or what economists call competition in laxity . . . has both undermined the control span of the state from without and fragmented it from within."

There are clearly certain necessary conditions that need to be met for the race-to-the-bottom process to be observed (Spar and Yoffie 1999, p. 565). The first is simply mobility: the race-to-the-bottom phenomenon may be particularly acute where the factors of production are highly mobile, as is the case with many industries within the new information economy. Hypothetically, vast quantities of information can be transmitted instantaneously for processing in jurisdictions that have lower regulatory, including privacy, standards.

The second condition is a genuine diversity of regulation that critically affects production costs. There can only be a race to the bottom where clearly different costs give firms an incentive to relocate their activities to less tightly regulated business environments. If the differences are negligible or unimportant, firms will generally be content to remain where they are or to base any relocation decisions on other factors. For states to provide these attractive incentives, there must accordingly be clear and multiple levels of regulatory action. It must be hypothetically possible for states to continue to minimize the regulatory burden. Obviously, if there are only a few finite ways to solve a particular policy problem, then the race will stop as soon as the lowest level is reached.

In short, a number of critical questions can be raised about this model. First, there are questions about the circumstances under which states would use regulation as an instrument to compete for capital or trade. Second, there are questions about the applicability of abstract, "rational actor" assumptions upon which some of this literature is based. Third, there are questionable assumptions about the ability of state actors to measure the consequences of their actions. These are cogent reasons to believe that an efficiency model based on cost-benefit calculus cannot, and should not, form the basis of regulatory decision-making (Swire 1996).

A second position, therefore, accepts the logic of the race-to-the-bottom argument, but also contends that this race is conditional on other facilitating factors. The race to the bottom is, therefore, not generally observed across all economic sectors, but can be halted, at least temporarily, by domestic political and economic constraints. We note three such constraints.

The first set of constraints relates to *the internal structure and dynamics of various industries*. The basic race-to-the-bottom thesis suggests that firms can and do hop across borders as soon as they perceive an economic advantage from a more favorable regulatory climate. This is clearly simplistic. Most firms cannot switch locations at will because they will incur substantial costs in doing so—sunk costs relating to existing capital investment, as well as transaction costs relating to the move itself, which are not only financial and tangible, but also invisible (Spar and Yoffie 1999, p. 568). These factors will vary from sector to sector. As a working hypothesis, Spar and Yoffie (1999, p. 570) suggest the following:

Firms will be most inclined to race when they produce homogenous, commodity type products; when the costs that matter most to them are sharply divergent across national borders; and when their sunk costs of investment and transaction costs of relocation are both relatively low. When these conditions are not in place, races to the bottom are less likely to occur.

The second set of constraints relates to the *structure of the international economy*. The race-to-the-bottom thesis is undoubtedly more persuasive in a model in which all economies are of relatively similar size and openness. In a world of highly differentiated economies, however, the regulatory position of the largest economies is likely to be more powerful. For example, no multinational with global aspirations can avoid investing in the United States, still the world's largest economy. Thus, the regulatory decisions of American policy-makers obviously carry more weight than do those of their counterparts in other countries. Given the political will, economies with the largest or most lucrative markets can raise regulatory standards in certain industries without fear of a flight of capital or a loss of trade. The EU can wield a similar clout when it acts in a unified manner. In general, if the standards in larger economies are relatively high, the pressure on smaller countries to deregulate will be correspondingly reduced. So the race to the bottom can only occur, it seems, if the standards in the larger economies are relatively low.

The third set of constraints relates to *political and social activism*. The race to the bottom may be slowed by transnational activists who can spotlight the behavior of firms and the lax standards of states. When firms go abroad, they take not only their capital investment, they also take their reputations, brand names, images, and so on. Activists in many countries are ready to use the media to shed the spotlight upon the socially irresponsible corporation and upon the weak regulations that facilitate such behavior. The "spotlight phenomenon" (Spar 1998) can expose questionable practices such as the use of child labor, the hiring of workers at below minimum wages, or the processing of personal data in electronic sweat shops. Under pressure, multinational firms are reluctantly forced to accept responsibility for the abuses perpetrated by foreign contractors and subsidiaries. Such pressures have led to global codes of conduct, standards, and seals that companies have been forced to adhere to. The race to the bottom is not, therefore, a process that can take place quietly and without cost.

These various sets of conditions may only serve, however, to slow the race to the bottom, or to ameliorate its worse effects. A third broad position rejects the assumptions behind the race-to-the-bottom argument entirely. Vogel's explanation of how international commerce can generate a "trading-up" of national regulatory standards is the most important reaction to that argument. In contrast to racing to the bottom—the "Delaware effect"—Vogel describes a "California effect" to denote the ratcheting upward of regulatory standards in competing political jurisdictions (Vogel 1995, pp. 5–8). He concludes that this pattern applies to regulatory activities in such diverse fields as animal hormones, genetically engineered crops, meat inspection, pharmaceutical regulation and inspection, fuel economy standards, leg-hold trap bans, eco-labeling, chemical testing standards, and ozone depletion. Vogel (1997, p. 57) argues that "[t]here does not appear to be a single instance in which either the United States or the EU lowered any health, safety, or environmental standard to make its domestic producers more competitive."

According to him, the "trading-up" pattern is driven by three separate influences. First, where the burdens of compliance fall disproportionately on foreign competitors, this may make domestic firms more willing to support stricter regulations than would have been the case in the absence of foreign competition. The liberalization of trade (in data or anything else) may actually give states an economic incentive to strengthen regulations. A second and related influence concerns market access. The stricter standards developed in some political jurisdictions force firms in other states with weaker domestic standards either to design products to meet the higher standards or to sacrifice export markets. Having made these initial investments, they now have a stake in encouraging their home markets to strengthen their standards as well, since their exports are already meeting those standards. A third influence relates to the politics of integration. In Vogel's view (1995, pp. 263–264), "[t]o the extent that treaties or trade agreements provide formal mechanisms for establishing harmonized or equivalent standards, they provide an opportunity for richer, more powerful countries to play a greater role in setting those standards. . . . [T]he more authority nations concede over the making of national regulatory standards, the more likely these standards will be strengthened."

The race-to-the-bottom thesis is based on an underlying premise that states might benefit by having divergent regulations. On the other hand, the trading-up thesis suggests that there is a point at which a more cooperative mode of regulation is in the interests of states to prevent or halt race-to-the-bottom behavior. Two factors explain this. First, compatible regulations facilitate trade and access to different markets; second, harmonized regulations reduce the cost of production. If a firm is forced to produce multiple versions of the same product, the unit costs are significantly increased. This argument says nothing, of course, about the level at which a coordinated compromise might be struck. Harmonization of standards could conceivably be struck at any point along a hypothetical scale of regulation, from extreme laxity on the one end to extreme strictness on the other (Swire 1996). Baldwin and Cave (1999, pp. 185–188) point out, for instance, that the EU's facilitation of this coordination or harmonization among Member States sometimes mitigates the competitive race to the bottom. It should be noted that coordinative activity need not necessarily produce higher standards. Many instruments of policy coordination may have a symbolic purpose and/or effect. Moreover, the trading-up argument is probably more relevant to product standards than to process standards; the incentive to harmonize production to that higher standard will be stronger where the economies of scale dictate that it is more efficient for a firm to meet the higher standard than to tolerate different products in different jurisdictions. Process standards, however, of which privacy protection is a clear example, are perhaps more difficult to enforce outside of a state's borders.

Empirical evidence of race-to-the-bottom or race-to-the-top processes is often dependent on guessing the motives behind certain corporate and governmental decisions. Of course, there is no reason to assume that these theories operate on the same linear and unidimensional scale. As we will see, the confirmation or disconfirmation of each of these hypotheses depends directly on how a particular policy sector is defined; and no public policy is inherently self-defining. Contributory explanations for races to the top or to the bottom will often be found in the empirical details of particular industries and markets. In determining which process might be at work in a given policy area, it is thus more important to determine whether the underlying conditions are likely to push corporate decisions about investment and government choices about regulation in one direction rather than another. Having outlined some of these conditions, therefore, let us examine the broad history of the attempt to regulate the international flows of personal data. Which of these positions best approximates and explains what we have seen with regard to privacy protection over the past thirty years?

Globalization and the Governance of Privacy: The Evidence

There are certainly powerful reasons to believe that a race-to-the-bottom dynamic might be very strong with respect to privacy protection policy. The main conditions seem to be met: the resources of production—personal data—are highly mobile, and there is a diversity of regulatory conditions, ranging from countries with absolutely no data privacy safeguards to those, mainly in Europe, with ostensibly very strong protections. There is also a thriving global market for the processing of data by contract, including personal data. Moreover, for companies in the new high-tech service sector, the sunk costs of capital investment and the transaction costs for relocation are likely to be low. Especially for any sector that might profit from the processing of identifiable personal data for marketing purposes, complying with privacy protection law entails costs. The complicated consent requirements imposed by data protection law inevitably increase the number of consumers who might refuse to consent to having their personal information disclosed in this way, thus reducing the value of the lists that are compiled and traded within the personal information market. For companies whose business is the processing of personal data, and for whom data protection regulations incur real costs, there would appear to be an incentive to relocate to those societies with no, or minimal, data protection regulations.

It is not surprising that such arguments are regularly raised during attempts to lobby against the passage of data protection laws. Decisions about Canadian regulation are instructive in this regard. The EU Data Protection Directive placed Canadian policy-makers in a dilemma about whether to trade up to the European standard or to follow the less interventionist approach of the United States, by far Canada's largest trading partner. Some provinces, influenced by industry lobbying, argued very strongly that a more stringent regulatory climate in Canada would lead to the industry's flight south of the border. A particularly interesting exchange occurred in 1998 between the province of Manitoba and the federal Department of Industry. The government of Manitoba asserted that it would only support data protection legislation for the private sector if "thorough research, preferably undertaken by an independent body, has demonstrated that Canadian businesses will not be placed at a comparative disadvantage as against American companies if the United States does not implement similar legislation . . . and that foreign investment in Canada will be unaffected" (Manitoba 1998). In response, the federal government offered a series of arguments for trading-up and pointed out that there was no evidence that jurisdictions with data protection law (including Québec) had lost investment or competitiveness due to privacy legislation. Similar arguments about loss of investment have also surfaced in Latin America as data protection has risen to the agendas of Argentina, Chile, Brazil, Mexico, and other states (Palazzi 2002).

It is very hard to find clear evidence of corporate-location decisions being driven by the presence or absence of data protection legislation. Occasionally, stories appear in the media about high-tech companies locating in offshore "havens." An Internet web server company called HavenCo[2] was set up in 2000 in the "Principality of Sealand," a former World War II anti-aircraft military fortress in the North Sea. Only authorized persons directly involved in the HavenCo project are permitted to land on the island. Sealand is ideal for web business, HavenCo argues, as there are no direct reporting or registration requirements: "Sealand has no laws governing data traffic, and the terms of HavenCo's agreement with Sealand provide that none shall ever be enacted." Closer analysis reveals, however, that this particular data haven is attractive precisely because of the secure environment and very tightly controlled access to outsiders: "HavenCo provides a place for secure e-Commerce, privacy-protected Internet services and uncensorable free speech." One also suspects that if HavenCo did fall foul of the UK's Data Protection Act in a serious way, there would be very little that the company could in effect do to resist regulatory intervention.

From time to time, there are media stories about computer professionals relocating to Caribbean islands to provide offshore information services. But again, the major incentives are obviously tax-related, rather than privacy-related.[3] No doubt less reputable outfits seek data havens to engage in more nefarious conduct. Those individuals engaged in sending unsolicited bulk e-mailing over the Internet—"spammers"—obviously locate their servers in countries where there are minimum regulations on many things, including data privacy. Perhaps the ultimate race-to-the-bottom scenario is reflected in an announcement in October 2000, that Skycorp Inc. had signed a Space Act Agreement with NASA to place the world's first Internet server in Space. The company plans to launch satellites full of Apple Computer Macintosh G4 Cubes running Apache web servers and using new wireless Internet technology.[4]

The evidence in contrast to these somewhat bizarre illustrations is, of course, overwhelming. As we have shown, the fair information principles now appear in a large number of national laws. They have been embraced in international agreements, in voluntary codes of conduct, in certifiable standards, and (with some variations) in the Safe Harbor Principles (Bennett and Grant 1999, p. 6). Many large companies are now appointing data protection or privacy officers to oversee their compliance with applicable standards, and professional associations of privacy professionals have now been institutionalized. A small industry offering privacy-protective services has developed, and many of the traditional accounting firms offer privacy auditing services. The EU Directive, with its insistence that data protection laws should be overseen by a "supervisory authority," has reinforced a process of convergence not only on the statutory principles, but also on the policy instruments through which those principles should be enforced (Bennett 1997a). There is also a growing consensus on the efficacious use of PETs, and examples of cryptographic researchers locating to jurisdictions with no controls over the export of such products.[5] This dynamic is consistent with a race-to-the-bottom argument, except that the absence of regulation for cryptography operates to advance, rather than impede, the progress of privacy.

In summary, there is clearly no race to the bottom. Despite the relative ease with which companies in electronic commerce could locate in jurisdictions with lax privacy safeguards, there has been no discernible attempt to escape from the advanced industrial states—at least not for reasons that relate to privacy protection. There is therefore no clear incentive for jurisdictions to race to the bottom in order to attract businesses seeking weak privacy safeguards. But does all the policy activity we have described constitute a race to the top? Does the convergence dynamic operate to harmonize data protection rules to the highest, rather than the lowest, common denominator—that is, to the standard embodied within the EU Directive? Let us return to Vogel's (1997) arguments for the trading-up of regulations in competitive jurisdictions.

Vogel's first explanation is that stricter regulations represent a source of competitive advantage for domestic firms, and that the latter then support them in the international arena if the burdens of compliance fall disproportionately on their foreign competitors. Thus the liberalization of trade may provide states with an incentive to strengthen regulations. One problem with this argument in the data protection case is that many European industries, particularly in direct-marketing and consumer credit, lobbied hard against the EU Directive; some even made common cause with American multinationals (Regan 1999).

Vogel's second explanation concerns market access: stricter product standards in some jurisdictions force foreign producers to design products to meet those standards or else lose export markets. To protect their investments, they have a stake in encouraging their state to upgrade its standards because their exports are already meeting those higher standards. This is obviously an important argument, with some validity in this case.[6] But the costs of making different automobiles to different emission standards, for instance, are generally a lot higher than the costs of complying with different privacy standards. Fundamentally, this debate comes down to one of consent: should one have to get data subjects' consent before using personal data for secondary purposes? The value of personal information for a major direct-marketing firm is probably a greater incentive to seek the lowest possible standard. If it has to design its systems to allow an opt-in in Germany, and an opt-out in the United States, so be it. The economies of scale are perhaps not strong enough to dictate an across-the-board trading-up dynamic.

Vogel's third explanation, however, is more plausible. This, we have seen, had to do with the politics of integration and the role of richer, more powerful countries in setting harmonized standards through treaties or trade agreements. Here, politics makes the difference. In the data protection case, the EU Directive was driven by the efforts of the Germans and the French. We have therefore seen considerable pressure brought to bear upon those states that lacked comprehensive privacy protection laws to adopt them, first within Europe and then outside. This pressure stemmed from officials within the European Commission, as well as from certain influential data protection commissioners, who now have the power to disrupt the international trade in personal information. Related to this, we would add another important factor relating to culture and history. Within the memory of a large proportion of the populations of many European countries, privacy has been a value that was threatened or sacrificed under totalitarian or authoritarian regimes, and its protection to a high level is therefore particularly prized. In many cases, therefore, the emotional appeal of rediscovering privacy is consistent with harder-headed economic considerations at the European level.

A related, and perhaps more satisfactory, explanation for the trading-up of standards in this particular case is provided by Shaffer (2000), who offers five separate reasons for the raising of privacy standards, although his analysis is limited to the United States. First, he argues that business demand for trade liberalization leads to a need to compete in Europe, and a concomitant need to conform their data processing standards to the EU level. The important implication of trade liberalization is the spillover effect, permitting US privacy advocates to highlight the lower level of privacy protection in the United States. Secondly, the authority of EU law is bolstered by the power of the European market, producing an ability in Europe to negotiate rules that govern firms' behavior. A third argument relates to the relative importance of privacy in the public consciousness, and the belief that privacy becomes a good that is increasingly demanded as individuals become richer. A fourth reason has to do with the externalities of data privacy policies, and the need within Europe to ensure that their laws are not undermined by the processing of personal data in offshore data havens; fears about a race to the bottom are therefore as significant as arguments for a race to the top. This factor is strengthened by the final reason, which relates to the application of international trade rules to data privacy questions. WTO rules, which otherwise constrain a country's ability to restrict imports and exports, provide for exemptions for data protection. As a result, "trade liberalization rules do not abate the pressure on the United States to raise effectively its data privacy standards. On the contrary, they constrain the ability of the United States to retaliate, again further facilitating a trading up of standards" (Shaffer 2000, p. 86).

Shaffer's analysis links the interests of European governments, private industry and privacy advocates. His argument is persuasive, that the EU Directive can be, and has been, used by privacy advocates as "leverage to force domestic regulators and businesses to raise privacy standards at home" (Shaffer 2000, p. 88). But his analysis does raise the question about the true effect of the "spotlight phenomenon," referred to earlier. As we see in chapter 8, in the privacy protection sector, there is a diverse range of advocacy interests, stretching from traditional civil liberties organizations, consumer associations and groups established to promote freedom in cyberspace, to more specialized groups involved solely with privacy protection. When privacy conflicts arise, they tend to be waged by a loose coalition of relatively small groups who come together for specific causes, generally via listservers and newsgroups, and then disband.[7] In few countries, however, are there powerful lobbying organizations whose sole interest is the protection of privacy. Most such groups also lobby on a range of civil liberties and consumer-related issues, some of which can sit uneasily alongside privacy. Moreover, the control of the spotlight tends to pass from one organization to another depending on the scale, complexity, and location of the practice being targeted.

There is, therefore, no consistent and concerted worldwide privacy movement that has anything like the scale, resources, or public recognition of organizations such as the Sierra Club or Amnesty International. The level of activism and the scale of publicity about privacy has clearly risen in the last decade, and high-profile campaigns against the worst abuses of personal data have risen in frequency and intensity. But it cannot yet be argued that the greater salience of the issue is attributable to the rise of a global social movement devoted exclusively to the advancement of the privacy value.[8] In addition, while the mass media— often in conjunction with advocacy groups—occasionally mount vigorous campaigns against erosions of privacy, their attitude towards this issue is often fickle; much of the public press is inherently ambivalent about privacy given their own commercially driven propensity to pry into private lives. In general terms, therefore, it would seem that Shaffer's trading-up explanation is broadly correct. But we have to be careful not to exaggerate the role of the advocates in spotlighting abuses or in pointing out the contradictory policies of firms who are willing to abide by tougher standards in Europe, but not in the United States.

One final qualification relates to the 2004 APEC Privacy Principles discussed in chapter 4. On the one hand these principles offer a set of "Asian-made" standards for countries in that region, and especially China, for whom privacy is often regarded as an alien and "Western" value.[9] They do offer an incentive to "trade-up" relative to the current regulatory positions in these countries. However, critics charge that the framework is weaker than the EU Directive in several key respects. It refers to the free flow of information as essential, and yet only speaks of "encouraging privacy protection." There is no data export limitation principle, nor is there any clear means of implementation and enforcement. Legislated solutions are not required. Countries may therefore rely upon a range of voluntary measures (such as codes of practice), the success of which is questionable (Greenleaf 2005). There is, therefore, a general suspicion that the APEC Privacy Principles are intended as an alternative, and a weaker, global standard to the EU Directive. The latter has inspired, if not a race to the top, at least a halting and meandering walk. The APEC principles may serve to slow and even reverse that trend.

The Governance of Privacy: The Contradictions

Can we reconcile this conclusion with some equally persuasive evidence that the level of personal surveillance is reaching unprecedented levels as a result of the convergence of political, administrative, capitalist, and technological pressures? At the same time as this intense policy activity has reached new heights, so too has the rhetoric concerning the levels of global surveillance, as well as the reality of heightened surveillance in face of perceived threats to nations and populations from terrorism, organized crime, illegal immigration, and other phenomena. A trading-up of standards seems to have been accompanied by an almost concomitant increase in the amount of personal information collected, processed, and distributed in personal databanks. Rule and Hunter (1999, p. 168) express the dilemma in this fashion:

> Throughout the Western democracies, misuse of personal data has come to be officially defined—at least for public consumption—as a wrong. Various forms of recourse are provided to those suffering such wrongs, ranging from litigation, as favored in the United States, to the sorts of direct intervention by privacy protection officials afforded in other countries. Surely, it would be held, the evolution of these protections gives assurance that the privacy abuses of yesteryear are now under check. Other commentators, ourselves included, take a less sanguine view. By almost any standard, the sheer scope of appropriation and use of personal data has grown vastly over the past generation.

The mechanisms for this appropriation are, of course, increasingly intrusive: the prevalence of video-surveillance cameras, the use of locational tracking devices, the development of genetic databanks, the insertion of spyware programs within commercially available software, the development of integrated health information systems based on electronic patient records, new forms of drug-testing, new methods for workplace surveillance, the proliferation of RFID chips in products, and so on. More generally, as the sociological literature reviewed in chapter 1 tells us, surveillance is an important condition of postmodernity. In his recent treatment of the subject, Lyon, for example, concentrates his analysis on the mundane practices in everyday life that track and monitor individual behavior, and in which we are all complicit. Surveillance always has two faces, he contends, because it always "carries with it some plausible justification that makes most of us content to comply" (Lyon 2001, p. 3).

How, then, can it be argued that standards for personal privacy protection are being traded up in the face of such overwhelming evidence? We have already rejected the hypothesis that personal surveillance practices have simply migrated to jurisdictions that do not have adequate privacy protections. We suggest a number of explanations to try to reconcile these interpretations.

First, it is likely that personal data processing practices would be a lot worse were it not for data protection regulations and regulators. This position is obviously difficult to substantiate in the absence of counterfactual evidence. But for each of the surveillance problems listed above, there are policy analysis, debate, recommendations, and sincere attempts to inject a countervailing privacy argument and interest. There are enough illustrations provided in Part II of this book to conclude that, under certain conditions, legal, self-regulatory, and technological policy instruments have constrained the acquisition and appropriation of personal data. However, we have to acknowledge that, especially in the context of modern campaigns against terrorism and the like, privacy protection, in many jurisdictions, is now more easily set aside in favor of other pressing policy imperatives, as we will argue more fully.

Second, it is obvious that the trading-up dynamic does not operate with equal force in different sectors. Privacy protection policy cuts across traditional sectoral categories, with the result that the market incentive of a bank will not be the same as those of an airline, or a retailer, for example. Furthermore, the dynamic tends to vary according to the type of information transferred. Business incentives vary depending on whether one is talking about consumer information, employee information, client information, or other kinds. Thus a complex multinational organization may have a very high incentive to self-regulate for some of the personal information it processes, and a lower incentive for others. As a general hypothesis, data protection legislation will be resisted when it is perceived that the costs of compliance (for example, in terms of obtaining consent for collecting, processing, and dissemination of personal data) are higher than the costs of resistance. But that resistance might take a number of forms, and be manifested during both the formation and implementation of data protection policy.

We must also remember that the "trading-up" logic can only apply to firms in the private sector. Public sector agencies cannot, of course, relocate—even though they might frequently outsource data processing to firms in foreign jurisdictions. Many of the examples of excessive surveillance are driven by public, rather than private, sector policy agendas. The literature that argues for the "end of privacy," which we discuss in chapter 1, is informed as much by observations of the surveillance state, than by the expropriation of personal data for private sector purposes (for example, Whitaker 1999). Nevertheless, these sectors are not independent of each other in practice, as much personal data flows across their boundaries. Moreover, it is unlikely that considerable differences in privacy levels between the two can constitute a stable situation. It may become politically anomalous for a government to uphold higher standards for the private sector while eroding privacy protections in the sphere of its own public policy agendas. But the perception of that anomaly may depend on the persuasiveness of the argument that states and peoples are facing unprecedented threats that require privacy protection to be set aside.

Third, and as we see in chapter 9, the trading-up of standards does not mean the trading-up of practices. There is a variable but palpable gap between the standards of an organization and the practices it pursues; we may have witnessed a ratcheting up of standards, but not of compliance. There is evidence to suggest that the private sector in both Europe and the United States is quite willing to tolerate a trading-up of standards, provided that there are no onerous enforcement and oversight mechanisms to ensure that those standards are complied with. An interesting illustration of this position is provided by the parallel attempt to negotiate a certifiable management standard for data protection through the International Standardization Organization (ISO), and latterly through the Comité Européen de Normalisation (CEN), discussed in chapter 6. Both initiatives have aroused vociferous and bitter opposition by multinational business interests on both sides of the Atlantic. The stated reason, that such an instrument would be redundant, is perhaps less important than the fear that such a standard would in fact force businesses engaged in the international transfer of personal data to say what they do, *and* to do what they say.

The contradiction between standards and practice is also manifested in the corporate behavior of some of the largest companies on the Internet. In July 2001, it was announced with great fanfare that Microsoft, Intel, Hewlett-Packard, and Procter & Gamble had recently pledged to provide European-grade privacy protection to their customers in the United States and around the world, even though no law requires them to do so.[10] In each case, the stated reason was that it was administratively burdensome for a company with a global reach to have to apply different standards in all the countries in which they operate. In registering to the Safe Harbor principles, these and the other companies thus calculated that the increased exposure to regulatory intervention was a price worth paying for the good publicity and the ability, at least on the surface, to apply a consistent set of privacy standards worldwide.

However, at the same time that Microsoft was making this announcement, it was also being severely criticized for the privacy implications of its new XP Operating System. Several consumer groups filed a complaint with the Federal Trade Commission alleging that the system of services, known as "Passport," "Hailstorm," and "Wallet" were designed to extract personal information from consumers unfairly and deceptively. In response, Microsoft made certain changes to these services, but these did not quell the fears of critics that the company was effectively building a central repository of consumer purchasing behavior that was very difficult for the unwary consumer to avoid. The case precipitated a typical public dispute of charge and counter-charge, as the implications of highly technical issues were "debated" in the media between the spokesmen for Microsoft and its critics. The case suggests that compliance with data protection norms is a highly interpretive exercise.

Finally, and in consequence, the contradiction is also explained by the fact that the abilities of democratic states to protect our personal information is perhaps as much dependent on decisions made in the laboratories of the Microsofts and Intels as in international negotiations and in national regulatory bodies, as our discussion of technological instruments in chapter 7 shows. Technological choices, such as whether to allow the latest Internet browsers to disable the "cookies" files, whether to allow "Web-bugs" on Word documents, whether to include a unique identifier within the latest generation of Pentium processors, or whether to record the search histories of those who "google" have inescapably social and political consequences.

Yet it is insufficient simply to try to assess the impact of technology on values such as privacy. The methodology of technology assessment often presupposes that the role of the social scientist is to examine the impacts or side effects, and possibly, to warn of adverse consequences in advance of technological development and application on culture, the environment, users, and so on. As Winner (1989) has argued, technologies are not merely aids to human activity but also powerful forces acting to reshape that activity and its meaning. The analysis has to go beyond causes and effects. The real question is how technologies become "deeply insinuated into people's perceptions, thoughts and behavior"— how they become an "indelible part of modern culture":

As they become woven into the texture of everyday existence, the devices, techniques, and systems we adopt shed their tool-like qualities to become part of our very humanity. In an important sense we become the beings who work on assembly lines, who talk on telephones, who do our figuring on pocket calculators, who eat processed foods, who clean our homes with powerful chemicals. (Winner 1989, p. 12)

Or who "surf the Internet," he might have added today.

In this meaning, technologies actually have political qualities. The details of technological form and architecture embody political consequences. In this light the initial analysis of legal scholars such as Reidenberg (1998) and Lessig (1999), discussed in chapter 7, is very useful, but their point needs extension. It suggests that to understand contemporary threats to privacy, we must direct our attention not just to the anteced-ent social forces, but to the artifacts themselves. Technologies embody political properties, both because the design or arrangement of a par-ticular technology can become a way of settling an issue in the affairs of a given community, and, more profoundly, because certain systems seem to require or to be compatible with only certain political arrange-ments (Winner 1989, p. 22).

Many of the practices that raise threats to personal privacy arise regardless of the privacy policy instruments in place. Those practices stem from the properties of the technology itself, which accumulate in individuals' lack of control over their personal information. That lack of control is produced by structure and agency operating in a coinciden-tal and inseparable manner, with intended and unintended consequences for the processing of personal information. Unacceptable levels of per-sonal information processing, therefore, are not side-effects or impacts, but are practices embedded within the very properties of the technolo-gies themselves. Following this logic, one of the proper roles for the social and political scientist is to examine how the architecture of infor-mation and communication technologies favors or disfavors certain values, be they freedom of speech, intellectual property, or privacy. In relation to the Internet, one can paint a picture in which an initial design that favored anonymous communication is slowly and surreptitiously being challenged by a variety of technological forces and organizational interests that threaten that essential privacy. Structurally, the initial valence of the Internet and the World Wide Web is being challenged, and a more privacy-invasive medium produced (Bennett 2001).

The importance of understanding the structural properties of certain technologies can also help us to contend with the set of contradictions with which we began. One can conceptualize a policy arena, on the one hand, in which the regulatory, self-regulatory, and technological policy instruments are debated and developed. But one can also conceptualize a parallel arena in which the dominant technology practices are con-structed and which normally pays little, or belated, attention to the privacy value regardless of the constant exhortations of privacy advo-cates and officials. Agre (1997) has pointed out that those practices become embedded in the "representational practice" of computing that has remained remarkably stable throughout the various generations of information technology development. The trading-up of data protection standards, and the development of privacy-enhancing technologies, are therefore confronting a set of practices within the systems-design environment that emphasizes the importance of the representation, and hence control, of the material world. "At stake is the sense in which a technical field has a history: what it inherits from past practice, how this inheritance is handed down, the collective thinking through which the field evolves, and how all this is shaped by the institutional contexts in which the work occurs" (Agre 1997, p. 57). Those practices have endured, regardless of the proliferation of regulatory, self-regulatory, and technological policy instruments devoted to the protection of privacy.

The Governance of Privacy in the Risk Society

There may well be a global race, or at least walk, to improve levels and standards of privacy protection, as we have argued. It follows a trajectory that acquires its slope and pace from an intricate and pluralistic set of processes and involves a range of policy actors, networks, and institutions operating at multiple levels. Largely reactive to changes in technologies, organizational purposes, and behavior, policy activity –and some technologies themselves—has occasionally anticipated change through precautionary modes of protection that befit a public policy area in pursuit of an important human value. Yet its trajectory is not alone in the world of processes that concern personal data, nor is it the most vigorous.

Let us look at the matter this way: the "trading up" of privacy protection is only one of several identifiable trajectories, and it is arguably not the most virile. The other discernible races to the top are those of the extensive, intensive processing of personal data; of the transformation of economic activity through the use of electronic communications and information infrastructures; and of the globalization of law enforcement and security objectives. All these escalations threaten the various values with which privacy is now associated.

Privacy protection thus aims to curb or to penalize certain personal-information processes that endanger privacy. If it seeks higher levels, it is in order to get on top of those activities, to guard against the dangers they bring, and to sanction those whose activities pose threats. However, the exploitation of personal data is powerfully fuelled along its own global trajectory, whether in the commercial sector or the public sector. The globalization of commerce through the flow of personal data across borders, and particularly through the Internet, is difficult enough to regulate with privacy instruments, as we have seen. But what has become a particularly prominent factor is that part of the public sector that has to do with law enforcement; public order; and global, national, or personal security. Control over the processing of personal data for surveillance is especially problematic in these nontransparent domains, given the exemptions that are available in data protection laws, the limitations of self-regulation, and the unavailability or proscription of individual-controlled PETs for these purposes. The targets for surveillance-related information processing are themselves discursively, and perhaps actually as well, constructed as the menacing race to the top by the forces of international organized crime, including the drugs trade, money-laundering and other financial fraud, computer crime, traffic in stolen goods and in persons, and—perhaps especially now—terrorism (Anderson et al. 1995). These have become matters of great concern, as safety and security have become major preoccupations of states, international actors, and individuals themselves, shaping policies and personal practices from macro to micro levels of social scale. In the domains of law-enforcement and security, privacy protection is perceived as assisting criminals in their race to the top more than as protecting innocent members of the public. The trajectory of privacy protection is therefore less likely to succeed under these circumstances.

Terrorism has had a powerful, even determining influence on these equations. Terrorism did not begin with the attacks of 11 September 2001 in the United States, nor with the Oklahoma City bombing some years earlier. It is an old story in Europe, the Middle East, and elsewhere. Terrorism had already exerted a strong influence on the other races to the top, in terms of hastening the coordination of antiterrorist activity and the development of information and intelligence resources in that campaign. Laws and other measures had already been put in place to meet the threat of terrorism, among other related challenges, and these had already affected the prospects for privacy protection, particularly concerning telecommunications and their interception. Many would argue that privacy protection has taken, and should take, a back seat in the face of terrorist threats. But the latter have taken on a qualitatively new dimension since 11 September 2001 (Lyon 2003), not least in the perception that they are global in nature and require global responses. New legal instruments have been developed since then in most advanced industrial states, to facilitate cooperation among national and international intelligence agencies, to ease the interception of communications, and to broaden powers of apprehension for "terrorist" related crimes.[11]

The supervention of security agendas through measures such as these revise earlier settlements of the "security versus privacy" debate that have been achieved with considerable difficulty over the past few years. They may even change the nature of the trade-off between privacy and other values that takes place in mundane civilian and consumer domains remote from the current climate of insecurity. New immunities from privacy protection have been found for the flow of personal data, not only in the pursuit of antiterrorist goals, but in ancillary activities that give evidence of "function creep" (Foundation for Information Policy Research 2001).

It is tempting to conclude, therefore, that the race-to-the-top trajectory is limited to those more mundane aspects of privacy protection. The development of techniques for protecting privacy in the everyday world of credit-card purchases, direct-marketing practices, or joined-up public services may appear to be a diversionary toy for privacy advocates and regulators to busy themselves with while the "real business" of heightening surveillance for internal security proceeds apace. For others, it may be seen as a luxury that leans too far in the direction of the transparent, customer- or citizen-friendly, and often consented sharing of personal information, out of kilter with the requirements of a dangerous world where the circulation of personal information and surveillance are indispensable to making life more secure. But the realms of commerce and the welfare state, and their rules for information practices, cannot be insulated from the world of security and surveillance. The shaping of specific business processes, including technologies for sharing or using data and also for protecting privacy, is also being affected by the pressure of these other policy considerations.

Any concluding inquiry about the governance of privacy under conditions of globalization can profit from being located within—but perhaps taking issue with—the social-science discourse about risk to which we refer in chapter 3. To be sure, that discourse—and especially that of the more recent "risk society"—long preceded the advent of terrorism on an international or global scale, and has not had these threats at the very forefront of its scope. But the trajectories of crime and terrorism have recently led to a ratcheting-up of the stakes of the risk society, and to a more global perspective. Beck (1999, pp. 5, 36) talks about "world risk society" as the latest stage of its development. In the "global age", he writes,

the theme of risk unites many other disparate areas of new transnational politics with the . . . new political economy of uncertainty, financial markets, transcultural conflicts over food and other products (BSE), emerging "risk communities," and, last but not least, the anarchy of international relations. . . . To the threat of military conflict between states is now added the (looming) threat of fundamentalist or private terrorism. It can less and less be ruled out that the private possession of weapons of mass destruction, and the potential they provide for political terror, will become a new source of dangers in the world risk society.

Moreover, the policing of risk society depends utterly upon surveillance and the exploitation of personal information in myriad ways and with profound consequences for territories, personal identities and careers, and financial or other securities, as Ericson and Haggerty (1997) have demonstrated. World risk society, it would follow, elevates these processes to the global level—precisely the level at which privacy protection's race to the top is poised to take place. Yet when risks to, or from, information and communication processes have been considered by analysts, the focus has been mainly on computer-related risks (Neumann 1995), including the Y2K phenomenon—the informatics Chernobyl that never happened—and the security-related issues of cybercrime (for example, Thomas and Loader 2000). We ourselves have addressed some of the issues of privacy-related risks, particularly as they relate to questions of social distribution and patterns of advantage and disadvantage (Raab and Bennett 1998; see also Bygrave 2001). Privacy impact assessments, and the concept of *sensitive* data, are based on implicit and largely unarticulated concepts of risk as well. But privacy risks, much less any "privacy risk society," have until very recently been far below the scholarly and practical radar; attempts to come to grips with it in policy formation are still groping in the dark (for example, UK Performance and Innovation Unit, Cabinet Office, 2002).

However, as argued elsewhere (Raab 2001), privacy and data protection discourse uses the language of "risk" as if the concept were unproblematic, and as if all risks were alike. Yet even if we are unable to estimate different degrees and kinds of risk inherent in transactions involving personal information, to say simply that "data-matching poses a threat to privacy," or that "people's privacy is at risk if databases are inaccurate"—whatever the truth in that—does not get us closer to a more nuanced understanding of what is more serious and what is less serious, or what is perceived to be the case, and why, to found regulatory policies and practices on. If this has been a problem at the organizational and national levels, it is perforce true at the global level. However, as our argument in chapter 3 indicates, we cannot easily separate objective and subjective dimensions of the concept of risk, or describe clearly the relationship between the two. No easy distinction can be drawn between "real risks" and "mistaken perceptions," nor can it be supposed that science can determine the former and explode the fallacies of the latter. This may be particularly so in fields such as information processes, in which human perception and agency shape the situations in which personal data are collected or transmitted, and in which regulatory policy must be geared at least as much to people's perceptions and fears as to any "objective" calculation of risk, even if the latter were conceptually and empirically possible.

Finally, whereas in regard to crime (or terrorism) and the fear of crime (or terrorism), the slogan "you can never be too careful" underpins much of the trajectory of law enforcement and security practices, it does not seem to underpin approaches to the reduction of privacy risks. These are not perceived as quite so serious, especially in the face of these other threats and fears whose alleviation may require, or at least be consistent with, invasions of privacy and other values of individual or social freedom.

Where does this leave our race to the top for privacy protection? We have advanced a number of arguments in these pages. We have problematized the traditional assumptions of a "privacy paradigm," which has been based on a state-centric view of the problem and the solution. We have contended that privacy is better seen as also a social value rather than just as an individual right being eroded by a set of impersonal structural forces. We have explored the conceptual implications of the decentering of privacy, as it comes to be used instrumentally to justify a variety of different values. We have investigated the policy implications of the decentering of privacy. The governance of privacy is exercised through a variety of institutional forms—public and private, domestic and transnational, with the result that in certain contexts the government regulators are not necessarily the most important actors, and the laws they enact not necessarily the most important instruments. As we have shown, the governance of privacy has become a complex phenomenon that involves a plurality of actors and a range of methods of operation and coordination. It is the details of those complexities, pluralities, and methods that are really important to understand, and to convert into policies and regimes for the governance of privacy.

On the positive side, this pluralism of policy goals and instruments ensures that the issue will remain on the public agenda. Too many interests, entrenched and otherwise, have a stake in privacy. It employs the staff of data protection agencies. It funds lawyers, consultants, and auditors. It provides ammunition for journalists. It justifies the existence of corporate privacy officers. It fuels the activities of many disparate advocacy groups. It would be disingenuous for us to deny that it also provides a fascinating range of scholarly questions for academics. There is an enormous amount and variety of disparate activity that surrounds this amorphous and flexible issue.

It is that fragmentation, however, that promotes the many trajectories of privacy protection in a global economy. The variety of privacy issues, and the plurality of institutional arenas within which they are addressed, means that different actors can observe progress in one place at one time, and regress in another place at the same or another time. In the Introduction, we outline four possible visions of privacy: the surveillance society, an incoherent and fragmented patchwork, a world of privacy haves and have-nots, and a trading-up to global privacy standards. Our analysis suggests the second scenario is the most plausible: a more chaotic future of periodic and unpredictable victories for the privacy value as the spotlight focuses on a particular practice for a brief period and then moves on (Bennett and Grant 1999, pp. 265–266).

The governance of privacy in the global economy through such multiple modes of regulation and coordination means that it is thoroughly misleading to try to observe a balance been privacy and surveillance on a global scale. Simply because privacy standards are being traded-up does not mean that surveillance practices are being correspondingly reduced. There are sufficient institutional arenas for the issue to advance sufficiently well in some, and at the same time to retreat elsewhere. This is precisely why we have argued that the language of "balancing" is mistaken, and the effort at measuring levels of privacy protection often misguided. The issue is simply too flexible, too dynamic, too pluralistic, too contradictory, and too fascinating to allow simplified conclusions about whether the issue is progressing or regressing at any one time. There is no one race to the top, just as there is no one race to the bottom. There are many races, many tops, and many bottoms as a host of actors, public and private, use or resist the expanding repertoire of privacy instruments to encourage or obstruct the more responsible use of personal information within modern organizations.

Notes

Preface

1. US National Science Foundation Grant no. SES-0083271; the other principal researchers are Michael Curry, David Phillips, and Priscilla Regan.

2. Canadian Social Sciences and Humanities Research Council (Grant no. 410-97-159700).

3. ESRC Grant no. L132251019 for a project titled *Privacy Protection in the Virtual Society*, under the ESRC's "Virtual Society?" Programme.

4. Charles Raab was closely associated with the ESRC project (Grant no. R000232639) titled *A System of European Police Co-operation After 1992*, under the direction of Malcolm Anderson, and with Monica den Boer, Peter Cullen, William Gilmore, and Neil Walker.

Introduction

1. A related conception, the "information polity" (Taylor and Williams 1991, Bellamy and Taylor 1998) focuses upon the effects of information and communications technologies in government and politics.

2. Terminology varies across countries and disciplines. We use the term *privacy protection policy* to describe the class of policies that are designed to regulate the collection, processing, and dissemination of individually identifiable information, even though we recognize that the word *privacy* has other behavioral and spatial dimensions beyond the processing of personal data. This concept also embraces and is roughly equivalent to the European term *data protection* (derived from the German *Datenschutz*). See Margulis (2003) for up-to-date analysis of these conceptual issues.

3. There are, of course, exceptions. See Bennett (1992) and Regan (1995). For a general discussion of the political science contribution to data protection, see van de Donk, Bennett, and Raab (1996).

4. For example, Westin (1967, pp. 31–32) identifies four states of privacy: solitude, intimacy, anonymity, and reserve. Flaherty (1989, pp. 7–8) lists thirteen *privacy interests*, which are the ultimate values upon which to construct data protection systems.

Chapter 1

1. An incomplete list would include Rosenberg (1969), Miller (1971), Raines (1974), Lemond and Fry (1975), Sobel (1976), Smith (1980), Bier (1980), Linowes (1989), Rothfeder (1992), Maclean (1995), Cavoukian and Tapscott (1997), Diffie and Landau (1998), Sykes (1999), Whitaker (1999), Garfinkel (2000), Rosen (1999), and Rosen (2004).

2. Madgwick (1968), Warner and Stone (1970), Thompson (1970), Madgwick and Smythe (1974), Hewitt (1977), Will (1983), Campbell and Connor (1986), Davies (1996), and Goldsmith (1997).

3. For example, *The Handmaid's Tale*; *Gattaca*; *Enemy of the State*. We note, however, the reversal of effect for the "Big Brother" label with regard to the overwhelmingly popular British television program and other "candid camera" productions that turn surveillance into mass entertainment.

4. The *Economist* was actually paraphrasing the chairman of Sun Microsystems, Scott McNeally, who allegedly declared in 1999: "You have zero privacy anyway, get used to it." The original source of this quote seems to have been lost amid the flurry of criticism that McNeally received.

5. See the review of new directions in surveillance theory in Lyon (2001), chapter 7. He identifies four strands of theory or orientation: the nation state, bureaucracy, "technologic," and political economy.

6. He argues that there are ten attributes of the new surveillance:

• it transcends distance, darkness, and physical barriers;
• it transcends time; its records can be stored, retrieved, combined, analyzed, and communicated;
• it has low visibility, or is invisible;
• it is often involuntary;
• prevention is a major concern;
• it is capital- rather than labor-intensive;
• it involves decentralized self-policing;
• it triggers a shift from targeting a specific suspect to categorical suspicion of everyone;
• it is more intensive, probing beneath surfaces, discovering previously inaccessible information;
• it is more extensive, covering not only deeper, but larger, areas.

Chapter 2

1. A range of data on the digital divide within and across countries can be found at: http://www.digitaldivide.org. See also the OECD's Workshop, The Digital Divide: Enhancing Access to ICTs, 7 December 2000, available at: http://www.oecd.org/dataoecd/22/11/2428340.pdf.

2. See http://www.doubleclick.com/us/products/abacus.

3. See chapter 7.

4. See http://www.oipcbc.org.

Chapter 3

1. This chapter draws upon Raab (1998a) and Raab and Bennett (1998).

2. For example, Sztompka (1999), Misztal (1996), Fukuyama (1995), Giddens (1991), Gambetta (1988), Barber (1983), and Luhmann (1979).

3. *Global Information Networks—Ministerial Conference*, Bonn, 6–8 July 1997, available at: http://europa.eu.int/ISPO/bonn/docs/theme_paper_en.pdf.

4. "Consumer Protection in the Electronic Marketplace," DSTI/CP(98)13/FINAL, background paper, available at: http://www.olis.oecd.org/olis/1998doc.nsf/LinkTo/DSTI-CP(98)13–FINAL.

5. Ibid., para. 13.

6. For example, Beck (1992, 1999), Renn (1998), Ericson and Haggerty (1997), Adams (1995), Luhmann (1993), Douglas (1992), Krimsky and Golding (1992), The Royal Society (1992), Douglas and Wildavsky (1982), and Lowrance (1976).

7. See Lloyd (1998), pp. 19–22 for a commentary on these provisions.

8. See http://www.biotech-info.net/precautionary.html and Tickner, Raffensperger, and Myers (n.d.).

9. Montague (1998).

10. An updated digest of some US poll findings and other resources can be found at: http://www.epic.org/privacy/survey/default.html. See also an updated reference list of surveys of privacy attitudes from several countries at: http://www.anu.edu.au/people/Roger.Clarke/DV/Surveys.html.

11. Some of these findings resonate with the categories of risk identified by 6 (1998, pp. 39–42) in his study of privacy and trust. These are risks of injustice (inaccuracy, unjust inference, function creep, reversal of the presumption of innocence), risks to personal control over personal data collection (surveillance, lack of consent to collection, denial of access to protective security procedures), and risks to dignity by exposure or embarrassment (lack of transparency of

decisions made about the person, physical intrusions, lack of anonymity, disclosure without consent).

12. 1994 figures are shown here because they were more detailed than those published in subsequent years. No survey results were published in the Registrar's 1995 Annual Report. The 1999 Annual Report (UK House of Commons 1999, p. 91) reports a reduction in the level of public trust across all types of organizations; that very high concern about the level of personal data held by companies had risen to the highest proportion—77 percent—since 1995; and that privacy protection was regarded as "very important" by 73 percent, the highest figure since 1992.

13. The Harris-Equifax figures for 1996 were 24 percent "fundamentalists," 16 percent "unconcerned," and 60 percent "pragmatists" (Harris-Equifax 1996, p. 13). The survey by The Henley Centre found 9 percent "fundamentalists," 8 percent "unconcerned," and 80 percent "pragmatists," although these proportions were only considered indicative (The Henley Centre 1995, pp. 87–88).

14. Westin adds, colorfully: "As in the earliest frontier days in America, the Internet abounds with modern-day cattlemen, sheep-herders, farmers, saloon keepers, whores, and hacker-gunmen, with the influences of the schoolmarm, minister, sheriff, and judge also struggling to be heard and felt" (Privacy & American Business 1997, p. xvi). The survey reports its findings about attitudes to this Wild West of cyberspace in considerable sociodemographic and other detail.

15. Partly in response to public opinion, the US Congress passed the Children's Online Privacy Protection Act in 1998.

16. See the discussion of "risk communication" in The Royal Society (1992), chap. 5.

17. These distinctions, in turn, are derived from the "grid/group" analytical construct in cultural theory; see Douglas and Wildavsky (1982) and, with specific application to privacy, 6 (1998), chap. 4.

Chapter 4

1. The declared purpose is "to protect human rights, pluralist democracy and the rule of law; to promote awareness and encourage the development of Europe's cultural identity and diversity; to seek solutions to problems facing European society (discrimination against minorities, xenophobia, intolerance, environmental protection, human cloning, Aids, drugs, organized crime, etc.); to help consolidate democratic stability in Europe by backing political, legislative and constitutional reform." See http://www.coe.int.

2. Resolution 74 (29) on the protection of individuals vis-à-vis electronic data banks in the public sector; Resolution 73 (22) on the protection of privacy of individuals vis-à-vis electronic data banks in the private sector at: http://www

.coe.int/T/E/Legal_affairs/Legal_co-operation/Data_protection/Documents/ International_legal_instruments/2CM.asp#TopOfPage.

3. See http://conventions.coe.int/general/v3IntroConvENG.asp.

4. "Complete List of the Council of Europe's Treaties," at: http://conventions .coe.int/Treaty/Commun/ListeTraites.asp?CM=8&CL=ENG.

5. Including several recommendations that bear upon the protection of personal data, but which are not included in the Council of Europe's list at: http:// www.coe.int/T/E/Legal_affairs/Legal_co-operation/Data_protection/Documents/International_legal_instruments/2CM.asp#TopOfPage. These are: Recommendation no. R (2002) 9 on the protection of personal data collected and processed for insurance purposes; Recommendation no. R (99) 5 for the protection of privacy on the Internet; Recommendation no. R (97) 18 on the protection of personal data collected and processed for statistical purposes; Recommendation no. R (97) 5 on the protection of medical data; Recommendation no. R (95) 4 on the protection of personal data in the area of telecommunication services, with particular reference to telephone services; Recommendation no. R (92) 3 on genetic testing and screening for health care purposes; Recommendation no. R (92) 1 on the use of analysis of deoxyribonucleic acid (DNA) within the framework of the criminal justice system; Recommendation no. R (91) 10 on the communication to third parties of personal data held by public bodies; Recommendation no. R (90) 19 on the protection of personal data used for payment and other operations; Recommendation no. R (90) 13 on prenatal genetic screening, prenatal genetic diagnosis, and associated genetic counseling; Recommendation no. R (90) 3 on medical research on human beings; Recommendation no. R (89) 2 on the protection of personal data used for employment purposes; Recommendation no. R (87) 15 regulating the use of personal data in the police sector; Recommendation no. R (86) 1 on the protection of personal data for social security purposes; Recommendation no. R (85) 20 on the protection of personal data used for the purposes of direct marketing; Recommendation no. R (83) 11 on the international recognition of national identity cards; Recommendation no. R (83) 10 on the protection of personal data used for scientific research and statistics; Recommendation no. R (83) 3 concerning the protection of users of computerized legal information services; Recommendation no. R (81) 1 on regulations for automated medical data banks.

6. "Amendments to the Convention for the Protection of Individuals With Regard to Automatic Processing of Personal Data (ETS no. 108) Allowing the European Communities to Accede" at: http://www.coe.int/T/E/Legal_affairs/ Legal_co-operation/Data_protection/Documents/International_legal_instruments/Amendements%20to%20the%20Convention%20108.asp#TopOfPage.

7. Council of Europe (2001) at: http://conventions.coe.int/Treaty/EN/Treaties/ HTML/181.htm. See the Explanatory Report at: http://conventions.coe.int/ Treaty/EN/Reports/HTML/181.htm.

8. "What is OECD" at: http://www.oecd.org/document/18/0,2340,en_2649_ 201185_2068050_1_1_1_1,00.html#The_OECD_what_is_it.

9. "Ministerial Declaration on the Protection of Privacy on Global Networks," Ottawa, 7–9 October 1998, at: http://www.oecd.org/dataoecd/39/13/1840065. pdf.

10. "What is the OECD Privacy Statement Generator?" at: http://www.oecd.org/document/39/0,2340,en_2649_201185_28863271_1_1_1_1,00.html#whatis.

11. A 1998 poll in *Business Week* claimed that 61 percent of non-Internet users cited privacy as a key reason for nonuse. *Business Week*, 16 March 1998, p. 102.

12. References are to the final text of the Directive published in October 1995. Directive 95/46/EC of the European Parliament and of the Council on the Protection of Individuals with regard to the Processing of Personal Data and on the Free Movement of Such Data. Brussels: OJ no. L281. 24 October 1995 (hereafter the "EU Data Protection Directive").

13. Very briefly, the process consisted of 1) the initiation of a draft proposal by the Commission of the European Communities (17 members appointed by the governments of the member states), 2) commentary on the draft by the European Parliament (518 members elected from member states) and by parliamentary committees, 3) revision by the Commission in the light of comments, 4) negotiation of a "common position" within the Council of Ministers (the executive body consisting of one member from each of the 12 member states with weighted votes), 4) final approval by the EU Parliament, and 5) publication.

14. There were many changes between 1990 and 1995. The principal changes relate to the abandonment of the distinction between public and private sector, the relaxation of requirements for informed consent (to allow a "negative option"), the exemption for journalistic and literary purposes, the application of these rules to manually processed data, the processing of sensitive data, and the role and independence of national supervisory authorities. See Simitis (1995).

15. See, for example, the documents of the Ministerial Conference on Global Information Networks held in Bonn, 6–8 July, 1997, at: http://europa.eu.int/ISPO/bonn/i_index.html. The Theme Paper was prepared by the German Economics Minister, Günter Rexrodt, and EU Commissioner Martin Bangemann. Its emphasis on the importance of confidence and trust was reflected in the Ministerial Declaration that emerged, and also formed part of the key principles in the Industrial Declaration and in the Users' Declaration. See Raab (1998a).

16. In addition, the Working Party has analyzed a number of technological issues from a similar perspective: airline computerized reservation systems, the platform for privacy preferences (P3P) and Open Profiling Standard (OPS), and a number of issues relating to the processing of personal data on the Internet. All Article 29 Working Party reports can be found at: http://europa.eu.int/comm/justice_home/fsj/privacy/workinggroup/wpdocs/2005_en.htm.

17. "Opinion 1/2001 on the Draft Commission Decision on Standard Contractual Clauses for the Transfer of Personal Data to Third Countries Under Article 26(4) of Directive 95/46" (WP 38), at: http://europa.eu.int/comm/justice_home/fsj/privacy/workinggroup/wpdocs/2001_en.htm.

18. All relevant Safe Harbor documents can be found at: http://www.export.gov/safeharbor.

19. See http://europa.eu.int/comm/justice_home/fsj/privacy/thridcountries/index_en.htm.

20. See http://www.bakercyberlawcentre.org/appcc/.

21. See http://www.bakercyberlawcentre.org/appcc/announce.htm.

22. Majone's (1996, pp. 23–26) discussion of self-regulation highlights the role that standardization and standard-setting organizations have played in the United States, Canada, Germany, and the EU, in fields where expertise and technical knowledge is particularly important.

23. ISO 17799 "is a comprehensive, current, internationally recognized, and auditable security management standard. It was originally developed by the British Standards Institute [as BS 7799] as a result of industry and government demand for a common framework for effective security management practice and inter-company trading. It is based on the best information security practices of leading international businesses and has met with acclaim. The standard applies to a wide range of organizations in industry and commerce and was first published in September 1998. A revised version, published late 1999, was approved as an ISO standard in late 2000." See http://healthnet.hnet.bc.ca/hds/approved_standards/iso_17799.html.

24. See http://www.iso.org/iso/en/comms-markets/consumers/iso+theconsumer-05.html.

25. "Opinion 1/97 on Canadian initiatives relating to the standardization in the field of privacy" (WP 2) at: http://europa.eu.int/comm/justice_home/fsj/privacy/workinggroup/wpdocs/1997_en.htm.

26. See the documentation available at: http://www.cenorm.be/isss.

27. See http://www.cenorm.be/cenorm/businessdomains/businessdomains/isss/activity/ipsefinalreport.pdf.

28. "Opinion 1/2002 on the CEN/ISSS Report on Privacy Standardisation in Europe" (WP 57) at: http://europa.eu.int/comm/justice_home/fsj/privacy/workinggroup/wpdocs/2002_en.htm.

29. See http://www.cenorm.be/cenorm/businessdomains/businessdomains/isss/activity/wsdppbp2005.pdf.

30. See http://26konferencja.giodo.gov.pl/data/rezolucje/en/rezolucja1.doc; http://www.istpa.org; http://www.datenschutz-berlin.de/doc/int/iwgdpt/index.htm.

31. Text on Nondiscrimination adopted by the Article 31 Committee on 31 May 2000 at: http://www.export.gov/safeharbor/nondiscrimArt31May00.htm.

32. Specifically, the "Shrimp-Turtle Case," which involved a US ban on foreign shrimp imports on account of a US finding of inadequate sea-turtle conservation policies in South East Asia (Shaffer 2000, p. 52). But see Pérez Asinari (2003).

33. It is worth noting, that even before the Directive came into force, the Spanish authorities in 1999 fined Microsoft almost $60,000 for breaching Spanish data protection controls by improperly collecting data from its European employees on a US website.

34. An important international business grouping is the "Global Business Dialogue on Electronic Commerce," http://www.gbde.org/.

Chapter 5

1. These arguments were particularly cogent in Canada; see Bennett (1996). They have, however, been less influential in the United States.

2. On a more abstract plane, Burkert (1996) identifies the functions of public-sector data-protection legislation as establishing material rules (information-handling principles), procedural elements (linking information-handling to consensus and verification processes), and institutionalization (establishing competition for legitimization with the administrative system).

3. This has been a feature of the German data protection landscape from the outset. It has since been adopted in the new Canadian legislation, as well as in the EU Directive.

4. This table does not purport to present a detailed inventory of general data protection laws. It merely presents an overview of diffusion, marking the first date of enactment of information privacy legislation in each country, either for the public sector or for both private and public sectors. Australia, Japan, and Canada each appear twice because these countries legislated sequentially for public and private sectors. Each of these countries has enacted a statute that incorporates the main privacy rights for data subjects and responsibilities for data controllers. The table omits subsequent amendments, replacements, and additions, and does not include the legislation of subnational jurisdictions, constitutional provisions, *habeas data* laws or other specific or sectoral laws. The years of enactment in some cases differ from the dates in which the laws came into force. The inclusion of a country in this table does not, of course, carry any implication that the law is effectively enforced. The table has been compiled from a number of sources, including various Newsletters of *Privacy Laws & Business,* as well as Electronic Privacy Information Center (2001).

5. Details of national legislation to January 2001 can be found at: http://www.coe.int/T/E/Legal_affairs/Legal_cooperation/Data_protection/.

6. This section draws upon Raab (1998b, 1998c).

7. These regulations date from, respectively, 1982, 1983, 1990, 1990, and 1991. See Brulin (1993).

8. See Overkleeft-Verburg (1995), Germany (1994, 1995), Austria (1994), Finland (1994, 1995), Norway Data Inspectorate (1996), Öman (1997), Denmark (1994, 1997), and Nielsen (1995).

9. This table has been compiled principally from Newsletters of *Privacy Laws & Business*, and presents the data protection agencies in all thirty OECD countries. It excludes those authorities that are not independent of government (such as that in Japan), or that do not operate at the national level. In addition, some important data protection agencies exist in countries that are not members of the OECD. In particular, we note the Hong Kong Office of the Privacy Commissioner for Personal Data, the Estonian Data Protection Inspectorate, and the data protection authorities of the Isle of Man, Guernsey, and Jersey. In Argentina, the Dirección Nacional de Proteccion de Datos Personales has been established under the 2000 Data Protection Act. See Palazzi (2002) for an overview of South American data protection law.

10. David Flaherty, when Commissioner in British Columbia, instigated a series of informal and supposedly nonthreatening "site visits" to many of the larger public institutions in the province. See discussion on site visits at: http://www.oipcbc.org/publications/annual_reports/1997AR/site97.html.

11. See http://www.privcom.gc.ca/information/guide_e.asp.

12. See Canada OPC (1989, 1990, 1992).

13. For instance, see a range of useful papers on issues such as smart cards, e-mail, intelligent transportation systems, cellular privacy, etc. at the website of the Ontario Information and Privacy Commissioner, at: http//www.ipc.on.ca. For French reports on biometrics, Radio Frequency Identification (RFID), workplace surveillance, etc. see the website of the CNIL, at: http://www.cnil.fr/index.php?id=40.

14. *Privacy Act*, Sec. 39 (1).

15. See http://www.informationcommissioner.gov.uk/eventual.aspx?/ID=8040&replacecontent=yes.

16. New Zealand Privacy Act 1993, Sections 46–53; Australia's Privacy Act 1988, Part III, has a similar effect. See htto://www.austlii.edu.au/au/legis/cth/consol_act/pa1998108.

17. Article 27 states: "1) The Member States and the Commission shall encourage the drawing up of codes of conduct intended to contribute to the proper implementation of the national provisions adopted by the Member States pursuant to this Directive, taking account of the specific features of the various sectors; and 2) Member states shall make provision for trade associations and other bodies representing other categories of controllers which have drawn up draft national codes or which have the intention of amending or extending existing national codes to be able to submit them to the opinion of the national authority. Member States shall make provision for this authority to ascertain,

among other things, whether the drafts submitted to it are in accordance with the national provisions adopted pursuant to this Directive. If it sees fit, the authority shall seek the views of data subjects or their representatives."

18. For instance, in the UK, fines may be levied on controllers convicted of an offense, in the year 2000–2001. There were twenty-three prosecutions resulting in twenty-one convictions, mainly for nonregistration. These were fewer than in the previous two years, reflecting other compliance policies and strategies pursued by the Information Commissioner, but six of the convicted received fines in the range £1000–3000 (UK House of Commons 2001, pp. 79–81). But short of prosecution and penalties, noncompliant data controllers may have action brought against them—in the UK, enforcement notices and information notices (Lloyd 1998, pp. 37–38); failure to comply with these notices constitutes an offense.

19. New Zealand, *Privacy Act 1993*, Sec. 82.

20. Laurie (2002, chapter 6) canvasses a property model in the context of genetic information and genetic materials.

Chapter 6

1. See http://www.privacyexchange.org for examples of company codes of practice, as well as for evidence of the variety of instruments that fall within this broad classification.

2. See http://www.iata.org; http://www.fedma.org; and http://www.icx.org.

3. See http://www.ecom.or.jp/ecom_e/.

4. The US Direct Marketing Association's rules can be found at: www.dmaconsumers.org/privacy.html.

Those of the Canadian Marketing Association (CMA—previously the Canadian Direct Marketing Association) are at: http://www.the-cma.org.

The Australian code is found at: http://www.adma.com.au.

The UK Direct Marketing Association's "preferences" services can be found at: http://www.dma.org.uk/content/Prf-Introduction.asp.

5. See www.donotcall.gov. A similar service has also been proposed in Canada.

6. The Association of Card Technologies in Canada is an example. See http://www.actcda.com. See also the Asia Pacific Smart Card Forum at http://www.smartcardforum.asn.au.

7. See the privacy principles of the Responsible Electronic Communications Alliance at: http://www.responsibleemail.org.

8. The American Library Association has issued a "Policy Concerning the Confidentiality of Personally Identifiable Information about Library Users" at: http://www.ala.org/alaorg/oif/pol_user.html.

9. An example is the privacy code of the Canadian Medical Association at: http://www.cma.ca.

10. See http://www.c-cure.be.

11. The dominant technical standard for mobile communications is the 801.11 standard.

12. See www.privacyassociation.org.

13. See http://www.dutchdpa.nl/downloads_audit/PrivacyAuditFramework.pdf.

14. See the materials in the "Japan Department" at: http://www .privacyexchange.org.

15. The materials on the legislation can be found on the website of the Australian Privacy Commissioner at: http://www.privacy.gov.au.

16. See http://www.cenorm.be/cenorm/businessdomains/businessdomains/isss/ activity/cen+isss+ws+dpp+open+meeting.asp.

17. There are some European equivalents to these schemes. For instance, the UK consumer magazine *Which* launched a "Web Trader" seal of approval in June 1999. See http://whichwebtrader.which.net/webtrader/.

A more general European scheme is the "Trusted Shops" seal at: http://www .trustedshops.de.

Both schemes, however, address a wider range of consumer protection issues than just privacy.

18. See http://www.privacyalliance.org.

19. See http://www.truste.org/about/member_list.php.

20. The credibility of the TRUSTe certification was brought into question in 1999 as a result of a complaint against Microsoft, specifically the registration process for Windows '98. TRUSTe investigated the complaint, but concluded that the breach of privacy protection was outside the initial license agreement. They could not, then, initiate an audit.

21. See http://www.bbbonline.org.

22. See http://www.webtrust.org.

23. See http://www.privacymark.jp.

24. The list is available at: http://web.ita.doc.gov/safeharbor/shlist.nsf/ webPages/safe+harbor+list.

25. See http://www.export.gov/safeharbor/sh_overview.html.

26. Some enterprises in Canada that process large amounts of personal data from government have adopted the CSA principles in this way.

27. See http://www.icx.org.

28. A graphic example relates to the CMA, which claims to represent around 75 percent of the direct-marketing activity in Canada. It is no accident that the CMA was one of the first associations to develop a privacy code, and the very first to call for legislation based on the CSA standard. The "free-riders" who

ignore basic consent requirements for the collection and disclosure of personal information were tainting the reputations of the more responsible players. The rational solution for the CMA was to attempt to raise the barrier for entry into the sector.

Chapter 7

1. Ethical issues are widely discussed in a number of organizations, institutes, and conferences of academics and computer professionals. See, for example, Association for Computing Machinery (ACM)'s General Code of Ethics at: http://www.acm.org/constitution/code.html; its Software Engineering Code of Ethics at: http://www.acm.org/serving/se/code.htm; the Centre for Computing and Social Responsibility's series of ETHICOMP conferences at: http://www.ccsr.cse.dmu.ac.uk; the International Center for Information Ethics at: http://icie.zkm.de; and the International Federation for Information Processing (IFIP) at: http://www.ifip.or.at and its Ethics Task Group publication (Berleur and Brunnstein 1996).

2. See: http://www2.europarl.eu.int/omk/OM-Europarl?PROG=REPORT&L=EN&PUBREF=-//EP//TEXT+REPORT+A5-2001-0374+0+DOC+SGML+V0//EN&LEVEL=3. The draft directive concerning the processing of personal data and the protection of privacy in the electronic communications sector is COM (2000) 385. This "opt-in" amendment was replaced by a Council of Ministers amendment requiring notice and choice; see http://www.iabuk.net, "Europe's Telecom Ministers Reject Opt-in Regime for Cookies," 12 December 2001.

3. See http://www.privacyfoundation.org. For further descriptions of, and antidotes against, spyware, see http://www.cexx.org/adware.htm.

4. See http://www.passport.com.

5. The history of this complaint is provided at: http://www.epic.org.

6. See http://www.pkilaw.com for a description of PKI. See also Brands (1999) for a critique of traditional PKI. It is also worth noting Clarke's (2000a) considerable skepticism about the effectiveness of PKI based on the ISO standard X509: "Conventional PKI, built around ISO standard X.509, has been, and will continue to be, a substantial failure. . . . Its key deficiencies are its inherently hierarchical and authoritarian nature, its unreasonable presumptions about the security of private keys, a range of other technical and implementation defects, confusions about what it is that a certificate actually provides assurance about, and its inherent privacy-invasiveness," at: http://www.anu.edu.au/people/Roger.Clarke/II/PKIMisFit.html.

7. See the description at: http://www.cse.dnd.ca/en/services/pki/pki.html.

8. Directive 1999/93/EC of the European Parliament and of the Council of 13 December 1999 on a Community framework for electronic signatures, L13/12, 19.1.2000, available at: http://www.qlinks.net/quicklinks/digsig1.htm.

9. See http://www.legislation.hmso.gov.uk/acts/acts2000/20000007.htm for explanatory notes on the Act, including its background and documentary history, important definitions of technical terms, and further online references.

10. See http://www.epic.org/privacy/tools.html.

11. A similar classification is provided by Lorrie Faith Cranor at: http://www.research.att.com/projects/p3p/p3p-www9.ppt.

12. An example would be the products available at: www.shyfile.net or www.pc-encrypt.com.

13. Other products utilizing proxy servers have been available at: http://www.safeweb.com, http://www.proxymate.com, and www.privacyinc.com. Examples of failed products include the so-called "onion-router" technique, and the model based on the principle that anonymity loves company, grouping users into large and geographically diverse "crowds."

14. The ZeroKnowledge products can be found at: http://www.freedom.net. It discontinued its pseudonymous browsing service in October 2001.

15. See http://www.thelimitsoft.com/cookie; http://www.rbaworld.com/Programs/CookieCruncher; and http://www.junkbuster.com; http://www.ampsoft.net/; www.historykill.com.

16. The most common spyware detection programs can be found at: www.lavasoftusa.com; www.safer-networking.org; www.noadware.net; and Microsoft's own antispyware program.

17. The Children's Online Privacy Protection Act of 1998.

18. See http://www.getnctwise.org.

19. For example, http://www.novell.com/products/; and http://www.lumeria.com.

20. See http://www.w3.org/P3P/ for an overview of the P3P project.

21. Ian Goldberg of Zero Knowledge Systems (ZKS) has presented a four-fold typology of PETs according to the necessary involvement of different agents: single-party (such as spam filters), centralized intermediary (such as anonymizer.com), distributed intermediary (such as the freedom network offered by ZKS), and server support (such as e-cash). He argues that the more successful PETs have been those that have not relied on the cooperation of a network of intermediaries, and cites this as the major reason why the landscape of PETs has changed very little from 1996 to 2001 (Goldberg 2002).

22. The W3C website lists around 500 major e-commerce sites as being P3P compliant: http://www.w3.org/P3P/compliant_sites.

23. One conclusion of a panel on "The Promise of Privacy-Enhancing Technologies," Computers, Freedom and Privacy Conference, San Francisco, 19 April 2002.

24. See http://pet-pisa.openspace.nl/pisa_org/pisa/index.html; and Borking and Raab (2001).

25. The full text of the Dutch legislation can be found at: http://home.planet .nl/~privacy1/wbp_en_rev.htm.

26. Biometrics are a range of techniques for identifying persons, based on physical characteristics. They typically include fingerprints, iris and retinal scans, DNA patterns, and hand geometry. These characteristics can be held in digitized form and used in transactions in conjunction with other tools, such as smart cards and other identification devices. There has been a keen interest in, and technical development of, biometrics in recent years, owing to their potential use in schemes of verification and authentication of people and claims. As with other technologies, however, biometrics are controversial, in part because their collection is physically intrusive, and robust privacy safeguards are regarded by data protectors as essential for their use. Clarke gives a broad definition and exemplification of biometrics, as well as a discussion of biometrics in the context of human identification systems and the policy implications of these systems (Clarke 1994).

27. See http://www.ipc.on.ca/docs/pri-biom.pdf. The city of Toronto biometric initiative has not been implemented as of the date of writing.

28. Jason Catlett, Technical Standards and Privacy: An Open Letter to P3P Developers at: http://www.junkbusters.com/standards.html. See the related criticism of P3P in June 2000 by the Electronic Privacy Information Center (EPIC) and Junkbusters at: http://www.epic.org/reports/prettypoorprivacy. html.

Chapter 8

1. This idea is explored in Raab (1993).

2. A brief discussion of coregulation as a concept referring to self-regulation by an industrial association with governmental oversight and/or ratification may be found in Ayres and Braithwaite (1992, p. 102). They give further Australian and British examples, and distinguish between coregulation and "enforced self-regulation," which operates between the state and the individual firm, involving more particularistic standards. See also Baldwin and Cave (1999, pp. 133–137).

3. In choosing these four variables, we are aware of other, sometimes more complex, typologies of regulatory and self-regulatory instruments that are not necessarily applicable across both instruments and jurisdictions. Priest (1998), for example, analyzes five models of self-regulation according to ten characteristics: government involvement, source of power, involvement of the public, accountability to government, rulemaking, adjudication, sanctions, offenses, membership, and judicial review. This analysis, while very useful, is too closely tied to the Canadian context. Therefore some of Priest's variables are not

equivalent for the purposes of comparative analysis. Baldwin and Cave (1999, pp. 126–133) give an entirely different set of categories that comprise the case for, and the worries about, self-regulation: expertise, efficiency, mandates, accountability, and fairness of procedures. As with Priest's categories, these leave out several of the points we wish to emphasize with regard to privacy protection across a broader range of policy instruments.

4. See the brief discussion of key features of legislation, including its scope, in Mellors and Pollitt (1984, pp. 205–207).

5. See http://www.govtalk.gov.uk/e-gov/consult_subject_document.asp?docnum=339.

6. See UK Cm 4310 (1999); UK Performance and Innovation Unit Cabinet Office (2002).

7. An example that casts doubt on this expectation is the US' Direct Marketing Association's (DMA) difficulty in getting its member organizations to comply with the DMA's "Privacy Promise." This was issued in 1999 following two years of DMA effort in getting members to comply. Seventeen companies had refused to endorse the promise, some of which "believed it was inappropriate for a trade organization to dictate their behavior in such a way" (Magill 2001).

8. In the US, the Electronic Privacy Information Center at: http://www.epic .org.

The Center for Democracy and Technology at: http://www.cdt.org.

The Privacy Rights Clearinghouse at: http://www.privacyrights.org.

The American Civil Liberties Union at: http://www.aclu.org.

Junkbusters at: http://www.junkbusters.com.

In the UK, the Foundation for Information Policy Research at: http://www .fipr.org.

Cyber-Rights and Cyber-Liberties at: http://www.cyber-rights.org.

Liberty at: http://www.liberty-human-rights.org.uk.

In the Netherlands, Bits of Freedom at: http://www.bof.nl.

In Hungary, the Hungarian Civil Liberties Union at: http://www.c3. hu/~hclu/.

Internationally, examples include the Global Internet Liberty Campaign at: http://www.gilc.org.

Privacy International at: http://www.privacyinternational.org/.

9. Colin Bennett has been funded (2004–2007) to conduct a comparative study of the phenomenon of privacy advocacy.

10. We are grateful to Perri 6 for his suggestions for a richer treatment of figure 8.2.

Chapter 9

1. An earlier attempt to grapple with the question of evaluation is found in Raab and Bennett (1996).

2. See http://www.tietosuoja.fi/27580.htm.

3. See http://www.datenschutz.ch/index/datenschutzbeauftragt.htm?id=9249.

4. Many companies in North America have appointed Chief Privacy Officers to take responsibility for the issue within the organization. An Association of Corporate Privacy Officers was launched in the US through the Privacy & American Business organization; see http://www.pandab.org/cpo2001.

The UK's National Association of Data Protection Officers (NADPO), an offshoot of the local authority sector, dates from 1993; see http://www.nadpo .org.uk/index.home.html.

5. See, for example, the Ontario Management Board Secretariat's *Privacy Impact Assessment Guidelines*, updated June 2001, at: http://www.gov.on .ca/MBS/english/fip/pia/.

6. The PIA policy and guidelines are available at: http://www.tbs-sct.gc.ca/ pubs_pol/ciopubs/pia-pefr/siglist_e.html.

7. These benefits are explained in greater detail in White (2001, p. 11).

Chapter 10

1. We are grateful to Michael Webb of the University of Victoria for framing the theoretical positions in this manner.

2. See http://www.havenco.com.

3. See Offshore Information Services located in Anguilla at: http://www .ofshore.com.ai/.

4. See www.skycorpinc.com/press.htm.

5. This was one reason why ZeroKnowledge Systems located in Montreal, rather than the United States.

6. There is an anticipated "California effect" with respect to recent attempts to enact strong financial privacy protection laws in California; see Speier (2002).

7. As an illustration, the recent complaint to the FTC against Microsoft was waged by no fewer than thirteen groups of this kind: The Electronic Privacy Information Center, the Center for Digital Democracy, the Center for Media Education, Computer Professionals for Social Responsibility, Consumer Action, the Consumer Federation of America, the Consumer Task Force for Automotive Issues, the Electronic Frontier Foundation, Junkbusters, the Media Access Project, Net Action, the Privacy Rights Clearinghouse, and the US Public Interest Research Group. All of these organizations are US-based, even though the implications of the Microsoft "Passport" technology are global.

8. We do note, however, the recent establishment of a pan-European privacy lobbying organization, European Digital Rights; see http://www.edri.org.

9. Privacy protection has reached the official agenda in China, though it tends to be integrated with wider measures to promote electronic commerce, including the prevention of child pornography, digital signature legislation, and computer security. These initiatives are part of a five-year plan implemented through the State Council Informatization Office (SCITO). In 2004, a study group formed to compare legal systems in different countries and to propose legislation (Pipe 2005).

10. Jeffrey Benner, "EU Drives Privacy Global," *Wired News*, 16 July 2001 at: http://www.wired.com/news/privacy/0,1848,44922,00.html.

11. For example, the USA Patriot Act of 2001; the UK's Anti-terrorism, Crime, and Security Act 2001; Canada's Anti-Terrorism Act of 2001; and Australian Security Intelligence Organisation Legislation Amendment (Terrorism) Act 2002.

Bibliography

Adams, J. (1995), *Risk*, UCL Press, London.

Agre, P. (1997), "Beyond the Mirror World: Privacy and the Representational Practices of Computing," in P. Agre and M. Rotenberg (eds.), *Technology and Privacy: The New Landscape*, The MIT Press, Cambridge, MA, pp. 29–61.

Agre, P., and Rotenberg, M. (1997), *Technology and Privacy: The New Landscape*, The MIT Press, Cambridge, MA.

Aldhouse, F. (1992) *Performance Measurement*, Office of the Data Protection Registrar, Wilmslow.

Allen, A. (1985), *Uneasy Access: Privacy for Women in a Free Society*, Rowman and Littlefield, Totowa, NJ.

Allen, A., and Mack, E. (1990), "How Privacy Got Its Gender," *Northern Illinois University Law Review* 10:441–478.

Almond, G. (1988), "Separate Tables: Schools and Sects in Political Science," *PS: Political Science and Politics* 21:828–842.

Almond, G., and Verba, S. (1965), *The Civic Culture*, Little Brown, Boston.

Almond, G., and Verba, S. (1980), *The Civic Culture Revisited*, Little Brown, Boston.

Alston and Bird, LLP (2001), The World's Privacy Laws: An International Privacy Library Compiled by Alston & Bird LLP, Alston and Bird, Washington, at http://www.alston.com.

American Library Association (ALA) (1991), *Policy Concerning the Confidentiality of Personally Identifiable Information about Library Users*, ALA, Chicago, at http://www.ala.org/ala/oif/statementspols/statementspolicies.htm#privacy.

Anderson, M., den Boer, M., Cullen, P., Gilmore, W., Raab, C., and Walker, N. (1995), *Policing the European Union: Theory, Law, and Practice*, Clarendon Press, Oxford.

Ariès, P., and Duby, G. (general eds.) (1985–1987), *Histoire de la Vie Privée*, Vols. 1–5, Seuil, Paris.

Arndt, H. (1949), "The Cult of Privacy," *Australian Quarterly* 21:69–71.

Ash, T. Garton (1997), *The File: A Personal History*, Vintage Books, New York.

Aurigi, A., and Graham, S. (1998), "The "Crisis" in the Urban Public Realm," in B. Loader (ed.), *Cyberspace Divide*, pp. 57–80.

Australia, Office of the Federal Privacy Commissioner (FPC) (1995), *Community Attitudes to Privacy—Information Paper Number Three*, Human Rights Australia, Sydney.

Australia, Office of the Federal Privacy Commissioner (FPC) (2001), *Privacy and the Community*, Sydney, Office of the Federal Privacy Commissioner, at http://www.privacy.gov.au/publications/rcommunity.html.

Austria (1994), "Legislative Developments Concerning Data Protection in Austria (1994)," presented to the 16th International Conference of Privacy and Data Protection Commissioners, The Hague, 6–8 September.

Ayres, I., and Braithwaite, J. (1992), *Responsive Regulation: Transcending the Deregulation Debate*, Oxford University Press, New York.

Bachrach, P., and Baratz, M. (1962), "Two Faces of Power," *American Political Science Review* 56:947–952.

Bainbridge, D. (1996), *The EC Data Protection Directive*, Butterworths, London.

Baldwin, R., and Cave, M. (1999), *Understanding Regulation: Theory, Strategy, and Practice*, Oxford University Press, Oxford.

Barber, B. (1983), *The Logic and Limits of Trust*, Rutgers University Press, New Brunswick, NJ.

Barrett, S., and Fudge, C. (eds.) (1981), *Policy and Action*, Methuen, London.

Beck, U. (1992), *Risk Society: Towards a New Modernity*, Sage, London.

Beck, U. (1999), *World Risk Society*, Polity Press, Cambridge.

Bellamy, C., and Taylor, J. (1998), *Governing in the Information Age*, Open University Press, Buckingham.

Beniger, J. (1986), *The Control Revolution: Technological and Economic Origins of the Information Society*, Harvard University Press, Cambridge, MA.

Bennett, C. (1988), "Different Processes, One Result: The Convergence of Data Protection Policy in Europe and the United States," *Governance: An International Journal of Policy and Administration* 1:415–441.

Bennett, C. (1991), "Computers, Personal Data, and Theories of Technology: Comparative Approaches to Privacy Protection in the 1990's," *Science, Technology, & Human Values* 16:51–69.

Bennett, C. (1992), *Regulating Privacy: Data Protection and Public Policy in Europe and the United States*, Cornell University Press, Ithaca.

Bennett, C. (1995), *Implementing Privacy Codes of Practice: A Report to the Canadian Standards Association*, Canadian Standards Association (CSA), PLUS 8830, Rexdale.

Bennett, C. (1996), "Rules of the Road and Level Playing-Fields: The Politics of Data Protection in Canada's Private Sector," *International Review of Administrative Sciences* 62:479–491.

Bennett, C. (1997a), "Convergence Revisited: Toward a Global Policy for the Protection of Personal Data," in P. Agre and M. Rotenberg, *Technology and Privacy: The New Landscape*, The MIT Press, Cambridge, MA, pp. 99–123.

Bennett, C. (1997b), *Prospects for an International Standard for the Protection of Personal Information: A Report to the Standards Council of Canada*, Standards Council of Canada, Ottawa, at http://web.uvic.ca/~polisci/bennett/research/iso.htm.

Bennett, C. (1997c), "Understanding Ripple Effects: The Cross-National Adoption of Policy Instruments for Bureaucratic Accountability," *Governance: An International Journal of Policy and Administration* 10:213–233.

Bennett, C. (1999), "Where the Regulated are the Regulators: Privacy Protection within the Contemporary Canadian State," in G. Doern, M. Hill, M. Prince and R. Schultz (eds.), *Changing the Rules: Canadian Regulatory Regimes and Institutions*, University of Toronto Press, Toronto, pp. 293–315.

Bennett, C. (2000), "An International Standard for the Protection of Personal Information: Objections to the Objections," paper presented to the 2000 conference of "Computers, Freedom & Privacy (CFP 2000)," 19 April, San Francisco, at http://www.acm.org/pubs/articles/proceedings/cas/332186/p33-bennett/p33-bennett.pdf.

Bennett, C. (2001), "Cookies, Web Bugs, Webcams and Cue Cats: Patterns of Surveillance on the World Wide Web," *Ethics and Information Technology* 3:197–210.

Bennett, C., and Grant, R. (eds.) (1999), *Visions of Privacy: Policy Choices for the Digital Age*, University of Toronto Press, Toronto.

Bennett, C., and Raab, C. (1997), "The Adequacy of Privacy: The European Union Data Protection Directive and the North American Response," *The Information Society* 13:245–263.

Berleur, J., and Brunnstein, K. (eds.) (1996), *Ethics of Computing*, Chapman and Hall, London.

Bier, W. (ed.) (1980), *Privacy: A Vanishing Value*, Fordham University Press, New York.

Bigelow, R. (1979), "Transborder Data Flow Barriers," *Jurimetrics* 20:8–17.

Bok, S. (1982), *Secrets: On the Ethics of Concealment and Revelation*, Oxford University Press, Oxford.

Boling, P. (1996), *Privacy and the Politics of Intimate Life*, Cornell University Press, Ithaca.

Borking, J. (2001), *Privacy Incorporated Software Agent: Proposal for Building a Privacy Guardian in the Electronic Age*, College Berscherming Persoongevens, The Hague.

Borking, J., and Raab, C. (2001), "Laws, PETs and Other Technologies for Privacy Protection," *The Journal of Information, Law and Technology* (JILT), 1 February, at www2.warwick.ac.uk/fac/soc/law/elj/jilt/2001_1/borking/.

Bouckaert, G. (1990), "The History of the Productivity Movement," *Public Productivity and Management Review* 14:53–89.

Bowker, G., and Star, S. (1999), *Sorting Things Out: Classification and its Consequences*, The MIT Press, Cambridge, MA.

Brands, S. (1999), *Rethinking Public Key Infrastructures and Digital Certificates: Building in Privacy*, Ponsen and Looijen, Utrecht.

Brenton, M. (1964), *The Privacy Invaders*, Coward-McCann, New York.

Brulin, H. (1993), "Protection des Données à Caractère Personnel en Belgique: Quelle Commission? Pour Quelle Vie Privée?," paper presented to the 15th International Conference of Privacy and Data Protection Commissioners, Manchester, 27–30 September.

Burkert, H. (1994), " 'Electronic Trust' and the Role of Law: A European Perspective," in K. Brunnstein and E. Raubold (eds.), *Applications and Impacts—Information Processing '94*, Proceedings of the IFIP 13th World Computer Congress, Hamburg, Germany, 28 August–2 September, Vol. 2, Elsevier, North Holland, pp. 239–447.

Burkert, H. (1996), "Data-Protection Legislation and the Modernization of Public Administration," *International Review of Administrative Sciences* 62:557–567.

Burkert, H. (1997), "Privacy Enhancing Technologies: Typology, Critique, Vision," in P. Agre and M. Rotenberg (eds.), *Technology and Privacy: The New Landscape*, The MIT Press, Cambridge, MA, pp. 125–143.

Bygrave, L. (2001), "Electronic Agents and Privacy: A Cyberspace Odyssey 2001," *International Journal of Law and Information Technology* 9:275–294.

Bygrave, L. (2002), *Data Protection Law: Approaching Its Rationale, Logic and Limits*, Kluwer Law International, New York.

Bygrave, L. (2004), Privacy Protection in a Global Context—A Comparative Overview," *Scandinavian Studies in Law* 47:319–348.

Cable Television Standards Council (CTSC) (1991), *Cable Television Customer Service Standards*, CTSC, Ottawa, at http://www.ctsc.ca/eng/standards/customerservice/.

Campbell, D., and Connor, S. (1986), *On the Record: Surveillance, Computers and Privacy*, Michael Joseph, London.

Canada, Government of Canada (1998), *Voluntary Codes—A Guide for Their Development and Use: A Joint Initiative of the Office of Consumer Affairs, Industry Canada, and the Regulatory Affairs Division, Treasury Board Secretariat*, Ministry of Supply and Services, Ottawa, at http://strategis.ic.gc.ca/epic/internet/inoca-bc.nsf/en/ca00863e.html.

Canada, Insurance Bureau of Canada (IBC) (1996), *Model Personal Information Code*, IBC, Toronto.

Canada, Office of the Privacy Commissioner (OPC) (1989), *Aids and the Privacy Act*, Minister of Supply and Services, Ottawa.

Canada, Office of the Privacy Commissioner (OPC) (1990), *Drug Testing and Privacy*, Minister of Supply and Services, Ottawa.

Canada, Office of the Privacy Commissioner (OPC) (1992), *Genetic Testing and Privacy*, Minister of Supply and Services, Ottawa.

Canada, Office of the Privacy Commissioner (OPC) (1995), *Annual Report 1994–95*, Canada Communications Group, Ottawa.

Canada, Office of the Privacy Commissioner (OPC) (1996), *Annual Report 1995–96*, Canada Communications Group, Ottawa.

Canada, Office of the Privacy Commissioner (OPC) (1999), *Annual Report 1998–99*, Minister of Public Works and Government Services Canada, Ottawa.

Canada, Office of the Privacy Commissioner (OPC) (2000), *Annual Report 1999–2000*, Minister of Public Works and Government Services Canada, Ottawa.

Canada, Stentor (1992), *Model Code for Fair Information Practices*, Stentor Telecom Policy Inc., Ottawa.

Canadian Bankers Association (CBA) (1996), *Privacy Model Code: Protecting Individual Bank Customers' Personal Information*, CBA, Toronto, at http://www.cba.ca/en/ViewDocument.asp?fl=3&sl=65&tl=133&docid=294.

Canadian Life and Health Insurance Association (CLHIA) (1993), *Right to Privacy Guidelines*, CLHIA, Toronto.

Canadian Medical Association (CMA) (1998), *Health Information Privacy Code*, CMA, Toronto, at http://www.cma.ca/index.cfm/ci_id/3216/la_id/1.htm.

Canadian Standards Association (CSA) (1996), *Model Code for the Protection of Personal Information*, CAN/CSA-Q830-96, CSA, Rexdale, at http://www.csa.ca/standards/privacy/code/Default.asp?language=English.

Canadian Standards Association (CSA) (1997), *Making the Privacy Code Work for You*, CSA, Rexdale, at http://www.csa.ca/standards/privacy/default.asp?load=code&language=English#privacy%20code.

Canadian Cable Television Standards Council (CTSC) (1991), *Cable Television Customer Service Standards*, CTSC, Ottawa, at http://www.ctsc.ca/eng/standards/customerservice/.

Castells, M. (1996), *The Rise of the Network Society*, Blackwell Publishers, Oxford.

Cavoukian, A., and Hamilton, T. (2002), *The Privacy Payoff: How Successful Businesses Build Consumer Trust*, McGraw-Hill Ryerson, Toronto.

Cavoukian, A., and Tapscott, D. (1995), *Who Knows? Safeguarding Your Privacy in a Networked World*, Random House, Toronto.

Center for Democracy and Technology (CDT) (2000), *Broadband Backgrounder: Public Policy Issues Raised by Broadband Technology*, at http://www.cdt.org/digi_infra/broadband/backgrounder.shtml.

Center for Democracy and Technology (CDT), and Ontario, Office of the Information and Privacy Commissioner (IPC) (2000), "P3P and Privacy: An Update for the Privacy Community," at http://www.cdt.org/privacy/pet/p3pprivacy.shtml.

Cerny, P. (1995), "Globalization and the Changing Logic of Collective Action," *International Organization* 49:595–625.

Charlesworth, A. (2000), "Clash of the Data Titans? US and EU Data Privacy Regulation," *European Public Law* 6:253–274.

Chaum, D. (1992), "Achieving Electronic Privacy," *Scientific American* 267:96–101.

Clarke, R. (1994), "Human Identification in Information Systems: Management Challenges and Public Policy Issues," *Information Technology and People* 7:6–37.

Clarke, R. (1999), "Introduction to Dataveillance and Information Privacy, and Definitions of Terms," at http://www.anu.edu.au/people/Roger.Clarke/DV/Intro.html.

Clarke, R. (2000a), "Beyond the OECD Guidelines: Privacy Protection for the 21st Century," at http://www.anu.edu.au/people/Roger.Clarke/DV/PP21C.html.

Clarke, R. (2000b), "Conventional Public Key Infrastructure: An Artefact Ill-Fitted to the Needs of the Information Society," at http://www.anu.edu.au/people/Roger.Clarke/II/PKIMisFit.html.

Clarke, R. (2001), "Cookies," at http://www.anu.edu.au/people/Roger.Clarke/II/Cookies.html#Dev.

Collingsworth, T., Goold, W., and Harvey, P. (1994), "Labor and Free Trade: Time for a Global New Deal," *Foreign Affairs* 73:8–13.

Council of Europe (CoE) (1981), *Convention for the Protection of Individuals with Regard to Automatic Processing of Personal Data (Convention 108)*, Council of Europe, Strasbourg.

Council of Europe (CoE) (1989), *New Technologies: A Challenge to Privacy Protection?* Council of Europe, Strasbourg.

Council of Europe (CoE) (2001), *Additional Protocol to the Convention for the Protection of Individuals with Regard to Automatic Processing of Personal Data, Regarding Supervisory Authorities and Transborder Data Flows*, Strasbourg 8/XI/2001, Council of Europe, Strasbourg, at http://www.conventions.coe.int/Treaty/EN/Treaties/Html/181.htm.

Culnan, M., and Bies, D. (1999), "Managing Privacy Concerns Strategically: The Implications of Fair Information Practices for Marketing in the Twenty-first Century," in C. Bennett and R. Grant (eds.), *Visions of Privacy: Policy Choices for the Digital Age*, University of Toronto Press, Toronto, pp. 149–167.

Danziger, J., Dutton, W., Kling, R., and Kraemer, K. (1982), *Computers and Politics: High Technology in American Local Governments*, Columbia University Press, New York.

Davies, S. (1996), *Big Brother: Britain's Web of Surveillance and the New Technological Order*, Pan Books, London.

Davies, S. (1999), "Spanners in the Works: How the Privacy Movement is Adapting to the Challenge of Big Brother," in C. Bennett and R. Grant (eds.), *Visions of Privacy: Policy Choices for the Digital Age*, University of Toronto Press, Toronto, pp. 244–267.

Denmark (1994), "Report from the Danish Data Protection Agency (DPA), doc. 1994-753-001, 26/07/94," presented to the 16th International Conference of Privacy and Data Protection Commissioners, The Hague, 6–8 September.

Denmark (1997), "Report from the Danish Data Protection Agency (DPA) August 1997, doc. 1996-74-201," presented to the 19th International Conference of Privacy and Data Protection Commissioners, Brussels, 17–19 September.

Dhont, J., Asinari, M.V.P., and Pouller, Y. (2004), *Safe Harbour Decision Implementation Study*, Centre de Recherche Informatique et Droit, Namur, Belgium.

Diffie, W., and Landau, S. (1998), *Privacy on the Line: The Politics of Wiretapping and Encryption*, The MIT Press, Cambridge, MA.

Direct Marketing Association (UK) (n.d.), *The New Information Trade*, Direct Marketing Association (UK) Ltd., London.

Dix, A. (1996), "The German Railway Card," address to the 18th International Conference of the Privacy and Data Protection Commissioners, Ottawa, 18–20 September.

Dix, A. (2000), "Infomediaries and Negotiated Privacy Techniques," paper presented to the 2000 "Conference of Computers, Freedom & Privacy (CFP 2000)," 19 April, Toronto.

Douglas, M. (1992), *Risk and Blame: Essays in Cultural Theory*, Routledge, London.

Douglas, M., and Wildavsky, A. (1982), *Risk and Culture*, University of California Press, Berkeley and Los Angeles.

Dumortier, J., and Goemans, C. (2000), *Data Privacy and Standardization*, discussion paper prepared for the CEN/ISSS Open Seminar on Data Protection, Brussels 23–24 March, at http://www.law.kuleuven.ac.be/icri/.

Dutton, W. (ed.) (1996), *Information and Communication Technologies: Visions and Realities*, Oxford University Press, Oxford.

Dutton, W. (ed.) (1999), *Society on the Line: Information Politics in the Digital Age*, Oxford University Press, Oxford.

Economist, The (1999), "End of Privacy," 351, no. 8117 (May 1): 16 and 105–107.

Eger, J. (1978), "Emerging Restrictions on Transnational Data Flow: Privacy Protection or Non-Tariff Trade Barriers?," *Law and Policy in International Business* 10:1055–1103.

Ekos Research Associates (1993), *Privacy Revealed: The Canadian Privacy Survey*, Ekos, Ottawa.

Ekos Research Associates (2001), *Business Usage of Consumer Information for Direct Marketing: What the Public Thinks, Public Interest Advocacy Centre*, Ottawa, at http://www.piac.ca/privacy1.htm.

Electronic Privacy Information Center (EPIC) and Privacy International (2001), *Privacy & Human Rights: An International Survey of Privacy Laws and Development*, EPIC, Washington DC.

Ellul, J. (1964), *The Technological Society*, Vintage Books, New York.

Ericson, R., and Haggerty, K. (1997), *Policing the Risk Society*, University of Toronto Press, Toronto.

Etzioni, A. (1999), *The Limits of Privacy*, Basic Books, New York.

European Commission (EC) (1990), *Proposal for a Council Directive Concerning the Protection of Individuals in Relation to the Processing of Personal Data*, OJ no. C. 277, 5. 11, (13 September 1990).

European Commission (EC) (1992), *Amended Proposal for a Council Directive on the Protection of Individuals with Regard to the Processing of Personal Data and on the Free Movement of Such Data*, OJ no. C 311, 27. 11 (15 October 1992).

European Commission (EC) (1995), *Council Definitively Adopts Directive on Protection of Personal Data*, European Commission Press Release, IP/95/822, 25 July.

European Commission (EC) (2001), *Commission Decision of 15 June 2001 on Standard Contractual Clauses for the Transfer of Personal Data to Third Countries, Under Directive 95/46/EC*, 2001/497/EC, OJ no. L181/19, 4 July.

European Commission (EC) (2004), *Commission Decision C(2004) 5271 Amending Decision 2001/497/EC as Regards the Introduction of an Alternative Set of Standard Contractual Clauses for the Transfer of Personal Data to Third Countries* J L385/74 of 27 December, at http://europa.eu.int/comm/justice_home/fsj/privacy/modelcontracts/index_en.htm.

European Union (EU) (1995), *Directive 95/46/EC of the European Parliament and of the Council on the Protection of Individuals with Regard to the Processing of Personal Data and on the Free Movement of Such Data*, Brussels, OJ no. L281, (The EU Data Protection Directive) (24 October 1995).

European Union (EU) (1997), *First Orientations on Transfers of Personal Data to Third Countries—Possible Ways Forward in Assessing Adequacy*, Working Party on the Protection of Individuals with Regard to the Processing of Personal Data, Brussels, WP 4, at http://europa.eu.int/comm/justice_home/fsj/privacy/.

European Union (EU) (1998), *Judging Industry Self-Regulation: When Does It Make a Meaningful Contribution to the Level of Data Protection in a Third Country?* Working Party on the Protection of Individuals with Regard to the Processing of Personal Data, Brussels, WP 7, at http://europa.eu.int/comm/justice_home/fsj/privacy/docs/wpdocs/1998/wp7_en.pdf.

Farrell, H. (2002), "Negotiating Privacy Across Arenas: The EU–US "Safe Harbor" Discussions," in A. Héritier (ed.), *Common Goods: Reinventing European and International Governance*, Rowman and Littlefield, Lanham, MD.

Finland (1994), "Finland: National Report 1993/94," presented to the 16th International Conference of Privacy and Data Protection Commissioners, The Hague, 6–8 September.

Finland (1995), "National Report 1994/95—Finland," presented to the 17th International Conference of Privacy and Data Protection Commissioners, Copenhagen 6–8 September.

Flaherty, D. (1972), *Privacy in Colonial New England*, University Press of Virginia, Charlottesville, VA.

Flaherty, D. (1989), *Protecting Privacy in Surveillance Societies: The Federal Republic of Germany, Sweden, France, Canada, and the United States*, University of North Carolina Press, Chapel Hill.

Flaherty, D. (1997), "Controlling Surveillance: Can Privacy Protection Be Made Effective?," in P. Agre and M. Rotenberg (eds.), *Technology and Privacy: The New Landscape*, The MIT Press, Cambridge, MA, pp. 167–192.

Flaherty, D. (2001), "Privacy Impact Assessments: An Essential Tool for Data Protection," in S. Perrin, H. Black, D. Flaherty, and T. Rankin, *The Personal Information Protection and Electronic Documents Act: An Annotated Guide*, Irwin Law Inc., Toronto, pp. 265–274.

Foucault, M. (1979), *Discipline and Punish: The Birth of the Prison*, Vintage Books, New York.

Foundation for Information Policy Research (FIPR) (2001), *Emergency Powers Allow Mass-Surveillance for Non-Terrorist Investigations*, FIPR Release 16/10/2001, at http://www.chiark.greenend.org.uk/pipermail/ukcrypto/2001-October/056931.html.

Fried, C. (1968), "Privacy," *Yale Law Journal* 77:475–493.

Fukuyama, F. (1995), *Trust: Social Virtues and the Creation of Prosperity*, The Free Press, New York.

Gambetta, D. (1988), *Trust: Making and Breaking Cooperative Relations*, Blackwell, New York.

Gandy, O. (1993), *Panoptic Sort: A Political Economy of Personal Information*, Westview Press, Boulder, CO.

Garfinkel, S. (2000), *Database Nation: The Death of Privacy in the 21st Century*, O'Reilly, Sebastopol, CA.

Gavison, R. (1980), "Privacy and the Limits of the Law," *Yale Law Journal* 89:421–471.

Gellman, R. (1993), "Fragmented, Incomplete and Discontinuous: The Failure of Federal Privacy Regulatory Proposals and Institutions," *Software Law Journal* 6:199–231.

Gellman, R. (1996), "Can Privacy be Regulated Effectively on a National Level? Thoughts on the Possible Need for International Privacy Rules," *Villanova Law Review* 41:129–172.

Gellman, R. (1997), "Conflict and Overlap in Privacy Regulation: National, International, and Private," in B. Kahin and C. Nesson (eds.), *Borders in Cyberspace*, The MIT Press, Cambridge, MA, pp. 255–282.

General Agreement in Trade and Services (GATS) (1994), *General Agreement on Tariffs and Trade*, The World Trade Organization, Geneva, at http://www.wto.org/english/tratop_e/serv_e/gatsintr_e.htm.

Germany (1994), "National Report 1993/1994," presented to the 16th International Conference of Privacy and Data Protection Commissioners, The Hague, 6–8 September.

Germany (1995), "National Report 1994/1995," presented to the 17th International Conference of Privacy and Data Protection Commissioners, Copenhagen, 6–8 September.

Giddens, A. (1991), *Modernity and Self-Identity*, Stanford University Press, Stanford, CA.

Gill, S. (1995), "Globalisation, Market Civilisation, and Disciplinary Neoliberalism," *Millennium: Journal of International Studies* 24:399–423.

Goldberg, I. (2002), "Privacy-Enhancing Technologies for the Internet, II: Five Years Later," in R. Dingledine and P. Syverson (eds.), *PET 2002—Workshop on Privacy Enhancing Technologies*, San Francisco.

Goldsmith, S. (1997), *Privacy: How to Live a Private Life Free From Big Brother's Interference*, Medina, Reading.

Greenleaf, G. (1995), "The 1995 EU Data Protection Directive on Data Protection—An Overview," *The International Privacy Bulletin* 3:1–21.

Greenleaf, G. (2003), "Australia's APEC Privacy Initiative: The Pros and Cons of 'OECD Lite,'" at http://www.bakercyberlawcentre.org/appcc/apec_ini.htm.

Greenleaf, G. (2005), "APEC's Privacy framework: A New Low Standard," *Privacy Law & Policy Reporter* 11:121–124.

Harris-Equifax (1991), *Harris-Equifax Consumer Privacy Survey 1991*, Equifax Inc., Atlanta, GA.

Harris-Equifax (1992), *Harris-Equifax Consumer Privacy Survey 1992*, Equifax Inc., Atlanta, GA.

Harris-Equifax (1993), *Harris-Equifax Health Information Privacy Survey 1993*, Equifax Inc., Atlanta, GA.

Harris-Equifax (1994), *Equifax-Harris Consumer Privacy Survey 1994*, Equifax Inc., Atlanta, GA.

Harris-Equifax (1996), *Equifax-Harris Consumer Privacy Survey 1996*, Equifax Inc., Atlanta, GA.

Held, D., McGrew, A., Goldblatt, D., and Perraton, J. (1999), *Global Transformations: Politics, Economics and Culture*, Stanford University Press, Stanford, CA.

Henkel, M. (1991), "The New UK 'Evaluative State,'" *Public Administration* 69, no. 1:121–136.

Henley Centre, The (1995), *Dataculture*, The Henley Centre, London.

Hewitt, P. (1977), *Privacy: The Information Gatherers*, National Council for Civil Liberties, London.

Hill, M. (1997), *The Policy Process in the Modern State*, 3rd ed., Prentice Hall, London.

Hine, C., and Eve, J. (1998), "Privacy in the Marketplace," *The Information Society* 14:253–262.

Hirst, P., and Thompson, G. (1996), *Globalization in Question: The International Economy and the Possibilities of Governance*, Polity Press, Cambridge, MA.

Hixson, R. (1987), *Privacy in a Public Society: Human Rights in Conflict*, Oxford University Press, New York.

Holvast, J., van Dijk, H., and Schep, G. (1989), *Privacy Doorgelicht*, Onderzocksrapport No. 71, SWOKA, 's-Gravenhage.

Hondius, F. (1975), *Emerging Data Protection in Europe*, North Holland Publishing, Amsterdam.

Hood, C. (1983), *The Tools of Government*, Macmillan, London and Basingstoke.

Hood, C. (1991), "A Public Management for all Seasons?," *Public Administration* 69:3–19.

Hood, C., Scott, C., James, O., Jones, G., and Travers, T. (1999), *Regulation Inside Government: Waste-Watchers, Quality Police, and Sleaze-Busters*, Oxford University Press, Oxford.

Hustinx, P. (1991), "The Role of Self-Regulation in the Scheme of Data Protection," paper presented to the 13th Conference of Data Protection Commissioners, Strasbourg.

Hustinx, P. (1994), "The Use and Impact of Codes of Conduct in the Netherlands," paper presented to the 16th Conference of Data Protection Commissioners, The Hague.

IBM-Harris, L. (2000), *IBM Multi-National Consumer Privacy Survey*, Louis Harris & Associates (Now Harris Interactive), New York, at ftp://www6 .software.ibm.com/software/security/privacy_survey_oct991.pdf.

Industry Canada (1994), "Privacy and the Canadian Information Highway: Building Canada's Information and Communications Infrastructure," *Information Highway Advisory Council*, Industry Canada, Ottawa.

Industry Canada (1998), "The Protection of Personal Information: Building Canada's Information Economy and Society," *Task Force on Electronic Commerce, Industry Canada, Justice Canada*, at http://www.ifla.org/documents/ infopol/canada/privacy.pdf.

International Labour Organization (ILO) (1997), *Protection of Workers' Personal Data: An ILO Code of Practice*, ILO, Geneva.

International Research Associates (INRA) (1997), *Information Technology and Data Privacy: Report Produced for the European Commission*, INRA, Brussels.

Italy, Garante per la Protezione dei Dati Personali (1997), The Italian Data Protection Act, Presidenza del Consiglio dei Ministri Dipartimento per l'Informazione e l'Editoria, Rome.

Japan, Ministry of International Trade and Industry (MITI) (1997), *Guidelines Concerning the Protection of Computer Processed Personal Data in the Private Sector*, Tokyo.

Kirby, M. (1999), "Privacy Protection: A New Beginning: OECD Principles 20 Years On," at http://www.austlii.edu.au/au/journals/PLPR/1999/41.html.

Kooiman, J. (ed.) (1993), *Modern Governance: New Government-Society Interactions*, Sage, London.

Kooiman, J. (2003), *Governing as Governance*, Sage, London.

Krimsky, S., and Golding, D. (eds.) (1992), *Social Theories of Risk*, Praeger, Westport, CT.

Kuhn, T. (1970), *The Structure of Scientific Revolutions*, 2nd ed., University of Chicago Press, Chicago.

Laperrière, R. (1999), "The 'Quebec Model' of Data Protection: A Compromise Between *Laissez-Faire* and Public Control in a Technological Era," in C. Bennett and R. Grant (eds.), *Visions of Privacy: Policy Choices for the Digital Age*, University of Toronto Press, Toronto, pp. 182–196.

Laudon, K. (1996), "Markets and Privacy," *Communications of the Association for Computing Machinery* 39:92–104.

Laurie, G. (2002), *Genetic Privacy: A Challenge to Medico-Legal Norms*, Cambridge University Press, Cambridge.

Lemond, A., and Fry, R. (1975), *No Place to Hide*, St. Martin's Press, New York.

Lessig, L. (1999), *Code and Other Laws of Cyberspace*, Basic Books, New York.

Levy, S. (2001), *Crypto: How the Code Rebels Beat the Government—Saving Privacy in the Digital Age*, Viking Penguin, New York.

Linowes, D. (1989), *Privacy in America: Is Your Private Life in the Public Eye?* University of Illinois Press, Urbana.

Lloyd, I. (1998), *A Guide to the Data Protection Act 1998*, Butterworths, London.

Loader, B. (ed.) (1998), *Cyberspace Divide: Equality, Agency and Policy in the Information Society*, Routledge, London.

Lowi, T. (1964), "American Business, Public Policy, Case Studies and Political Theory," *World Politics* 16:677–715.

Lowrance, W. (1976), *Of Unacceptable Risk: Science and the Determination of Safety*, William Kaufmann, Inc., Los Altos, CA.

Luhmann, N. (1979), *Trust and Power*, Wiley, Chichester.

Luhmann, N. (1993), *Risk: A Sociological Theory*, Walter de Gruyter, Berlin.

Lukes, S. (1974), *Power: A Radical View*, Macmillan, London and Basingstoke.

Lyon, D. (1994), *The Electronic Eye: The Rise of Surveillance Society*, University of Minnesota Press, Minneapolis.

Lyon, D. (2001), *Surveillance Society: Monitoring Everyday Life*, Open University Press, Buckingham.

Lyon, D. (2003), *Surveillance after September 11*, Polity Press, Cambridge.

Lyon, D., and Zureik, E. (eds.) (1996), *Computers, Surveillance and Privacy*, University of Minnesota Press, Minneapolis.

MacKenzie, D., and Wajcman, J. (eds.) (1999), *The Social Shaping of Technology*, 2nd ed., Open University Press, Buckingham.

Maclean, D. (1995), *Privacy and its Invasion*, Praeger, Westport.

Madgwick, D. (1968), *Privacy Under Attack*, National Council for Civil Liberties, London.

Madgwick, D., and Smythe, T. (1974), *The Invasion of Privacy*, Pitman, London.

Magill, K. (2001), "DMA to Publish, Enforce E-Mail Guidelines," *DM News*, 7 November 2001.

Majone, G. (1996), "Regulation and its Modes," in G. Majone, *Regulating Europe*, Macmillan, London, pp. 9–27.

Majtényi, L. (2001), "The Cause of Data Protection in East Central Europe," in L. Majtényi (ed.), *The Door Onto the Other Side: A Report on Information*

Rights, Office of the Parliamentary Commissioner for Data Protection and Freedom of Information, Budapest, pp. 319–340.

Manitoba (1998), Protection of Personal Information in the Marketplace: A Discussion Paper, April.

Margulis, S. (2003), "Contemporary Perspectives on Privacy: Social, Psychological, Political," Journal of Social Issues 59, no. 2.

Marx, G. (1988), Undercover: Police Surveillance in America, University of California Press, Berkeley.

Marx, G. (1999), "Ethics for the New Surveillance," in C. Bennett and R. Grant (eds.), Visions of Privacy: Policy Choices for the Digital Age, University of Toronto Press, Toronto, pp. 38–67.

Mayer-Schönberger, V. (1997), "Generational Development of Data Protection in Europe," in P. Agre and M. Rotenberg (eds.), Technology and Privacy: The New Landscape, The MIT Press, Cambridge, MA, pp. 219–241.

McCloskey, H. (1980), "Privacy and the Right to Privacy," Philosophy 55:17–38.

Mellors, C., and Pollitt, D. (1984), "Legislating for Privacy: Data Protection in Western Europe," Parliamentary Affairs 37:199–215.

Mill, J. Stuart (1859), Three Essays, Oxford University Press, Oxford.

Miller, A. (1971), The Assault on Privacy: Computers, Data Banks and Dossiers, University of Michigan Press, Ann Arbor.

Misztal, B. (1996), Trust In Modern Societies: The Search for the Basis of Social Order, Polity Press, Cambridge.

Montague, P. (1998), "The Precautionary Principle," Rachel's Environment and Health Weekly 586, at: http://www.biotech-info.net/rachels_586.html.

Moore, Jr., B. (1984), Privacy: Studies in Social and Cultural History, M.E. Sharpe, Armonk, NY.

Morris, J., and Berman, J. (2000), "The Broadband Internet: The End Of The Equal Voice?" at: http://www.cdt.org/publications/broadbandinternet.pdf.

National Consumer Council (2000), E-Commerce and Consumer Protection: A Report by the National Consumer Council, Ref. PD38/2000, National Consumer Council, London.

Negroponte, N. (1995), Being Digital, Knopf, New York.

Neumann, P. (1995), Computer-Related Risks, ACM Press (Addison-Wesley), New York.

Nielsen, L. (1995), "Use of Medical Data on the Labour Market: a Danish Draft Bill," presented to the 17th International Conference of Privacy and Data Protection Commissioners, Copenhagen, 6–8 September.

Nissenbaum, H. (2004) "Privacy as Contextual Integrity," Washington Law Review 79:119–158.

Norris, C., and Armstrong, G. (1999), *The Maximum Surveillance Society: The Rise of CCTV*, Berg, Oxford.

Norway, The Data Inspectorate (1996), *The Data Inspectorate and the Protection of Privacy in Norway*, The Data Inspectorate, Oslo.

Ogus, A. (1994), *Regulation: Legal Form and Economic Theory*, Clarendon Press, Oxford.

Ohmae, K. (1990), *The Borderless World: Power and Strategy in the Interlinked Economy*, Harper Business, New York.

Olson, M. (1971), *The Logic of Collective Action: Public Goods and the Theory of Groups*, Harvard University Press, Cambridge, MA.

Oman, S. (1997), "The EC Directive on Data Protection and Swedish Law—An Introduction," in W. Kilian (ed.), *EC Data Protection Directive—Interpretation/Application/Transposition Working Conference*, S. Toeche-Mittler Verlag, Darmstadt.

Ontario, Office of the Information and Privacy Commissioner (IPC) (1994), *Privacy Protection Makes Good Business Sense*, Information and Privacy Commissioner, Toronto, at: http://www.ipc.on.ca/scripts/index_.asp?action=31&N_ID=1&P_ID=11287&U_ID=0.

Ontario, Office of the Information and Privacy Commissioner (IPC) (1999), *E-mail Encryption Made Simple*, Information and Privacy Commissioner, Toronto, at: http://www.ipc.on.ca/docs/encrypt.pdf.

Ontario, Office of the Information and Privacy Commissioner (IPC) (2001), *Privacy Diagnostic Tool (PDT)*, Information and Privacy Commissioner, Toronto, at: http://www.ipc.on.ca/scripts/index_.asp?action=31&P_ID=12081&N_ID=1&PT_ID=15&U_ID=0.

Ontario, Office of the Information and Privacy Commissioner (IPC) and Netherlands Registratiekamer (1995), *Privacy-Enhancing Technologies: The Path to Anonymity*, Information and Privacy Commissioner and Registratiekamer, at: http://www.ipc.on.ca/scripts/index_.asp?action=31&N_ID=1&P_ID=11361&U_ID=0.

Ontario, Office of the Information and Privacy Commissioner (IPC) and Netherlands Registratiekamer (1999), *Intelligent Software Agents: Turning a Privacy Threat into a Privacy Protector*, Information and Privacy Commissioner and Registratiekamer, at: http://www.ipc.on.ca/scripts/index_.asp?action=31&N_ID=1&P_ID=11413&U_ID=0.

Ontario, Office of the Information Privacy Commissioner (IPC) and Australia, Office of the Federal Privacy Commissioner (2000), *Web Seals: A Review of Online Privacy Programs: A Joint Paper by Ontario's Information and Privacy Commissioner and the Federal Privacy Commissioner of Australia, for Presentation to the 22nd International Conference on Privacy and Personal Data Protection*, Venice, Italy, at: http://www.ipc.on.ca/scripts/index_.asp?action=31&N_ID=1&P_ID=11441& U_ID=0.

Organisation for Economic Co-operation and Development (OECD) (1981), *Guidelines on the Protection of Privacy and Transborder Flows of Personal Data*, OECD, Paris, at: http://www.oecd.org/document/18/0,2340,en_2649_34255_1815186_1_1_1_1,00.html.

Organisation for Economic Co-operation and Development (OECD) (1985), *Declaration on Transborder Data Flows*, OECD, Paris, at: http://www.oecd.org/document/25/0,2340,en_2649_34255_1888153_1_1_1_1,00.html.

Organisation for Economic Co-operation and Development (OECD) (1992), *Guidelines for the Security of Information Systems*, OECD, Paris, at: http://www.oecd.org/document/42/0,2340,en_2649_34255_15582250_1_1_1_1,00.html.

Organisation for Economic Co-operation and Development (OECD) (1997), *Cryptography Policy: The Guidelines and the Issues*, OECD, Paris, at: http://www.oecd.org/document/11/0,2340,en_2649_34255_1814731_1_1_1_1,00.html.

Organisation for Economic Co-operation and Development (OECD) (1998), Directorate for Science, Technology and Industry, *The Economic and Social Impact of Electronic Commerce—Preliminary Findings and Research Agenda*, OECD, Paris, at: http://www.oecd.org/dataoecd/3/12/1944883.pdf.

Organisation for Economic Co-operation and Development (OECD) (1999), Directorate for Science, Technology and Industry, *Inventory of Instruments and Mechanisms Contributing to the Implementation and Enforcement of the OECD Privacy Guidelines on Global Networks*, OECD, Paris, at: http://www.olis.oecd.org/olis/1998doc.nsf/linkto/dsti-iccp-reg(98)12–final.

Organisation for Economic Co-operation and Development (OECD) (2001), Directorate For Science, Technology and Industry, "A Study of Privacy Enhancing Technologies," *Working Party on Information Security and Privacy: Committee for Information, Computer and Communications Policy*, OECD, Paris, at: http://www.olis.oecd.org/olis/2001doc.nsf/LinkTo/dsti-iccp-reg(2001)6–final.

Organisation for Economic Co-operation and Development (OECD) (2002a), Directorate For Science, Technology and Industry, *OECD Guidelines for the Security of Information Systems and Networks: Towards a Culture of Security*, OECD, Paris, at: http://www.oecd.org/document/42/0,2340,en_2649_33703_15582250_1_1_1_1,00.html.

Organisation for Economic Co-operation and Development (OECD) (2002b), Directorate For Science, Technology and Industry, "Inventory of Privacy-Enhancing Technologies," *Working Party on Information Security and Privacy: Committee for Information, Computer and Communications Policy*, OECD, Paris, at: http://www.olis.oecd.org/olis/2001doc.nsf/LinkTo/dsti-iccp-reg(2001)1–final.

Organisation for Economic Co-operation and Development (OECD) (2003), Directorate for Science, Technology and Industry, *Inventory of Instruments and Mechanisms Contributing to the Implementation and Enforcement of the OECD Privacy Guidelines on Global Networks*, OECD, Paris, at: http://www.oecd.org/dataoecd/12/54/2092454.pdf.

Overkleeft-Verburg, G. (1995), *De Wet Persoonsregistraties—Norm, Toepassing en Evaluatie* (English Summary), Tjeenk Willink, Zwolle.

Packard, V. (1964), *The Naked Society*, David McKay, New York.

Palazzi, P. (2002), *La Transmisión Internacional de Datos Personales y la Protección de la Privacidad: Argentina, América latina, Estados Unidos y la Unión Europea*, AD-HOC, Buenos Aires.

Parent, W. (1983), "Privacy, Morality and the Law," *Philosophy and Public Affairs* 12:269–288.

Parker, R. (1974), "A Definition of Privacy," *Rutgers Law Review* 27:275–296.

Pateman, C. (1970), *Participation and Democratic Theory*, Cambridge University Press, Cambridge.

Pateman, C. (1983), "Feminist Critiques of the Public/Private Dichotomy," in S. I. Benn and G. F. Gaus (eds.), *Public and Private in Social Life*, St. Martin's Press, New York, pp. 281–303.

Pérez Asunari, M. (2003), "The WTO and the Protection of Personal Data: Do EU Measures Fall Within GATS Exception? Which Future for Data Protection Within the WTO E-Commerce Context?," paper presented to the 18th BILETA Conference: "Controlling Information in the Online Environment," April, at: http://www.bileta.ac.uk/Document%20Library/1/The%20WTO%20and%20the%20Protection%20of%20Personal%20Data.%20Do%20EU%20Measures%20Fall%20within%20GATS%20Exception.pdf.

Perrin, S., Black, H., Flaherty, D., and Rankin, T. (2001), *The Personal Information Protection and Electronic Documents Act: An Annotated Guide*, Irwin Law Inc., Toronto.

Pew Internet & American Life Project (2000), *Trust and Privacy Online: Why Americans Want to Rewrite the Rules*, Pew Internet & American Life Project, Washington DC, available at: http://www.pewinternet.org/PPF/r/19/report_display.asp.

Pierre, J. (ed.) (2000), *Debating Governance: Authority, Steering, and Democracy*, Oxford University Press, Oxford.

Pipe, R. (2005), "China Prepares for New Privacy Law," *Privacy Laws and Business Newsletter,* no. 76, January–February, p. 11.

Plesser, R., and Cividanes, E. (1991), *Privacy Protection in the United States: A 1991 Survey of Laws and Regulations Affecting Privacy in the Public and Private Sector Including a List of All Relevant Officials*, Piper & Marbury, Washington DC.

Pollitt, C. (1988), "Bringing Consumers into Performance Measurement: Concepts, Consequences and Constraints," *Policy and Politics* 16:77–87.

Pool, I. (1983), *Technologies of Freedom: On Free Speech in an Electronic Age*, Harvard University Press, Cambridge, MA.

Posner, R. (1978), "An Economic Theory of Privacy," *Regulation*, May/June, pp. 19–26.

Poster, M. (1990), *The Mode of Information*, Polity Press, New York.

Pounder, C., and Kosten, F. (1995), "The Data Protection Directives," *Data Protection News* 21:2–38.

Pressman, J., and Wildavsky, A. (1973), *Implementation: How Great Expectations in Washington are Dashed in Oakland*, 2nd ed., University of California Press, Berkeley.

Priest, M. (1997–1998), "The Privatization of Regulation: Five Models of Self-Regulation," *Ottawa Law Review* 29:233–302.

Privacy & American Business (1994), *Handbook of Company Privacy Codes*, Bell Atlantic, Hackensack, NJ.

Privacy & American Business (1997), *Commerce, Communication, and Privacy Online: A National Survey of Computer Users*, conducted for Privacy & American Business by Louis Harris & Associates and Dr. Alan F. Westin, Privacy & American Business, Hackensack, NJ.

Prosser, W. (1960), "Privacy," *California Law Review* 48:383–423.

Public Interest Advocacy Centre (PIAC) (1995), *Surveying Boundaries: Canadians and their Personal Information*, Ottawa, PIAC.

Raab, C. (1993), "Data Protection in Britain: Governance and Learning," *Governance* 6:43–66.

Raab, C. (1995), "Connecting Orwell to Athens? Information Superhighways and the Privacy Debate," in W. van de Donk, I. Snellen and P. Tops (eds.), *Orwell in Athens: A Perspective on Informatization and Democracy*, IOS Press, Amsterdam, pp. 195–211.

Raab, C. (1996), "Implementing Data Protection in Britain," *International Review of Administrative Sciences* 62:493–511.

Raab, C. (1997a), "Co-Producing Data Protection," *International Review of Law, Computers and Technology* 11:11–42.

Raab, C. (1997b), "Privacy, Democracy, Information," in B. Loader (ed.), *The Governance of Cyberspace*, Routledge, London, pp. 155–174.

Raab, C. (1998a), "Electronic Confidence: Trust, Information and Public Administration," in I. Snellen and W. van de Donk (eds.), *Public Administration in an Information Age: A Handbook*, IOS Press, Amsterdam, pp. 113–133.

Raab, C. (1998b), "Sectoral Approaches to Data Protection," *Privacy & Informatie*, no. 2, pp. 60–64.

Raab, C. (1998c), "Sectoral Data Protection in Europe," paper presented to the 1998 Conference on Personal Data Protection in Europe and in Hungary, Budapest, 28–29 January.

Raab, C. (1999a), "From Balancing to Steering: New Directions for Data Protection," in C. Bennett and R. Grant (eds.), *Visions of Privacy: Policy Choices for the Digital Age*, University of Toronto Press, Toronto, pp. 68–93.

Raab, C. (1999b), "National Privacy Laws: United Kingdom," in C. Prins and E. Louwers (eds.), *International Computer Law*, Publication 318, Release 14, Matthew Bender, New York, pp. 83–96.

Raab, C. (1999c), "La Transposition de la Directive Européenne sur la Protection des Données Personnelles au Royaume-Uni," *Revue Française d'Administration Publique*, no. 89, pp. 21–36.

Raab, C. (2001), "Electronic Service Delivery in the UK: Proaction and Privacy Protection," in J. Prins (ed.), *Designing E-Government: On the Crossroads of Technological Innovation and Institutional Change*, Kluwer Law International, Boston and The Hague, pp. 41–62.

Raab, C., and Bennett, C. (1994), "Protecting Privacy Across Borders: European Policies and Prospects," *Public Administration* 72:95–112.

Raab, C., and Bennett, C. (1996), "Taking the Measure of Privacy: Can Data Protection be Evaluated?," *International Review of Administrative Sciences* 62:535–556.

Raab, C., and Bennett, C. (1998), "The Distribution of Privacy Risks: Who Needs Protection?" *The Information Society* 14:263–274.

Raab, C., Bennett, C., Gellman, R., and Waters, N. (1998), *Application of a Methodology Designed to Assess the Adequacy of the Level of Protection of Individuals with Regard to Processing Personal Data: Test of the Method on Several Categories of Transfer*, Office for Official Publications of the European Commission, Luxembourg, at: http://europa.eu.int/comm/justice_home/fsj/privacy/studies/method-adequacy_en.htm.

Raines, J. (1974), *Attack on Privacy*, Judson Press, Valley Forge, PA.

Regan, P. (1995), *Legislating Privacy: Technology, Social Values and Public Policy*, University of North Carolina Press, Chapel Hill.

Regan, P. (1999), "American Business and the European Data Protection Directive: Lobbying Strategies and Tactics," in C. Bennett and R. Grant (eds.), *Visions of Privacy: Policy Choices for the Digital Age*, University of Toronto Press, Toronto, pp. 199–216.

Regan, P. (2002), "Privacy as a Common Good in the Digital World," *Information, Communication and Society* 5:382–405.

Reidenberg, J. (1993), "Rules of the Road for Global Electronic Highways: Merging the Trade and Technical Paradigms," *Harvard Journal of Law and Technology* 6:1–20.

Reidenberg, J. (1995), "Setting Standards for Fair Information Practice in the US Private Sector," *Iowa Law Review* 80:497–511.

Reidenberg, J. (1997), "Governing Networks and Rule-Making in Cyberspace," in B. Kahin and C. Nesson (eds.), *Borders in Cyberspace*, The MIT Press, Cambridge, MA, pp. 84–105.

Reidenberg, J. (1998), "Lex Informatica: The Formulation of Information Policy Rules Through Technology," *Texas Law Review* 76:552–593.

Reidenberg, J. (2000), "Resolving Conflicting International Data Privacy Rules in Cyberspace," *Stanford Law Review* 52:1315–1371.

Reinicke, W. (1998), *Global Public Policy: Governing Without Government?* Brookings Institution, Washington DC.

Renn, O. (1998), "Three Decades of Risk Research: Accomplishments and New Challenges," *Journal of Risk Research* 1:49–71.

Rhodes, R. (1997), *Understanding Governance: Policy Networks, Governance, Reflexivity and Accountability*, Open University Press, Buckingham.

Rockart, J., and Short, J. (1991), "The Networked Organization and the Management of Interdependence," in M. Scott Morton (ed.), *The Corporation of the 1990s: Information Technology and Organizational Transformation*, Oxford University Press, New York, pp. 189–219.

Rosen, J. (2001), *The UnWanted Gaze: The Destruction of Privacy in America*, Vintage Books, New York.

Rosen, J. (2004), *The Naked Crowd: Reclaiming Security and Freedom in an Anxious World*, Random House, New York.

Rosenberg, J. (1969), *The Death of Privacy*, Random House, New York.

Rotenberg, M. (2000), "What Larry Doesn't Get: Fair Information Practices and the Architecture of Privacy," *Stanford Technology Law Review*, at: http://stlr.stanford.edu/STLR/Articles/01_STLR_1/index.htm.

Rothfeder, J. (1992), *Privacy for Sale*, Simon and Schuster, New York.

Royal Society, The (1992), *Risk: Analysis, Perception and Management*, London, The Royal Society.

Rule, J. (1974), *Private Lives and Public Surveillance: Social Control in the Computer Age*, Schocken Books, New York.

Rule, J., and Hunter, L. (1999), "Towards Property Rights in Personal Data," in C. Bennett and R. Grant (eds.), *Visions of Privacy: Policy Choices for the Digital Age*, University of Toronto Press, Toronto, pp. 168–181.

Rule, J., McAdam, D., Stearns, L., and Uglow, D. (1980), *The Politics of Privacy: Planning for Personal Data Systems as Powerful Technologies*, Elsevier, New York.

Samarajiva, R. (1996), "Surveillance by Design: Public Networks and the Control of Consumption," in R. Mansell and R. Silverstone (eds.), *Communication by Design: The Politics of Information and Communication Technologies*, Oxford University Press, Oxford, pp. 129–156.

Schattschneider, E. (1960), *The Semi-Sovereign People*, Holt, Rinehart and Winston, New York.

Schoeman, F. (ed.) (1984), *Philosophical Dimensions of Privacy: An Anthology*, Cambridge University Press, New York.

Schoeman, F. (1992), *Privacy and Social Freedom*, Cambridge University Press, Cambridge.

Schwartz, P. (1999), "Privacy and Democracy in Cyberspace," *Vanderbilt Law Review* 52:1609–1702.

Schwartz, P. (2000), "Beyond Lessig's *Code* For Internet Privacy: Cyberspace Filters, Privacy Control and Fair Information Practices," *Wisconsin Law Review* 2000:743–788.

Schwartz, P., and Reidenberg, J. (1996), *Data Privacy Law: A Study of United States Data Protection*, Michie, Charlottesville, VA.

Seipp, D. (1978), *The Right to Privacy in American History*, Harvard University Program on Information Resources Policy, Cambridge, MA.

Selznick, P. (1985), "Focusing Organizational Research on Regulation," in R. Noll (ed.), *Regulatory Policy and the Social Sciences*, University of California Press, Berkeley, pp. 363–367.

Sennett, R. (1977), *The Fall of Public Man*, Knopf, New York.

Shaffer, G. (2000), "Globalization and Social Protection: The Impact of EU and International Rules in the Ratcheting Up of US Privacy Standards," *Yale Journal of International Law* 25:1–88.

Shapiro, A. (1999), *The Control Revolution: How the Internet is Putting Individuals in Charge and Changing the World We Know*, Century Foundation, New York.

Shils, E. (1956), *The Torment of Secrecy*, Free Press, Glencoe, IL.

Sieghart, P. (1976), *Privacy and Computers*, Latimer, London.

Simitis, S. (1987), "Reviewing Privacy in an Information Society," *University of Pennsylvania Law Review* 135:707–746.

Simitis, S. (1995), "From the Market to the Polis: The EU Directive on the Protection of Personal Data," *Iowa Law Review* 80:445–469.

Smith, J. (1994), *Managing Privacy: Information Technology and Corporate America*, University of North Carolina Press, Chapel Hill.

Smith, R. (1979), *Privacy: How to Protect What's Left of It*, Anchor Press, Garden City, NJ.

Smith, R. (1993), *War Stories: Accounts of Persons Victimized by Invasions of Privacy*, Privacy Journal, Providence, RI.

Sobel, L. (ed.) (1976), *War on Privacy*, Facts on File Inc., New York.

Spar, D. (1998), "The Spotlight and the Bottom Line: How Multinationals Export Human Rights," *Foreign Affairs* 77:7–12.

Spar, D., and Yoffie, D. (1999), "Multinational Enterprises and the Prospects for Justice," *Journal of International Affairs* 52:557–581.

Speier, J. (2002), "Keynote Address," paper presented to the 2000 conference of "Computers, Freedom & Privacy (CFP 2002)," 19 April, San Francisco.

Stewart, B. (1996), "Privacy Impact Assessments," *Privacy Law & Policy Reporter* 3–4, at: http://www.austlii.edu.au/au/journals/PLPR/1996/39.html.

Strange, S. (1996), *The Retreat of the State: The Diffusion of Power in the World Economy*, Cambridge University Press, Cambridge.

Swire, P. (1996), "The Race to Laxity and the Race to Undesirability: Explaining Failures in Competition Among Jurisdictions in Environmental Law," *Yale Law and Policy Review* 67:67–110.

Swire, P. (1997), "Markets, Self-Regulation, and Government Enforcement in the Protection of Personal Information," *Privacy and Self-Regulation in the Information Age*, United States (US), Department of Commerce National Telecommunications and Information Administration, Washington DC, pp. 3–19.

Swire, P., and Litan, R. (1998), *None of Your Business: World Data Flows, Electronic Commerce, and the European Privacy Directive*, Brookings Institution, Washington DC.

Sykes, C. (1999), *The End of Privacy*, St. Martin's Press, New York.

Székely, I. (ed.) (1991), *Information Privacy in Hungary: Survey Report and Analysis*, Hungarian Institute for Public Opinion Research, Budapest.

Sztompka, P. (1999), *Trust: A Sociological Theory*, Cambridge University Press, New York.

Taylor, J., and Williams, H. (1991), "Public Administration and the Information Polity," *Public Administration* 69:171–190.

Thomas, D., and Loader, B. (eds.) (2000), *Cybercrime: Law Enforcement, Security and Surveillance in the Information Age*, Routledge, London.

Thompson, A. (1970), *Big Brother in Britain Today*, Michael Joseph, London.

Tickner, J., Raffensperger, C., and Myers, N. (n.d.) *The Precautionary Principle in Action: A Handbook*, Science and Environmental Health Network, Windsor, ND, at: http://www.biotech-info.net/handbook.pdf.

Todd, D. (2001), *Politicizing Privacy: "Focusing Events" and the Dynamics of Conflict*, unpublished Master's Thesis, University of Victoria.

Toffler, A. (1981), *The Third Wave*, Bantam Books, New York.

Trubow, G. (1992), "The European Harmonization of Data Protection Laws Threatens US Participation in Trans Border Data Flow," *Northwestern Journal of International Law and Business* 13:159–176.

United Kingdom (UK), Central Information Technology Unit (CITU) (2000), *e-government—A Strategic Framework for Public Services in the Information Age*, Cabinet Office, London.

United Kingdom (UK), Cm 3438 (1996), *government.direct*, The Stationery Office, London.

United Kingdom (UK), Cm 4310 (1999), *Modernising Government*, The Stationery Office, London.

United Kingdom (UK), Her Majesty's Treasury (1988), *Output and Performance Measurement in Central Government: Technical Guide*, HM Treasury, London.

United Kingdom (UK), Home Office (1995), *Identity Cards—A Consultation Document*, CM 2879, Her Majesty's Stationery Office, London.

United Kingdom (UK), House of Commons (1990), *Information Commissioner: Annual Report of the Data Protection Registrar. First Report of the Home Affairs Committee*, The Stationery Office, London.

United Kingdom (UK), House of Commons (1994), *The Tenth Report of the Data Protection Registrar*, (HC 453), Her Majesty's Stationery Office, London.

United Kingdom (UK), House of Commons (1999), *The Fifteenth Annual Report of the Data Protection Registrar*, (HC 575), The Stationery Office, London.

United Kingdom (UK), House of Commons (2001), *Annual Report and Accounts for the Year Ending 31 March 2001* (HC 2), The Stationery Office, London.

United Kingdom (UK), National Audit Office (1993), *Data Protection Controls and Safeguards, Report by the Comptroller and Auditor General*, (HC 899), The Stationery Office, London.

United Kingdom (UK), Performance and Innovation Unit, Cabinet Office (2002), *Privacy and Data-Sharing: The Way Forward for Public Services*, Cabinet Office, London, at: http://www.number-10.gov.uk/su/privacy/11.htm.

United Nations (UN) (1990), *Guidelines Concerning Computerized Personal Data Files*, Resolution A/RES/45/95 adopted by the General Assembly on 14 December 1990, at: http://www.un.org/documents/ga/res/45/a45r095.htm.

United States (US), Department of Commerce National Telecommunications and Information Administration (NTIA) (1997), *Privacy and Self Regulation In The Information Age*, Department of Commerce, NTIA, Washington, DC.

United States (US), Department of Commerce National Telecommunications and Information Administration (NTIA) (2000), *Falling Through the Net: Toward Digital Inclusion*, Department of Commerce, NTIA, Washington DC.

United States (US), Senate Committee on the Judiciary (2000), "Know the Rules, Use the Tools—Privacy in the Digital Age: A Resource for Internet Users," at: http://www.hipaadvisory.com/programs/privacy.pdf.

United States (US), Privacy Protection Study Commission (PPSC) (1977), *Protecting Privacy in an Information Society*, Government Printing Office, Washington DC.

van de Donk, W., Bennett, C., and Raab, C. (eds.) (1996), "Symposium on the Politics and Policy of Data Protection," *International Review of Administrative Sciences* 62:513–534.

Vogel, D. (1986), *National Styles of Regulation: Environmental Policy in Great Britain and the United States*, Cornell University Press, Ithaca.

Vogel, D. (1995), *Trading Up: Consumer and Environmental Regulation in a Global Economy*, Harvard University Press, Cambridge, MA.

Vogel, D. (1997), *Barriers or Benefits? Regulation in Transatlantic Trade*, Brookings, Washington DC.

Warner, M., and Stone, M. (1970), *The Data Bank Society: Organizations, Computers, and Social Freedom*, Allen and Unwin, London.

Warren, S., and Brandeis, L. (1890), "The Right to Privacy," *Harvard Law Review* 4:193–220.

Webb, K. ed. (2004), *Voluntary Codes: Private Governance, the Public Interest and Innovation*, Carleton Research Unit for Innovation, Science and Environment, Ottawa.

Weise, K. (1992) "How Volkswagen Manages Data Protection Auditing in Germany," *Privacy Laws & Business (PLB)* 22:19–22.

Weiss, L. (1997) "Globalization and the Myth of the Powerless State," *New Left Review* 225:3–27.

Westin, A. (1967), *Privacy and Freedom*, Atheneum, New York.

Westin, A. (1996), "Testimony before the Subcommittee on Domestic and International Monetary Policy of the Committee on Banking and Financial Services," US House of Representatives, Washington DC, 11 June.

Westwood, J. (1999), "Life in the Privacy Trenches: Experiences of the British Columbia Civil Liberties Association," in C. Bennett and R. Grant (eds.), *Visions of Privacy: Policy Choices for the Digital Age*, University of Toronto Press, Toronto, pp. 231–243.

Whitaker, R. (1999), *The End of Privacy: How Total Surveillance is Becoming a Reality*, New Press, New York.

White, F. (2001), "The Use of Privacy Impact Assessments in Canada," *Privacy Files* 4, no. 7:1–11.

Will, I. (1983), *The Big Brother Society*, Harrap, London.

Wilson, I. (1999), "Asia Pacific Forum Promotes Privacy in the Region," *Privacy Laws & Business Newsletter (PLB)* 51:18–19.

Winner, L. (1977), *Autonomous Technology: Technics-Out-Of-Control as a Theme in Political Thought*, The MIT Press, Cambridge, MA.

Winner, L. (1989), *The Whale and the Reactor: A Search for Limits in the Age of High Technology*, University of Chicago Press, Chicago.

Young, J. (ed.) (1978), *Privacy*, Wiley, New York.

6, Perri (1994), "Trust, Social Theory and Public Policy," unpublished paper on file with authors.

6, Perri (1998), *The Future of Privacy, Volume 1: Private Life and Public Policy*, Demos, London.

6, Perri and Briscoe, I. (1996), *On the Cards: Privacy, Identity and Trust in the Age of Smart Technologies*, Demos, London.

6, Perri, with Lasky, K., and Fletcher, A. (1998), *The Future of Privacy, Volume 2: Public Trust in the Use of Private Information*, Demos, London.

Index